T0393100

THE HANDBOOK OF CLIMATE CHANGE LEADERSHIP IN ORGANISATIONS

Climate change is one of the most significant and challenging problems we face today, and many organisations have recognised their responsibility in reducing emissions and environmental degradation and regenerating biodiversity. However, conventional leadership has failed to respond adequately to the magnitude of the threat, and a profound change in corporate leadership is required to substantively cut emissions and change climate policy to minimise further destructive environmental impact. This book sets out the qualities and approaches needed by leaders to successfully develop and implement climate change mitigation and adaptation policies.

Bringing together the foremost experts in climate change leadership from business, leadership, psychology and coaching backgrounds, this book addresses the failures of current leadership practice and proposes a variety of models of how climate change leadership capabilities can be effectively developed in organisations. It is structured around four concepts: foundations, which includes models of environmental, ecological and evolutionary leadership; transitions, which looks at transformational and ethical models that are being repurposed for the age of sustainability; progressions, which explores innovative models that are being developed for the current age including systems, adaptation and maturity-based models of leadership; and actions, which includes models of sustainable goal setting and climate leadership coaching and development.

The book is written for corporate leaders, researchers and educators and will be an invaluable addition to the leadership curriculum and executive development programmes to help the next generation of leaders respond to global challenges.

Doug MacKie has over 30 years' experience as an organisational and business psychologist, working in the UK, Europe and Australasia. He has researched and accelerated the development of leadership, team and organisational capability in boards, CEOs and C-Suite executives within many of the top 100 companies in the UK and Australia.

'The concept of the good ancestor asks how we want our grandchildren's children to regard us — what was the legacy we left to them? Leaders, in every sphere of life, have the responsibility to be good ancestors and that in today's world means leading in the context of climate change. In this book, they will find more than exhortation to do the right thing — they will find practical examples of how to lead on climate change. This book is essential reading for any leader wanting to make his or her great-grandchildren proud of them!'

Prof David Clutterbuck, *Special Ambassador, European Mentoring and Coaching Council; visiting professor, Henley Business School; Distinguished Research Fellow, The Conference Board*

'The climate crisis calls for leadership from all of us, meaning we have to get to the edge of our comfort zone and then take one more step. This handbook has something for every leader to support their courage in navigating the unknown, whether by understanding their own cognitive biases or learning how to become a leader of systemic change beyond their own organisation, setting science-based targets or seeing the world as a complex adaptive system.'

Nigel Topping, *UN Climate Change High Level Climate Champion, COP26*

THE HANDBOOK OF CLIMATE CHANGE LEADERSHIP IN ORGANISATIONS

Developing Leadership for the Age of Sustainability

Edited by
Doug MacKie

LONDON AND NEW YORK

Designed cover image: © Getty Images / borchee

First published 2024
by Routledge
4 Park Square, Milton Park, Abingdon, Oxon OX14 4RN

and by Routledge
605 Third Avenue, New York, NY 10158

Routledge is an imprint of the Taylor & Francis Group, an informa business

British Library Cataloguing-in-Publication Data
A catalogue record for this book is available from the British Library

Library of Congress Cataloging-in-Publication Data
Names: MacKie, Doug, editor.
Title: The handbook of climate change leadership in organisations : developing leadership for the age of sustainability / edited by Doug MacKie.
Description: Abingdon, Oxon ; New York, NY : Routledge, 2024. | Includes bibliographical references and index. |
Identifiers: LCCN 2023021374 (print) | LCCN 2023021375 (ebook) |
ISBN 9781032352220 (hardback) | ISBN 9781032380056 (paperback) |
ISBN 9781003343011 (ebook)
Subjects: LCSH: Social responsibility of business. | Leadership. | Climate change mitigation—Social aspects. | Climate change mitigation—Economic aspects.
Classification: LCC HD60 .H333 2024 (print) | LCC HD60 (ebook) |
DDC 658.4/08—dc23/eng/20230630
LC record available at https://lccn.loc.gov/2023021374
LC ebook record available at https://lccn.loc.gov/2023021375

ISBN: 978-1-032-35222-0 (hbk)
ISBN: 978-1-032-38005-6 (pbk)
ISBN: 978-1-003-34301-1 (ebk)

DOI: 10.4324/9781003343011

Typeset in Joanna
by codeMantra

CONTENTS

CONTRIBUTORS

Paul W.B. Atkins, PhD, is a researcher, speaker and facilitator. He is a visiting associate professor with the Crawford School of Public Policy (Australian National University). His research has focused on interventions to reduce stress while enhancing relationships, well-being, perspective-taking and cooperation in groups and organisations. Paul is a registered organisational psychologist with a PhD in psychology from Cambridge University. He is the lead author of *Prosocial: Using Evolutionary Science to Build Productive, Equitable, and Collaborative Groups* and co-founder and vice president of Prosocial World, a not-for-profit organisation focused on enhancing cooperation and trust in purpose-driven groups globally. www.paulatkins.net

Christopher Beehner is a business professor at Seminole State College of Florida. He earned a doctor of business administration from Northcentral University and a master of public administration from City University of Seattle. Prior to joining academia, Chris worked in leadership roles in supply chain management in the electrical equipment industry. Chris is recognised globally as a sustainable business and sustainability leadership expert, having presented at numerous conferences and published multiple books, chapters and articles. He is a community fellow at the University of Central Florida (UCF) Center for Global Economic and

Environmental Opportunity and a research fellow at the Earth Charter International. A native of Pittsburgh, Pennsylvania, Dr Beehner currently lives in Central Florida with his wife and two sons.

Kristina Bogner is an interdisciplinary researcher enthusiastic about fostering just sustainability transitions. Kristina is assistant professor working in Organisations and Sustainability at the Copernicus Institute of Sustainable Development, Utrecht University. Her main research interests are transition processes and transformations towards sustainability, in general, as well as education, knowledge and learning for the transformation towards sustainability; for example, towards a sustainable knowledge-based bioeconomy, in particular. In her work, she focuses on the transition of higher education institutions, including transformative research and education, as well as on emotions and coping as collective meaning-making in transitions-in-the-making. https://www.uu.nl/staff/KBBogner

Jonathan Boston is Emeritus Professor of public policy at Victoria University of Wellington. He has published widely on a range of matters including public management, social policy, climate change policy, tertiary education policy and comparative government. Jonathan has served as director of the Institute for Governance and Policy Studies and director of the Institute of Policy Studies. His recent research has focused on the challenge of governing for the long term in the face of strong presentist tendencies in democratic policymaking. During 2022–2023 he was a member of an Expert Working Group on Managed Retreat for the Ministry for the Environment in Aotearoa New Zealand.

David J. Brown is a professor of biology and environmental sciences at Marietta College. He received his doctorate from Duke University. His research interests include mapping deposition of heavy metals in the environment and studying effects of exposure to metals at the molecular and whole-animal level. He developed an interest in conservation and leadership and has taught short courses on these topics in four countries in Central and South America. He has assisted in the development of two master's programmes in sustainability leadership, and he will serve as the director of the master's in sustainability leadership at Marietta College.

Frederik Dahlmann is associate professor of strategy and sustainability at Warwick Business School, UK. His research focuses on understanding how companies respond to global sustainability challenges in their business strategies, management practices and corporate governance systems. Specifically, he examines the factors that shape how companies address climate change and reduce corporate carbon emissions. Fred is also interested in the emerging phenomenon of the purpose ecosystem and its role within wider earth system governance and sustainability transformations. Finally, his research is concerned with the ethical implications of the Anthropocene for business and managers.

Joel A. DiGirolamo is the vice president of research and data science for the International Coaching Federation (ICF), where he leads the organisation's efforts to study the science and profession of coaching. Joel has published numerous articles, book chapters and white papers on coaching research. He has more than 30 years of staff and management experience and is the author of two books, *Leading Team Alpha* and *Yoga in No Time at All*. Joel holds a master's degree in industrial and organisational psychology, an MBA and a bachelor's degree in electrical engineering. He is an associate editor for *Consulting Psychology Journal*.

William (Willy) Donaldson is associate professor of management at Christopher Newport University. He is the director of the CNU Luter Business Institute and director of the Biotechnology and Management Program. Willy has over 35 years of experience as a board member and CEO, has been president of eight companies and helped start dozens of companies. He is the founder and president of Strategic Venture Planning, a management consulting firm that assists boards, investors, families and senior management teams to maximise results. His books include *Simple_Complexity* (Morgan James, 2017) and *Estimated Time of Departure* (Atia Press, 2021).

Anna Eckardt is managing partner at MyLearningBoutique, an organisational development consultancy in Switzerland. She works on the integration of CSR into organisational design and strategy execution, focusing on transforming decision-making processes and behaviours of leaders. Anna is a visiting lecturer for Sustainability & Strategy at the

Stockholm School of Economics (Sweden) and affiliated researcher with IMD (Switzerland). Her research on strategy, sustainability and compliance has been published in books and in peer-reviewed journals, and she has been awarded several internationally recognised awards. Anna holds a master in law (University in Bonn/Germany) and a PhD in management (Zeppelin University/Germany).

Donald Eubank is cofounder of the sustainable business advisory firm Read the Air, where he serves as key advisor to organisations that are integrating sustainability into their core strategy and designing decarbonisation initiatives. Donald has worked across the IT, finance and media industries in Asia, launching new business lines and divisions with start-ups and multinationals. He is co-author of *Leading Sustainably: The Path to Sustainable Business and How the SDGs Changed Everything* from Routledge, an advisor to Doshisha University's Values Research Center, a three-time judge for the Global Corporate Sustainability Awards and a guest lecturer at Ban Ki-moon's ESG Academy.

Alexander Herwix is a design-oriented researcher who aims to contribute to the flourishing of humanity from a critical pragmatist perspective. He is currently finishing his PhD in information systems at the University of Cologne and working as an interdisciplinary researcher at the Faculty of Education at Leipzig University. His work focuses on improving humanities capacity to responsibly engage with societal transitions across multiple levels of aggregation (e.g., narratives, individuals, groups, institutions) with a special interest in the role of digital technologies, philosophy and education.

Rik Irons-Mclean leads global strategy for sustainability enablement at Microsoft, with a previous role as UK industry strategy lead for manufacturing, energy and resources. Before Microsoft, Rik worked at Cisco for 13 years, with global roles in energy and resource industries, IoT and security. Rik has spoken at multiple conferences, is a published book author and has written multiple industry papers and magazine articles. He has sat on boards and groups for energy, manufacturing, sustainability and digital twins. Rik holds an MBA and the MIEMA and CEnv sustainability accreditations and is part of the Australian Climate Leaders Coalition. uk.linkedin.com/in/rikironsmclean

Christopher D. Ives is associate professor in the School of Geography at the University of Nottingham. He is an interdisciplinary sustainability scientist with research interests in urban social–ecological systems, sustainability transformations, religion and spirituality and values for nature. Chris obtained his PhD from Macquarie University in 2012 for research on urban ecology and environmental planning. He subsequently held research positions at the University of Melbourne, RMIT University and Leuphana University Lueneburg. Chris is programme director of the MSc in environmental leadership & management at the University of Nottingham and is a fellow of the Higher Education Academy and the Royal Geographical Society.

Brad Jackson is professor of leadership and governance at the University of Waikato Management School. Brad has co-authored eight leadership books including *A Very Short, Fairly Interesting and Reasonably Cheap Book About Studying Leadership*, *Revitalising Leadership* and *The Board as the Nexus Between Leadership and Governance* and *Responsible Leadership in Corporate Governance*. He also co-edited the *Sage Handbook of Leadership* and *Major Works in Leadership*. Brad's current research explores the interrelationship between leadership and governance practices in promoting sustainable economic, environmental and social innovation and the application of place-based approaches to foster cross-sectoral leadership development and education.

Talib Karamally is pursuing his MSc in industrial/organizational psychology at Western University. His research focuses on mindfulness interventions in the workplace, nature relatedness and environmental leadership development. Prior to his studies at Western University, Talib worked in organisational development and has experience implementing positive psychology interventions in organisations. He has experience facilitating courses on mindfulness meditation, happiness and resilience. Additionally, he has experience designing leadership development programmes and facilitating team building sessions using assessment tools.

Steve Kempster is Professor Emeritus at Lancaster University Management School and is an associate partner of the Regenerative Alliance. He has published broadly on leadership learning, leadership of purpose and responsible leadership, with five books and many articles and chapters.

Steve leads the Good Dividends project (www.gooddividends.com) – formed from an interdisciplinary group of academics drawn from five universities in Europe and Australasia – with the objective of enabling business leaders to develop their business models towards realising 'good dividends' and becoming regenerative. Currently, Steve is the director of the Lancaster University Made Smarter and Evolve Digital programmes linking digitalisation with regenerative outcomes – funded by the UK Government.

Beate Klingenberg, PhD, MBA, is an interdisciplinary, international and passionate educator and researcher with a background in physical chemistry and business. Her mission is to help individuals and organisations on their path towards sustainability. Her areas of research include the sustainability mindset indicator, knowledge management for sustainability, as well as the interface of operations management and financial performance. She holds a position as professor of business administration (sustainability and supply chain management) at the FOM School of Economics & Management, in Mannheim, Germany. In the past, she was professor of management at Marist College (US) and Istituto Lorenzo de'Medici (Italy).

Nancy E. Landrum, PhD, is a professor of sustainable business transformation at Munich Business School (Germany) and a visiting professor of sustainability management at Les Roches Global Hospitality Education (Switzerland). Dr Landrum is widely published in books, journals and media. Dr Landrum has received awards for sustainability research, teaching and service, including two Fulbright awards. She previously taught at Loyola University Chicago, University of Arkansas at Little Rock and Morehead State University and has been a visiting scholar in Europe and Asia. Her interests are in sustainable business, biomimicry, strong sustainability, ecological economics and circular economy.

Doug MacKie has over 30 years' experience as an organisational and business psychologist and executive coach working in the UK, Europe and Australasia. He has researched and accelerated the development of leadership, team and organisational capability in boards, CEOs and C-Suite executives within many of the top 100 companies in the UK and Australia. He is an associate program director with the prestigious

Melbourne Business School and has and has helped to develop and integrate executive coaching into their leadership development programmes. He is an active researcher on strength-based leadership, team effectiveness and sustainability leadership. He is the author of the definitive guide *Strength-Based Leadership Coaching in Organisations* (2016) and is a co-editor of *The Practitioners Handbook of Team Coaching* (2019). He established the Centre for Climate Change Leadership in Organisations in 2020 and can be contacted at doug@csaconsulting.biz.

Sasha Maher is lecturer of sustainability at the University of Auckland's Business School. Prior to joining the university in 2021, Sasha held senior policy and business executive roles in industry and an environmental NGO. She has a PhD in anthropology and management from the University of Auckland. Sasha's research explores organisational and leadership responses to climate change adaptation, with a specific focus on corporate political activities, disclosure and risk.

Daina Mazutis is an associate professor of strategy at the Telfer School of Management (University of Ottawa) where she also holds the Endowed Professorship in Ethics, Responsibility and Sustainability (ERS) and co-directs the Globalization, Governance and Sustainability (GGS) Area of Strategic Impact (ASI). Daina's research on leadership, strategy and sustainability has been published in several edited books as well as peer-reviewed journals and has been honoured with numerous prestigious awards. She holds an MBA from the University of Ottawa and a PhD from the University of Western Ontario (Ivey) and is a graduate of the ICD Directors Education Program.

Robert M. McManus is the executive director of Applied Leadership and professor of Leadership at Muskingum University (Ohio). He is the co-author of *Understanding Leadership: An Arts and Humanities Perspective* and is the lead editor of *Ethical Leadership: A Primer*. McManus has designed two master of arts programs in sustainability leadership and has published on the intersection between leadership and environmental sustainability. He is an award-winning educator, author and executive coach and has travelled extensively teaching on leadership. McManus holds a PhD in communication as well as a master of business administration.

Katrin Muff is director of the Institute for Business Sustainability in Lucerne, Switzerland, and professor of practice at the LUISS Business School in Rome, Italy. She consults leaders and boards in business sustainability and strategic transformation and runs an executive programme together with Thomas Dyllick. Her book *Five Superpowers for Co-Creators* provides insights about issue-centered multi-stakeholder processes. She brings 20 years of international strategic and general management experience in Europe, Australia, North America and Russia and a decade of leadership in business education. www.KatrinMuff.com

Johanna Nalau is an award-winning climate adaptation scientist at Griffith University who thrives on finding clues to how humans can better see into the future and make decisions on how we adapt to climate change. She specialises in adaptation heuristics, which are rules of thumb that guide how we think about adaptation and the decisions we make. Dr Nalau is a lead author for the Intergovernmental Panel on Climate Change (IPCC) 6th Assessment report in Working Group II, an Australian Research Council DECRA fellow (2019–2022) and Science Committee co-chair of the World Adaptation Science Programme at United Nations. Dr Nalau firmly believes that good leadership enables better lives and better decisions across organisations and scientific fields and is a key ingredient in fostering innovation.

Gonzalo Palomo-Vélez is an assistant professor of social psychology at the Universidad de O'Higgins, Chile. His research focuses on the study of the evolutionary, social and psychological motives that underlie people's pro-environmental behaviours.

Benjamin W. Redekop is professor of leadership studies at Christopher Newport University in Newport News, Virginia. He teaches courses in the President's Leadership Program at CNU, including Environmental Leadership and Outdoor Leadership. His books include *Common Sense and Science From Aristotle to Reid* (Anthem, 2020), *Innovation in Environmental Leadership: Critical Perspectives* (co-editor; Routledge, 2018), *Leadership for Environmental Sustainability* (editor; Routledge, 2010), *Power, Authority, and the Anabaptist Tradition* (co-editor; Johns Hopkins University Press, 2001) and *Enlightenment and Community* (McGill–Queen's University Press, 2000). He lives in Newport News with his wife Fran and daughter Katarina.

Kevin Reeves is an experienced technologist and senior leader across UK economic infrastructure. As industry executive for energy & utilities at Microsoft UK, Kevin is responsible for developing the UK industry strategy for energy and utilities, working as part of the leadership team in manufacturing and resources. Kevin supports the development of new digitally enabled markets, helping Microsoft continue its transformation from a technology vendor to a trusted partner. Within industry, Kevin is a digital lead within the Construction Leadership Council, supporting the acceleration of digital transformation across the built environment, working across government, industry and academia. As an honorary research fellow at Warwick Manufacturing Group, Kevin supports leading research in the field of trusted data sharing, to ensure the UK maintains its position as a globally leading centre of excellence in cyber security.

Isabel Rimanoczy, EdD, is an academic who has made it her life purpose to promote change accelerators. She developed the Sustainability Mindset through her research. She created LEAP!, a cohort of academics promoting a holistic sustainability mindset. She has authored more than 15 books around the Sustainability Mindset. Isabel was scholar in residence at Huizenga School of Business and Entrepreneurship, Nova Southeastern University, Florida. She has been a visiting lecturer at Kingston University (UK), Universidad de Navarra (Spain) and Al Akhawayn University (Morocco). She earned her doctorate at Columbia University and is a licensed psychologist from Universidad de Buenos Aires.

Jennifer L. Robertson is an associate professor in the DAN Department of Management and Organizational Studies at Western University. Jennifer's research focuses on psychological issues involved in organisational environmental sustainability and the nature and prediction of leadership. Professor Robertson's scholarship in this area has been internationally recognised through an Emerald Citations of Excellence Award and an Emerald Literati Award. Together with Dr Julian Barling, she is the editor of the book *The Psychology of Green Organizations.*

Rian Satterwhite serves as director of the Office of Service Learning & Leadership at the University of Nevada, Las Vegas and teaching faculty at Claremont Lincoln University. Author of numerous chapters and articles, he co-edited the book *Innovation in Environmental Leadership: Critical Perspectives* and has served in numerous roles within professional associations, including founding chair of the ILA Sustainability Leadership Member Community. His work and publications focus on how to develop the skills and mindsets necessary to prepare leaders and leaderful systems for the collective, wicked challenges of climate change.

Michael P. Schlaile is a postdoctoral researcher at Leibniz Centre for Agricultural Landscape Research, working on sustainability-oriented transformation and innovation processes in the bioeconomy. He is also affiliated with the University of Hohenheim as an external habilitation candidate and as a research fellow with Cusanus Hochschule für Gesellschaftsgestaltung, where he recently held the position of project coordinator. He is also visiting professor at the University of Insubria's Department of Economics and member of the Turkish–German University's flying faculty. His interdisciplinary research revolves around the three strongly interwoven research areas: complexity and evolution, innovation and transformation and sustainability and responsibility. www.michael-schlaile.de/en/

Mark Van Vugt is a professor of evolutionary psychology and organizational psychology at the Vrije Universiteit Amsterdam, the Netherlands, and a research associate at the Department for Politics and International Relations, University of Oxford, UK. His expertise is in evolutionary perspectives on human social behaviour and in applications of evolutionary psychology to fields such as leadership, politics, business and management and sustainability.

Jenny Wilkinson is a freelance development consultant and lecturer. Co-founder of Goodman Wilkinson Associates Ltd (training and development), she has extensive experience of delivering accredited leadership qualifications in association with the Institute of Leadership and Management (ILM). Jenny lectures at De Montfort University in digital design, business planning and leadership in the creative industries and is a senior fellow of the Higher Education Academy. Jenny has a doctorate in interaction design, and her main research area is user experience and interaction design, with a particular focus on digital media and its potential to engage people with cultural heritage.

FOREWORD

Georg Kell
Chairman, Arabesque
Founder, UN Global Compact

Corporate climate change leadership is in high demand as the imperative to reduce harmful emissions is increasingly recognised. Governments and societies at large have long failed to sufficiently price harmful emissions to incentivise low carbon investments and production, and consumers are only slowly changing wasteful behaviour. As of today, subsidies for fossil fuels, direct and indirect, far exceed the amount of total investments in renewable energy according to IMF studies. For over 2 decades now, voluntary business initiatives have tried to establish the business case for climate leadership. A growing number of companies are setting goals towards net zero emissions, and investors are increasingly pricing climate risks into their decision making. Yet, emissions continue to rise overall, and international climate diplomacy is taking a back seat as political rivalry, economic nationalism and fragmentation are on the rise.

The good news is that the solutions needed are in principle mostly available. And there are indications that the much-needed big transformations towards emission-free and environmentally friendly practices are on the rise at least in some parts of the world. There is also much greater awareness today to prepare for the negative consequences of climate change. In some countries the challenge of climate change has already become an issue that influences national policymaking. Extreme weather and natural disasters are increasingly waking up societies and forcing their hands, prepared or not. Yet, the pace of change is slow and not enough to avoid worse consequences in the future. Some of the damage done already seems hard to reverse, as the dramatic loss of biodiversity and the degradation of soil and water indicates.

In this messy world where old systems and mindsets and behaviours – formed over generations during the industrial era – still control most levers of decision making in both the public and private domains, and where the political will for international cooperation is at low point, a special focus on climate business leadership at the firm level is most relevant. Business is striving to survive within given political and societal contexts and has to play along to thrive. In the current setting, for example, most businesses that have pledged carbon net zero will go bankrupt unless policy frameworks change and emission reductions are positively priced sufficiently. But business is not just a passive player. It has a huge influence in shaping policy frameworks through lobbying and by making technology choices and investment decisions that shape outcomes for years to come. Businesses continuously compete with each other and seek to survive and thrive. They can be either a defender of old systems that pollute and exploit the natural environment or they can be an innovator of new systems that thrive on low carbon and low negative environmental impact. But all too often they are both at the same time.

Better understanding what business climate leadership means in this dynamic setting of a fragmenting world and how climate leadership can be fostered is a critical question of our time. Exploring this challenge requires more than context understanding and analysis. It involves bigger questions of valuation and values, time-bound shifts of perspectives, assumptions and beliefs about the future and, above all, organisational challenges. It also involves imagination about a safe and healthy future and the courage to ride cyclical waves of short-termism that continue to define much of our economic and social lives while working towards a different future.

Probing this question from different perspectives holds the promise to unlock more climate leadership while overcoming barriers. Common to all perspectives is the recognition that a new era has already begun where the human impact on the natural environment is of geophysical force. There is no exit strategy or escaping the consequences of our actions. Facing this reality challenges much of our traditional belief systems and values. But the complexity of the challenge at hand should not paralyse us. On the contrary, it should motivate us to double down on our quest to foster climate change leadership in organisations.

PREFACE

The concept of *handbook* emerged from the twin and opposing forces of optimism and frustration – optimism that organisations can be, and frequently are, forces for good in the world, with their catalysing of innovation, provision of meaning and purpose, development of professional identities and delivery of goods and services that help humanity flourish, and frustration that this is not always the case. Organisations can be the harbingers of stress and disappointment, the repositories of unrealised talent and the creators of silos whose myopic and competitive perspectives encourage the catastrophic and wilful ignorance of their externalities.

Slowly and over time these externalities have grown, unheeded by our evolutionally orientated cognition that concentrates its focus on the immediate until, in the blink of a geological eye, anthropogenic climate change is upon us. So how to respond to this emerging reality of our capacity for self- and planetary destruction in the age of the Anthropocene? It's clear that our capabilities, including leadership, and our institutions are struggling to keep up with the complexity and significance of the challenge. Seduced by cheap energy and affordable consumption, the idea of changing this dependency or revaluing prosperity seems beyond even our most progressive leaders.

And yet, slowly, awareness is growing of the unsustainability of our current predicament. In researching for this book, two themes kept re-emerging in the data – themes that would not only prevent human flourishing but could lead to societal collapse. These themes, inequality and resource depletion, historically predictive of so many societal collapses, are two of many indicators that are currently blinking red on humanity's dashboard, and yet so few organisations are orientating their considerable resources and capabilities to solving the external challenges that we collectively face.

The book aims to amplify the voice of those that are and suggests that the leadership skills and capabilities required for such a transformation exceed by some margin what contemporary models have to offer. The optimism comes from the confidence that organisations and their leadership can and are being repurposed for the age of sustainability. It is to the facilitation of that transition and to the attainment of sustainable prosperity that this book is dedicated.

Dr Doug MacKie
23 February 2023
Brisbane

1

AN INTRODUCTION TO CLIMATE CHANGE LEADERSHIP IN ORGANISATIONS

Doug MacKie

Chapter Summary

Human activity is causing climate change, resource depletion and environmental degradation at an unprecedented rate. Organisations including corporations are responsible for a significant proportion of direct and indirect emissions that are contributing to anthropogenic global warming, biodiversity loss and environmental pollution. Corporate leadership has spectacularly failed to address these issues and now requires a fundamental repurposing for the age of sustainability. This chapter introduces the foundations, transitions and progressions necessary for effective climate change leadership in organisations. Corporations are both a significant source of anthropogenic global warming and the repositories of significant resources and talent that can be repurposed to address the existential issue of climate change. Biases that have for so long protected business leaders from the long-term, glacial and perceptual challenging consequences of our consumption are breaking down in the face of incontestable evidence of adverse and potentially

DOI: 10.4324/9781003343011-1

catastrophic planetary impact. Business can be both a significant cause of climate change and instrumental in the transformations necessary to mitigate the adverse social and environmental impact of corporate activity and promote sustainable flourishing and planetary regeneration.

Introduction

We have a complex and at times conflicting relationship with organisations. They are the crucibles of positive innovation, identity formation and career fulfilment and, yet, simultaneously are significant contributors to the dark side of human progress. Organisations in general and corporations in particular play a significant and ongoing role in climate change, unsustainable resource depletion, biospheric degradation and social inequality (Heede, 2014; Hoffman, 2021; Intergovernmental Panel on Climate Change, 2014; Steffen et al., 2015). The statistics are stark and arresting and fundamentally challenge both contemporary business models and the economic context in which they operate: An ecological footprint that requires the productive capacity of 1.75 planets (WWF, 2022); planetary boundaries for biodiversity loss, carbon emissions and freshwater use that have been breached for the first time in human history (Rockstrom et al., 2009); 1 billion people living in extreme poverty (World Bank, 2015); 7% of the richest population accounting for 50% of the world's carbon emissions (Pearce, 2009); a 69% decrease in monitored wildlife populations around the globe between 1970 and 2018 (WWF, 2022); and a ratio of 300:1 between CEO pay and that of the average worker in the United States (Mishel & Davis, 2015).

These are not the statistics of a flourishing society supported by a responsible and sustainable corporate sector. And yet the Sustainable Development Goals (SDGs) necessary for a transition to a more equitable and sustainable society have been painstakingly documented with six priority domains identified, including increasing well-being, environmental and biospheric regeneration, reducing inequality, increasing decarbonisation and sustainable industries (Dixson-Decleve et al., 2022; Sachs et al., 2019). Whilst emissions reduction is the primary focus of industry it is increasingly apparent that a sustainable industrial and corporate sector is predicated on a thriving biosphere and flourishing society (Folke et al., 2016). The interconnectedness of these domains is one of the core components of systems leadership (Chapter 14) supporting the position that emissions reduction is a necessary but not sufficient goal for the contemporary climate change leader. Closing the leadership gap between the current reality and the vision of the SDGs is the primary purpose of this book.

The Context and Purpose of Business

The business context for climate change leaders is undergoing a radical transformation. The core purpose of organisations is rapidly evolving from the creation of wealth for the privileged few towards a focus on solving the problems of people and planet (Dyllick & Muff, 2016; Mayer, 2018). Organisational responses to climate change have been categorised in a number of ways. Business has been conceptualized as both the problem in its denial of externalities and promotion of shareholder primacy and the potential solution with its significant capacity to contribute to sustainable development (Jeanrenaud et al., 2017). Depending on the response, a number of future scenarios have been proposed. The first is business as usual where the focus on incremental change denies the systemic risk or the gravity of the situation, leading to the second scenario, aptly named *barbarisation*. Here chronic inequality and resource depletion lead to societal collapse and a complete breakdown of the economic model in which all organisations operate (Motesharrei et al., 2014). The third scenario is termed *the great transition*, where the transformation of organisations and their values leads to the restoration of natural systems, the decoupling of economic growth from resource depletion and the development of a sustainable prosperity (Tellus Institute, 2023). Corporations have an unprecedented opportunity to contribute to this transition, but the leadership capability necessary to catalyse such a reformation is in short supply (Cannon et al., 2015; M. Metcalfe & Hinske, 2022). Business is a key mediator between the fundamental assumptions of the individual and society and the future scenarios outlined above. Multiple business surveys suggest that the gap between intention and actions remains significant and corporations sit between sceptical incrementalism and a reformed modernist approach where green transitions rather than radical transformations are the received wisdom (Hulme, 2022; UN Global Compact [UNGC] & Accenture, 2019).

Whilst a detailed economic analysis of the context in which corporations are operating is beyond the scope of this book, there are some significant contextual changes that are catalysing the current reformation in business purpose (Jacobs & Mazzucato, 2016). There is an emerging consensus that some of the fundamental tenets of shareholder capitalism are coming under welcome and much-needed scrutiny, with core assumptions like the superiority of private sector innovation, the benefit of organisational self-interest over external regulation and the desirability of unrelenting economic growth in all sectors of society coming under sustained, informed and erudite attack (T. Jackson, 2021; Piketty, 2016). However, it was the awareness of increasing resource depletion and growing economic inequality within advanced economies that signalled most clearly the need for a fundamental review of the economic conditions in which all corporations were operating given that these two variables were most predictive of societal collapse in the long term (Motesharrei et al., 2014). There are currently underway multiple attempts to reform capitalism that recognise its capability for wealth creation but woeful record at equitable distribution and environmental preservation, including inclusive, stakeholder, regenerative, conscious and nurturing capitalism (Biglan, 2020; Elkington, 2020; Henderson, 2020; Stoknes, 2021). This reformation of the economic context has proved decisive in creating the necessary conditions for the rethinking of the purpose of business and the development of positive impact organisations.

The structure, values, purpose and leadership of positive impact organisations are beginning to be articulated with case studies now emerging of the type of organisations capable of leading the great transition (Polman & Winston, 2021; Chapter 2). There have been several attempts to restructure business away from a narrow and extractive focus aimed at shareholder renumeration and towards a net positive benefit for society (Elkington, 2020; Mayer, 2018). What these approaches have in common is a fundamental revision of the purpose of the organisation that starts with the sustainable confrontation of global challenges and that emphasises prosocial values, social benefit and environmental stewardship (Crooke et al., 2015; George et al., 2021). With such explicit articulation of the type of business models compatible with a transition to a sustainable and regenerative future, tensions have followed specifically around time frame, inclusion and dematerialization (Applebaum, 2021). Short-term focus on profit and growth is contrasted with a longer-term focus on social, environmental and economic impacts, whilst stakeholder capitalism routinely includes the environment and future generations as key components of inclusive prosperity (Henderson, 2020).

Many businesses that are committed to progressing on the sustainability transition implicitly take an ecomodernist perspective where the reduction in resource intensity and faith in future technologies such as carbon capture and storage play a major role (Hulme, 2022). One of the challenges of the ecomodernist approach is that its success is dependent on an absolute decoupling of economic growth and environmental footprint combined with a radical increase in resource productivity (Stoknes, 2021). Given that the marginal green growth to date has largely been achieved through outsourcing of environmentally polluting industries, the absolute and meaningful reduction in resource intensity would require a radical transformation from the current estimations of recycled materials that currently sits around 9% to embrace a much more circular economy (Hickel & Kallis, 2020; T. Jackson, 2021). It is fair to say that current views on the plausibility of this transition range from the optimistic to the highly contested (Wright & Nyberg, 2015).

Necessary Components of Positive Organisations

Organisations provide the context and culture in which leadership occurs. Positive impact organisations by their definition provide a very different context for leaders to operate within than those organisations orientated towards shareholder primacy. As well as a compelling purpose that is socially orientated, future focused and regenerative rather than extractive, positive impact organisations require a fundamental reorganization in structure, strategy, leadership and outcomes (Elkington, 2021; Polman & Winston, 2021; Chapter 2). There are already several movements underway that have articulated the positive organization, from shared value to net positive, blueprint for a better business and UNGC. What these various approaches have in common is a commitment to purpose beyond shareholder primacy, accountability for all consequences and impacts, positive returns for all stakeholders, a focus on radical collaboration between and within sectors, the need for external verification of progress on sustainable goals and a focus on the longer term stewardship of the environment as the crucible in which all business is done (Elkington, 2021; Muff, 2021; Polman & Winston, 2021; UNGC, 2023).

Contemporary organisations represent a continuum of sustainability from the recalcitrant laggards at one end to the net positives at the other. The leadership required to facilitate the organisational shift along this continuum is the core purpose of this book. Strong sustainability requires the broadening of purpose and value creation that starts with an external perspective focusing on problems to solve rather than opportunities to exploit and the intent to move from doing no harm to positive regeneration (Chapter 2, Chapter 12). There is also a requirement to increase efficiency of resource consumption, promote a circular economy and responsible consumption and improve circular material flows and renewable energy utilisation (de Oliveira Neto et al., 2018). According to Muff (Chapter 2), these positive impact organisations have four strategic differentiators: governance alignment, a sustainability culture, higher or social purpose and external validation of their positive impact. Sustainable development goals and science-based targets are currently the gold standard of external validation (Chapter 17).

Sustainable Prosperity

There is, however, a broader recognition that complex global sustainability challenges cannot be solved by technology and governance alone and that, increasingly, the focus is on the subjective domain or inner dimension of mindsets, values, beliefs, worldviews and emotions (Wamsler & Brink, 2018). This shift from the outer to the inner domain is supported by the significant volume of research that confirms that materialistic values and lifestyles are associated with poor outcomes for both personal well-being and planetary health (Isham & Jackson, 2022; Kasser, 2016). This research builds on a well-known phenomenon in the science of well-being that has repeatedly found that after a relative small level of income, there is no further relationship become material wealth and subjective reports of happiness (Easterlin, 2003). In fact, subjective well-being is strongly correlated with flow states where the individual is completely absorbed in an activity that, critically, unlike materialistic values, can be achieved without a negative cost to the environment (B. Jackson, 2019). In addition, there is evidence that flow states are mediated by effective self-regulation, one of the core constructs of effective leadership (Chapter 19) and significantly less present in those with more materialist values. The focus on inner transformation through a mindful, self-centred and considered approach to sustainability has received further support from attempts to link stages in human awareness with the evolution of business and society (Scharmer & Kaufer, 2013). Models of leadership maturity make similar claims regarding how core competencies of sustainable leadership unfold during the ontogeny of the leader (Rooke & Torbert, 2005).

Barriers to Effective Corporate Action

Multiple barriers to effective corporate action on climate change have been suggested from the individual, the interpersonal to the ideological. Our evolved preferences and abilities are not designed to attend to distant, incremental and impersonal threats affording climate change denialists opportunities to question environmental trends, attributions and impacts (Hulme, 2022). All cognition is mediated through an evolved system replete with biases, shortcuts and algorithms adapted to an environment of relative stasis, short-term focus and high predictability (Mazutis & Eckardt, 2017; Chapter 5). Threats and challenges that do not fit these evolved parameters are easier to ignore, dismiss and disregard due to the reduced moral intensity of their impact (Gifford, 2011; Mazutis & Eckardt, 2017). Enhancing the moral intensity of climate change through bias mitigation can be achieved through the framing of the costs of inaction, the focus on positive emotions and the enhancement of empathy for future generations (Markowitz & Shariff, 2012). These cognitive biases that inhibit the registration, intensity and relevance of climate change signals almost certainly mediated the gap between the environmental rhetoric and emissions reality of many corporations (UNGC & Accenture, 2019). However, such cognitive biases are not only active in the C-suites and boardrooms of corporations. They are also present in the consumers, employees, suppliers, communities and investors that comprise stakeholder capitalism (Biglan, 2020).

Other barriers to action are more ideological in nature. Despite gross domestic product being only ever intended as a measure of goods and services over a period of time, it is frequently used as a proxy for national well-being despite providing no information on environmental impact, income distribution and resource depletion (Biglan, 2020; Hoffman, 2015). A final theme running through the multiple barriers to effective corporate action is the concept of self-regulation, which is fundamental in managing the unsustainable gratifications of stakeholders. This deficit in self-regulation leads directly to the cultivation of expectations and norms that are incompatible with a sustainable business and the promotions of strategy, processes and products that are directly or indirectly contributing to environmental degradation.

The Failure of Contemporary Leadership

Contemporary corporate leadership has evolved within a context of shareholder primacy, purposeful agnosticism and ethical indifference (Tourish, 2013). Many models with an individual and agency-based orientation have been co-opted in the business context in the uncritical pursuit of shareholder returns and the denial of the true cost of negative externalities. Business schools have been complicit in this promotion of heroic leadership whilst ignoring the environmental context in which organisations sit (Hoffman, 2016). In particular, models of authentic, exceptional and heroic leadership that cultivate excessive optimism, risk minimization and self-enhancement have been accused of the cultivation of narcissistic tendencies and the decontextualised projection of personal preferences onto followers and the organisation (Ibarra, 2015). Such approaches have been termed Prozac leadership for their tendency to promote illusory optimism, excessive positivity and a disregard of risk and anticipation of setbacks (Alvesson & Einola, 2019; Collinson, 2012). Table 1.1 outlines some of the key distinctions between contemporary and post-conventional models of leadership.

The unsustainabilities of mainstream leadership have been eruditely articulated in the following domains (Bendell et al., 2018). Firstly, the purpose of leadership is critical and must be operationalised. This concept has been succinctly expressed by Evans (2011) as 'leadership is only as good as the purpose it serves' (p. 3). Secondly, 'heroic' individualism is no longer fit for purpose in the management of complex, wicked and multifaceted challenges. The focus has now moved from leaders to leadership and how this is distributed amongst followers whose strengths have been consistently underutilised in heroic models (Tourish, 2020). Thirdly, leadership is the domain of the many, not the few. Models of talent and capability that see leadership as a fixed and scarce resource have given way to those that emphasise abundance, malleability and collaboration. The strengths-based approach has been a major facilitator of this transition (MacKie, 2016). Fourthly, the construct of leadership is broadening from the individual personality of the leader to a focus on performance, process, purpose and

Table 1.1 Climate Change Leadership Versus Contemporary Leadership

Criteria	*Contemporary Leadership*	*Climate Change Leadership*
Purpose	Agnostic/economic advantage	Sustainable human flourishing
Boundaries	Open/undefined	Planetary
Agency	Individual	Societal
Values	Growth/individualism	Environmentalism
Context	Minimised	Emphasised
Ethics	Optional and relative	Foundational and directive
Complexity	Unitary	Systemic
Stakeholders	Singular and exclusive	Multiple and inclusive
Impact	Economic	Net positive
Sustainability	Peripheral	Core
Political	Acquisition	Distribution
Leadership	Heroic individualism	Distributed and systemic
Horizon	Immediate	Evolutionary and distal
Worldview	Anthropocentric	Ecocentric
Focus	Achievement	Obligations
Maturity	Conventional	Post-conventional
Responsibility	Narrow and amoral	Broad and moral
Power	Focused and hierarchical	Distributed and inclusive

place (Case et al., 2015; B. Jackson, 2019). In addition to these recognised unsustainabilities, there are further reasons to be concerned about the capacity of contemporary leadership to address problems of such complexity and interconnectedness as climate change (Grint, 2010). Far from developing leaders capable of managing complex and systemic challenges, organisational structure may in fact be creating situationally destructive leadership, with evidence that components of the dark triad (Machiavellianism, psychopathy and narcissism) are not only overrepresented in the business context but may increase as a function of exposure to corporate environments. Indeed, the presence of psychopathy in corporations is estimated to be four times that of the general population (Mathieu et al., 2014). What is also apparent is that managers and leaders who score highly on the dark triad are simply less concerned about environmental and sustainability issues (Pelster & Schaltegger, 2022). Character development and the cultivation of prosocial values are core components of climate change leadership development (Chapter 19).

The distinction between conventional and post-conventional leadership, whilst mapping a significant shift in the corporate leadership paradigm, does risk the creation of a straw man for the purposes of emphasis (Schein, 2017). Whilst much of contemporary leadership theory has been focused on the great man theories of individual attributes and fixed and scarce models of talent and exceptional contribution that supported and encouraged hierarchical organisation structures, this in itself was an aberration from the phylogeny of leadership that indicated a much more egalitarian and distributed origin for the concept of leadership that has emerged over our evolutionary history (Van Vugt & Ronay, 2014). Nonetheless, conventional models that emphasise individual exceptionalism and excessive positivity do expose themselves to the vagaries of those with excessive personal ambition, Machiavellianism and other traits of the 'dark side' that have undoubtedly contributed the litany of corporate scandals that continue to signal, along with climate change inaction, that conventional leadership models within corporations are no longer fit for purpose.

However, it is not just leadership theory that has been complicit in the development of models and theories independent of their naturalistic and environmental context (Western, 2018). Leadership development has also largely ignored the environment as a key stakeholder in education of corporate leaders (Hoffman, 2016). In fact, not only are leaders not explicitly taught the fundamentals of sustainability leadership at many business schools but the experience of attending them it itself appears to cultivate more materialistic and self-interested values (Crossan et al., 2013). In addition, the issues of character and prosocial values are rarely addressed in business school curricula, leading to the development of values and norms that are inconsistent with responsible leadership and environmental stewardship. Attempts are underway to reform the leadership education process, with Business Schools for Climate Leadership (BS4CL) and the Principles of Responsible Management Education making significant progress is reforming curricula to align with climate mitigation and the SDG's more broadly (BS4CL, 2023; Wall et al., 2020).

Repurposing Contemporary Leadership

Many contemporary models of leadership are in transition, adapting to the changing demands of the business context and the ongoing criticism of the critical leadership studies movement and the broader shifts in cultural expectations of business and organisational leadership (MacKie, 2021; Robertson & Barling, 2015). Strengths-based approaches, for example, have developed from value-neutral approaches that emphasised subjective self-enhancement and the unfettered utilisation of individual strengths to approaches that require that leadership strengths be utilised both to benefit followers and for a purpose that is self-transcendent and generative of a broader positive impact (MacKie, 2016, 2019). Strengths-based approaches also democratised leadership, promoting models of talent that were more abundant, inclusive and growth oriented (Biswas-Deiner et al., 2017), a trend that is entirely compatible with enhancing sustainability but still missing the recognition of operating within a complex and fragile ecological system. Other attempts at repurposing contemporary models include environmentally specific transformational leadership, which has taken one of the most widely researched and applied models (Sosik & Jung, 2011) and oriented it towards the specific generation of positive environmental behavior within organisations (Robertson & Barling, 2017). Implicit in attempts at repurposing are the growing awareness of the importance of social purpose, stakeholder inclusivity, positive impact, the complexity of current challenges and consequent distribution of leadership across teams and organisations to drive collective problem solving.

The Emergence of Post-Conventional Leadership Models

The sustained criticism of contemporary leadership models, chronic and ongoing corporate inaction on climate change and the litany of corporate scandals and rampant inequality have promoted a flourishing of innovation in the leadership development space. These models can be categorised into foundational, transitional and progressive models of leadership. Foundational models like environmental and evolutionary approaches emphasise core components of our evolutionary origins like altruism and cooperation as well as seek inspiration from the natural world in terms of balance and biomimicry (Hutchins, 2022). Transitional models including transformational, sustainable and responsible leadership offer a mechanism whereby contemporary models such as transformational leadership can be repurposed to meet the emerging demands of stewardship and stakeholder engagement that contemporary corporations require. Progressive models like adaptive leadership, systems leadership and place-based approaches seek to redress the damage done by decades of inaction on climate change and develop the systemic capabilities that will increasingly focus moral opprobrium on those who attempt to benefit the entitled few at the expense of social and planetary well-being.

Given the relatively recent emergence of post-conventional models, the data on their effectiveness are unsurprisingly embryonic. Most of the available data are qualitative in form, usually derived from surveys and semi-structured interviews. In a naturalistic inquiry of 75 corporate leaders, Schein (2017) found what differentiated sustainability leaders was their ecological worldview, their systemic thinking, curiosity, long-term horizons and the expansion of their circle of care. The UN Global Compact and Russel Reynolds (2019) surveyed the CEOs of 55 companies performing well against sustainability criteria and inferred the presence of a sustainability mindset that included systems thinking, stakeholder inclusion, disruptive innovation and a long-term commitment to change. The UNGC and Accenture (2019) conducted a review of 173 companies on criteria of growth, sustainability, profitability and trust. They found that only 35% were transformational; that is, superior on both business and ESG (environment, society and governance) metrics. Transformational leaders in this context were differentiated by the diversity of their operations, a high sense of accountability, attention to social impact, a divestment from fossil fuels and a technical and research focus. Finally, Stillman (2021) conducted 29 open interviews in four business sectors and concluded that phronesis, systems theory and culture were the critical determinants of sustainability. In terms of predicting organisational stages of sustainability, Muff (2021) conducted a regression analysis on 13 case studies and concluded that leadership indicators including sustainability integration, risk taking, clear vision and capacity to inspire were the significant predictors. Stakeholder management was also a significant predictor, with message consistency, engagement and supply chain integration proving significant in the prediction of higher levels of sustainability.

Post-conventional models face a number of significant challenges if they are to attain the requisite criterion validity of having a significant and positive impact on meaningful dependent variables, including emissions reduction, responsible consumption and biospheric regeneration. Existing research suggests that the development of a sustainability mindset, systemic thinking, awareness of the natural context, stakeholder inclusion, a long-term perspective, ecocentric values, ethical and integrated decision making, a clear vision of sustainability and capacity to inspire others are all significant prerequisites of effective climate change leadership. In addition, there is a recognition that many of the existing surveys have focused on CEO behaviour, but visionary and inspiring leaders are in short supply, and leadership is increasingly distributed amongst their followers, teams and employees more generally. This democratisation of leadership unlocks and engages significant amounts of sustainability capital within organisations and reduces the reliance on high-impact but low-frequency visionary leaders.

The *Handbook* aims to address these challenges and is structured around the concepts of foundations, transitions, progressions and actions in climate change leadership.

- *Foundations* include models of environmental, ecological and evolutionary leadership that articulate both the cognitive biases that inhibit action and the interdependent and systemic components of a flourishing biosphere. They invoke questions of natural leadership and biomimicry.
- *Transitions* include models of leadership, including transformational and ethical, that are being repurposed for the age of sustainability. This includes the cultivation of sustainability mindsets that are predicated on foundations including values, virtues and strengths.
- *Progressions* include models that are being innovated and developed for the age of sustainability, including systems, adaptation and maturity-based models. This includes concepts of life span development, radical collaboration and future orientation to effectively manage both mitigation and adaptation.
- *Actions* includes models of sustainable goal setting, developing climate change leadership and a case study on the specific impact of digital technology in enhancing cooperation on hydrogen uptake within industrial clusters.

Discussion Points

- In what way is the climate changing for business? What are some of the factors creating this change?

- Is contemporary leadership fit to manage complex and wicked problems like climate change?
- What are some of the core characteristics of post-conventional leadership?

Further Reading

Hulme, M. (2022). *Climate change*. Routledge.

Polman, P., & Winston, A. (2021). *Net positive: How courageous companies thrive by giving more than they take*. Harvard Business Press.

Wright, C., & Nyberg, D. (2015). *Climate change, capitalism, and corporations*. Cambridge University Press.

References

Alvesson, M., & Einola, K. (2019). Warning for excessive positivity: Authentic leadership and other traps in leadership studies. *The Leadership Quarterly, 30*(4), 383–395.

Applebaum, R. A. (Ed.). (2021). *Leadership in sustainability: Perspectives on Research policy, and practice*. Fielding University Press.

Bendell, J., Little, R., & Sutherland, N. (2018). The seven unsustainabilities of mainstream leadership. In B. W. Redekop, D. R. Gallagher, & R. Satterwhite (Eds.), *Innovation in environmental leadership* (pp. 13–31). Routledge.

Biglan, A. (2020). *Rebooting capitalism: How we can forge a society that works for everyone*. Values to Action.

Biswas-Diener, R., Kashdan, T. B., & Lyubchik, N. (2017). Psychological strengths at work. In L. G. Oades, M. F. Steger, A. Delle Fave, & J. Passmore (Eds.), *The Wiley Blackwell handbook of the psychology of positivity and strengths-based approaches at work* (pp. 34–47). John Wiley & Sons.

BS4CL. (2023). Business Schools for Climate Leadership. https://sites.google.com/view/bs4cl/home

Cannon, S., Morrow-Fox, M., & Metcalf, M. (2015). The strategist competency model: The future of leadership development. In M. Sowcik, A. C. Andenoro, M. McNutt, & S. E. Murphy (Eds.), *Leadership 2050: Critical challenges, key contexts, and emerging trends* (pp. 189–206). Emerald.

Case, P., Evans, L. S., Fabinyi, M., Cohen, P. J., Hicks, C. C., Prideaux, M., & Mills, D. J. (2015). Rethinking environmental leadership: The social construction of leaders and leadership in discourses of ecological crisis, development, and conservation. *Leadership, 11*(4), 396–423.

Collinson, D. (2012). Prozac leadership and the limits of positive thinking. *Leadership, 8*(2), 87–107.

Crooke, M., Csikszentmihalyi, M., & Bikel, R. (2015). Leadership in a complex world. *Organizational Dynamics, 2*(44), 146–155.

Crossan, M., Mazutis, D., Seijts, G., & Gandz, J. (2013). Developing leadership character in business programs. *Academy of Management Learning & Education, 12*(2), 285–305.

de Oliveira Neto, G. C., Pinto, L. F. R., Amorim, M. P. C., Giannetti, B. F., & de Almeida, C. M. V. B. (2018). A framework of actions for strong sustainability. *Journal of Cleaner Production, 196*, 1629–1643.

Dixson-Declève, S., Gaffney, O., Ghosh, J., Randers, J., Rockstrom, J., & Stoknes, P. E. (2022). *Earth for all: A survival guide for humanity*. New Society Publishers.

Dyllick, T., & Muff, K. (2016). Clarifying the meaning of sustainable business: Introducing a typology from business-as-usual to true business sustainability. *Organization & Environment, 29*(2), 156–174.

Easterlin, R. A. (2003). Explaining happiness. *Proceedings of the National Academy of Sciences, 100*(19), 11176–11183.

Elkington, J. (2021). *Green swans: The coming boom in regenerative capitalism*. Greenleaf Book Group.

Evans, T. (2011). Leadership without domination? Toward restoring the human and natural world. *Journal of Sustainability Education, 2*(1), 1–16.

Folke, C., Biggs, R., Norström, A. V., Reyers, B., & Rockström, J. (2016). Social–ecological resilience and biosphere-based sustainability science. *Ecology and Society, 21*(3), 41.

George, G., Haas, M. R., McGahan, A. M., Schillebeeckx, S. J., & Tracey, P. (2021). Purpose in the for-profit firm: A review and framework for management research. *Journal of Management, 49*(6), 1841–1869.

Gifford, R. (2011). The dragons of inaction: Psychological barriers that limit climate change mitigation and adaptation. *American Psychologist, 66*(4), 290.

Grint, K. (2010). Wicked problems and clumsy solutions: The role of leadership. In S. Brookes & K. Grint (Eds.), *The new public leadership challenge* (pp. 169–186). Palgrave Macmillan UK.

Heede, R. (2014). *Carbon majors: Accounting for carbon and methane emissions 1854–2010 methods & results report*. https://climateaccountability.org/pdf/MRR%209.1%20Apr14R.pdf

Henderson, R. (2020). *Reimagining capitalism in a world on fire*. Penguin UK.

Hickel, J., & Kallis, G. (2020). Is green growth possible? *New Political Economy, 25*(4), 469–486.

Hoffman, A. J. (2015). *How culture shapes the climate change debate*. Stanford University Press.

Hoffman, A. J. (2021). Business education as if people and the planet really matter. *Strategic Organization, 19*(3), 513–525.

Hulme, M. (2022). *Climate change*. Routledge.

Hutchins, G. (2022). Leading by nature for flourishing future-fit business: Embracing an OD in the service of life-affirming futures. *Organization Development Review, 54*(1), 57–64.

Ibarra, H. (2015). The authenticity paradox. *Harvard Business Review, 93*(1/2), 53–59.

Intergovernmental Panel on Climate Change. (2014). *Climate change 2014: Synthesis report. Contribution of Working Groups I, II and III to the Fifth Assessment Report of the Intergovernmental Panel on Climate Change* [Core Writing Team, R. K. Pachauri & L. A. Meyer (Eds.)].

Isham, A., & Jackson, T. (2022). Finding flow: Exploring the potential for sustainable fulfilment. *The Lancet Planetary Health, 6*(1), e66–e74.

Jacobs, M., & Mazzucato, M. (Eds.). (2016). *Rethinking capitalism: Economics and policy for sustainable and inclusive growth*. John Wiley & Sons.

Jackson, B. (2019). The power of place in public leadership research and development. *International Journal of Public Leadership, 15*(4), 209–223.

Jackson, T. (2021). *Post growth: Life after capitalism*. John Wiley & Sons.

Jeanrenaud, S., Jeanrenaud, J. P., & Gosling, J. (Eds.). (2017). *Sustainable business: A one planet approach*. Wiley Global Education.

Kasser, T. (2016). Materialistic values and goals. *Annual Review of Psychology, 67*, 489–514.

MacKie, D. (2016). Positive leadership development. In L. G. Oades, M. F. Steger, D. E. Fave, & J. Passmore (Eds.), *The Wiley Blackwell handbook of the psychology of positivity and strengths-based approaches at work* (pp. 297–316). Wiley.

MacKie, D. (2019). Shared leadership and team coaching. In C. Clutterbuck, J. Gannon, S. Hayes, I. Iordanou, K. Lowe, & D. MacKie (Eds.), *The practitioner's handbook of team coaching* (pp. 53–62). Routledge.

MacKie, D. (2021). Strength-based coaching and sustainability leadership. In W. A. Smith, I. Boniwell, & S. Green (Eds.), *Positive psychology coaching in the workplace* (pp. 375–396). Springer.

Markowitz, E. M., & Shariff, A. F. (2012). Climate change and moral judgement. *Nature Climate Change, 2*(4), 243–247.

Mathieu, C., Neumann, C. S., Hare, R. D., & Babiak, P. (2014). A dark side of leadership: Corporate psychopathy and its influence on employee well-being and job satisfaction. *Personality and Individual Differences, 59*, 83–88.

Mayer, C. (2018). *Prosperity: Better business makes the greater good*. Oxford University Press.

Mazutis, D., & Eckardt, A. (2017). Sleepwalking into catastrophe: Cognitive biases and corporate climate change inertia. *California Management Review, 59*(3), 74–108.

Metcalf, M., & Hinske, C. (2022). Circular economy leadership. In H. Lehmann, C. Hinske, V. de Margerie, & A. Slaveikova Nikolova (Eds.), *The impossibilities of the circular economy: Separating aspirations from reality* (pp. 103–123). Taylor & Francis.

Mishel, L., & Davis, A. (2015). *CEO pay has grown 90 times faster than typical worker pay since 1978*. Economic Policy Institute. https://policycommons.net/artifacts/1409216/ceo-pay-has-grown-90-times-faster-than-typical-worker-pay-since-1978/2023480/

Motesharrei, S., Rivas, J., & Kalnay, E. (2014). Human and nature dynamics (HANDY): Modeling inequality and use of resources in the collapse or sustainability of societies. *Ecological Economics, 101*, 90–102.

Muff, K. (2021). Learning from positive impact organizations: A framework for strategic innovation. *Sustainability, 13*(16), 8891.

Pearce, F. (2009). Consumption dwarfs population as main environmental threat. Yale Environment 360. https://e360.yale.edu/features/consumption_dwarfs_population_as_main_environmental_threat

Pelster, M., & Schaltegger, S. (2022). The dark triad and corporate sustainability: An empirical analysis of personality traits of sustainability managers. *Business Ethics, the Environment & Responsibility, 31*(1), 80–99.

Piketty, T. (2016). *Chronicles: On our troubled times*. Penguin UK.

Polman, P., & Winston, A. (2021). *Net positive: How courageous companies thrive by giving more than they take*. Harvard Business Press.

Robertson, J. L., & Barling, J. (Eds.). (2015). *The psychology of green organizations*. Oxford University Press.

Robertson, J. L., & Barling, J. (2017). Contrasting the nature and effects of environmentally specific and general transformational leadership. *Leadership & Organization Development Journal, 38*(1), 22–41.

Rockström, J., Steffen, W., Noone, K., Persson, Å., Chapin, F. S., Lambin, E. F.,... & Foley, J. A. (2009). A safe operating space for humanity. *Nature, 461*(7263), 472–475.

Rooke, D., & Torbert, W. R. (2005). Seven transformations of leadership. *Harvard Business Review, 83*(4), 66–76.

Sachs, J. D., Schmidt-Traub, G., Mazzucato, M., Messner, D., Nakicenovic, N., & Rockström, J. (2019). Six transformations to achieve the sustainable development goals. *Nature Sustainability, 2*(9), 805–814.

Scharmer, C. O., & Kaufer, K. (2013). *Leading from the emerging future: From ego-system to eco-system economies*. Berrett-Koehler.

Schein, S. (2017). *A new psychology for sustainability leadership: The hidden power of ecological worldviews*. Routledge.

Sosik, J. J., & Jung, D. (2011). *Full range leadership development: Pathways for people, profit and planet*. Psychology Press.

Steffen, W., Broadgate, W., Deutsch, L., Gaffney, O., & Ludwig, C. (2015). The trajectory of the Anthropocene: The great acceleration. *The Anthropocene Review*, 2(1), 81–98.

Stillman, P. (2021) Creating an organizational culture of sustainability. In R. P. Appelbaum (Ed.), *Leadership in sustainability* (pp. 89–109). Fielding.

Stoknes, P. E. (2021). *Tomorrow's economy: A guide to creating healthy green growth*. MIT Press.

Tellus Institute. (2023). Home page. www.tellus.org

Tourish, D. (2013). *The dark side of transformational leadership: A critical perspective*. Routledge.

Tourish, D. (2020) Beyond heroic leadership. https://assets.publishing.service.gov.uk/government/uploads/system/uploads/attachment_data/file/926853/NLC-thinkpiece-Effective-Leadership-TOURISH.pdf

UN Global Compact. (2023). The SDGs. https://www.unglobalcompact.org/

UN Global Compact & Accenture. (2019). Architects of a better world. The UN Global Compact–Accenture CEO study on sustainability. https://unglobalcompact.org/library/5715

UN Global Compact & Russel Reynolds Associates. (2020). *Leadership for the decade of action*. https://www.russellreynolds.com/en/insights/reports-surveys/leadership-for-the-decade-of-action

Van Vugt, M., & Ronay, R. (2014). The evolutionary psychology of leadership: Theory, review, and roadmap. *Organizational Psychology Review*, *4*(1), 74–95.

Wall, T., Mburayi, L., & Johnson, N. (2020). Principles of responsible management education. *Quality Education*, 640–653.

Wamsler, C., & Brink, E. (2018). Mindsets for sustainability: Exploring the link between mindfulness and sustainable climate adaptation. *Ecological Economics*, *151*, 55–61.

Western, S. (2018). The eco-leadership paradox. In B. W. Redekop, D. R. Gallagher, & R. Satterwhite (Eds.), *Innovation in environmental leadership: Critical perspectives* (pp. 48–60). Routledge.

World Bank. (2015). Poverty overview. http://www.worldbank.org/en/topic/poverty/overview

Wright, C., & Nyberg, D. (2015). *Climate change, capitalism, and corporations*. Cambridge University Press.

WWF. (2022). Living planet report 2022. https://www.wwf.org.uk/our-reports/living-planet-report-2022

Part I

FOUNDATIONS

2

FROM ESG MANAGEMENT TO POSITIVE IMPACT CREATION

THE DUAL MINDSET TRANSFORMATION[1]

Prof. Dr. Katrin Muff

The Institute for Business Sustainability (www.theibs.net)

Chapter Summary

The pressure is on for business to embrace sustainability: mandatory ESG (environmental, social and governance) reporting, regulatory changes, increased customer sensitivity and pressure from within leave current CEOs little choice. And yet, it is critical to differentiate between an ESG-based risk management approach and true sustainability that aims at both ensuring reducing negative impacts and generating important positive value for society and the planet. The difference between these approaches has been measured in a first-ever CEO impact rating of largest Swiss organizations. Our research shows that this shift from

1 This chapter first appeared as an article in ***Organization Development Review*, Special Issue: One Giant Leap, Volume 54, Issue 1, published Spring 2022**. The text and images have not been changed from the original.

DOI: 10.4324/9781003343011-3

risk management to impact orientation involves: 1) a strategic innovation, and 2) a dual mindset transformation. The first can be mapped with the Positive Impact Measurement Framework that outlines eight innovation strategies. The second requires an outside-in leadership mindset and a co-creative organization mindset, both can be measured in four distinct aspects. Mindsets are transforming in parallel with new generations that have been entering the corporate workforce. To become Positive Impact Organizations, it is important to: a) gain strategic clarity in terms of reducing negative impact versus increasing positive impact; b) setting relevant 2030 Goal making net zero a must and measuring positive impact products & service as a percentage of revenue; c) understanding the status quo to adapt the transformation to the organizational change readiness and its current degree of sustainability; and d) succeeding the transformation process by implementing the strategic innovation and enabling the dual mindset transformation. This work presents both an invitation and framework for Organizational Development (OD) practitioners to support organizations through the transformations needed in the world today. **Keywords:** Positive Impact Organizations, Positive Impact Measurement Framework, Net Zero Organizations, Dual Mindset Transformation

---

The Challenge for Business & The Opportunity for Organizational Development (OD)

Business is facing increasing pressure from external and internal stakeholders regarding its sustainability efforts. Investors are demanding ESG (environmental, social and governance) reports, the European Union is launching a series of new regulatory frameworks such as the Green Deal, the EU Corporate Sustainability Reporting Directive including the taxonomy for sustainable activities and the Sustainable Finance Disclosure Regulation. Customers are increasingly aware and sensitized on sustainability matters and are adapting their purchasing choices, creating significant market segment shifts. And then there are the kids of corporate leaders who are driving different conversations at the kitchen table, as CEOs willingly admit (Dunn, 2019). The changing demographic in organizations is also seeing a shift with the baby boomers retiring and the Generation X taking charge, pushed by the Millennials and Gen Y. This is resulting in values-driven innovations that result in organizations adopting new purposes that are society-oriented. The decade of action has kicked in and, in many ways this trend toward elevated organizational purposes aligns with the humanistic values that have long been articulated by the field of Organization Development (Margulies & Raia, 1972). As such, the opportunity for the field of Organization Development (OD) to support organizations through this transformation and impact the future trajectory of our society is vast. The challenges businesses are facing today call for alignment of strategy, structure, people, rewards, metrics, and management processes—the exact work in which OD specializes. Ultimately, this work is at the very heart of the work OD has defined for itself, that is working "collaboratively with organizations and communities to develop their system-wide capacity for effectiveness and vitality" (O'Brien & Jackson, 2021, pg. 12).

Clarifying ESG Versus Positive Impact Focus

As we look at the work to be done within organizations today on this massive transformation (previously called "change management"), it is important to differentiate between green washing and truly sustainable efforts within organizations. An important distinction that enables us to recognize this difference is the perspective an organization takes when creating new products and services (Dyllick & Muff, 2016). We call it the difference between an inside-out and an outside-in perspective.

- **Inside-out:** How well is the organization prepared to reduce its sustainability risks and to benefit from its sustainability opportunities? This question is best answered with a traditional risk management and is currently measured through ESG reporting.
- **Outside-in:** Does the organization contribute positively to solving important societal and environmental issues? This question is addressed in the way the organization develops its new product and service offerings and is measured by attributing the revenue to various UN Sustainable Development Goals (SDGs) (United Nations, 2021).

These two perspectives can be displayed in a two-dimensional matrix, whereby the ESG-based risk management is contrasted against the SDG-based impact orientation (see Figure 2.1). The ability to measure the positive impact orientation of an outside-in perspective is critical to entice the

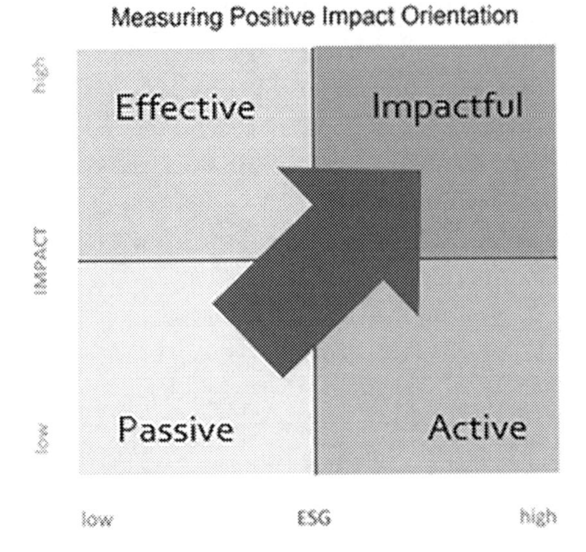

Figure 2.1 Comparing ESG risk management against SDG impact orientation

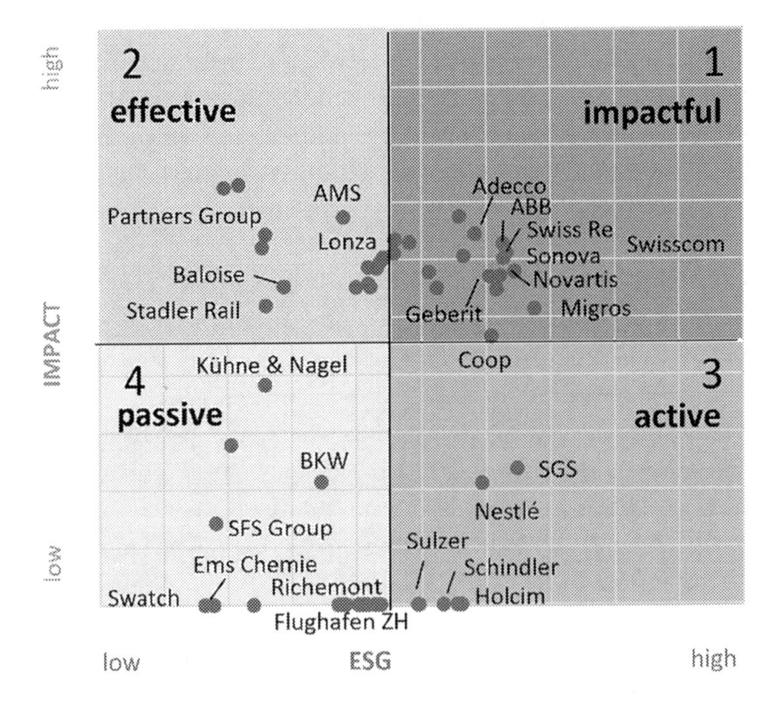

Figure 2.2 Mapping the top 50 Swiss business organizations on the ESG vs. Impact scale

transformation needed so that organizations don't consider their societal duty done when they announce future net zero goals.

In Switzerland, the largest 50 employers and stock-quoted businesses were recently rated against these two measurements. The ESG category was measured using Standard & Poor's ESG data developed by oekom[1]. The SDG category was measured using the ISS SDG data which was developed by truecost[2]. While the SDG impact data is still in development, the comparison published in the renowned Swiss business journal Bilanz (for German language) and PME (for French language) generated an important public discussion about these two approaches to sustainability. We treasure what we measure, Paul Polman has once said, and this is exactly what this new rating does (see Figure 2.2).

Translating a Positive Impact Orientation Into Business

There are two ways Positive Impact Organizations embed their outside-in thinking in their business. First, they embrace their negative impact on the environment and acknowledge the need to eliminate their negative impact. This results in calls for becoming "net zero", meaning that businesses commit to at least compensate their negative CO2 footprint. Looking at the global net zero emissions pathway shows how important it is to take reduction and compensation measures now. Action in the next three to seven years will make the difference between a livable future or a world that will experience climate catastrophes as their new normal.

And yet, cutting CO2 emissions is but a first important step. As we have defined in our research, "truly sustainable business shifts its perspective from seeking to minimize its negative impacts to understanding how it can create a significant positive impact in critical & relevant areas for society & the planet" (Dyllick & Muff 2016, 165–166). This positive impact is created primarily through products and services as well – of course – by being a socially just and sustainable employer and producer. It implies orienting product and service innovation towards solving the SDGs. Paul Polman and Andrew Winston describe these two journeys in their recent book "Net Positive" (October 2021). It goes without saying, achieving this change in perspective from inside-out to outside-in depends on a mindset transformation. This is precisely the space where OD can contribute change management theories and practices to catalyze this transformation within organizations. The following four steps outline a framework for the transformation needed to support organizations with the integration of sustainability into their core.

- Step 1: The organization needs **strategic clarity** regarding its aims. The guiding change question here is: Does the organization seek to simply reduce its negative impact as it is in an industry that is causing harm through CO2 or other emissions; or is the organization seeking to increase its positive impact by focusing its product innovation on societal and environmental challenges such as the SDGs? OD practitioners can work with sustainability experts to help organizations clarify and understand the vast difference between these two pathways.
- Step 2: Once clarified, the organization needs to set **relevant goals for 2030**. This decade of action is our last moment to bend the curve so that our children's children grow up in a world they can safely enjoy. Relevant 2030 goals can be expressed twofold: 1) reducing negative impact and 2) expanding positive impact. Organizations must recognize that achieving net zero is a non-negotiable must. While many organizations will start by compensating their emissions, this target will clarify it as the operational priority it must become. In addition, those organizations that are aiming at generating a positive impact, can set a 2030 goal that measures their positive impact products & service as a percentage of their total revenue. The percentage will depend on the starting base of the company at the moment of goal setting. Research confirms that companies that set ambitious goals have a significantly higher chance in reaching their goal than companies that set modest goals. The message is clear: goals must be inspirational! This is something that the field of OD has long known; that positive images lead to positive actions (Cooperrider, 1999).
- Step 3: Before getting started, we have learned that the organization needs to **understand its status quo**. As OD practitioners know, transformation journeys are challenging and knowing one's starting base and once capacity for change are essential to identify appropriate processes. Two assessments can clarify things enormously. The "change readiness" survey is an excellent tool to host a discussion among the leadership team. It identifies the current and the desired culture of the

organization along two important dimensions: organizational flexibility vs. stability on one hand, and internal vs. external focus. The resulting mapping allows for a focused discussion about potential changes in governance and decision-making, which are – if ignored – the biggest potential obstacles of transformational success. The "True Business Sustainability" assessment helps an organization establish where it is in terms of sustainability. It differentiates between green-washing and true sustainability and it assesses an organization's inside-out vs. outside-in perspective. The purpose of the assessment is to serve as a starting base for an in-depth internal discussion about an organization's sustainability status. Both assessments are available for free online: https://sdgx.org/online-assessments/

- Step 4: Last but not least, we are ready to get started for **a successful transformation process** – which is the work that OD specializes in. There are two key aspects that ensure success in the transformation: 1) the *what*, which relates to selecting the most fruitful strategic innovation focus, and 2) the *how*, which focuses on what it takes to create the dual mindset transformation so that the leadership and the organization is able to transform. The following two sections are dedicated to describing these two aspects of the transformation process, which have proven critical to implement the strategic goals in the organization.

The 'What' of Transformation: Strategic Innovation

Five years of researching Positive Impact Organizations (PIOs) has taught us that these organizations are different from traditional organizations in four distinct ways: 1) The have a sustainability culture including a leader and relevant performance measures in place; 2) they are externally validated by relevant external stakeholders; 3) they have a higher purpose that is translated in their products and services; and 4) their governance is aligned to support their sustainability vision. Furthermore, we have identified four related change challenges these organizations had to overcome in order to become PIOs:

- Change Challenge #1: The **priority challenge** which is observed in the organizational culture. Positive impact organizations with an advanced sustainability culture are inspired and led by a leader or a leadership team that gets the outside–in perspective of sustainability. Such organizations often attract employees who carry a desire to create positive impact in their hearts. Their compensation system is aligned with broader sustainability goals and the organization measures its ambitious sustainability goals. This priority ensures that in times of a crisis, the sustainability topic does not get put on the back-burner.

- Change Challenge #2: The **engagement challenge** to achieve a positive external validation. Positive impact organizations benefit from a positive external recognition of their sustainability efforts have learned to excel in how to engage with external stakeholders. Although traditional firms often consider external stakeholders are a potential danger and handle them with "silver gloves", truly sustainable firms have learned their lessons in how to engage authentically with critical civil society players and how to integrate constructive external views in their operational decision-making processes. Such open stakeholder engagement becomes the source of entirely new "outside-in" ideas that the organization can translate into new business opportunities.
- Change Challenge #3: The **positioning challenge** to accomplish the organization's higher purpose. Positive impact organizations have rewritten their purpose in a way to demonstrate their desire to create a positive impact for society and the planet. What differentiates advanced sustainability organizations from other firms with impact-oriented purpose statement is the fact that they have translated such a purpose into their products and services. They have reconsidered and identified markets which are relevant to them. Other firms have often not been able to make this translation from a lofty purpose to an amended or expanded product or service offering and they not only risk facing credibility issues but also cannot benefit from the opportunities such a new purpose potentially holds for them.
- Change Challenge #4: The **integration challenge** of a governance alignment. Positive impact organizations have implemented alignment in governance are able to attract suitable investors and are likely to have a board that is more supportive of a progressive sustainability agenda. This makes it significantly easier to integrate sustainability deeply within the organization." (Muff, 2021)

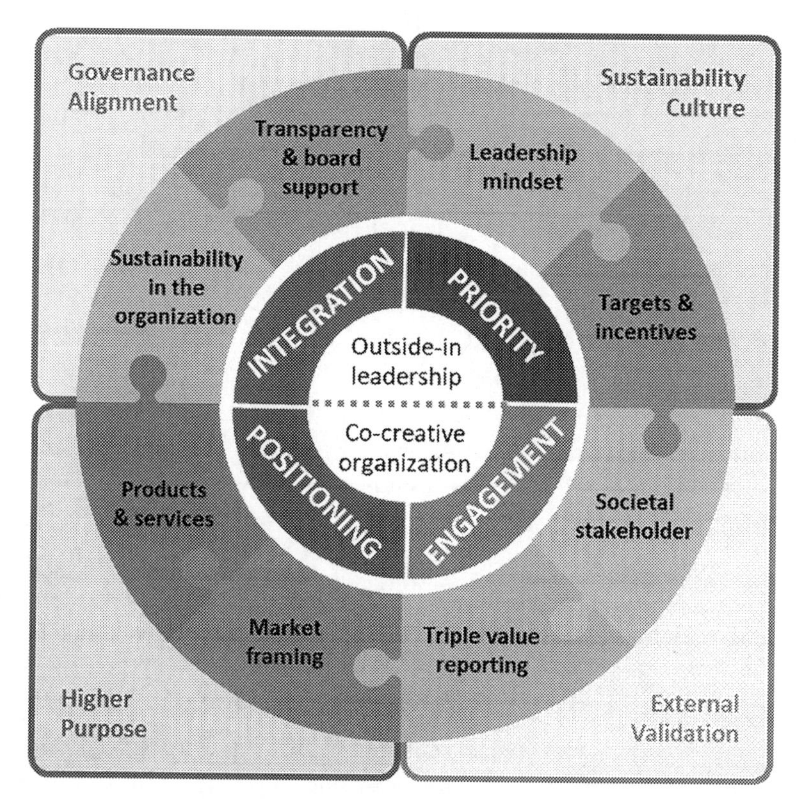

Figure 2.3 The Strategic Innovation Canvas of Positive Impact Organizations

There are different ways of overcoming these challenges and our research has identified eight successful innovation strategies (see Figure 2.3). These strategies can also serve as a guiding framework for OD interventions to influence organizations toward becoming PIOs.

Strategies for Change Challenge #1: The **priority challenge**

1. **Leadership mindset** is one predictor of success of a Positive Impact Organization. The mindset ranges from opportunity seekers to integrators of sustainability, all the way to idealists, that put the societal and planetary well-being at the center of their corporate vision (Bukhari, 2015). Working to educate leaders of the difference between

an inside-out and an outside-in perspective can be a critical intervention strategy for influencing system-wide change.

2. **Targets and incentives** including relevant non-financial, sustainability performance indicators are highly relevant in assessing the degree to which an organization has embraced a sustainability culture. Early sustainability organizations tend to create short term, qualitative targets. Advanced sustainability organizations set smart targets and some non-financial incentives for management. True sustainability organizations find answers in how to create value for stakeholders and society and as a result create both moonshot goals as well as smart, science-based targets and sustainability incentives for all employees, management, and board members. OD as a field is well equipped to support organizations clarifying and aligning targets and incentives in new ways.

   Strategies for Change Challenge #2: The **engagement challenge**

3. The **societal stakeholder** is a new way for the organization to see itself in society. The range of options goes from viewing external stakeholders, to reaching out to stakeholders along the value chain, to ultimately adopting the perspective that as an organization, we are ourselves just one of many responsible stakeholders in society. Fortunately, OD has vast techniques for helping organizations engage the voices of diverse stakeholders.
4. The **triple value reporting** indicates how sustainable an organization is. It ranges from undertaking selective reporting, to reporting on all material aspects, to ultimately engage in the unchartered territory of attempting to report on the societal and environmental value, including negative and positive impacts.

   Strategies for Change Challenge #2: The **positioning challenge**

5. **Market framing** indicates the degree of outside-in thinking in the organization and its purpose. Initially, an organization react to outside pressures in existing markets, later on, an organization may explore new market opportunities and emerging segments inside or outside existing markets. Ultimately, the organization transform existing markets or define entirely new markets as a result of seeking to solve existing societal and environmental challenges, resulting in potential repositioning of future products and services. OD is well versed in

supporting organizations through strategic reflections for such reframing; practitioners are advised to collaborate with sustainability experts to ensure that the size of the challenge can be properly understood.

6. **Products and services** are central to the repositioning of an organization. The development range goes from considering selective improvements of existing products and services, to undertaking systematic improvements across the product and service range, including the whole life-cycle, to ultimately develop products and services that generate a net positive impact on sustainability challenges, along several time horizons (Malnight, Buche and Dhanaraj, 2019). OD practitioners have the skills to facilitate such explorations with multiple stakeholders and are advised to collaborate with relevant experts in product and service innovation and in particular in sustainability and SDG-impact to frame the results appropriately.

   Strategies for Change Challenge #2: The **integration challenge**

7. **Sustainability in the organization** assesses the integration of sustainability is integrated into a hierarchy and structure. The range starts with the creation of a staff function and continues with integrating sustainability responsibilities across departments and divisions. Ultimately, it is about reorganizing the organization around its purpose of addressing a certain societal challenge, creating multi-functional teams that co-create dedicated positive impact products and services together with external partners.
8. **Transparency and board support** allow measuring the degree of sustainability integration. It ranges from defensive policies to protect against sustainability risks to a fully transparent integration of triple-bottom line objectives into policies and an inclusion of relevant societal stakeholders into decision-making processes across the organization, including the board, which is work that falls well within OD's realm of competencies.

We have translated these insights into a strategic innovation process that organizations of any type and size can use to implement a positive impact orientation into their business. The process was prototyped with businesses across all relevant sectors and was field-tested since. We call it SDGXCHANGE and it works both online and with in-person workshops. We train consultants interested in using the methodology so that they can advise their clients in how to embed sustainability into their organizations. We offer all tools as open-source solutions. We want this to spread quickly as we want business to transform. More information is available at: www.SDGX.org, complete with proven tools to help organizations create the change we need in the world today.

The 'How' of Transformation: The Dual Mindset Transformation

Any of the eight innovation strategies serve to overcome the identified four challenges that are required to be resolved to realize the four strategic differentiators of PIOs: a sustainability culture, an external validation, a higher purpose and a governance alignment. When we analyzed the organizations during their transformation journey to become PIOs, we could identify two predictors of success during that transformation. If an organization had these two factors in place, it was only a question of time until they were able to create a positive impact. The two factors are not of strategic nor of organizational nature; they relate to the mindset of the leadership and to that of the organization (see Figure 2.4). We learned that an organization has a mindset too, not just a leader. We shall explore the two of them here further.

At the individual level of leaders, we are looking for an outside-in leadership mindset. A leader with this mindset has redefined their own role and as a consequence the role of their organization in society. Such leaders experience themselves as one with the world and as a result they broaden their focus to serve the common good. They seek to provide a positive contribution to society and the planet, and they align their organizational

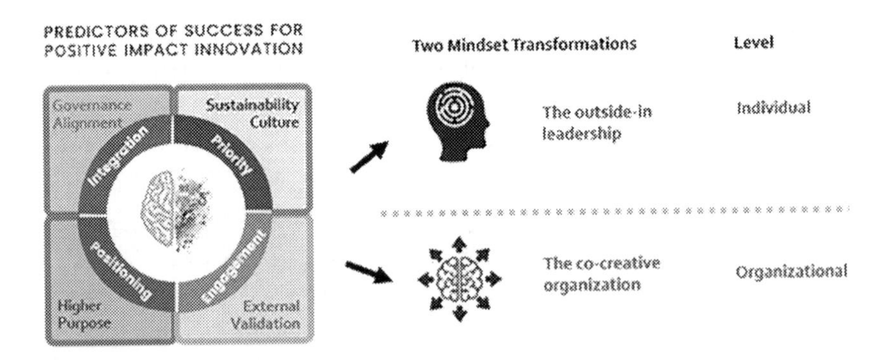

Figure 2.4 The two predictors of success: outside-inside leadership and co-creative organization

processes to ensure the long-term well-being of the organization. These insights are supported by related research suggesting that sustainability minded leaders have an ecological worldview that comes with a high degree of eco-literacy and clarity regarding their contribution for society. Such leaders often develop a spiritual intelligence that springs from how they see themselves in nature and in how mindful they with others (Rimanoczy, 2020).

At the organizational level, we have discovered the co-creative organization mindset. PIOs excel in how openly they engage with their external stakeholders. They are externally oriented and able to work as fluently outside of their boundaries as internally across divisions. Multi-stakeholder processes have shown that co-creative organizations successfully work with stakeholders outside of their traditional boundaries, living their positive impact purpose by co-creating innovative solutions with them. Organizational mindsets can be best observed in smaller groups. For example, a way to observe that systems thinking is alive is to see the "both/and" approach applied in discussions. Such teams demonstrate a high degree of emotional intelligence, which includes self-awareness and the capacity to reflect. They are interconnected and capable to engage in purpose-driven innovation.

The transformation from a traditional mindset to a positive impact mindset can be described at the leadership level as transforming from "me" to "we", and at the organizational level as transforming from "competition" to "co-creation". This sounds easy and evident; yet shifting from a closed to an open stance at the individual level or from being risk aware to being opportunity aware is not for the faint-hearted (see Figure 2.5).

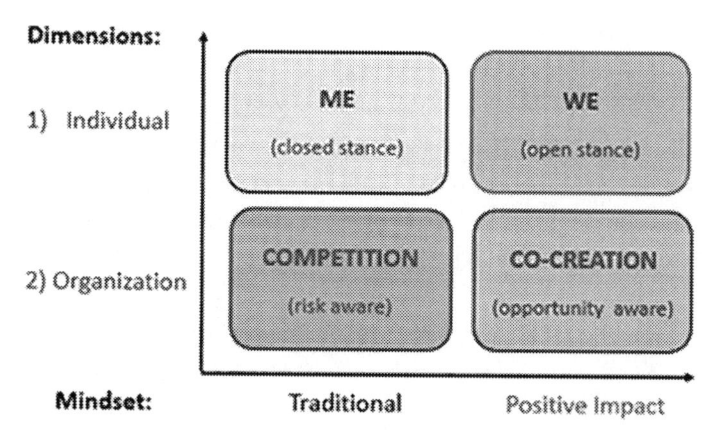

Figure 2.5 The two mindset transformations from traditional to positive impact

Research into mindset transformation has revealed interesting insights into what it takes get from a traditional to a positive impact mindset (Muff, 2018). The Outside-In Leadership Mindset Transformation consists of four aspects, two are visible (external), two are often hard to perceive (internal). This shift could be called as moving from an egocentric to and eco-centric worldview.

- The **internal aspects** concern a transformation from being internally closed to becoming internally directed; and from being externally directed to externally open. Internally directed can also be called being "values-based", which is quite the opposite of being externally directed, which is sometime also called acting like a flag in the wind.
- The **external aspects** can be observed as a transformation from being self-focused to becoming other-focused; and from acting from comfort-centered preference to embracing a purpose-centered attitude. It is often quite easy to assess others in where they are on these two scales, albeit it is worth pointing out that depending on the type of pressure, most persons can become self-focused.

The Co-creative Organization Mindset Transformation can also be described in these four aspects, two are visible (external), two are often hard to perceive (internal). This transformation is also called as moving from a state of competition to a state of co-creation.

- The **internal aspects** relate to the transformation from being tribe-oriented to being issue-oriented; and from rejecting differences to embracing differences.
- The **external aspects** can be observed in how an organization live its values. It is reflected in how an organization treat other organizations with different values. The transformation can be defined as moving from competing values to co-creating values. This can also be observed in how the organization operates. The transformation ranges from operating disconnectedly to operating in a connected way with other players.

This may also sound like much and a bit overwhelming. It may be helpful to remember that in any organization today, there are already different

Figure 2.6 The current and emerging generations in a typical organization

mindsets of different generations present. A typical organization today has four generations in-house that need to work together and these four generations come with very different mindsets (see Figure 2.6). This reflection is not meant to categorize people into boxes, rather it is meant to help understand and recognize different mindsets. I find it helpful to consider a particular generation, lets take Gen Y, as an expression of the decade and a half in which they are born. The shift from Gen Z, which was focused on the status symbol latest tech gadgets to Gen Y, which is purpose-oriented and demands equal treatment of all minorities, is a shift of awareness and consciousness across a certain part of society of these times. The 2nd decade of the 21st century saw movements like "me too", "Fridays for Future" and "black life matters" become important influences that shaped our society. Anybody in society, irrespective into which generation they are born, has been affected by these influences.

A Call for Action

If you are a business leader, an OD practitioner, or a next-gen future leader, I hope the message is clear: step up and help the organizations you are involved in embrace and integrate positive impact in their core business activities. Yes, it will involve new processes and new innovation strategies. It will also require an ability to work inter- and trans-disciplinary. For OD practitioners in particular, this means reaching out to experts in fields of new subjects such as SDG-impact and sustainability from an opportunity-creation rather than just a risk-management perspective, as well as more traditional fields such as innovation and strategy. And, just as importantly, it will require a leadership and an organization mindset transformation that is nothing short of a revolution. The tools and measurement frameworks exist. The innovation strategies for the transformation needed in our organizations connect directly to the field of OD. What I am suggesting here is purpose-orientation of OD in service of helping organizations to provide positive value to society and our planet. What we need is you – a courageous change agent that will translate insights of lessons learned described here into concrete action. Remember, these four steps to embed a positive impact into organizations:

1. Create Strategic Clarity (Reducing negative impact, Increasing positive impact)
2. Set Relevant 2030 Goals (Net zero is a must, Positive impact products & service as % of revenue)
3. Understanding the Status Quo (Change readiness, Degree of sustainability)
4. Succeeding the Transformation Process (Strategic Innovation, The Dual Mindset Transformation)

The insights presented in this thought piece are based on published, open access research (link here). Please reach out to me if you have questions. I am dedicating my life to help find answers to enable business to realize its positive business potential – the world depends on it!

Notes

1 See: https://www.intentionalendowments.org/oekom_research_inc
2 See: https://www.marketplace.spglobal.com/en/datasets/trucost-sustainable-development-goals-analytics-(163)

References

Bukhari, N. Pebbles (PVT) Ltd sustainable real estate develops: Building hope. In *Award-Winning Case Studies 2015*; Muff, K., Ed.; A Special Issue of Building Sustainable Legacies; Greenleaf Publishing: Sheffield, UK, 2015.

Cooperrider, D.L. (1999). Positive Image, Positive Action: The Affirmative Basis of Organizing. In Cooperrider, D., Sorenson, P., Whitney, D., and Yaeger T.

(Eds). *Appreciative Inquiry: An Emerging Direction for Organization Development* (pp. 29–53). Champaign IL: Stipes Publishing.

Dunn, K. (2019). CEOs are Facing Fierce Pressure on Climate Change – From their own kids. Fortune: Nov 25. Retrieved Dec 27, 2021 from: https://fortune.com/2019/11/25/ceos-climate-change-kids/

Malnight, T.W.; Buche, I.; Dhanaraj, C. (2019). *Put Purpose at the Core of Your Strategy—It's How Successful Companies Redefine Their Businesses.* Harvard Business Review. Sept/Oct: 70–79.

Margulies, N., & Raia, A. P. (1972). Organizational development: Values, process, and technology. New York: McGraw-Hill.

Muff, K. (2021). Learning from Positive Impact Organizations: A Framework for Strategic Innovation. *Sustainability.* 13(16): 8891.

Muff, K. (2018). Five Superpowers for Co-Creators: How Change Makers and Business Can Achieve the Sustainable Development Goals. Routledge: Sheffield, UK.

O'Brien, J. & Gilpin-Jackson, Y. (2021). What is the Definition of OD? *Organization Development Review*: 53(1): 12–20.

Polman, P. and Winston, A. (2021). Net Positive: How Courageous Companies Thrive by Giving More. Harvard Business Review Press.

Rimanoczy, I. (2020). The Sustainability Mindset Principles: A Guide to Developing a Mindset for a Better World; Routledge: London, UK; New York, NY, USA.

United Nations. (2021). *Sustainable Development Goals Report.* Retrieved December 27, 2021 from https://unstats.un.org/sdgs/report/2020/The-Sustainable-Development-Goals-Report-2020.pdf

3

OVERCOMING COGNITIVE BIASES THAT CONTRIBUTE TO CORPORATE CLIMATE CHANGE INERTIA

Anna Eckardt and Daina Mazutis

Chapter Summary

Climate change has long been identified as one of the most significant environmental, social and economic risks to individuals, governments, businesses and the planet. And yet immediate and deep emissions reductions across all industrial sectors have not materialised (Intergovernmental Panel on Climate Change, 2022; World Economic Forum, 2022). What might be causing this corporate climate change inertia? In this chapter, we illustrate how cognitive biases prevent business leaders from accurately perceiving the importance of climate change, preventing them from paying attention to, and ultimately acting on, climate-related issues. While other institutional and organisational factors also contribute to inaction, the role of managerial cognitive biases should not be underestimated. As the research reviewed and synthesised herein suggests, the effects of framing, anchoring, availability and professional identity biases can have a profound impact on how climate change is perceived by organisational leaders. The larger goal of this

DOI: 10.4324/9781003343011-4

chapter, however, is to go beyond purely descriptive accounts of cognitive biases by also presenting a list of mitigating interventions that could be implemented within the organisation to counter these biases. In doing so, we hope to illustrate how business leaders can better pay better attention to the strategic importance of climate change.

Introduction

Despite the plethora of calls from the scientific community over the last several decades for an urgent and immediate corporate response to the imminent negative effects of global warming, most organisations continue to run their operations as though climate change is not an issue. And while the press reports on yet another update from the International Panel on Climate Change, deep emissions reductions across all sectors have not materialised. Rather, despite 27 years of COP meetings (Conference of the Parties of the United Nations Framework Convention on Climate Change), there has been very little actual progress from businesses located in the very same signatory countries that pledged meaningful climate action before the turn of the last century.

We argue, therefore, that at this moment most businesses are continuing to sleepwalk into a climate disaster (Mazutis & Eckardt, 2017). For example, in Europe, recent research has demonstrated that the current strategic course of European companies is more in line with a 2.7°C increase in global temperatures by 2100 than in line with the 1.5°C required as being 'safe' for our ecosystems to survive (CDP, 2022). Not surprisingly, then, this same report found that as of 2021, (only) 56% of European companies in their sample even had a transition plan to net zero emissions, meaning that 44% of organisations do not yet even have a plan to tackle an issue that has been identified as critical for more than 30 years.

In parallel, governments continue to provide perverse subsidies to the fossil fuel industry, the largest contributor to the industrial greenhouse gas (GHG) emissions that cause global warming. Between 2015 and 2019 alone, G20 member countries (all of whom were signatories to COP21) have subsidised coal, oil and gas and fossil fuel power to the tune of over $3.3 trillion. And governments are not the only ones fuelling this disaster – the *Fossil Fuel Finance Report* 2022, for example, found that that the world's 60 largest commercial and investment banks have poured another $4.6 trillion into fossil fuel projects in the 6 years following the adoption of the Paris Agreement at COP21 in 2016 (BankTrack et al., 2022).

These and many other examples make us wonder how it is possible that despite the global scientific consensus (American Meteorological Society, 2003; Cook et al., 2016; Intergovernmental Panel on Climate Change, 2007; National Academy of Sciences Committee on the Science of Climate Change, 2021; National Aeronautics and Space Administration, 2016) that climate change will have huge consequences not just for the planet in general but on corporate operations specifically, business leaders continue to fail to adjust their strategic priorities to incorporate the impact of climate change. Why have companies not recognised the magnitude of the issue and adjusted their operations to prevent a climate change catastrophe in the future?

We argue that one of the reasons behind corporate climate change inertia has to do with specific cognitive biases that derail the quality of managerial attention towards the issue and diminish the capacity of decision makers to focus on and sustain their attention towards the issue over time. While there are certainly many other contextual factors operating at individual, organisational and even institutional levels that have contributed to organisational climate change inertia (Slawinski et al., 2015), we suggest that a closer look at the cognitive mechanisms behind how climate change is perceived and judged by business leaders can help us understand the attentional voids (Mazutis et al., 2022) contributing to the glacial pace of organisational change. In so doing, we take a distinctly upper echelon view of leadership (vs. trait- or personality-based perspectives), where the managerial cognition processes of an organisation's top executives (CEO, top management team) impact the strategic decisions being made (Finkelstein et al., 2009). In the context of climate change, we find that the existing discourse around the issue prevents business leaders from noticing, identifying and recognising it as a sufficiently important and critical strategic issue. As a result, climate change gets screened out of managerial attentional engagement processes, thereby also ultimately hindering the implementation of more sustainable solutions.

In this chapter, we first explore the underlying reasons for why business leaders fail to pay attention to climate change by elaborating on the cognitive biases that affect perceptions of climate change specifically. We describe and illustrate how these biases effect the selective attention processes in organisations but also provide examples of successful mitigating interventions that can be implemented as debiasing tactics. In this manner, we present practical ideas about how leaders can more mindfully overcome the phenomenon of cognitive biases contributing to corporate climate change inertia.

Theory and Concepts

Managerial Attention to Strategic Issues

For more than 50 years, organisation theory has focused on finding a solution to the major (and ever growing) challenge of how to effectively support managers coping with high volumes of information by correctly directing their attention towards critical issues (Ocasio et al., 2022). It is against this backdrop that Herbert Simon (1973, p. 270) remarked that 'the scarce resource is not information; it is processing capacity to attend to information. Attention is the chief bottleneck in organisational activity, and the bottleneck becomes narrower and narrower as we move to the tops of organisations ...'. For strategy scholars such as Alfred Chandler, the solution to this information processing challenge lay in delegating the multitude of daily operational decisions to specific divisions within the organisation to protect their top managers from attentional overload and allow them to focus on strategy (Chandler, 1962). However, since then, organisational contexts have significantly evolved, making it necessary for managers to pay equal attention to strategically valuable information coming from multiple stakeholders (Ocasio et al., 2022). Therefore, managers are exposed to even more cues, both from outside and from within their own organisation, leading to a significant increase of cognitive effort that needs to be deployed to engage in accurate sensemaking. The flipside of this phenomenon is that this increase of cognitive effort further constrains how much information leaders can attend to at a given point in time.

When a strategic issue (such as climate change) falls outside the scope of normal business activity and requires greater deliberation, it must sufficiently stand out or be considered critical for the decision maker to be willing to focus their limited and potentially already stretched attentional capacity to engage in dealing with it (Eckardt & Mazutis, 2020). As part of executive job demands, leaders of business organisations should be attuned to noticing and scanning their operating environments for important changes in social, technological, environmental, economic or other signals that might affect organisational competitiveness and performance. Information about climate change–related risks such as energy security, water scarcity, supply chain security, higher costs of raw materials, increased likelihood of natural disasters, constantly changing regulatory and legal requirements around carbon and GHG emissions, etc., should hence come to the attention of the corporate decision makers. In theory, the attention of business leaders to climate change–related cues, developed through continuous and interactive interplay between scanning and engagement with strategy insights coming from the top to the bottom, should not only ensure attentional stability (the ability to keep their focus on the issue over time) but also maintain attentional vividness (the ability to pay attention to both the breadth of the issue as well as its details; Rerup, 2009). Unfortunately, this attentional perception, engagement and focus with climate change as a strategic issue has largely failed to materialise. For example, a recent study showed that even though 84% of global leaders claim to be very 'concerned' or 'worried' about the climate risk outlook, a full 77% of these same leaders say that their companies' efforts to mitigate climate change have not started or are only in early development (World Economic Forum, 2022). This perception vs. action gap is our specific area of inquiry.

We argue that perceptual cognitive biases affect the way in which business leaders notice, scan for, encode and subsequently interpret climate change as a 'strategic cue' worth attending to. This in turn can inhibit sensemaking and attentional quality (stability and vividness) and lead to attentional voids; that is, the complete absence of engagement with the issue in the context of their strategic decision-making process (Mazutis et al., 2022). We illustrate this challenge in Figure 3.1 via a separation between the largely automatic processes of selective attention and the more intentional processes of attentional engagement and choice (Ocasio et al., 2022). Importantly, we include in our model the potential for deliberate interventions that can mitigate the effects of these cognitive biases and help leaders to 'pay attention to' issues such as climate change that might otherwise fail to get noticed.

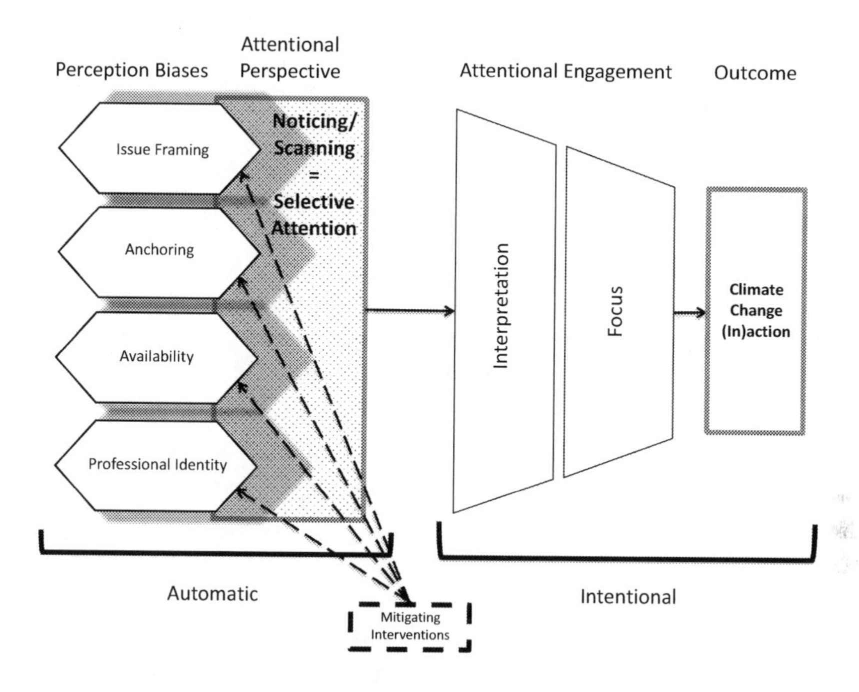

Figure 3.1 An Attention-Based View of Climate Change (In)action

Cognitive Biases and Climate Change Inaction

Research on cognitive biases is prolific (see Ariely, 2008; Bazerman & Tenbrunsel, 2011; Finkelstein et al., 2008; Haidt, 2001; Thaler & Sunstein, 2008). Studies from multiple disciplines including psychology, philosophy, economics, sociology and business have identified hundreds of cognitive biases that impact how individuals make decisions. Our focus here is on an assortment of cognitive biases that affect how issues are perceived. Perceptual cognitive biases impact the attentional perspective; that is, they interfere with cognitive structures that generate heightened awareness and focus over time to relevant stimuli and responses. This is important because the attentional perspective not only affects automatic and intentional information processing – cognitive aspects – but it also has motivational effects on action (Kaplan & Henderson, 2005).

We focus on issue framing, anchoring, availability and professional identity biases that specifically effect noticing and scanning processes contributing to selective attention as identified in Figure 3.1. We believe that these biases can prevent decision makers from noticing and encoding stimuli that would otherwise allow them to recognise climate change as a critical issue within their business context in the first place (for an overview of all of the types of bias categories, refer to Mazutis & Eckardt, 2017).

Issue Framing

Issue framing has been shown to affect how people interpret a given topic and can include how an issue is worded textually or presented graphically. For example, because in the early part of this century there was deliberate move away from referring to the issue of rising GHG emissions and their consequences as 'global warming' to the more controllable and less emotional term 'climate change', organisational leaders were less likely to perceive the urgency and magnitude of consequences associated with the impending climate disaster. In addition, the media continues to portray climate change as something that will occur in a distant time and place, with unknown consequences and ambiguous impacts. This framing reduces the likelihood that organisational leaders will perceive climate change as a critical cue that should be of importance to current business practices. By framing global warming using vague language (e.g., global temperatures are expected to rise between 2°C and 5°C sometime in the future), it becomes cognitively easier to discount what seems to be a relatively small and distant temperature increase; these nebulous cues therefore influence selective attention, allowing organisational leaders to efficiently 'weed out' (Nicolini & Korica, 2021) climate change stimuli.

Anchoring

Similarly, these 'small estimates' serve as textual anchors which are numerical or positional statements that prime how issues are interpreted and hence impact how leaders pay attention to what they are paying attention to (Lovallo & Sibony, 2012; Strack et al., 1988). That is, a wide body of research has found that simply suggesting a starting value (the anchor) for issues such as salary negotiations or house purchases, for example, influences subsequent interpretations and outcomes. With regards to climate change, these low anchors (of 2°C–5°C warmer) can prevent organisational leaders from being immediately concerned about the implications of the possible scale and scope of a climate catastrophe: if we can cope with even larger temperature fluctuations during the year, it becomes difficult to imagine the terrible impact that a 2°C increase could have on one's business.

The vague and distant anchors around the time horizons associated with climate change communication (an issue which will occur 'in the coming decades' or 'in approximately 30 years from now') is similarly problematic. These temporal anchors lower the urgency of climate change by increasing the distance between cause and effect, allowing organisational leaders to defer paying attention to this issue. Setting global carbon reduction goals for the year 2030 or 2050 creates long time frames, further suggesting that social consensus supports focussing any intentional engagement and action in the future (versus focusing attention, engagement and action on the issue now). Very few current business leaders will be in their same roles in 25 years and forced to face the consequences of their own lack of attentional perspective, engagement and focus on climate change. In summary, the way in which climate change has been framed and anchored in the popular discourse as 'only 2°C' or 'something to worry about in 30 years' has fed perception biases that have contributed to the lack of attentional engagement and focus given to this issue by business leaders in a corporate context.

Availability Biases

Noticing and scanning processes are also influenced by unconscious availability biases which impact the vividness and saliency of informational cues. Availability biases are mental shortcuts or simplifying strategies that describe the human tendency to depend on immediate top-of-mind examples when considering a specific topic, concept or decision (Schwarz et al., 1991; Tversky & Kahneman, 1979). The underlying assumption of this bias is that if something can be recalled, it must be important, or at least more important than other stimuli which are not as readily recalled. Subsequently, under the availability heuristic, people tend to pay attention to more recent information. For example, research has demonstrated that vivid information is more likely to be stored and remembered, which makes it, by definition, easier to access and hence to have available when scanning for environmental cues (Nisbet & Ross, 1980). Information or events are perceived as more vivid when they are closer to us both physically and psychologically (proximity). They are also more vivid when the threat of an event will affect us now or in the immediate future (temporal immediacy). Similarly, the saliency of an issue will depend on how this issue stands out relative to other issues when it comes to noticing stimuli in the attention perception phase.

One of the implications of these availability biases is that vivid and salient but improbable events tend to receive more than their due weight in selective attention processes. Unfortunately, the opposite is also true: Probable or even certain events, such as the impact of climate change to business, which are less vivid and less salient, are less 'available' and will consequently be overlooked in the scanning phase. A leader's capacity to appropriately perceive the plausibility, frequency and magnitude of climate change therefore depends on how readily they can imagine its consequences relative to other important business issues and hence notice these as problems requiring subsequent attentional engagement and strategic action.

Given the fact that climate change is not a single phenomenon but rather a complex interplay of a multitude of different factors that are changing the Earth's climate overall, the ability to perceive the salience of the cues is diminished. For example, while the occurrence of hefty weather events such as record snowfalls or more frequent floods, hurricanes and typhoons receives media attention because these events are presented as single, unrelated events, though they may be vivid and salient for those directly impacted, the lack of proximity and/or low magnitude of consequences for businesses not impacted make them unavailable when it comes down to perceiving climate change as a strategic issue requiring attention and action. Unless a corporation has suffered direct or indirect concrete losses from climate change–related events such as droughts, floods or hurricanes in a short and memorable time frame, these cues will remain unavailable in executive noticing and scanning processes.

Professional Identity Biases

Finally, business leaders often rationalise climate change inaction by citing normative and coercive pressures that 'prevent' organisations from adopting more aggressive mitigation strategies than minimally necessary to be compliant with law. Managers describe their beliefs as in line with 'industry trends' and their fiduciary duty towards the shareholder within the profit maximisation paradigm. As a consequence, they perceive more aggressive climate change initiatives as something that would put their company at a competitive disadvantage (Hofmann & Bazerman, 2005). This is an example of professional identity bias for the management profession (Lindner, 1987).

A professional identity bias describes a perspective that narrows one's field of vision by focusing on the norms and conventions of a single profession. Perpetuated by decades of teaching profit-maximising management theories in universities and business schools, the shareholder maximisation norm has become the central tenet of every business activity and hence a core part of a business leader's professional identity (Ghoshal, 2005; Stout, 2012). For example, we know from previous research (e.g., Hawkins & Cocanougher, 1972) that business students found questionable business practices less important than did non-business students. Similarly, Jordan (2009) found that second-year MBA students showed significantly lower moral awareness than did first-year MBA students, suggesting that moral awareness decreases with the increased exposure to business studies. As a consequence, by perpetuating the myth that business, society and the biosphere are mutually independent, this professional bias constrains how business leaders perceive climate change issues (Starik & Rands, 1995); under this paradigm, social and environmental impacts are considered as irrelevant externalities and therefore not noticed or selectively 'weeded out' of more deliberate attentional focus.

While these examples of perceptual cognitive biases are by no means exhaustive, they are representative of automatic 'thinking errors' that contribute to the lack of attention business leaders pay to climate change in organisational contexts, preventing climate change cues from being picked up as strategic issues. Because these biases play such a critical role at the beginning of the attentional engagement process, they in turn limit the range of strategic alternatives considered and bias the attentional channels and structures created within organisations to address the issue. A central question then becomes what, if anything, can be done to overcome these cognitive biases and increase the likelihood that business leaders will pay attention to climate change as a strategic issue? Research has demonstrated that just being aware of one's biases is insufficient to prevent decision-making errors. As such, we focus next on deliberate, mindful mitigating tactics that business leaders can implement to ensure that climate change cues do not get unintentionally overlooked and excluded from the attentional engagement and focus that they deserve.

Overcoming Perceptual Biases: Methods, Techniques and Applications

The first step in countering the effects of cognitive biases is to acknowledge that they exist and likely play a role in selective perception and attention processes. By labelling and identifying the biases, we are able to move the engagement with the topic of climate change out of the realm of 'automatic' or unconscious to a stage where it can be intentionally addressed through the deliberate implementation of mitigating tactics. Debiasing interventions tackle the perceptual biases of issue framing, anchoring, availability and professional identity bias by intensifying the magnitude, immediacy and proximity of the effect of climate change risks and opportunities on business operations. By making climate change impacts more concrete, more immediate, more proximate and more available, leaders are more likely to perceive and scan for cues about climate change, thereby triggering the rest of the attentional engagement and focus processes.

Cognitive biases that short-circuit accurate perceptions of the urgency, immediacy or necessity to address climate change are at the heart of the failure of business leaders to attend to the issue in the noticing/scanning phase of attentional engagement. Mitigating tactics therefore must serve to augment these dimensions of climate change in such a way that increases the cues associated with the health and well-being of the firm and its stakeholders.

We propose ten easy tactics that can be deployed to increase the probability that climate change appears on the radar of business leaders in a more regular way. That is, once a leader acknowledges that these perceptual biases are narrowing the scope of their attentional perspective, there are many deliberate actions that can be taken to mitigate the potentially negative effects of these biases. We offer ten tactics ranging from more externally focused initiatives, through more mesolevel organisational tactics that can be implemented in any business:

1. **Change the frame:** As much as climate change has traditionally been framed as a multifaceted risk to geographically distant future

generations, business leaders can reframe how climate change is having an impact on the organisation here and now. For decades management scholars have debated 'the business case for sustainability', which has focused primarily on establishing tenuous and vague correlations between sustainable solutions and profits. Lessons from debiasing tactics, however, suggest that the argument could be more effectively reframed as the need to mitigate the very real, concrete and immediate losses to profits that are likely to accrue to an organisation that ignores impending climate change risks. For example, large investors like the Norwegian Pension Fund and Blackrock are divesting from fossil fuels and insisting on reporting the CO_2 emissions of their investment portfolios. Business leaders can use these changes in the external environment to establish a clear correlation between the necessity to address the company's own CO_2 emissions if they want to have access to attractive funding, or any access to capital at all. This would actively reframe climate change as something affecting far-away 'others' in a distant future to an issue that needs immediate attention here and now, thus broadening the attentional perspective and subsequent attentional engagement.

2. **Join industry-level sustainability coalitions:** Joining industry-level sustainability coalitions can also expose organisational leaders more regularly to climate change cues and ultimately help alter ingrained professional identity biases by establishing new business norms. Climate change action is often perceived as costly, and first movers fear competitive disadvantage. Joining forces and committing to certain actions as part of an industry group (coalition) can alleviate the fear of 'losing out' towards laggards, when being progressive in proactively doing 'more'. For example, the industry-led and United Nations–hosted Net Zero Banking Alliance initially brought together 43 of the world's biggest banks, providing a forum for strategic coordination of the finance sector towards the alignment of their portfolios with the 2°C Paris goal. It was designed to ensure that banks engage with their clients' transition towards decarbonisation, promoting real economy transition. Similarly, the Green Hydrogen Catapult Coalition reunites the world's biggest hydrogen producers to halve the current costs of hydrogen below the tipping point, which will make green hydrogen the energy source of choice across other CO_2-intensive and critical

sectors such as fertiliser production and power generation. These are just two examples that illustrate how actors in a given industry can collectively become engaged around climate change issues in a regular business context, thereby mitigating the availability and professional identity biases around the perceptual importance of climate change.

3. **Invoke other identity frames:** The power of identity frames to alter how we perceive situations has been well established. As such, rather than invoking only shareholder maximisation norms, business leaders can instead tap into other identity frames that are more supportive of long-term climate change goals. Nike, for example, invoked the company's innovation and competition culture to design more environmentally sustainable shoes, rather than trying to invent a new purely sustainable professional identity (Howard-Grenville & Bartels, 2012). Alternatively, emphasising the role of history and past employees in producing the present group's identity has been shown to enhance intergenerational identification and thus help promote environmental sustainability (Plunkett Tost & Wade-Benzoni, 2012). This broadening of professional identity beyond the confines of the singular pursuit of financial returns can thus mitigate perceptual biases preventing climate change cues from being noticed as salient.
4. **Use simulations and experiential exercises:** To make climate change even more salient and 'available', exposure to simulations or experiential exercises can also be helpful. For example, designing service-learning opportunities such as work exchange programs in countries experiencing severe climate change impacts can render social and environmental responsibility and sustainability more salient to executives (Pless et al., 2011). If physical travel is not feasible or reasonable, the use of climate change simulations in executive training programs can increase knowledge of the issue in a manner that alleviates availability bias by making climate change considerations more readily accessible in future decision-making contexts. It also normalises climate change as an important issue from a professional identity perspective, thereby also broadening a leader's attentional perspective.
5. **Implement joint evaluation:** Business leaders can also insist on joint evaluation of both small and large strategic initiatives. Research suggests that when one is presented with just the losses or just the gains of initiatives, the losses will almost always be more salient; however,

if a combination option is introduced, where the gains and losses are presented together, this option will prevail (Shu & Bazerman, 2012). Insisting that any new initiative include not only the financial gains/losses but also the environmental and social gains/losses simultaneously would equalise the stimuli and the effectiveness of these cues. Conversely, if sustainability is relegated to a department that is independent of (and subservient to) finance, the two will compete for selective attention. At the more macro level, therefore, how organisational design and decision making are structured within the organisation can have a profound impact on what gets perceived as important within the firm.

Once leaders have reframed the climate change as an issue that is important to the organisation, there are many ways to embed the importance of the issue within the organisational context in such a way that it stays top of mind in the attentional perception, interpretation, and focus process. To further increase the importance of climate change cues within the organisation, a range of mesolevel mitigating tactics can also be deployed. For example:

6. **Change the trim tab:** The trim tab refers to a small flap on a larger boat rudder that, when activated, changes the direction of immense vessels. The analogy has been used in organisational and systems theory to suggest that small changes in complex structures can incite significant transformations. For example, we know that 'what gets measured, gets managed'. To make climate change cues more salient, organisational leaders can reformulate performance scorecards to incorporate long-term climate change objectives. This one small trim tab tactic would trigger the relevancy of climate change to immediate decisions and undoubtedly change the way in which climate change issues are perceived and interpreted within organisations.
7. **Establish stretch targets:** Importantly, organisational leaders can also set these climate change goals around 'gold standard' stretch goals (e.g., zero emissions, zero waste, 100% renewables, etc.), rather than anchoring climate change goals to incremental improvements. Research suggests that simply being exposed to higher anchors results in respondents setting higher energy performance goals; even no anchor, it seems, is better than low anchors, which tend to drive declared targets downwards (Klotz, 2011). When organisations accept 'reducing

emissions by 5%' or 'cutting GHGs by 7%', they are unconsciously tethering their performance to low anchors. In contrast, innovative, transformational companies are announcing zero-emission goals or zero-waste targets which drastically alter how climate change is perceived, interpreted and acted upon within the organisation. Unilever, for example, made headlines in 2010 when it announced that it would double the size of the business while halving its environmental footprint by 2020. This aggressive target changed how managers perceived the temporal immediacy of climate change within the company. Large multinationals from GE to GM have also committed to zero-landfill facilities, again changing the anchors internally from reduction to elimination. Truly imaginative companies, stretch their anchors even further. California's Newlight Technologies, for example, is committed to being carbon negative, not just carbon neutral, in that their resin compounding processes actually remove harmful GHGs from the air and turn them into plastic.

8. **Steal from the safety culture playbook:** Many organisations have designed safety interventions for daily tasks that would otherwise be routine or automatic to increase the conscious attention paid to safety hazards. Using active decision support techniques such as safety checklists, safety items on meeting agendas, safety considerations embedded in worksheets and other visual reminders (e.g., posters) in decision-making settings increases the availability of these cues and helps keep commitments to important objectives (Ariely, 2008). Similarly, deliberately designing climate change–related goals (e.g., carbon reduction targets) for routine organisational practices (e.g., meeting agendas, internal newsletters, procurement forms, human resources training and development manuals, lunch room menus, etc.) would make these cues more salient and more likely to be perceived as important, thereby augmenting attentional engagement with the issue.
9. **Change the signposts:** In addition, deliberately changing the signposts – key numbers, dates or objectives – to be more in line with climate change issues can help mitigate anchoring biases. For example, to counter short-term budget pressures anchored in yearly budget reports, Harvard University set up a Green Campus Initiative which provides funds that support projects that have longer pay-back periods, and which might therefore otherwise get overlooked. Similarly, in 2009,

Unilever announced that it would eliminate the quarterly report to allow for the longer time frames required to implement some of its ambitious sustainability goals. Changing the signposts broadens the perception of temporal anchors in favour of climate change action.

10. **Implement behavioural nudges:** Similar to implementing active decision support techniques, behavioural nudges are subtle yet deliberate changes in one's environment that can alter how an issue is perceived and therefore prime individuals to make more effective decisions. For example, graphic images of diseased lungs and gums on cigarette packages are designed to heighten the risks of smoking at the purchase decision moment (Thaler & Sunstein, 2008). These types of behavioural nudges, also known as *choice architecture*, can likewise be used to heighten the perception of climate change as a critical issue. For example, relabelling a garbage can as 'landfill' (accompanied by a photo of a dump) has been shown to reduce the amount of waste that gets thrown into such containers by drawing an individual's attention to the consequences of their actions at the time of action Introducing other immediate feedback mechanisms in organisations (e.g., thermostats that tell you the cost of running an air conditioner during a heat wave) can also change behaviour by making the magnitude of consequences more readily available (Thaler & Sunstein, 2008). Behavioural nudges can therefore serve to mitigate availability biases by broadening attentional perception.

In our consulting and executive teaching experience, we have often heard business leaders say that they would really like to do something about sustainability and climate change and yet they feel that this is impossible. The objective of presenting several potential mitigating tactics is to illustrate that there are many ways in which leaders can tackle the hidden causes of climate change inertia resulting from unconscious cognitive biases. There is great potential to use some very simple interventions to make climate-related business issues more salient and trigger more intentional attentional engagement that spurs action.

Conclusion

The purpose of this chapter has been to illustrate how cognitive biases can prevent leaders from paying attention to climate change as an important issue. Because of perceptual biases, climate change cues do not get noticed and hence do not receive additional attentional engagement that would ensure attentional focus and corporate climate change action. While many other institutional and organisational contextual factors undoubtedly also contribute to this problem, the role of cognitive biases should not be underestimated. Although it is impossible to quantify the exact proportion of decisions that are affected by these biases, as the research cited herein suggests, the effects of issue framing, anchoring and availability biases alone can have a profound impact on sustainability-related decisions. The larger goal of this chapter therefore was also present several possible mitigating interventions that could be implemented by strategic leaders within their organisations to counter the effects of these biases. In so doing, we hope to have contributed to the discourse about climate change solutions in general to help business leaders avoid the potential detrimental effects of cognitive biases.

Discussion Points

- What is the role of leadership in perpetuating corporate climate change inertia?
- How can governance play a role to support sustained attention to climate change in organizations?
- What are some interventions that could be implemented in organizations to mitigate against these biases?

Suggested Reading

Bazerman, M. H., & Moore, D. A. (2012). *Judgment in managerial decision making*. John Wiley & Sons.

Thaler, R. H., & Sunstein, C. R. (2008). *Nudge: Improving decisions about health, wealth, and happiness*. New Haven: Yale University Press.

References

American Meteorological Society. (2003). Climate change research: Issues for the atmospheric and related sciences. *Bulletin of the American Meteorological Society, 84*, 508.

Ariely, D. (2008). *Predictably irrational: The hidden forces that shape our decisions*. Harper.

BankTrack, Rainforest Action Network, Indigenous Environmental Network, Oil Change International, Reclaim Finance, & Sierra Club. (2022). *Banking on climate chaos – fossil fuel finance report 2022.* https://www.bankingonclimatechaos.org/wp-content/uploads/2023/06/BOCC_2023_06-27.pdf

Bazerman, M. H., & Tenbrunsel, A. (2011). *Blind spots: Why we fail to do what's right and what to do about it.* Princeton University Press.

CDP. (2022, September) Missing the Mark: 2022 analysis of global CDP temperature ratings. *CDP Disclosure Insight Action.* https://cdn.cdp.net/cdp-production/cms/reports/documents/000/006/544/original/Missing_the_Mark_-_CDP_temperature_ratings_analysis_2022.pdf?1662412411

Chandler, A. D. (1962). *Strategy and structure: Chapters in the history of the industrial enterprise.* The MIT Press.

Cook, J., Oreskes, N., Doran, P. T., Anderegg, W. R. L., Verheggen, B., Maibach, E. W, Carlton, J., Lewandowsy, S., Skuce, A. G., Green, S. A., Nuccitelli, D., Jacobs, P., Richardson, M., Winkler, B., Painting, R., & Rice, K. (2016). Consensus on consensus: A synthesis of consensus estimates on human-caused global warming. *Environmental Research Letters, 11*(4), 1–7.

Eckardt, A., & Mazutis, D. (2020). Banking for a low carbon future: Explaining climate change responses in a low-salience industry. *Academy of Management Proceedings, 2020*(1), 18435. https://doi.org/10.5465/AMBPP.2020.178

Finkelstein, S., Hambrick, D. C., & Cannella, A. A. (2009). *Strategic leadership: Theory and research on executives, top management teams, and boards.* Oxford University Press.

Finkelstein, S., Whitehead, J., & Campbell, A. (2008). *Think again: Why good leaders make bad decisions and how to keep it from happening to you.* Harvard Business Review Press.

Ghoshal, S. (2005). Bad management theories are destroying good management practices. *Academy of Management Learning & Education, 4*(1), 75–91.

Haidt, J. (2001). The emotional dog and its rational tail: a social intuitionist approach to moral judgment. *Psychological Review, 108*(4), 814.

Hawkins, D. I., & Cocanougher, A. B. (1972). Student evaluations of the ethics of marketing practices: The role of marketing education. *Journal of Marketing, 36*, 61–64.

Hofmann, A., & Bazerman, M. H. (2005). Changing environmental practice: Understanding and overcoming the organizational and psychological barriers (Harvard NOM Working Paper No. 05-04; Harvard Business School Working Paper No. 05–043; Ross School of Business Paper No. 923).

Howard-Grenville, J., & Bartels, S. (2012). Organizational culture and environmental action. In P. Bansal & A. Hoffman (Eds.), *The Oxford handbook of business and the natural environment* (pp. 194–210). Oxford University Press.

Intergovernmental Panel on Climate Change. (2007). 2007: Summary for policymakers. In S. Solomon, D. Qin, M. Manning, Z. Chen, M. Marquis, K. B. Avery, M. Tignor, & H. L. Miller (Eds.), *Climate change 2007: The physical science basis. Contribution of Working Group I to the Fourth Assessment Report of the Intergovernmental Panel on Climate Change*. Cambridge University Press. https://www.ipcc.ch/site/assets/uploads/2018/02/ar4-wg1-spm-1.pdf

Intergovernmental Panel on Climate Change. (2022). *Climate change 2022: Impacts, adaptation, and vulnerability. Contribution of Working Group II to the Sixth Assessment Report of the Intergovernmental Panel on Climate Change* [H.-O. Pörtner, D. C. Roberts, M. Tignor, E. S. Poloczanska, K. Mintenbeck, A. Alegría, M. Craig, S. Langsdorf, S. Löschke, V. Möller, A. Okem, & B. Rama (Eds.)]. Cambridge University Press.

Jordan, J. (2009). A social cognition framework for examining moral awareness in managers and academics. *Journal of Business Ethics, 84*, 237–258.

Kaplan, S., & Henderson, R. (2005). Inertia and incentives: Bridging organizational economics and organizational theory. *Organization Science, 16*(5), 509–521. https://doi.org/10.1287/orsc.1050.0154

Klotz, L. (2011). Cognitive biases in energy decisions during the planning, design and construction of commercial buildings in the United States: An analytical framework and research needs. *Energy Efficiency, 4*, 271–284.

Lindner, S. H. (1987). On cogency, professional bias, and public policy: An assessment of four views of the injury problem. *The Milbank Quarterly, 65*(2), 276–230.

Lovallo, D., & Sibony, O. (2012). Re-anchor your next budget meeting. *Harvard Business Review*. https://hbr.org/2012/03/can-you-re-anchor-your-next-bu

Mazutis, D., & Eckardt, A. (2017). Sleepwalking into catastrophe: Cognitive biases and corporate climate change inertia. *California Management Review, 59*(3), 74–108. https://doi.org/10.1177/0008125617707974

Mazutis, D., Hanly, K., & Eckardt, A. (2022). Sustainability (is not) in the boardroom: Evidence and implications of attentional voids. *Sustainability, 14*(14), 8391. https://doi.org/10.3390/su14148391

National Academy of Sciences Committee on the Science of Climate Change. (2021) *Climate change science: An analysis of some key questions*. National Academy Press.

National Aeronautics and Space Administration. (2016). How do we know climate change is real? http://climate.nasa.gov/evidence/

Nicolini, D., & Korica, M. (2021). Attentional engagement as practice: A study of the attentional infrastructure of healthcare chief executive officers. *Organization Science, 32*(5), 1273–1299. https://doi.org/10.1287/orsc.2020.1427

Nisbett, R., & Ross, L. (1980). *Human inference: Strategies and shortcomings of social judgment*. Prentice Hall.

Ocasio, W., Yakis-Douglas, B., Boynton, D., Laamanen, T., Rerup, C., Vaara, E., & Whittington, R. (2022). It's a different world: A dialog on the attention-based view in a post-Chandlerian world. *Journal of Management Inquiry, 32*(2), 107–119. https://doi.org/10.1177/10564926221103484

Pless, N. M., Maak, T., & Stahl, G. K. (2011). Developing responsible global leaders through international service-learning programs: The Ulysses experience. *Academy of Management Learning & Education, 10*(2), 237–260.

Plunkett Tost, L., & Wade-Benzoni, K. A. (2012). Intergenerational beneficence and the success of environmental sustainability initiatives in organizational contexts. In P. Bansal & A. Hoffman (Eds.), *The Oxford handbook of business and the natural environment* (pp. 176–193). Oxford University Press.

Rerup, C. (2009). Attentional triangulation: Learning from unexpected rare crises. *Organization Science, 20*(5), 876–893.

Schwarz, N., Bless, H., Strack, F., Klumpp, G., Rittenauer-Schatka, H., & Simons, A. (1991). Ease of retrieval as information: Another look at the availability heuristic. *Journal of Personality and Social Psychology, 61*(2), 195–202.

Shu, L., & Bazerman, M. H. (2012). Cognitive barriers to environmental action: Problems and solutions. In P. Bansal & A. Hoffman (Eds.), *The Oxford handbook of business and the natural environment* (pp. 161–175). Oxford University Press.

Simon, H. A. (1973). Applying information technology to organization design. *Public Administration Review, 33*(3), 268–278.

Slawinski, N., Pinkse, J., Busch, T., & Banerjee, S. B. (2015). The role of short-termism and uncertainty avoidance in organizational inaction on climate change: A multi-level framework. *Business & Society, 56*(2), 253–282. doi:10.1177/ 0007650315576136

Starik, M., & Rands, G. P. (1995). Weaving an integrated web: Multilevel and multisystem perspectives of ecologically sustainable organizations. *Academy of Management Review, 20*(4), 908–935.

Stout, L. A. (2012). *The shareholder value myth: How putting shareholders first harms investors, corporations, and the public*. Berrett-Koehler.

Strack, F., Martin, L., & Schwarz, N. (1988). Priming and communication: Social determinants of information use in judgments of life satisfaction. *European Journal of Social Psychology, 18*(5), 429–442.

Thaler, R. H., & Sunstein, C. R. (2008). *Nudge: Improving decisions about health, wealth, and happiness*. Yale University Press.

Tversky, A., & Kahneman, D. (1979). Availability: A heuristic for judging frequency and probability, *Cognitive Psychology, 5*(2), 207–232.

World Economic Forum. (2022). *The global risk report 2022* (17th ed.).

4

AN EVOLUTIONARY PERSPECTIVE ON CORPORATE SUSTAINABILITY TRANSITIONS

A PROSOCIAL APPROACH[1]

Michael P. Schlaile, Alexander Herwix, Kristina Bogner and Paul W.B. Atkins

Chapter Summary

Companies can actively contribute to large-scale systemic changes towards more sustainable modes of production and consumption by engaging with their own *corporate sustainability transitions*. This, however, requires new forms of organisational leadership. In this chapter, we make a three-fold contribution to the question of how this might be realised. First, we apply the multi-level perspective on sustainability transitions to the corporate level and conceptualise how the relational orientation towards reference systems plays a key role when working towards sustainability at five different but interrelated levels. Second, we introduce a prosocial leadership approach that builds on and synthesises work from contextual behavioural science,

DOI: 10.4324/9781003343011-5

evolutionary science and cooperation science (especially the work by Elinor Ostrom) into a flexible approach for facilitating cooperation across scales. Third, we highlight how such an approach may help to address some of the challenges arising in corporate sustainability transitions and present case vignettes that show how these approaches are reflected in practice.

Introduction

The urgency and magnitude of current social–ecological problems is palpable. Humanity has already transgressed most of the planetary or Earth system boundaries (e.g., Rockström et al., 2023). Yet, we can still observe 'business as usual' and a lock-in into unsustainable modes of production and consumption in most areas of our societies (Simoens et al., 2022).

One reason for such self-reinforcing but unsustainable behaviour lies in the *paradigms* – broad frameworks for action – that companies use to define problems, search for solutions and define success (Dosi & Nelson, 2016). Paradigms become explicit in the *business models* that articulate a company's purpose and how it means to propose, create, deliver and capture *value*. While business models are often used for analysis, comparison or communication about how a firm does business, they can also be used to manage and transform (the orientation of) corporate activities more deeply. Business models for sustainability (or *dedicated business models*; Urmetzer, 2021), for instance, transcend the conventional understanding of the value creation, delivery and capture process. Especially in the combination of different archetypes of sustainable business models, the traditional focus on profit and economic growth is replaced by a prioritised integration of social, environmental and economic values into the business purpose and processes as well as dedicated relationships and interactions with stakeholders (e.g., Norris et al., 2021). Sustainable business models can thus contribute to the re-purposing of business activities for the benefit of society, the environment and the long-term well-being of all stakeholders (e.g., through adopting a stewardship role; Bocken et al., 2014) as part of so-called sustainability transitions.

In the literature on socio-technical systems, sustainability transitions are conceived of as 'multidimensional and co-evolutionary processes that involve changes in technology, user practices, business models, policies and governance approaches, and cultural meanings' with the goal of achieving sustainability across sectors and at all scales of society (Geels, 2018, n.p.; see also Schlaile & Urmetzer, 2021, for an overview).[2] Taking up a sustainability transitions perspective coincides with an understanding of companies as systems nested within larger systems. In this regard, Urmetzer (2021) argued, for example, that companies have the potential (as well as the responsibility) to not only *adapt* their purpose to the grand global challenges ahead but also actively *contribute* to the dedication of the larger system towards sustainability (see also Schlaile, Urmetzer, et al., 2021, on a related note). In this context, companies and other *incumbents*[3] are often accused of more or less intentionally perpetuating the status quo. Dyllick and Muff (2016) spoke of 'the big disconnect' and argued that there is a broad range of what is typically considered as *business sustainability*, including companies that contribute effectively to sustainability and those that do not. Hence, current scientific discussions prompt us to paint a more nuanced picture about how incumbents can actively contribute to desired systemic changes (e.g., see Turnheim & Sovacool, 2020).

Nonetheless, successfully orchestrating the development and implementation of more sustainable forms of proposing, creating, delivering and capturing value while navigating the broader dynamics of nested systems of systems requires new forms of organisational leadership. Many contemporary approaches to leadership seem to neglect the need for deep organisational reconfiguration, thus inadvertently perpetuating corporate inertia (e.g., Joseph et al., 2019; Rivera & Clement, 2019, on a related note). Yet, fortunately, novel leadership concepts have been and are being devised by both researchers and practitioners that acknowledge the complex systemic interconnectedness, transformative potential and responsibilities of business organisations and their decision makers in times of grand global challenges. Such approaches include but are not limited to *conscious leadership* (Mackey & Sisodia, 2013), *ecological leadership* (e.g., Chapter 7), *green leadership* (e.g., Chapter 9) *integral leadership* (Volckmann, 2014), *regenerative leadership* (Hutchins, 2022), *responsible leadership* (Maak & Pless, 2022; see also Chapter 10) or, alternatively, *responsible global leadership* (Mendenhall et al., 2020), *shamanic leadership* (Waddock, 2019), *sustainability* and/or *environmental leadership* concepts that acknowledge complexity (e.g., Chapters 6, 8 and 13) and *system leadership* (Beehner, 2020; Chapter 14).

With this chapter, we aim to contribute to these debates by contextualising and introducing a *prosocial leadership* approach, [4] articulated most prominently by Paul Atkins, David Sloan Wilson, and Steven Hayes (Atkins et al., 2019; Gillard et al., 2022; Hayes, Atkins, & Wilson, 2022), to the domain of sustainability transitions. This Prosocial approach can, in our view, serve as a promising multi-disciplinary and scientifically grounded 'facilitation toolkit' that can help corporations become active contributors to sustainability transitions by helping them to engage with their own *corporate sustainability transitions*. To this end, in the next section, we build on the (extended) multi-level perspective known from the sustainability transitions literature (Geels, 2011; Göpel, 2016; Schlaile et al., 2022) to define and explicate our understanding of corporate sustainability transitions and their associated challenges. This helps us to set the ground for introducing the Prosocial approach as a combination of evidence-based interventions and potential remedy for some of these challenges. We then describe two case vignettes to illustrate some of the opportunities and challenges associated with the Prosocial approach before we draw our conclusions.

Theory: Corporate Sustainability Transitions and the Prosocial Approach

The Challenges of Corporate Sustainability Transitions

Introducing the Extended Multi-Level Perspective

We use the term *corporate sustainability transition* (CST) to refer to the changes in corporations – including paradigmatic changes in a corporation's business model (how the organisation proposes, creates, delivers and captures value), culture and structures (e.g., governance, organisational form, routines, narratives and institutional logics), practices and processes – that are driving and driven by the sustainability transitions of the encompassing socio-technical and social–ecological systems. To make sense of CSTs, we draw on an extended version of the multi-level perspective (MLP), which is a middle-range framework that describes sustainability transitions as multilevel phenomena where actors interact across multiple levels of aggregation to challenge, alter, reconfigure and potentially replace socio-technical systems over time (Geels, 2011). As such, it can be viewed as a generic lens that emphasises the complex, multi-layered, and (co)evolutionary nature of change processes in socio-technical systems. The MLP is not an explanatory theory or model in any particular context, nor is it a descriptive or prescriptive stage model of how to orient a corporation towards sustainability (in the latter regard, see Landrum, 2018, on discussions on stages of corporate sustainability). Although the MLP has been developed for and is usually applied to studying socio-technical transitions at the societal level (e.g., transitions of the mobility or energy system of a particular country or region), we apply the framework to sustainability transitions at the corporate level. This step is possible as the MLP is compatible with general evolutionary and multilevel selection theory that recognizes the fractal nature of nested systems of systems (Schlaile et al., 2022; Waring et al., 2015). In essence, it does not really matter to the MLP whether we are talking about a country or a business ecosystem because the patterns, relationships and dynamics it highlights exist at both scales. Applying the MLP to the corporate level helps us to get a holistic, multilevel picture on key challenges associated with achieving sustainability in such settings. Our framing is thus related to recent (re)conceptualisations of business sustainability (especially 'business sustainability 3.0' as discussed by Dyllick & Muff, 2016). To elaborate on our understanding of CST, we particularly draw on the *extended* MLP (Göpel, 2016; Schlaile et al., 2022), which suggests (at least) five levels and associated interactions through which CSTs can be investigated (see Figure 4.1):

1. The *meta level* focuses on the analysis and curation of distinct narratives, worldviews, and paradigms shaping the behaviours of actors (e.g., humans, machines or organisations).

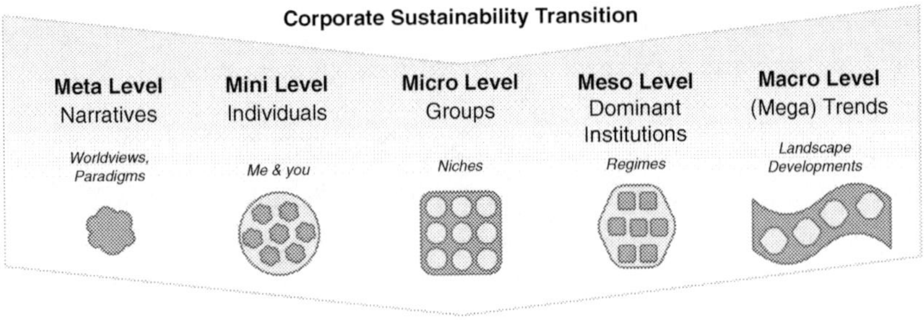

Figure 4.1 The Extended MLP Based on Schlaile et al. (2022) and Göpel (2016) Applied to CST

2. The *mini level* focuses on the analysis and guidance of individual actors' behaviours.
3. The *micro level* focuses on the analysis and management of groups and collectives as spaces for (experimental) interactions between individual actors in a CST.
4. The *meso level* focuses on the analysis and governance of dominant institutions that order the relationships between groups.
5. The *macro level* focus on the analysis and anticipation of overarching (mega) trends (e.g., societal and Earth system developments) that may impact a CST.

As illustrated in Figure 4.1, in our adaptation of the MLP to CST, the levels build on each other to create five kinds of actants that are defined by their level of aggregation. This framing is related to the multi-actor perspective explored in Avelino and Wittmayer (2016) and allows us to explore the complex interplay of actants in CST within and across levels. We arrive at five layers because this arguably presents a sweet spot for acknowledging the breadths of actants involved in CST in a holistic manner while still being manageable in terms of conceptual complexity (Göpel, 2016; Schlaile et al., 2022). In the following subsections, we explain how each of the five levels of the extended MLP can be used to make sense of and inform CSTs. In particular, we highlight selected organisational challenges that threaten CSTs and that can be addressed using a prosocial leadership approach.

Meta Level: Focus on Narratives, Worldviews, Paradigms

Taking the perspective of the meta level, we are interested in understanding the *narratives, worldviews and paradigms* that are involved in a specific CST. Narratives, worldviews and paradigms provide instructional guidance for actors and are thus significant culturally evolved shapers of valued behaviours (Göpel, 2016; Schlaile, 2021; Schlaile et al., 2022). As Figure 4.2 illustrates, it can be useful to classify narratives with regard to the relational orientation and strategy that they dispose actors to take towards others. Specifically, we argue that narratives, worldviews and paradigms are culturally evolved cognitive or semantic frameworks that prompt actors to use a certain mix of *cooperative* (or mutualistic), *competitive* and *exploitative* (or antagonistic) *strategies* when interacting with a particular *reference system*

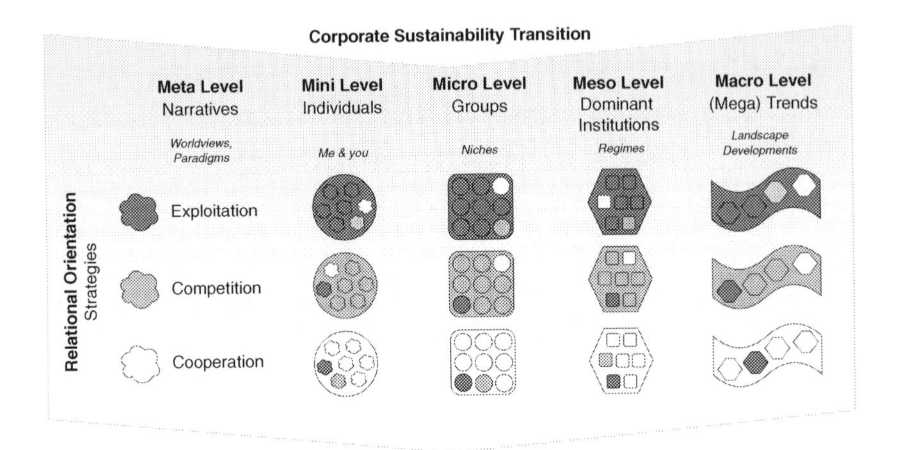

Figure 4.2 Relational Orientation in the Extended MLP Based on Schlaile et al. (2022) and Göpel (2016)

(e.g., competitors, stakeholders or also the Earth system; see also Abatecola et al., 2020; Breslin et al., 2021). This relationship is multilevel and scale invariant in the sense that, given a particular reference system, it is possible to identify distinct relational orientations at all levels of a CST (i.e., mini, micro, meso and macro levels). Taking the Earth system as the reference system, a CST involving an oil company may be faced with growing societal demands for a cooperation orientation at the macro level, exploitation-oriented dominant institutions at the meso level, a set of small cooperation-oriented groups where sustainability innovators interact at the micro level and a majority of employees who are competition oriented (i.e., mostly concerned with advancing in their jobs rather than having a strong cooperation or exploitation orientation towards the Earth system) at the mini level.

A major challenge for CSTs that emerges from the meta level is the need to develop storytelling capabilities (see also Maak & Pless, 2022; Riedy & Waddock, 2022) that are able to successfully manage and align relational orientations towards a variety of valued reference systems (e.g., competitors, stakeholders, the Earth system) across levels. Or, put simply, narratives, worldviews and paradigms of CST participants and stakeholders must be aligned in such a way that sustainability can become imaginable. This requires highly adaptive management and leadership processes that continuously (re-)fit stories and the underlying (micro)narratives to recipients (see also Maak & Pless, 2022; Riedy & Waddock, 2022; Waddock, 2019). Each of the relational orientations may have a place in this effort; however, research suggests that for the maintenance of sustainable institutions, as a rule of thumb, it seems useful to aim for a cooperative orientation when- and wherever possible (e.g., Waring et al., 2015; Wilson et al., 2020). This stands in contrast to the often still prevailing neoliberal narrative, which builds on the core assumption that humans are inherently selfish and thus promotes competition as the most important and promising relational orientation for organising economic affairs (see also Hutchins, 2022, on a related note). Because both perspectives can lead to important insights in certain contexts, we argue for a flexible narrative which is centred around the recognition that humans can be highly prosocial under the right conditions.

Mini Level: Focus on the Behaviours of Individual Actors

At the mini level, we are interested in understanding and guiding the *behaviours of individual actors.* The perspective of the mini level focuses on individuals and their agency, which is important for making sense of CSTs because outcomes at all levels are ultimately emerging from the behaviours and interactions of individuals. Drawing an analogy from CSTs to biological systems and multilevel selection (Waring et al., 2015), individual actors can be viewed as the carriers of complex systems of social and behavioural rules, narratives and instructions (e.g., genes and cultural traits), which can stabilise in patterns that manifest in (un)sustainable behaviours (Price & Shaw, 1998; Schlaile, 2021). Thus, leaders in the context of CSTs do well to consider and leverage known patterns and heuristics underlying individuals' behaviours to facilitate and support behaviour change in mutually desired directions or at least identify (both personal and organisational) mindset barriers to behaviour change (see also Hutchins, 2022). Examples include analysing patterns in corporate culture to unveil the (mis)fit between 'unwritten rules of the game', behaviour of members of the organisation and expected changes in the larger ecosystem (Price & Shaw, 1998; Schlaile, Bogner, & Muelder, 2021). Two major challenges at the mini level are (a) finding or creating opportunities for behaviour change that are ethically acceptable and have a meaningful positive impact on a CST and

(b) developing the capability to effectively facilitate and support individual behaviour change where desirable.

Micro Level: Focus on Groups as Spaces for Interaction

At the micro level, we are interested in identifying and managing groups as spaces for interactions between individual actors. The micro-level perspective is essential for understanding CSTs because transformative moves towards sustainability require changes in social relations and, in turn, access to spaces where such changes can be fostered and experimented with (Pel et al., 2020). The traditional MLP makes this relationship explicit by highlighting how groups can bring forth (social) innovations that may challenge dominant institutional structures at the meso level. As such, the micro level requires balancing the need for strong cooperation and cohesion within groups with the capacity to hold a potentially competitive or even exploitative relational orientation towards dominant institutions at the meso level. The strategic fostering and growing of innovative groups in a potentially hostile environment are a core challenge for successful CSTs. Taking manufacturing firms as an example, the establishment of separate innovation units within the corporation has become a common practice to experiment with and nurture innovations and innovative practices in a supportive environment before integrating them more deeply with the rest of the company (Blindenbach-Driessen & van den Ende, 2014).

Meso Level: Focus on Dominant Institutions

At the meso level of a CST, we are interested in understanding and governing regimes of dominant institutional structures that order the relationships between groups. The meso-level perspective is important for understanding CSTs because it looks at how innovative sustainability initiatives are shaping and being shaped by the context of the encompassing (often still unsustainable) business environment. It is particularly interested in how (social) innovations challenge, alter, reconfigure and potentially replace the existing organisational form, rules, values and logics that govern a corporation. In addition, the meso perspective can help us to better understand why particular unsustainable behaviours and business models have become dominant and self-reinforcing; for instance, due to the tendency of humans to imitate the behaviour of peers and people who are perceived as important or successful and due to the tendency of humans to habituate behaviour they perceive as rewarding (see also Chapter 5).

Two major challenges for CSTs at this level are (a) choosing a useful scope for the regime one is interested in and (b) managing the complexity that is associated with attempts to facilitate regime change. First, choosing a regime scope for a CST is not always straightforward because changes towards more sustainable value creation, delivery and capture are generally only achievable if the whole corporate supply chain is considered. Thus, decisions about which organisations and stakeholders are considered as being part of a CST need to be made and justified (see also Urmetzer, 2021). Second, facilitating regime change is highly complex because the more people are involved and the more resources are at stake, the more important but difficult communication becomes and the more potential for conflict exists. Thus, ways to manage the relationships between groups need to be developed that appreciate the complexity inherent to large scale socio-technical and social-ecological systems.

Macro Level: Focus on (Mega) Trends

At the macro level, we are interested in anticipating the overarching *landscape developments* that may impact a particular CST. For instance, the Earth system gives us increasingly strong signals (e.g., pandemics, floods, forest fires, biodiversity loss, etc.) that our societies' unsustainable modes of production and consumption are severely damaging to our habitats, and thereby to us. The macro-level perspective helps us view CSTs in the light of the bigger picture of societal and Earth system change. This illustrates why organisations engaged in CSTs do well to consider the macro level for planning the long-term but also the short-term definitions of value proposition, creation, delivery, and capture. The COVID-19 pandemic is one of these landscape developments that vividly illustrates how companies' abilities to create, deliver, and capture what they define as value depends on the macro level (i.e., business-as-usual strategies were challenged by global supply chain disruptions). Still, cognitive biases of leaders might prevent them from correctly anticipating these mega trends and lead to inertia (Mazutis & Eckardt, 2017). The two main challenges we see at this level are (a) identifying the landscape developments that are most relevant to the CSTs at hand and (b) anticipating the interplay between CSTs and the broader landscape developments, which often include shocks that originate outside of the corporations of interest (e.g., pandemics, wars).

The Prosocial Approach

Although it is impossible for organisational leaders to *directly steer* the complex (co)evolutionary processes that constitute CSTs in defined directions, there are opportunities for using interventions to *facilitate* systemic changes (Schlaile, Urmetzer, et al., 2021). Such interventions include proven methods from psychology and evolutionary science to support behavioural and cultural change in mutually desired directions (Wilson et al., 2014). Rather self-evidently, systemic changes such as CSTs require a cooperation-oriented collective effort supported by self-reflective behavioural reorientations on the individual level. The prosocial leadership approach we considered (Atkins et al., 2019) recognises these needs and addresses them with findings from evolutionary theory and evidence-based interventions from contextual behavioural science. It thus presents a promising candidate approach for addressing some of the key CST challenges we have raised in the previous sections.

At this point, it should be noted that the Prosocial approach has multiple facets: For example, it can be viewed as (a) an *evolutionary perspective* on the tensions between individual self-interest and collective interests, (b) a *practical approach* to facilitate positive change in groups, (c) a *research effort* to study the evolution of psychological flexibility and cooperation within and across groups, and (d) a *community of practice* of trained facilitators. Although these facets are all intertwined, in this section we focus on giving a brief overview of the scientific background and the practical approach with an eye to how the Prosocial approach can contribute to CSTs. Readers interested in more detail on the foundations of the Prosocial approach are referred to Atkins et al. (2019), Gillard et al. (2022) and Hayes et al. (2022).

Awareness of our Internal Thoughts and Feelings

The first central pillar of the Prosocial approach is a focus on facilitating internal reflection and behaviour change. It is built on contextual behavioural science and some of the tools developed in *acceptance and commitment training* (ACT), which focuses on the development of *psychological flexibility*

(Hayes, 2019; Hayes et al., 2012).[5] Psychological flexibility involves 'consciously moving in the direction of values even in the presence of difficult thoughts and feelings' (Atkins et al., 2019, p. 56).[6] Essentially, values are represented on the meta level of the MLP and can be expressed, for example, in narratives (Riedy & Waddock, 2022). One important tool that can aid in the development of psychological flexibility is the ACT matrix (Polk & Schoendorff, 2014). The ACT matrix provides a simple framework for making sense of difficult situations that helps to structure and shape narratives towards value-directed action (see Figure 4.3). In essence, the ACT matrix helps participants to reflect in a structured way about a particular challenge or situation that they are involved in (e.g., how to react to a new sustainability initiative that is demanding a lot of attention and resources at work). It encourages participants to bring the values to mind that they want to embody while at the same time making space for holding and accepting the difficult thoughts and feelings that may get in the way of them realising their values (Polk & Schoendorff, 2014). By doing so, the ACT matrix encourages a mindful reflection about useful behaviours and potential coping strategies when difficult thoughts and feelings invariably arise.

The ACT matrix can be used to reflect about individual but also group behaviours. When taking the perspective of a group, the individual group members are encouraged to transcend their own perspectives by shifting into a collective group mindset. Rather than focusing on what they personally value, the group version of the ACT matrix focuses on what 'we' – as

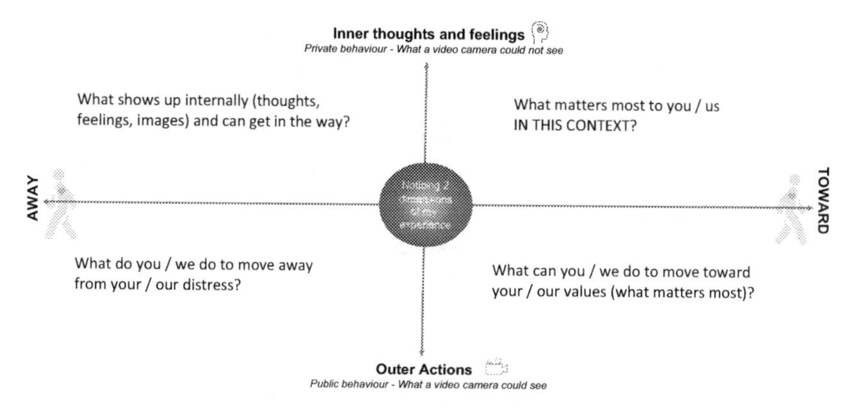

Figure 4.3 Sample ACT Matrix (courtesy of ProSocial World, Creative Commons License)

a group – collectively value. For instance, the ACT matrix could be used in a board meeting to help identify, from the perspective of each individual board member, what they think the board should collectively value and what they fear can get in the way of the board realising those values. Doing such an exercise may surface unspoken or even suppressed thoughts and ideas and thus potentially lends itself to the development of new and more effective behavioural strategies. In sum, the ACT matrix can be seen as a versatile and potentially powerful tool for gaining awareness of internal thoughts and feelings as well as relational orientations of individuals and groups.

The Quality of Our Relationships

Another central pillar of the Prosocial approach is the work by Nobel laureate Elinor Ostrom (Ostrom, 1990), which led to the identification of eight core design principles (CDPs) for sustainable self-organising groups in the context of the governance of common pool resources. These CDPs were later generalised to all groups involving humans (Wilson et al., 2013) and applied – especially as part of the Prosocial approach – to various types of organisations (Wilson et al., 2020), ranging from schools and other educational contexts (Eirdosh & Hanisch, 2020; Gillard et al., 2022) to national aid workers (Read, 2020) and government agencies (Atkins & Styles, 2020). The eight CDPs are summarised in Figure 4.4 (the original terminology used by Ostrom is mentioned in italics for the sake of integrity, based on Wilson et al., 2013). One key characteristic of the CDPs is that they are inherently multilevel in that they explicitly and simultaneously consider cooperation *within* and *between* groups. Thus, the CDPs are by design scale invariant, meaning that they are generally applicable to groups of groups, which is what makes them particularly useful when considering complex nested social phenomena such as CSTs.

In practice, the CDPs are generally used to analyse and determine areas of improvement in organisational structures. For instance, Figure 4.4 shows a spoke diagram of the CDPs that can be used to rate and track the extent to which the CDPs are being implemented in an organisational setting. The CDPs may be particularly useful for identifying and dealing with collective action challenges such as opportunism and free-rider problems. In such situations, the CDPs can act as *boundary objects* that facilitate discourse

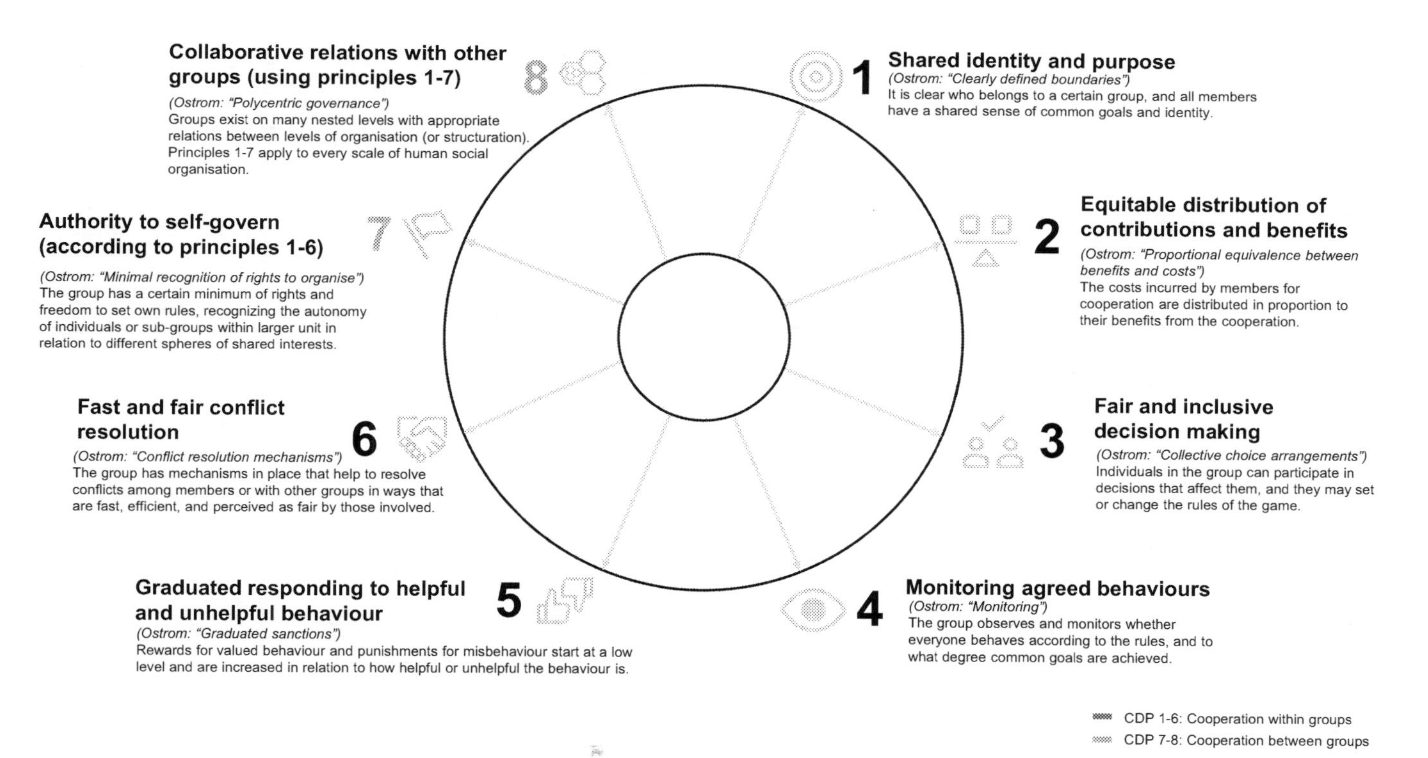

Figure 4.4 The CDPs as a Spoke Diagram (Own Representation Based on Atkins et al., 2019; Eirdosh & Hanisch, 2020; Wilson et al., 2013)

among involved individuals and groups by pointing towards broad evidence-based guidance for how to foster more sustainable self-organisation and cooperation across scales.

The Cultural Agreements We Create

The Prosocial approach can be understood as a process of applied cultural evolution (Atkins et al., 2019) that synthesises tools to manage cognition, cooperation and culture into a flexible framework and toolkit. For example, the ACT matrix can be combined with the CDPs to generate useful insights into the values, emotions and narratives (meta) of individuals (mini) or groups at different levels (micro, meso) regarding each of the CDPs. Applying the ACT matrix to CDP 2 (i.e., equitable distribution of contributions and benefits), for instance, can help an organisational unit (e.g., a team) identify which narrative of fairness or justice dominates for them as a group, what gets in the way and how they can create arrangements that lead to fair outcomes. The group may realise that some members of the team only feel valued when everyone is treated equally (*equality-based*), other team members may insist on being treated (e.g., paid) in proportion to their input (*equity-based*), whereas again others are, for example, in a dire personal situation and may currently require more support from their peers to feel valued and treated fairly (*needs-based*). Based on these revealed narratives, the group can involve all members to come to a fair agreement (CDP 3), which can be monitored (CDP 4) and reinforced/sanctioned (CDP 5).

As one can tell by this illustrative example, applying the Prosocial approach should not expected to be easy and quick if substantial progress in CST is the goal. The approach should rather be understood as advocating for a deliberate and ongoing engagement with the roles that we, individually and collectively, play in business and in life. Difficult questions around what 'sustainability' means for us and how it can be realised even when things get tough are bound to come up. Together with the multilevel understanding of CST, the Prosocial approach provides us with a lexicon, principles and tools that we can learn to use and adapt to facilitate change in mutually desired directions in and around us. In this perspective, CSTs cannot be enforced; they can only emerge from the cultural agreements we create.

Assessment: The Evidence Base for the Prosocial Approach

Although there is strong evidence for the importance of the CDPs for organisationally beneficial outcomes (Hayes, Atkins, & Wilson, 2022; Wilson et al., 2020) and the efficacy of ACT has been demonstrated by many studies (e.g., Hayes, Ciarrochi, et al., 2022), only limited academic studies have been done on the effects of interventions that take up both the ACT matrix and the CDPs simultaneously. In practice, however, successful applications of the Prosocial approach have been documented. One of the most prominent cases of successful applications of the Prosocial approach is the work by Commit and Act, which is an organisation dedicated to empowering vulnerable populations in Sierra Leone (Commit and Act, 2022). They explicitly and effectively used the Prosocial approach in their fights against domestic violence and Ebola (Ebert & Brandon, 2020; Stewart et al., 2017). Moreover, the case study on national aid workers in Uganda by Read (2020) provides a glimpse into ways in which the Prosocial approach can have positive effects on the development of psychological flexibility, trust, self-management and engagement with a team. Similar support for the Prosocial approach's positive influence has been provided by applications in government agency settings (Atkins & Styles, 2020). These results suggest that the Prosocial approach can also act as a useful modular platform for successful sustainability-oriented interventions as it can be flexibly combined and complemented with other findings, methods and interventions from evolutionary and contextual behavioural sciences (Wilson et al., 2014). For instance, this book chapter illustrates the potential application areas of the Prosocial approach through the lens of CST. However, more applications of the Prosocial approach and future research in the context of sustainability transitions would be desirable to further adapt the Prosocial approach to sustainability transitions practice.

Application: How the Prosocial Approach May Help to Address the Challenges of CSTs

In Table 4.1, we summarise how the Prosocial approach may help to address the challenges of CSTs that we have raised in the preceding sections. This list of challenges is illustrative of the potential we see for prosocial leadership approaches in the context of CSTs; it is not meant to be exhaustive.

Table 4.1 How the Prosocial Approach May Help to Address the Challenges of CSTs

MLP Level	Major Challenges	How the Prosocial Approach May Help

Meta	Developing storytelling capabilities to manage and align relational orientations towards a variety of important reference systems across levels	• The ACT matrix …
		  • suggests a systematic structure for crafting narratives around important and difficult situations to support value-directed action even in the face of challenges.
		  • can be used to elicit motivating values and difficult thoughts and feelings that may get in the way of value-directed action, which can inform the content of stories.
		• The CDPs provide a list of core mechanisms for facilitating cooperation that can inform the content of stories and challenge the dominant economic narrative focussing on selfishness. Contextual behavioural science questions the narrative that we should get rid of our negative feelings through consumption, and it helps us to identify other forms of value that are non-commercial.

Mini	Finding or creating opportunities for behaviour change that are ethically acceptable and have a meaningful positive impact on a CST	• The ACT matrix can be used to elicit motivating values and difficult thoughts and feelings in relation to specific behaviours.
		• The CDPs can be used …
		  • as a broad frame of reference for identifying ethically acceptable behaviours in a particular context.
		  • to structure a systematic search for behaviour change opportunities in a particular context.

	Developing the capability to effectively facilitate and support individual behaviour change where desirable	• ACT tools can be used to develop psychological flexibility and facilitate value-directed action towards desired outcomes. • The CDPs can be used as a broad frame of reference for identifying desired sustainability-oriented behaviours in a particular context.
Micro	Strategic fostering and growing of innovative groups	• Combine the CDPs, ACT tools and additional compatible components for systematic group facilitation towards desired outcomes. • Use the CDPs to design and enact governance arrangements that enable self-organisation and polycentric decision making.
Meso	Choosing a useful scope for the regime one is interested in	• Psychological flexibility helps to see regimes and institutions as socially constructed and, therefore, socially changeable. • The CDPs provide a list of core mechanisms for facilitating cooperation that can be used to assess relationships between regime actors. This can help to identify clusters and other patterns in regimes that may be helpful for identifying a useful scope and managing the complexity associated with regime change.
	Managing the complexity associated with attempts to facilitate regime change	
Macro	Identifying landscape developments that are most relevant to the CST at hand	• Psychological flexibility helps us to respond to the threat of landscape changes. Instead of being locked into despair or overwhelm, we can connect with what matters most and choose deliberate and collective actions. • The CDPs provide a list of core mechanisms for facilitating cooperation as a starting point for identifying potentially relevant (e.g., cooperation-threatening) landscape developments as well as considering how a CST may affect and be affected by landscape developments.

CASE STUDY: SUSTAINABILITY-ORIENTED USE OF THE PROSOCIAL APPROACH IN PRACTICE

In the following two boxes, we give some examples and illustrations of a sustainability-oriented use of the Prosocial approach in practice based on personal conversations with two experienced ProSocial facilitators and leaders.[7]

EXAMPLE 1

The first example is a non-profit endeavour from the United Kingdom that started with an initial group of 10 people in spring 2020, who already held a 'shared purpose ..., wanting to do something for the environment, thinking about their ... children or their grandchildren' (CDP 1; i.e., shared identity and purpose). The group is now a polycentric organisation (CDP 8; i.e., collaborative relations with other groups), consisting of several subgroups, which emerged from the initial reluctance of group members to take responsibility due to time constraints and other duties (CDP 2; i.e., equitable distribution of contributions and benefits), so 'it was [important to find] a way to ... make that more distributed ... [for example, by] asking people who were particularly passionate about things to take the lead for that area. And that ... grew their willingness to take on that responsibility'. The framing around choice instead of command helped the group members to realise that 'there is agency and it's connecting with people's values'. Similarly important was the framing around possibilities and potential rather than problems. The authority to self-govern (CDP 7) is reflected in the fact that 'people [within the subgroups] do have the authority to make decisions'. At the same time, 'fair and inclusive decision making where... all have a say' (CDP 3; i.e., fair and inclusive decision making) is also taken seriously as they 'make decisions as a whole group when they're important'.

The group has strong relationships with dominant institutional actors at the meso level that are responsible for policies and allocating funds. Initially, however, these institutional actors exhibited an antagonistic relational orientation, as 'they had a bit of a "who are these people?" kind of attitude, maybe [felt] a bit threatened by us as well, whereas now, it's much more of a working relationship' that is also supported by the fact that an institutional representative attends the group's meetings. These meetings occur on a regular basis and the agenda is now (though this has not always been the case) co-created by means of a shared online document, thus also reflecting fair and inclusive decision making (CDP 3; i.e., fair and inclusive decision making). Moreover, these meetings are designated spaces to report and monitor progress (CDP 4; i.e., monitoring agreed behaviours) and to celebrate helpful behaviours (CDP 5; i.e., graduated responding to helpful and unhelpful behaviour).

It is also noteworthy that the organisation has a cooperative stakeholder relationship with a local business that supports and hosts some of their sustainability efforts, but 'they're not in it to make lots of money, they're in it to ... bring life back to the village, to bring people together again'. At one point, a competitive or perhaps even somewhat exploitative relational orientation of one individual was revealed when leadership noticed that the person was 'referring to the group as ... *you* rather than *us*, ... they were positioning themselves outside of the group.' Eventually, 'this person stopped attending meetings or responding to emails,' so 'I chose to contact them to see ... what was going on with them' (aiming for fast and fair conflict resolution; CDP 6). They conducted an (implicit) ACT matrix that revealed unhelpful thoughts and feelings that led to the individual realising that that the organisation 'wasn't for them; to some degree they were in it to boost their own self esteem rather than helping the group as a whole'.

Some of the key findings from this first case vignette are that the shared identity and purpose (CDP 1) was the initial attractor, while some of main challenges revolved around equitable distribution of contributions and benefits (CDP 2) as well as the authority to self-govern (CDP 7) and collaborative relations with other groups (CDP 8), when decisions had to be postponed due to dominant institutional actors having a much longer time horizon (e.g., in this example, 6 months) for their decisions and allocations of funds.

The second example is from an ongoing sustainability-oriented initiative in Colombia that started in 2020. Below are excerpts from a written Q&A:

EXAMPLE 2

Q: Did the groups you helped to facilitate with the Prosocial approach already have a common identity/purpose (CDP1)?

A: These initial groups all had affinity towards the general themes of regeneration, landscape restoration, nature preservation and healthy local economy. But they were fragmented and mostly did not know about each other. We went through a process that informally embodied the ACT matrix and insights from contextual behavioural science to make explicit the personal agendas for each person and seek alignment around collective purposes.

Q: Which part(s) of the process would you regard as having been most successful in your context (e.g., ACT/CDPs)?

A: All of them. We continually interweaved all of the CDPs (and are still doing so more than 2 years later) and while the ACT matrix is never made explicit, it is always part of the pattern level of thinking that shapes our group processes.

Q: Which elements (e.g., CDPs) were most challenging ones to achieve?

A: It is difficult to say – because we never separated one CDP from another in any formal way. Our processes consistently hold holism and systemic perspectives that move across and among the CDPs. This said, we are in a context with very intense cultural trauma and histories of violence. Thus, we are very sensitive to the psychological triggers that cause trust to break down or for a member of our group to depart as an expression of trauma.

Q: Have you experienced a divergence of values such as different interpretations of sustainability or regeneration in your group, and what did you do about it?

A: We continuously have divergent views about these concepts and hold the space for celebrating and honouring their differences. It is this capacity for deep trust at the level of CDP 1 [i.e., shared identity and purpose] combined with a lot of emotion regulation and psychological flexibility among our group members that makes this possible.

Q: Based on your experience with the Prosocial approach, what would be most important in a corporate context to facilitate sustainability transitions?

A: The most important insight I have to share from my practice with Prosocial is that it is not sufficient to have one or a few members be fluent in the language of the ACT matrix or CDPs. All members need to have both levels of understanding: (1) that the group is practicing being prosocial and (2) that each group member is working to improve their own psychological and social capacities for cooperation. Only when this is explicit as part of the culture does it enable sustained evolution of the group in a conscious manner.

Conclusion

With this chapter, we contribute to the development of a prosocial leadership approach that can be used by both researchers and corporate leaders to better make sense of and engage with CSTs – multilevel processes of sustainability-oriented organisational reorientation. We have drawn on the extended MLP known from sustainability transitions research and adapted the framework to the corporate context. We have also presented the Prosocial approach and discussed how it can serve as a potential remedy for some of the challenges arising at the various levels of CSTs. Our conceptual discussions, the examples cited in the Assessment section and our two case vignettes from non-profit organisations suggest that components of the Prosocial approach can serve as a valuable and flexible multilevel framework for strengthening psychological flexibility and cooperation among both individuals in groups and groups within larger groups such as corporations. Nevertheless, while the individual components of the Prosocial approach have an established scientific basis, the combined approach is still in its infancy and needs to be researched and developed further; for example, through ethnography, participatory action research or more long-term and large-scale quantitative studies of applications of the Prosocial approach within corporations (or other types of organisations) with explicit attention paid to its potential to support and facilitate pro-environmental behaviour, sustainability outcomes or even full-scale organisational reorientation in the sense of CSTs.

Discussion Points for Corporate Leaders

- Think about using the ACT matrix and the CDPs with a group. Which groups in your organisation would you start with?

- How could you use the ACT matrix to identify your leadership values and the thoughts and feelings (and corresponding behaviours) that might keep you from reaching your valued goals?
- How can you make use of the CDPs to understand whether your groups share identity and purpose and whether they have governance structures that enable them to contribute to CSTs?
- How can your value proposition, creation, delivery and capture be reoriented as part of a CST (e.g., reconsider key partners, key resources and key activities; go explicitly beyond a focus on customers and consider all stakeholders their relationships; and explicitly include societal and environmental values in your considerations)?

Notes

1 Michael P. Schlaile and Alexander Herwix contributed equally to this work and should be considered co-first authors.

2 Depending on the research community, one also finds the notion of *sustainability transformations* (Linnér & Wibeck, 2019), which has been argued by some researchers to convey a different and more fundamental notion of change; here, however, we use sustainability *transitions* as the umbrella term.

3 Incumbents are understood here as established individual and collective actors (e.g., firms) that are deeply embedded in markets and socio-economic structures.

4 Note that we write 'Prosocial approach' when we refer to the approach developed by Atkins et al. (2019) instead of the adjective prosocial. However, we suggest that our discussions can also inform the application of other prosocial leadership approaches.

5 In a clinical context, ACT refers to acceptance and commitment *therapy*.

6 Psychological flexibility has six dimensions (acceptance, defusion, being present, a noticing self, values and committed action), which can be measured and represented using the 'hexaflex' model (Chantry, n.d.).

7 We thank Richard Coates and Joe Brewer for sharing their thoughts and experiences.

Suggested Reading

Atkins, P. W. B., Wilson, D. S., & Hayes, S. C. (2019). *Prosocial: Using evolutionary science to build productive, equitable, and collaborative groups*. Context Press.

Bocken, N. M. P., Short, S. W., Rana, P., & Evans, S. (2014). A literature and practice review to develop sustainable business model archetypes. *Journal of Cleaner Production, 65*, 42–56.

Göpel, M. (2016). *The great mindshift.* Springer.

Hayes, S. C. (2019). *A liberated mind: How to pivot toward what matters.* Avery.

Schlaile, M. P., Kask, J., Brewer, J., Bogner, K., Urmetzer, S., & De Witt, A. (2022). Proposing a cultural evolutionary perspective for dedicated innovation systems: Bioeconomy transitions and beyond. *Journal of Innovation Economics & Management, 38*(2), 93–118.

Wilson, D. S., Ostrom, E., & Cox, M. E. (2013). Generalizing the core design principles for the efficacy of groups. *Journal of Economic Behavior & Organization, 90*, S21–S32.

References

Abatecola, G., Breslin, D., & Kask, J. (2020). Do organizations really co-evolve? Problematizing co-evolutionary change in management and organization studies. *Technological Forecasting and Social Change, 155*, 119964. https://doi.org/10.1016/j.techfore.2020.119964

Atkins, P. W. B., & Styles, R. (2020). Solid evidence for ProSocial within government agency settings. ProSocial World Community. https://www.prosocial.world/posts/solid-evidence-for-prosocial-within-government-agency-settings

Atkins, P. W. B., Wilson, D. S., & Hayes, S. C. (2019). *Prosocial: Using evolutionary science to build productive, equitable, and collaborative groups.* Context Press.

Avelino, F., & Wittmayer, J. M. (2016). Shifting power relations in sustainability transitions: A multi-actor perspective. *Journal of Environmental Policy & Planning, 18*(5), 628–649. https://doi.org/10.1080/1523908X.2015.1112259

Beehner, C. G. (2020). *System leadership for sustainability.* Routledge.

Blindenbach-Driessen, F., & van den Ende, J. (2014). The locus of innovation: The effect of a separate innovation unit on exploration, exploitation, and ambidexterity in manufacturing and service firms. *Journal of Product Innovation Management, 31*(5), 1089–1105. https://doi.org/10.1111/jpim.12146

Bocken, N. M. P., Short, S. W., Rana, P., & Evans, S. (2014). A literature and practice review to develop sustainable business model archetypes. *Journal of Cleaner Production, 65*, 42–56. https://doi.org/10.1016/j.jclepro.2013.11.039

Breslin, D., Kask, J., Schlaile, M. P., & Abatecola, G. (2021). Developing a coevolutionary account of innovation ecosystems. *Industrial Marketing Management, 98*, 59–68. https://doi.org/10.1016/j.indmarman.2021.07.016

Chantry, D. (n.d.). ACT ADVISOR Psychological Flexibility Measure. https://contextualscience.org/files/ACT%20ADVISOR%20Psychological%20Flexibility%20Measure.pdf

Commit and Act. (2022). Commit and Act. https://www.commitandact.org/

Dosi, G., & Nelson, R. R. (2016). Technological paradigms and technological trajectories. In M. Augier & D. J. Teece (Eds.), *The Palgrave encyclopedia of strategic management* (pp. 1–12). Palgrave Macmillan. https://doi.org/10.1057/978-1-349-94848-2_733-1

Dyllick, T., & Muff, K. (2016). Clarifying the meaning of sustainable business: Introducing a typology from business-as-usual to true business sustainability. *Organization & Environment, 29*(2), 156–174. https://doi.org/10.1177/1086026615575176

Ebert, B., & Brandon, E. (2020). Violence against women in Sierra Leone: Can a Prosocial approach help reduce it? ProSocial World Community. https://web.archive.org/web/20220629195030/https://community.prosocial.world/b2/violence-against-women-in-sierra-leone-can-a-prosocial-approach-h

Eirdosh, D., & Hanisch, S. (2020). Can the science of Prosocial be a part of evolution education? *Evolution: Education and Outreach, 13*(1), 5, s12052-020-00119–7. https://doi.org/10.1186/s12052-020-00119-7

Geels, F. W. (2011). The multi-level perspective on sustainability transitions: Responses to seven criticisms. *Environmental Innovation and Societal Transitions, 1*(1), 24–40. https://doi.org/10.1016/j.eist.2011.02.002

Geels, F. W. (2018). Socio-technical transitions to sustainability. In H. H. Shugart (Ed.), *Oxford research encyclopedia of environmental science*. Oxford University Press. https://doi.org/10.1093/acrefore/9780199389414.013.587

Gillard, D., Jackson-Brown, F., Stanley-Duke, M., Atkins, P., Anderson, B., Balfour, E., & Cooper, P. (2022). The Prosocial framework: Theory, practice and applications within schools. *Educational Psychology Research and Practice, 8*(1), 1–11. https://doi.org/10.15123/UEL.8V1V8

Göpel, M. (2016). *The great mindshift*. Springer.

Hayes, S. C. (2019). *A liberated mind: How to pivot toward what matters*. Avery.

Hayes, S. C., Atkins, P., & Wilson, D. S. (2022). Prosocial: Using an evolutionary approach to modify cooperation in small groups. In R. A. Houmanfar, M. Fryling, & M. P. Alavosius (Eds.), *Applied behavior science in organizations* (pp. 197–223). Routledge. https://doi.org/10.4324/9781003198949-9

Hayes, S. C., Ciarrochi, J., Hofmann, S. G., Chin, F., & Sahdra, B. (2022). Evolving an idionomic approach to processes of change: Towards a unified personalized science of human improvement. *Behaviour Research and Therapy, 156*, 104155. https://doi.org/10.1016/j.brat.2022.104155

Hayes, S. C., Pistorello, J., & Levin, M. E. (2012). Acceptance and commitment therapy as a unified model of behavior change. *The Counseling Psychologist, 40*(7), 976–1002. https://doi.org/10.1177/0011000012460836

Hutchins, G. (2022). *Leading by nature: The process of becoming a regenerative leader.* Wordzworth.

Joseph, J., Orlitzky, M., Gurd, B., Borland, H., & Lindgreen, A. (2019). Can business-oriented managers be effective leaders for corporate sustainability? A study of integrative and instrumental logics. *Business Strategy and the Environment, 28*(2), 339–352. https://doi.org/10.1002/bse.2238

Landrum, N. E. (2018). Stages of corporate sustainability: Integrating the strong sustainability worldview. *Organization & Environment, 31*(4), 287–313. https://doi.org/10.1177/1086026617717456

Linnér, B.-O., & Wibeck, V. (2019). *Sustainability transformations: Agents and drivers across societies.* Cambridge University Press.

Maak, T., & Pless, N. M. (2022). Responsible leadership: A relational approach. In N. M. Pless & T. Maak, *Responsible leadership* (2nd ed., pp. 39–60). Routledge. https://doi.org/10.4324/b22741-4

Mackey, J., & Sisodia, R. (2013). *Conscious capitalism: Liberating the heroic spirit of business.* Harvard Business Review Press.

Mazutis, D., & Eckardt, A. (2017). Sleepwalking into catastrophe: Cognitive biases and corporate climate change inertia. *California Management Review, 59*(3), 74–108. https://doi.org/10.1177/0008125617707974

Mendenhall, M. E., Žilinskaitė, M., & Stahl, G. K. (Eds.). (2020). *Responsible global leadership: Dilemmas, paradoxes, and opportunities.* Routledge.

Norris, S., Hagenbeck, J., & Schaltegger, S. (2021). Linking sustainable business models and supply chains – Toward an integrated value creation framework. *Business Strategy and the Environment, 30*(8), 3960–3974. https://doi.org/10.1002/bse.2851

Ostrom, E. (1990). *Governing the commons: The evolution of institutions for collective action.* Cambridge University Press.

Pel, B., Haxeltine, A., Avelino, F., Dumitru, A., Kemp, R., Bauler, T., Kunze, I., Dorland, J., Wittmayer, J., & Jørgensen, M. S. (2020). Towards a theory of transformative social innovation: A relational framework and 12 propositions. *Research Policy, 49*(8), 104080. https://doi.org/10.1016/j.respol.2020.104080

Polk, K. L., & Schoendorff, B. (Eds.). (2014). *The ACT matrix: A new approach to building psychological flexibility across settings & populations.* Context Press.

Price, I., & Shaw, R. (1998). *Shifting the patterns: Breaching the memetic codes of corporate performance.* Management Books 2000.

Read, D. C. (2020). *Getting along in the field: The Prosocial process as a mediator of emotional contagion and behavioral entrainment in reducing tension within national aid worker teams*. Saybrook University.

Riedy, C., & Waddock, S. (2022). Imagining transformation: Change agent narratives of sustainable futures. *Futures, 142*, 103010. https://doi.org/10.1016/j.futures.2022.103010

Rivera, J., & Clement, V. (2019). Business adaptation to climate change: American ski resorts and warmer temperatures. *Business Strategy and the Environment, 28*(7), 1285–1301. https://doi.org/10.1002/bse.2316

Rockström, J., Gupta, J., Qin, D., Lade, S. J., Abrams, J., Andersen, L. S., McKay, D. I. A., Bai, X., Bala, G., Bunn, S. E., Ciobanu, D., DeClerck, F., Ebi, K., Gifford, L., Gordon, C., Hasan, S., Kanie, N., Lenton, T. M., Loriani, S., ... Zhang, X. (2023). Safe and just Earth system boundaries. *Nature*. Advance online publication. https://doi.org/10.1038/s41586-023-06083-8

Schlaile, M. P. (Ed.). (2021). *Memetics and evolutionary economics: To boldly go where no meme has gone before*. Springer. https://doi.org/10.1007/978-3-030-59955-3

Schlaile, M. P., Bogner, K., & Muelder, L. (2021). It's more than complicated! Using organizational memetics to capture the complexity of organizational culture. *Journal of Business Research, 129*, 801–812. https://doi.org/10.1016/j.jbusres.2019.09.035

Schlaile, M. P., Kask, J., Brewer, J., Bogner, K., Urmetzer, S., & De Witt, A. (2022). Proposing a cultural evolutionary perspective for dedicated innovation systems: Bioeconomy transitions and beyond. *Journal of Innovation Economics & Management, 38*(2), 93–118. https://doi.org/10.3917/jie.pr1.0108

Schlaile, M. P., & Urmetzer, S. (2021). Transitions to sustainable development. In W. Leal Filho, A. M. Azul, L. Brandli, A. Lange Salvia, & T. Wall (Eds.), *Encyclopedia of the UN Sustainable Development Goals: Decent work and economic growth* (pp. 1067–1081). Springer. https://doi.org/10.1007/978-3-319-95867-5_52

Schlaile, M. P., Urmetzer, S., Ehrenberger, M. B., & Brewer, J. (2021). Systems entrepreneurship: A conceptual substantiation of a novel entrepreneurial 'species'. *Sustainability Science, 16*(3), 781–794. https://doi.org/10.1007/s11625-020-00850-6

Simoens, M. C., Leipold, S., & Fuenfschilling, L. (2022). Locked in unsustainability: Understanding lock-ins and their interactions using the case of food packaging. *Environmental Innovation and Societal Transitions, 45*, 14–29. https://doi.org/10.1016/j.eist.2022.08.005

Stewart, C., Ebert, B., & Bockarie, H. (2017). Commit and act in Sierra Leone. In R. G. White, S. Jain, D. M. R. Orr, & U. M. Read (Eds.), *The Palgrave handbook of sociocultural perspectives on global mental health* (pp. 657–678). Palgrave Macmillan UK. https://doi.org/10.1057/978-1-137-39510-8_31

Turnheim, B., & Sovacool, B. K. (2020). Forever stuck in old ways? Pluralising incumbencies in sustainability transitions. *Environmental Innovation and Societal Transitions, 35*, 180–184. https://doi.org/10.1016/j.eist.2019.10.012

Urmetzer, S. (2021). Dedicated business models. *Journal of Business Models, 9*(2), 87–108. https://doi.org/10.5278/JBM.V9I2.3459

Volckmann, R. (2014). Generativity, transdisciplinarity, and integral leadership. *World Futures, 70*(3–4), 248–265. https://doi.org/10.1080/02604027.2014.934644

Waddock, S. (2019). Shaping the shift: Shamanic leadership, memes, and transformation. *Journal of Business Ethics, 155*(4), 931–939. https://doi.org/10.1007/s10551-018-3900-8

Waring, T. M., Kline, M. A., Brooks, J. S., Goff, S. H., Gowdy, J., Janssen, M. A., Smaldino, P. E., & Jacquet, J. (2015). A multilevel evolutionary framework for sustainability analysis. *Ecology and Society, 20*(2), art34. https://doi.org/10.5751/ES-07634-200234

Wilson, D. S., Hayes, S. C., Biglan, A., & Embry, D. D. (2014). Evolving the future: Toward a science of intentional change. *Behavioral and Brain Sciences, 37*(4), 395–416. https://doi.org/10.1017/S0140525X13001593

Wilson, D. S., Ostrom, E., & Cox, M. E. (2013). Generalizing the core design principles for the efficacy of groups. *Journal of Economic Behavior & Organization, 90*, S21–S32. https://doi.org/10.1016/j.jebo.2012.12.010

Wilson, D. S., Philip, M. M., MacDonald, I. F., Atkins, P. W. B., & Kniffin, K. M. (2020). Core design principles for nurturing organization-level selection. *Scientific Reports, 10*(1), 13989. https://doi.org/10.1038/s41598-020-70632-8

5

GUIDANCE TO GREEN ACTION

ENVIRONMENTAL LEADERSHIP THROUGH THE LENS OF EVOLUTIONARY PSYCHOLOGY

Gonzalo Palomo-Vélez and Mark Van Vugt

Chapter Summary

Mitigating environmental problems requires not only individual action and commitment to sustainability but also strong leadership to mobilise individuals, coordinate collective efforts and resolve conflicts among relevant agents and parties. But what do people look for in a strong environmental leader? Building from evolutionary models of leadership and followership, we posit that what followers regard as ideal environmental leaders depends critically on what they believe is required to deal with a particular ecological threat (e.g., pollution, water conservation, biodiversity loss). Specifically, we argue that some aspects of the environmental problems we are facing resemble those of recurrent problems faced by early humans and, as such, activate the same fundamental follower needs. Because of this, different environmental problems may result in different leader preferences. While a dominant and authoritarian leader might be appealing to followers when they seek active protection in an immediate environmental crisis, such as a nuclear

DOI: 10.4324/9781003343011-6

disaster or oil spill, they may want a guiding and visionary leader in dealing with environmental problems when outcomes are delayed and therefore more uncertain, such as climate change. In addition, when environmental threats are primarily seen as distributive problems – who is going to pay for the green taxes? – they might want a leader who is fair and high in integrity. In this contribution, we examine how different environmental challenges tap into different basic follower needs, thereby affecting what people regard as ideal environmental leadership. We distinguish between three fundamental follower needs that might be relevant to different environmental issues, namely, protection, guidance and fairness. Finally, we elaborate on theory-based recommendations, reflect on whether leaders who meet context-specific follower needs actually produce better environmental results and provide suggestions to further develop this literature.

Guidance to Green Action: Environmental Leadership Through the Lens of Evolution

Mitigating environmental problems requires coordinated efforts between many relevant parties (K. Chan et al., 2020; Margerum & Robinson, 2016; Nilsson et al., 2016). Individual action, while important (Nielsen et al., 2021), is likely not enough to tackle complex environmental issues such deforestation, biodiversity loss and freshwater scarcity (Mann, 2019; Pörtner et al., 2022). Similarly, when ecological disasters like oil spills and nuclear accidents happen, joint efforts from multiple organisations are needed to minimise their negative environmental and social consequences (Ripoll Gallardo et al., 2015; Tang et al., 2017). As such, effectively facing environmental crises typically calls for a cross-sectoral approach and demands collaboration across multiple actors, including international organisations and states (Bodin, 2017; Vogler & Stephan, 2007; Wurzel et al., 2019) as well as the private sector and local communities (Gilligan & Vandenbergh, 2020).

In this context, it is not surprising that strong leadership – by which we mean a leader figure who is able to mobilise large groups of followers for the purpose of organising collective action – is needed to coordinate efforts between, for instance, relevant stakeholders and the public and to resolve conflicts and disputes that might arise in the process of environmental decision making (Martiskainen, 2017; Van Veelen, 2018). But what makes a strong environmental leader? Early theorising depicts environmental leaders as visionaries who prioritise the protection of the natural environment in their decision making and who go beyond just following environmental regulations, assuming an active role as environmental stewards (Flannery & May, 1994). This being said, more recent literature seems to suggest that there is no broad agreement on what constitutes strong environmental leadership. Indeed, while some scholars have drawn parallels between environmental leadership and specific leadership styles (e.g., transformational leadership; Ardoin et al., 2015; Danter et al., 2000), research suggests that what makes a good environmental leader is generally difficult to grasp as the concept has evolved overtime (Akiyama et al., 2013). Indeed, while anecdotal examples of environmental leaders are abundant, they also seem to vary considerably when it comes to their leadership style, traits and skills (Akiyama et al., 2013; Arnold et al., 2009; Liefferink & Wurzel, 2017; Runhaar et al., 2008).

Take Greta Thunberg and Elon Musk as examples. The first is a young vocal leader from Sweden who – despite her non-elite status and lack of expert knowledge credentials – became known worldwide for her environmental activism, motivating people of all ages but specially the youth to participate in the 'Fridays for Future' movement (Sommer et al., 2019). The second is a rather eccentric billionaire who, through cutting-edge sustainable innovation and environmental entrepreneurship, gained international recognition and motivated millions into moving from conventional cars to electric ones (Thomas & Maine, 2019). These two contrasting examples of environmental leaders seem to suggest that what people regard as strong environmental leadership might depend not only on the characteristics of the leader itself but also on the specific context and the extent to which such characteristics are perceived as relevant to tackle the environmental threats at hand. Greta's youth and lack of formal political connections, for instance, might signal a sense of fairness and commitment to environmental causes to a younger generation disenchanted with the political system. Elon's status and overwhelming success on sustainable innovation, on the other hand, might convey a high degree of competence, tapping into his followers' needs for guidance to navigate uncertain climate futures, and his leadership style – if you follow his social media interactions – may be seen as quite directive and domineering.

In the present chapter, based on evolutionary models of leadership and followership, we argue that what people regard as ideal environmental leaders depends critically on what they believe is required to deal with a particular environmental challenge. In other words, we posit that the specifics of different environmental threats or opportunities will likely influence the kind of styles, traits and skills people search for in environmental leaders. While our approach is mostly based on evolutionary reasoning, the idea that people have preconceived notions of what might constitute good leadership for a specific situation (i.e., ideal leader prototypes) is also present in traditional leadership models such as in implicit leadership theories (Lord et al., 1984). Yet, these theories ultimately have to turn to evolution to explain where these ideal leadership prototypes originate from.

In this chapter, we first briefly review literature on leadership and followership from an evolutionary perspective. Thereafter, we examine how different environmental challenges might tap into different fundamental follower needs and ultimately affect the kind of styles, traits and skills people prefer to see in environmental leaders (see Table 5.1 for an overview of the follower needs discussed here and traits associated with their leadership preferences). Finally, we provide theory-based recommendations for practice and discuss whether these evolved context-specific preferences are, indeed, related to the environmental performance of leaders and suggests possible paths for future research.

Evolutionary Approaches to Leadership and Followership

An evolutionary approach to human nature posits that our psychology was shaped in a functional way through a process of evolution via natural and sexual selection (Barkow et al., 1995; Neuberg et al., 2010). This implies that evolutionary approaches in psychology study people's psychological tendencies and behaviours – for instance, eating, mating, parenting or cooperating – in terms of their adaptive function for survival and reproduction (Buss, 2005, 2019). However, evolutionary perspectives do not necessarily assume that these evolved psychological tendencies are still adaptive in today's modern environments – selection, after all, favored them because they provided benefits in an environment that was different from today's in many respects (Li et al., 2018; Penn, 2003). Humans evolved as nomadic hunter-gatherers living in small kinship-based groups

Table 5.1 Fundamental Follower Needs, Their Environmental Triggers and Traits in Environmental Leaders That Satisfy Such Needs, as Well as Examples of Threats That Endanger Followers' Environmental Action and Recommendations to Overcome Them

Fundamental Follower Need	*Examples of Environmental Problems as Triggers*	*Features That Activate the Need*	*Preferred Traits in Environmental Leaders*	*Examples of Potential Threats to Followers' Environmental Action*	*Examples of Recommendations for Leaders to Engage Followers in Environmental Action*
Protection	Nuclear disaster, flood, wildfire	Requires immediate action, poses imminent threat	Dominance, authoritarianism	Strong negative emotions (e.g., fear) might lead to feelings of helplessness	Strategic messaging stressing the need of immediate action (to induce mobilising emotion) along with clear description of solutions (to increase self-efficacy)
Guidance	Climate change, deforestation, biodiversity loss	Involves high complexity, multifactorial, has no single solution	Competence, prestige, commitment, a role model	Heuristically following leaders with little to no technical skills (e.g., charismatic leaders), following non-competent leaders	Coordinating consensus among different communicators (including leaders) regarding scientifically accurate climate information (to combat misinformation)
Fairness	Energy transitions, green taxes	Involves dispute resolution, requires distribution of benefits/costs	Warmth, integrity, trustworthiness, fairness	Participation schemes that are seen as not taking public input seriously can evoke resistance	Ensuring that participation instances are fair and involve actual decision-making power

(Penn, 2003). Nowadays we live in densely populated areas (e.g., cities), interacting with many genetic strangers, and in places where food and resources can be easily found in nearby supermarkets and grocery stores. Evolutionarily speaking, all of these changes occurred within a really short period of time – probably since the advent of agriculture – and therefore it is possible that our core psychology simply has not been adapted to these new environments (evolutionary mismatch hypothesis; Li et al., 2018).

Following this reasoning, evolutionary theories posit that both leading and following are adaptive strategies that evolved because they helped to solve recurrent problems of group living in ancestral environments (e.g., co-ordination of group movement, conflict resolution), yet not necessarily in modern environments (Bastardoz & Van Vugt, 2019; de Waal-Andrews & Van Vugt, 2020; Van Vugt et al., 2008; Van Vugt & Ronay, 2014). This evolutionary time lag, or mismatch, could help understand why people sometimes follow leaders that seem ill-equipped to handle the challenge. Think about the preference for strong, aggressive, authoritarian leaders elected during times of war or political instability, for instance. A physical conflict between tribes (Bowles, 2006) may elicit a preference for following a leader who goes up-front in battle, someone who is aggressive and physically strong. Yet such preferences may have nothing to do with leader effectiveness in modern hybrid warfare when wars are fought in front of a computer screen.

This notion of individuals having evolved an adaptive followership psychology that reacts to situational threats and opportunities is nothing new (Kenrick, Griskevicius, et al., 2010; Kenrick, Neuberg, et al., 2010; Schaller et al., 2017). Previous research has demonstrated the value of evolutionary psychology theories to understand universal human needs in domains like consumption (Durante & Griskevicius, 2016; Griskevicius & Kenrick, 2013), food and mate preferences (Buss, 2015; Folwarczny et al., 2023), conservation (Penn, 2003) and pro-environmental behaviours (Palomo-Vélez & Van Vugt, 2021; Van Vugt et al., 2014). In the case of leadership, evolutionary psychology offers a unifying framework to study the selection pressures that have shaped modern leadership preferences and tendencies. For instance, evolutionary leadership theory (ELT; Van Vugt & Ronay, 2014) proposes that leading and following strategies evolved among humans (and other social species) as psychological mechanisms that operate as fast-and-frugal heuristics (e.g., if in danger, follow a strong leader). ELT also provides insights into the origin of different leadership types. Dominance-based leaders influence followers because they are able inflict costs on them, whereas prestige-based leaders influence followers by their ability to confer benefits on followers (Van Vugt & Smith, 2019).

ELT describes three fundamental follower needs that are activated in different evolutionary-relevant situations: (a) guidance into a shared direction, (b) protection against physical and social threats, and (c) judicious dispute settlement (i.e., the triad model of followership, Figure 5.1; de Waal-Andrews & Van Vugt, 2020). These motivational needs operate as heuristics or 'if–then' decision rules requiring certain environmental inputs to become salient, resulting in certain outputs that aid with the selection of appropriate leaders to alleviate the specific environmental challenge. Building from the ELT, here we argue that different features of environmental challenges (inputs) – for instance, how imminent the threat is (e.g., nuclear disaster) – activate a specific follower need ('if there is a nuclear attack, we want a leader to protect us') and motivate people to favor some leaders over others (outputs). Importantly, favoring some leaders over others because of evolutionarily relevant follower needs may influence the extent environmental challenges are effectively dealt with. Indeed, while anthropological evidence suggests that conservation actions are rather scarce among people living in small scale societies (Smith & Wishnie, 2000), other literature indicates that for societies like these (i.e., the Tsimane in Bolivia and the Nyangatom in Ethiopia), the emergence of some (types of) leaders can help to effectively overcome collective action problems such as the overexploitation of natural resources (Glowacki & von Rueden, 2015).

In the following we discuss three fundamental follower needs as identified by ELT, how they are activated by specific environmental threats and how they affect what kind of leaders people want to overcome these threats.

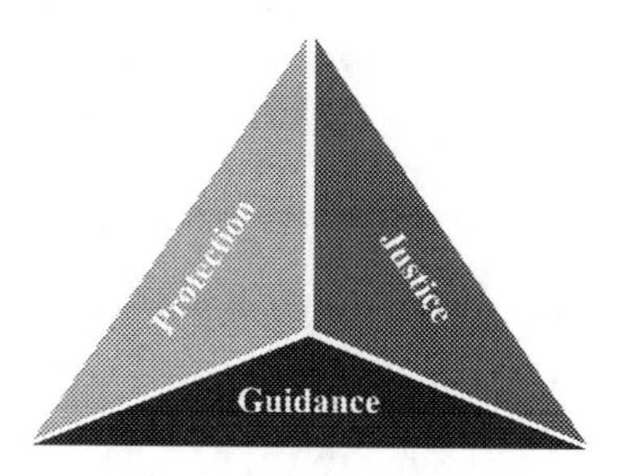

Figure 5.1 Graphical Representation of the Triad Model of Follower Needs

Protection and Environmental Challenges Posing Imminent Threats

Environmental crises such as nuclear accidents, floods, landslides, wildfires and catastrophic weather events (e.g., hurricanes, tornadoes) usually require immediate action and crisis management. Human psychology evolved to rapidly respond to imminent threats to survival and therefore features of environmental crises of rapid onset that require swift action may trigger a suite of adaptive responses. This first implies that environmental threats should probably induce a strong emotional reaction such as fear and, secondly, in terms of followership, they should seek out leaders who could effectively protect them and their kin.

First, literature does suggest that environmental problems posing imminent threats induce strong emotional reactions. Avoidant emotions such as fear and disgust are key to our human threat detection and threat management system (Neuberg et al., 2011), and there is research indicating that the former – via the human olfactory system – could be functionally relevant to react to stimuli often associated with environmental hazards such as smoke from fires and degraded air quality (K. Q. Chan et al., 2016; Stevenson, 2010). Similarly, recent research suggests that fear of contamination – a key feature of the emotion disgust (Tybur et al., 2013) – explains why most people are often ambivalent about nuclear power. Particularly, people high in disgust sensitivity were more likely to oppose to nuclear energy, and those who were reassured that radioactivity was not contagious showed less fear of radiation (Hacquin et al., 2022).

Furthermore, research indicates that environmental issues that call for immediate action are generally perceived as personally threatening by the public (Champ et al., 2013; Huang et al., 2013). For instance, after the Fukushima nuclear disaster, people rated their risk of dying due to nuclear power plants and nuclear waste higher than the risk of dying from smoking, riding a motorcycle and travelling by plane (Ho et al., 2014). Similarly, other research indicates that feelings of fear motivate opposition to nuclear power (Hartmann et al., 2013) and that direct exposure to wildfires increases expressions of fear in social media (Loureiro et al., 2022). More generally, scholars have noted that, particularly in the case of extreme weather events, direct experience with climate change–related disasters often induces acute emotional responses in people that might lead to either heightened concern or withdrawal due to emotional distress (Davidson & Kecinski, 2022). It should be noted, however, that owing to people's cognitive biases (e.g., accessibility bias, vividness bias), extreme weather events might increase environmental concern only among those who are directly affected (Mazutis & Eckardt, 2017) – and even among them, behavioural effects (i.e., voting for a green party) might be rather small (Garside & Zhai, 2022).

Do environmental issues that pose an imminent physical threat activate protection needs among followers? Whereas most research has focused on how social threats (e.g., intergroup conflict) or economic threats (e.g., recession) increase support for dominant leaders (Kakkar & Sivanathan, 2017; Laustsen & Petersen, 2017; Nettle & Saxe, 2021; Van Vugt & Spisak, 2008) and on how protection motives may lead to stereotyping and prejudice against outgroup members (Schaller et al., 2003), some literature suggests that similar patterns emerge when people are faced with life-threatening environmental threats. Recent experimental research, for example, shows that protection motives might be at work and motivate discrimination to outgroup members when people evaluate environmental refugee policies. In particular, Americans supported policies favoring the resettlement of refugees fleeing from climate disasters (e.g., low-lying coastal countries becoming inhabitable due to the rise in sea level) less when these were expected to migrate from abroad as compared to those coming from coastal areas of the United States (Stanley et al., 2022). Moreover, other literature indicates that exposure to rapid-onset environmental crises that pose an imminent physical threat to people also relates to anti-democratic attitudes and practices. For instance, using national survey data on Chile's 8.8 Richter scale earthquake in 2010, Carlin et al. (2014) showed that people who reported greater earthquake-related damage in their neighborhoods tended to lower their support for democratic institutions and values and increase their support for military coups. Similarly, longitudinal research suggests that higher exposure to news about the 2009 L'Aquila earthquake in Italy led to increased levels of right-wing authoritarianism – an attitude that reflects the need for order, social control, security and strong, authoritarian leadership – and this shift in authoritarian values was strongest among those who were relatively low in right-wing authoritarianism before the seismic event (Russo et al., 2020). Thus, it seems that when people are confronted with environmental problems that pose an imminent threat to their safety, people tend to increase their support for strong, dominant leaders as well as favor members of their own group (vs. outgroup members).

Guidance to Navigate Complex Environmental Challenges

Unlike nuclear accidents and earthquakes, some environmental issues are distant, slow-moving, uncertain and complex problems that require a systematic and evidence-based approach. Climate change is probably the best example of this type of environmental challenge. Being one of most pressing and complex issues of our time, the intricate social, economic and environmental impacts of climate change preclude the use of one-size-fits-all strategies (Nielsen et al., 2021; Pörtner et al., 2022). Complex, multifactorial environmental threats should elicit the need for leaders who are perceived as having both motivation and commitment to environmental causes but also the knowledge and skills to effectively guide environmental action. In other words, when facing complex environmental challenges, followers' need for guidance may be activated and therefore they should value competence in a leader more. Literature from evolutionary psychology suggests that the need for guidance evolved in response to recurrent problems of group movement whereby the most experienced, most knowledgeable individual took the lead (de Waal-Andrews & Van Vugt, 2020). Indeed, competent leadership – that is, leadership based on prestige, respect and admiration due to a person's skills and/or knowledge (Henrich & Gil-White, 2001; Van Vugt & Smith, 2019) – was likely key to solve evolutionary-relevant problems where people needed to choose among multiple alternative courses of action (de Waal-Andrews & Van Vugt, 2020; Van Vugt & Ronay, 2014).

Do people look for particularly competent leaders when confronted with complex and intricate environmental problems? Research indicates that conservationists are more likely to be selected as group leaders in resource dilemmas, and they are perceived as more respected, having more influence and of higher status than less environmentally restrained individuals (Hardy & Van Vugt, 2006). Further, prestigious traits like competence seem to be valued especially in a leader when people are confronted with complex environmental problems. For instance, vision, charisma, commitment and reputation are often identified as desirable personality traits of environmental leaders to tackle climate change (Evans et al., 2015). Based on case studies of successful agricultural and natural resource projects, Biggs (2008) suggested that environmental leaders require technical expertise and knowledge as well as a good reputation based on evidence of long-term professional concern and commitment to social issues. Moreover, recent research suggests that having committed environmental leaders can inspire others into climate action. Specifically, research indicates that those who are more familiar with Greta Thunberg report higher intentions to mitigate climate change via collective actions – and this occurs even after accounting for people's general support to climate activism (Sabherwal et al., 2021).

Particularly competent leaders are not only preferred when followers are faced with complex environmental issues, but a leader's competence also predicts the leader's effectiveness. Strong environmental leadership – represented by the presence of locally respected, motivated individuals with entrepreneurial skill – was the most important predictor of success among 130 co-managed sustainable fisheries (Gutiérrez et al., 2011). Similarly, people also rely more on those who hold expert credentials when it comes to solving complex environmental issues. For instance, when asked about how much they trust different sources of scientific information about the environment, people ranked well-respected science television channels such as Discovery Channel and university scientists as the most trustworthy sources (Brewer & Ley, 2013). Further, other research shows that trust in climate scientists predicts intentions to uptake both low- and high-impact environmental behaviours (Cologna et al., 2022) and that effects like this would more reliably occur when people do not expect climate scientists to have a 'hidden agenda' apart from providing the public with expert information (Rabinovich et al., 2012). Thus, when it comes to environmental issues that are complex and uncertain and where there is likely no single solution, people tend to look for leaders who signal competence as well as other prestige-based traits such as demonstrating a high degree of environmental commitment.

Fairness to Deal With Resource Allocation Issues in Environmental Problems

Disputes over food, territory and mates probably characterised the environment in which our ancestors evolved – though accumulating evidence also suggests that such disputes did not always end in violence (Boehm, 2012).

To minimise the chance of escalation, human psychology likely evolved ways to reduce within-group aggression (De Waal, 2000). Conflict management may have been facilitated by leaders with a strong sense of fairness and integrity to act as peacekeepers (Van Vugt et al., 2008). Preferences for fair and trustworthy leaders might mitigate against leaders using their privileged position to get benefits for themselves or their kin (Bøggild & Petersen, 2016). Leaders who show procedural fairness (e.g., equity in the procedures used to yield a decision) are trusted more (De Cremer et al., 2006), and fairness serves as a heuristic for followers when deciding whether they can rely on a leader (Janson et al., 2008; van Knippenberg et al., 2007).

Environmental issues often involve trade-offs between costs and benefits of mitigation measures, and the extent to which these measures are perceived as fair is an important consideration (e.g., Jenkins et al., 2016). Think about renewable energy transitions. While transitioning to cleaner energy production is essential to mitigate climate change (International Energy Agency, 2019), literature suggests that the public is unlikely to support such a transition if distribution between costs (e.g., more expensive energy bills for some groups) and benefits (e.g., greener, more habitable environments for everyone) is seen as unfair (Leer Jørgensen et al., 2020; Perlaviciute & Steg, 2014; Wüstenhagen et al., 2007). Experimental evidence shows that letting people participate in major aspects of hypothetical energy projects leads to higher public acceptability, and such effect derives from a higher perceived procedural fairness (Liu et al., 2020).

Do people favor environmental leaders with a strong sense of fairness? Early works indicate that, when faced with a naturally occurring resource dilemma such as the 1991 California water shortage, people were more likely to support leaders' water conservation decisions when the environmental decision-making processes were perceived as fair (Tyler & Degoey, 1995). More recent qualitative work in the context of an offshore wind farm in the United States showed that process leaders' (i.e., resource managers, developers) perceived procedural fairness as key to building followers' trust in the project, which ultimately affected its public acceptability. Semi-structured interviews with process leaders showed that signaling the ability to work for the public interest and providing opportunities for engagement and participation increased participants' trust in them, which in turn facilitated building trust in the environmental project and acceptability of its outcomes (Dwyer & Bidwell, 2019). Thus, when faced with environmental issues involving distributional problems, leaders perceived as particularly trustworthy and high in integrity are favored more.

Theory-Based Recommendations and Applications

Based on our review, multiple recommendations for increasing environmental leaders' effectiveness, as well as improving the alignment between leadership preferences and sustainability targets, can be drawn. For instance, while we noted that inducing acute affective responses to imminent environmental threats might backfire, making people withdraw because of emotional distress, literature suggests that leaders might harness followers' protection needs via threat- and fear-based communication to encourage climate action. Mixing persuasive messages that evoke fear of rapid-onset environmental problems but also self-efficacy could provide followers with a sense of urgency and avoid making them feel helpless (Brosch, 2021; Markowitz & Guckian, 2018). Similarly, research from intergroup leadership literature (e.g., Hogg, 2015) suggests that our tendency to stereotype and reject outgroup members due to protection motives might not need to impair climate refugee policies aiming to support those fleeing from abroad. Indeed, attitudes against foreign climate refugees (vs. local ones) are driven especially from the symbolic threats they pose (i.e., holding different values; Stanley et al., 2022) and, as such, leaders may use strategic messaging and framing to encourage support for climate refugee policies. For instance, environmental leaders could make foreign climate refugees seem more similar to locals by appealing to a superordinate identity or a common goal (e.g., 'we are all people from Earth', 'we must face climate disasters together') or stressing the value of collaboration on climate issues (e.g., 'different experiences bring different knowledge'; see Hogg, 2015).

Because of followers' need for guidance, our review suggests that people look for competence in leaders and for accurate sources of environmental information when faced with intricate and complex environmental problems. While looking for information is probably a good strategy when faced with complex environmental issues, this could also be problematic as much research has highlighted the dangers of following opinion leaders who disseminate climate misinformation (Treen et al., 2020; van der Linden et al., 2017). One strategy to increase the spread of accurate climate information is via highlighting its consensual nature. The gateway belief model suggests that high perceived scientific agreement regarding the origins of climate change is key in driving public responses to climate change (van der Linden et al., 2015). Articulated action and coordination in the climate information shared by relevant climate actors (e.g., nongovernmental organisations, universities, and science communicators) is likely highly relevant to secure followers' reliance on highly competent environmental leaders, such as scientists or committed folks such as Greta Thunberg. Increasing perceptions of consensus regarding climate change seems to even be able to persuade those who are still sceptical, making it a potentially great strategy for environmental leaders aiming to reach difficult audiences (Goldberg et al., 2022).

Finally, when it comes to followers' need for fairness, environmental leaders should make sure that interventions to tackle environmental problems do not further increase the social and economic inequalities within society (e.g., green tax benefits only for homeowners). Further, leadership should develop participation and consultation schemes that increase perceptions of trustworthiness and thereby positively influence support for their proposed environmental policies and projects. Indeed, letting people have a say in environmental projects often leads to higher support for such projects (e.g., Liu et al., 2020). Yet not every form of participation increases perceptions of fairness. Environmental leaders must ensure that the ways in which people can have a say in the decision-making process of environmental projects involve more than just providing them with information. For public participation schemes to increase perceived fairness and therefore acceptability of environmental projects and policies, leaders need to provide followers with decision-making power, safeguard that opinions expressed are able to capture the diversity of voices that will be affected by decisions and make arrangements so people can deliberate over matters long enough to go beyond the (possible) initial inertia of their own positions (Perlaviciute, 2022).

Limitations and Future Developments on an Evolutionary Approach to Environmental Leadership

Whereas our short review shows that different features of environmental issues tap into different fundamental follower needs and differentially influence their support for environmental leaders with particular qualities and personalities, this does not mean that the preferred leaders will be effective in coordinating efforts to mitigating the environmental problems at hand. For instance, the hierarchical nature of leader–follower relations might corrupt leaders who start out as fair and trustworthy leaders. Indeed, a resource dilemma experiment revealed that when there is high variance in resource use among followers, the appointed leaders showed less restraint, and this was partly explained because they felt entitled to harvest more from the common resource (Stouten et al., 2005). Thus, power corrupts. Similarly, although personal commitment to environmental issues is valued in environmental leaders, possibly because it is a signal of people's willingness to guide others, research suggests that interventions aimed to increase such commitments might not lead to green action. Ernst et al. (2017), for instance, showed that after attending a climate and conservation program for young leaders, the changes in students' sense of personal responsibility and commitment to environmental causes did not predict their environmental actions. Further, even though environmental knowledge might be perceived as a credential signal of competence among leaders, previous research indicates that the explanatory power of having objective knowledge about environmental issues in conservation behaviour is rather low (Frick et al., 2004). Finally, the heuristics that followers use to evaluate leaders might also trick them into following less-than-ideal leaders. Literature on charismatic leadership, for example, shows that people have a hard time discriminating reliable from false cues of charisma (Grabo et al., 2017; Schjoedt et al., 2013). These examples suggest actor-observer incongruences in terms of what followers regard as ideal environmental leaders and how effective they are. Future research should evaluate in which situations followers' preferences for environmental leaders translate into effective leadership.

Furthermore, given the complexity of many environmental issues, such as climate change, they are usually handled by governments rather than individual leaders. Indeed, much of the environmental literature focuses on judgements that people make about how much they trust governments, corporates and other institutions – as opposed to presidents and managers – when evaluating the acceptability of projects that have environmental consequences (Bronfman et al., 2008, 2012; Palomo-Vélez et al., 2023). Future research should evaluate to what extent the fundamental follower needs discussed here also predict preferences for different types of institutions and formal leadership roles. Moreover, given that literature that directly evaluates whether specific features of environmental problems tap into fundamental follower needs is scarce, future research should systematically test whether manipulating the specific features and contexts of environmental issues discussed in this chapter influences followers' preferred leader characteristics in the predicted ways. For example, if we were to pit an acute environmental problem (e.g., wildfires) against a long-term problem (e.g., climate change), would we see different leaders with different qualities and personalities being preferred by voters?

Finally, future research should also explore whether, in addition to the three fundamental needs, other follower needs might relate to environmental leadership preferences. For instance, people's evolved motivation for status acquisition (e.g., Schaller et al., 2017) might make high-status individuals attractive as environmental leaders. Indeed, building on costly signaling theory (Zahavi & Zahavi, 1999) and literature on conspicuous conservation (Griskevicius et al., 2010; Noel et al., 2019; Palomo-Vélez et al., 2021), it could be argued that driving a Tesla potentially improves your own status by associating yourself with a high-status figure like Elon Musk. Similarly, people's fundamental affiliation needs might also affect the kind of environmental leaders they prefer. Recent literature has highlighted the role of identification with the groups people belong to in promoting climate action (Bouman et al., 2021; Wang et al., 2021). It might be that leaders who fulfil followers' social identity needs are considered as more appealing and exert more influence among followers (e.g., being part of a green activist movement like Extinction Rebellion). Future studies could build on these ideas and evaluate empirically whether the activation of people's status or affiliation needs makes them prefer other kinds of traits and behaviours in environmental leaders than dominance, competence and warmth.

Discussion Points

- To what extent does an evolutionary perspective on environmental leadership offer novel insights and predictions not commonly derived from other approaches, such as environmental psychology?
- What other fundamental follower needs might be activated by specific features of environmental problems and therefore influence leader preferences?

Suggested Reading

Van Vugt, M., & Ahuja, A. (2011). *Naturally selected: The evolutionary science of leadership*. HarperBusiness.

Buss, D. (2015). *The Handbook of Evolutionary Psychology*. John Wiley & Sons, Inc.

References

Akiyama, T., An, K. J., Furumai, H., & Katayama, H. (2013). The concept of environmental leader. In T. Mino & K. Hanaki (Eds.), *Environmental leadership capacity building in higher education: Experience and lessons from Asian program for incubation of environmental leaders* (pp. 19–40). Springer Japan. https://doi.org/10.1007/978-4-431-54340-4_2

Ardoin, N. M., Gould, R. K., Kelsey, E., & Fielding-Singh, P. (2015). Collaborative and transformational leadership in the environmental realm. *Journal of Environmental Policy & Planning, 17*(3), 360–380. https://doi.org/10.1080/1523908X.2014.954075

Arnold, H. E., Cohen, F. G., & Warner, A. (2009). Youth and environmental action: Perspectives of young environmental leaders on their formative influences. *The Journal of Environmental Education, 40*(3), 27–36. https://doi.org/10.3200/JOEE.40.3.27-36

Barkow, J. H., Cosmides, L., & Tooby, J. (1995). *The adapted mind: Evolutionary psychology and the generation of culture*. Oxford University Press.

Bastardoz, N., & Van Vugt, M. (2019). The nature of followership: Evolutionary analysis and review. *The Leadership Quarterly, 30*(1), 81–95. https://doi.org/10.1016/j.leaqua.2018.09.004

Biggs, S. (2008). Learning from the positive to reduce rural poverty and increase social justice: Institutional innovations in agricultural and natural resources research and development. *Experimental Agriculture, 44*(1), 37–60. https://doi.org/10.1017/S0014479707005959

Bodin, Ö. (2017). Collaborative environmental governance: Achieving collective action in social-ecological systems. *Science, 357*(6352), eaan1114. https://doi.org/10.1126/science.aan1114

Boehm, C. (2012). Ancestral hierarchy and conflict. *Science, 336*(6083), 844–847. https://doi.org/10.1126/science.1219961

Bøggild, T., & Petersen, M. B. (2016). The evolved functions of procedural fairness: An adaptation for politics. In T. K. Shackelford & R. D. Hansen (Eds.), *The evolution of morality* (pp. 247–276). Springer International. https://doi.org/10.1007/978-3-319-19671-8_12

Bouman, T., van der Werff, E., Perlaviciute, G., & Steg, L. (2021). Environmental values and identities at the personal and group level [Special issue]. *Current Opinion in Behavioral Sciences, 42*, 47–53. https://doi.org/10.1016/j.cobeha.2021.02.022

Bowles, S. (2006). Group competition, reproductive leveling, and the evolution of human altruism. *Science, 314*(5805), 1569–1572. https://doi.org/10.1126/science.1134829

Brewer, P. R., & Ley, B. L. (2013). Whose science do you believe? Explaining trust in sources of scientific information about the environment. *Science Communication, 35*(1), 115–137. https://doi.org/10.1177/1075547012441691

Bronfman, N. C., Jiménez, R. B., Arévalo, P. C., & Cifuentes, L. A. (2012). Understanding social acceptance of electricity generation sources. *Energy Policy, 46*, 246–252. https://doi.org/10.1016/j.enpol.2012.03.057

Bronfman, N. C., Vázquez, E. L., Gutiérrez, V. V., & Cifuentes, L. A. (2008). Trust, acceptance and knowledge of technological and environmental hazards in Chile. *Journal of Risk Research, 11*(6), 755–773. https://doi.org/10.1080/13669870801967184

Brosch, T. (2021). Affect and emotions as drivers of climate change perception and action: A review [Special issue]. *Current Opinion in Behavioral Sciences, 42*, 15–21. https://doi.org/10.1016/j.cobeha.2021.02.001

Buss, D. M. (2005). *The handbook of evolutionary psychology*. John Wiley & Sons.

Buss, D. M. (2015). Mating. In D. M. Buss (Ed.), *The handbook of evolutionary psychology* (pp. 251–257). John Wiley & Sons. https://doi.org/10.1002/9780470939376.part3

Buss, D. M. (2019). *Evolutionary psychology: The new science of the mind* (6th ed.). Routledge.

Carlin, R. E., Love, G. J., & Zechmeister, E. J. (2014). Natural disaster and democratic legitimacy: The public opinion consequences of Chile's 2010 earthquake and tsunami. *Political Research Quarterly, 67*(1), 3–15. https://doi.org/10.1177/1065912913495592

Champ, P. A., Donovan, G. H., & Barth, C. M. (2013). Living in a tinderbox: Wildfire risk perceptions and mitigating behaviours. *International Journal of Wildland Fire, 22*(6), 832–840.

Chan, K., Boyd, D. R., Gould, R. K., Jetzkowitz, J., Liu, J., Muraca, B., Naidoo, R., Olmsted, P., Satterfield, T., Selomane, O., Singh, G. G., Sumaila, R., Ngo, H. T., Boedhihartono, A. K., Agard, J., de Aguiar, A. P. D., Armenteras, D., Balint, L., Barrington-Leigh, C., ... Brondízio, E. S. (2020). Levers and leverage points for pathways to sustainability. *People and Nature, 2*(3), 693–717. https://doi.org/10.1002/pan3.10124

Chan, K. Q., Holland, R. W., van Loon, R., Arts, R., & van Knippenberg, A. (2016). Disgust and fear lower olfactory threshold. *Emotion, 16*, 740–749. https://doi.org/10.1037/emo0000113

Cologna, V., Berthold, A., & Siegrist, M. (2022). Knowledge, perceived potential and trust as determinants of low- and high-impact pro-environmental behaviours. *Journal of Environmental Psychology, 79*, 101741. https://doi.org/10.1016/j.jenvp.2021.101741

Danter, K., Griest, D., Mullins, G., & Norland, E. (2000). Organizational change as a component of ecosystem management. *Society & Natural Resources, 13*(6), 537–547. https://doi.org/10.1080/089419200050114592

Davidson, D. J., & Kecinski, M. (2022). Emotional pathways to climate change responses. *WIREs Climate Change, 13*(2), e751. https://doi.org/10.1002/wcc.751

De Cremer, D., van Dijke, M., & Bos, A. E. R. (2006). Leader's procedural justice affecting identification and trust. *Leadership & Organization Development Journal, 27*(7), 554–565. https://doi.org/10.1108/01437730610692416

De Waal, F. B. M. (2000). Primates – A natural heritage of conflict resolution. *Science, 289*(5479), 586–590. https://doi.org/10.1126/science.289.5479.586

de Waal-Andrews, W., & Van Vugt, M. (2020). The triad model of follower needs: Theory and review. *Power, Status and Hierarchy, 33*, 142–147. https://doi.org/10.1016/j.copsyc.2019.07.006

Durante, K. M., & Griskevicius, V. (2016). Evolution and consumer behavior. *Consumer Behavior, 10*, 27–32. https://doi.org/10.1016/j.copsyc.2015.10.025

Dwyer, J., & Bidwell, D. (2019). Chains of trust: Energy justice, public engagement, and the first offshore wind farm in the United States. *Energy Research & Social Science, 47*, 166–176. https://doi.org/10.1016/j.erss.2018.08.019

Ernst, J., Blood, N., & Beery, T. (2017). Environmental action and student environmental leaders: Exploring the influence of environmental attitudes, locus of control, and sense of personal responsibility. *Environmental Education Research, 23*(2), 149–175. https://doi.org/10.1080/13504622.2015.1068278

Evans, L. S., Hicks, C. C., Cohen, P. J., Case, P., Prideaux, M., & Mills, D. J. (2015). Understanding leadership in the environmental sciences. *Ecology and Society, 20*(1). https://doi.org/10.5751/ES-07268-200150

Flannery, B. L., & May, D. R. (1994). Prominent factors influencing environmental activities: Application of the environmental leadership model (ELM). *The Leadership Quarterly, 5*(3), 201–221. https://doi.org/10.1016/1048-9843(94)90012-4

Folwarczny, M., Otterbring, T., Sigurdsson, V., Tan, L. K. L., & Li, N. P. (2023). Old minds, new marketplaces: How evolved psychological mechanisms trigger mismatched food preferences. *Evolutionary Behavioral Sciences, 17*(1), 93–101. https://doi.org/10.1037/ebs0000288

Frick, J., Kaiser, F. G., & Wilson, M. (2004). Environmental knowledge and conservation behavior: Exploring prevalence and structure in a representative sample. *Personality and Individual Differences, 37*(8), 1597–1613. https://doi.org/10.1016/j.paid.2004.02.015

Garside, S., & Zhai, H. (2022). If not now, when? Climate disaster and the Green vote following the 2021 Germany floods. *Research & Politics, 9*(4). https://doi.org/10.1177/20531680221141523

Gilligan, J. M., & Vandenbergh, M. P. (2020). A framework for assessing the impact of private climate governance. *Energy Research & Social Science, 60*, 101400. https://doi.org/10.1016/j.erss.2019.101400

Glowacki, L., & von Rueden, C. (2015). Leadership solves collective action problems in small-scale societies. *Philosophical Transactions of the Royal Society B: Biological Sciences, 370*(1683), 20150010. https://doi.org/10.1098/rstb.2015.0010

Goldberg, M. H., Gustafson, A., van der Linden, S., Rosenthal, S. A., & Leiserowitz, A. (2022). Communicating the scientific consensus on climate change: diverse audiences and effects over time. *Environment and Behavior, 54*(7–8), 1133–1165. https://doi.org/10.1177/00139165221129539

Grabo, A., Spisak, B. R., & Van Vugt, M. (2017). Charisma as signal: An evolutionary perspective on charismatic leadership [Special issue]. *The Leadership Quarterly, 28*(4), 473–485. https://doi.org/10.1016/j.leaqua.2017.05.001

Griskevicius, V., & Kenrick, D. T. (2013). Fundamental motives: How evolutionary needs influence consumer behavior. *Journal of Consumer Psychology, 23*(3), 372–386. https://doi.org/10.1016/j.jcps.2013.03.003

Griskevicius, V., Tybur, J. M., & Van den Bergh, B. (2010). Going green to be seen: Status, reputation, and conspicuous conservation. *Journal of Personality and Social Psychology, 98*, 392–404. https://doi.org/10.1037/a0017346

Gutiérrez, N. L., Hilborn, R., & Defeo, O. (2011). Leadership, social capital and incentives promote successful fisheries. *Nature, 470*(7334), 386–389. https://doi.org/10.1038/nature09689

Hacquin, A.-S., Altay, S., Aarøe, L., & Mercier, H. (2022). Disgust sensitivity and public opinion on nuclear energy. *Journal of Environmental Psychology, 80*, 101749. https://doi.org/10.1016/j.jenvp.2021.101749

Hardy, C. L., & Van Vugt, M. (2006). Nice guys finish first: The competitive altruism hypothesis. *Personality and Social Psychology Bulletin, 32*(10), 1402–1413. https://doi.org/10.1177/0146167206291006

Hartmann, P., Apaolaza, V., D'Souza, C., Echebarria, C., & Barrutia, J. M. (2013). Nuclear power threats, public opposition and green electricity adoption: Effects of threat belief appraisal and fear arousal. *Energy Policy, 62*, 1366–1376. https://doi.org/10.1016/j.enpol.2013.07.058

Henrich, J., & Gil-White, F. J. (2001). The evolution of prestige: Freely conferred deference as a mechanism for enhancing the benefits of cultural transmission. *Evolution and Human Behavior, 22*(3), 165–196. https://doi.org/10.1016/S1090-5138(00)00071-4

Ho, J.-C., Lee, C.-T. P., Kao, S.-F., Chen, R.-Y., Ieong, M. C. F., Chang, H.-L., Hsieh, W.-H., Tzeng, C.-C., Lu, C.-F., Lin, S.-L., & Chang, P. W. (2014). Perceived environmental and health risks of nuclear energy in Taiwan after Fukushima nuclear disaster. *Environment International, 73*, 295–303. https://doi.org/10.1016/j.envint.2014.08.007

Hogg, M. A. (2015). Constructive leadership across groups: How leaders can combat prejudice and conflict between subgroups. In S. R. Thye & E. J. Lawler (Eds.), *Advances in group processes* (Vol. 32, pp. 177–207). Emerald. https://doi.org/10.1108/S0882-614520150000032007

Huang, L., Zhou, Y., Han, Y., Hammitt, J. K., Bi, J., & Liu, Y. (2013). Effect of the Fukushima nuclear accident on the risk perception of residents near a nuclear power plant in China. *Proceedings of the National Academy of Sciences, 110*(49), 19742–19747. https://doi.org/10.1073/pnas.1313825110

International Energy Agency. (2019). *Global energy & CO_2 status report 2019*. https://www.iea.org/reports/global-energy-co2-status-report-2019

Janson, A., Levy, L., Sitkin, S. B., & Lind, E. A. (2008). Fairness and other leadership heuristics: A four-nation study. *European Journal of Work and Organizational Psychology, 17*(2), 251–272. https://doi.org/10.1080/13594320701746510

Jenkins, K., McCauley, D., Heffron, R., Stephan, H., & Rehner, R. (2016). Energy justice: A conceptual review. *Energy Research & Social Science, 11*, 174–182. https://doi.org/10.1016/j.erss.2015.10.004

Kakkar, H., & Sivanathan, N. (2017). When the appeal of a dominant leader is greater than a prestige leader. *Proceedings of the National Academy of Sciences, 114*(26), 6734–6739. https://doi.org/10.1073/pnas.1617711114

Kenrick, D. T., Griskevicius, V., Neuberg, S. L., & Schaller, M. (2010). Renovating the pyramid of needs: Contemporary extensions built upon ancient foundations. *Perspectives on Psychological Science, 5*(3), 292–314. https://doi.org/10.1177/1745691610369469

Kenrick, D. T., Neuberg, S. L., Griskevicius, V., Becker, D. V., & Schaller, M. (2010). Goal-driven cognition and functional behavior: The fundamental-motives framework. *Current Directions in Psychological Science, 19*(1), 63–67. https://doi.org/10.1177/0963721409359281

Laustsen, L., & Petersen, M. B. (2017). Perceived conflict and leader dominance: Individual and contextual factors behind preferences for dominant leaders. *Political Psychology, 38*(6), 1083–1101. https://doi.org/10.1111/pops.12403

Leer Jørgensen, M., Anker, H. T., & Lassen, J. (2020). Distributive fairness and local acceptance of wind turbines: The role of compensation schemes. *Energy Policy, 138*, 111294. https://doi.org/10.1016/j.enpol.2020.111294

Li, N. P., Van Vugt, M., & Colarelli, S. M. (2018). The evolutionary mismatch hypothesis: Implications for psychological science. *Current Directions in Psychological Science, 27*(1), 38–44. https://doi.org/10.1177/0963721417731378

Liefferink, D., & Wurzel, R. K. W. (2017). Environmental leaders and pioneers: Agents of change? *Journal of European Public Policy, 24*(7), 951–968. https://doi.org/10.1080/13501763.2016.1161657

Liu, L., Bouman, T., Perlaviciute, G., & Steg, L. (2020). Public participation in decision making, perceived procedural fairness and public acceptability of renewable energy projects. *Energy and Climate Change, 1*, 100013. https://doi.org/10.1016/j.egycc.2020.100013

Lord, R. G., Foti, R. J., & De Vader, C. L. (1984). A test of leadership categorization theory: Internal structure, information processing, and leadership perceptions. *Organizational Behavior and Human Performance, 34*(3), 343–378. https://doi.org/10.1016/0030-5073(84)90043-6

Loureiro, M. L., Alló, M., & Coello, P. (2022). Hot in Twitter: Assessing the emotional impacts of wildfires with sentiment analysis. *Ecological Economics, 200*, 107502. https://doi.org/10.1016/j.ecolecon.2022.107502

Mann, M. (2019, September 12). Lifestyle changes aren't enough to save the planet. Here's what could. *Time*. https://time.com/5669071/lifestyle-changes-climate-change/

Margerum, R. D., & Robinson, C. J. (2016). *The challenges of collaboration in environmental governance: Barriers and responses*. Edward Elgar.

Markowitz, E. M., & Guckian, M. L. (2018). 3—Climate change communication: Challenges, insights, and opportunities. In S. Clayton & C. Manning (Eds.), *Psychology and climate change* (pp. 35–63). Academic Press. https://doi.org/10.1016/B978-0-12-813130-5.00003-5

Martiskainen, M. (2017). The role of community leadership in the development of grassroots innovations. *Environmental Innovation and Societal Transitions, 22*, 78–89. https://doi.org/10.1016/j.eist.2016.05.002

Mazutis, D., & Eckardt, A. (2017). Sleepwalking into catastrophe: Cognitive biases and corporate climate change inertia. *California Management Review, 59*(3), 74–108. https://doi.org/10.1177/0008125617707974

Nettle, D., & Saxe, R. (2021). 'If men were angels, no government would be necessary': The intuitive theory of social motivation and preference for authoritarian leaders. *Collabra: Psychology, 7*(1), 28105. https://doi.org/10.1525/collabra.28105

Neuberg, S. L., Kenrick, D. T., & Schaller, M. (2010). Evolutionary social psychology. In S. T. Fiske, D. T. Gilbert, & G. Lindzey (Eds.), *Handbook of social psychology* (Vol. 2, 5th ed., pp. 761–796). John Wiley & Sons. https://doi.org/10.1002/9780470561119.socpsy002021

Neuberg, S. L., Kenrick, D. T., & Schaller, M. (2011). Human threat management systems: Self-protection and disease avoidance. *Threat-Detection and Precaution: Neuro-Physiological, Behavioral, Cognitive and Psychiatric Aspects, 35*(4), 1042–1051. https://doi.org/10.1016/j.neubiorev.2010.08.011

Nielsen, K. S., Clayton, S., Stern, P. C., Dietz, T., Capstick, S., & Whitmarsh, L. (2021). How psychology can help limit climate change. *American Psychologist, 76*, 130–144. https://doi.org/10.1037/amp0000624

Nilsson, M., Griggs, D., & Visbeck, M. (2016). Policy: Map the interactions between Sustainable Development Goals. *Nature, 534*(7607), 320–322. https://doi.org/10.1038/534320a

Noel, L., Sovacool, B. K., Kester, J., & Zarazua de Rubens, G. (2019). Conspicuous diffusion: Theorizing how status drives innovation in electric mobility. *Environmental Innovation and Societal Transitions, 31*, 154–169. https://doi.org/10.1016/j.eist.2018.11.007

Palomo-Vélez, G., Contzen, N., Perlaviciute, G., & Steg, L. (2023). Trust in institutions and public acceptability of risky energy production: Testing the causal relationships in the context of Groningen earthquakes. *Energy Research & Social Science, 96*, 102927. https://doi.org/10.1016/j.erss.2022.102927

Palomo-Vélez, G., Tybur, J. M., & Van Vugt, M. (2021). Is green the new sexy? Romantic of conspicuous conservation. *Journal of Environmental Psychology, 73*, 101530. https://doi.org/10.1016/j.jenvp.2020.101530

Palomo-Vélez, G., & Van Vugt, M. (2021). The evolutionary psychology of climate change behaviors: Insights and applications [Special issue]. *Current Opinion in Psychology, 42*, 54–59. https://doi.org/10.1016/j.copsyc.2021.03.006

Penn, D. J. (2003). The evolutionary roots of our environmental problems: Toward a Darwinian ecology. *The Quarterly Review of Biology, 78*(3), 275–301. https://doi.org/10.1086/377051

Perlaviciute, G. (2022). Contested climate policies and the four Ds of public participation: From normative standards to what people want. *WIREs Climate Change, 13*(1), e749. https://doi.org/10.1002/wcc.749

Perlaviciute, G., & Steg, L. (2014). Contextual and psychological factors shaping evaluations and acceptability of energy alternatives: Integrated review and research agenda. *Renewable and Sustainable Energy Reviews, 35*, 361–381. https://doi.org/10.1016/j.rser.2014.04.003

Pörtner, H.-O., Roberts, D. C., Adams, H., Adler, C., Aldunce, P., Ali, E., Begum, R. A., Betts, R., Kerr, R. B., & Biesbroek, R. (2022). *Climate change 2022: Impacts, adaptation and vulnerability. IPCC Sixth Assessment Report.* Cambridge University Press. doi:10.1017/9781009325844

Rabinovich, A., Morton, T. A., & Birney, M. E. (2012). Communicating climate science: The role of perceived communicator's motives. *Journal of Environmental Psychology, 32*(1), 11–18. https://doi.org/10.1016/j.jenvp.2011.09.002

Ripoll Gallardo, A., Djalali, A., Foletti, M., Ragazzoni, L., Della Corte, F., Lupescu, O., Arculeo, C., von Arnim, G., Friedl, T., Ashkenazi, M., Fisher, P., Hreckovski, B., Khorram-Manesh, A., Komadina, R., Lechner, K., Stal, M., Patru, C., Burkle, F. M., & Ingrassia, P. L. (2015). Core competencies in disaster management and humanitarian assistance: A systematic review. *Disaster Medicine and Public Health Preparedness, 9*(4), 430–439. https://doi.org/10.1017/dmp.2015.24

Runhaar, H., Tigchelaar, C., & Vermeulen, W. J. V. (2008). Environmental leaders: Making a difference. A typology of environmental leaders and recommendations for a differentiated policy approach. *Business Strategy and the Environment, 17*(3), 160–178. https://doi.org/10.1002/bse.520

Russo, S., Mirisola, A., Dallago, F., & Roccato, M. (2020). Facing natural disasters through the endorsement of authoritarian attitudes. *Journal of Environmental Psychology, 68*, 101412. https://doi.org/10.1016/j.jenvp.2020.101412

Sabherwal, A., Ballew, M. T., van der Linden, S., Gustafson, A., Goldberg, M. H., Maibach, E. W., Kotcher, J. E., Swim, J. K., Rosenthal, S. A., & Leiserowitz, A. (2021). The Greta Thunberg effect: Familiarity with Greta Thunberg predicts intentions to engage in climate activism in the United States. *Journal of Applied Social Psychology, 51*(4), 321–333. https://doi.org/10.1111/jasp.12737

Schaller, M., Kenrick, D. T., Neel, R., & Neuberg, S. L. (2017). Evolution and human motivation: A fundamental motives framework. *Social and Personality Psychology Compass, 11*(6), e12319. https://doi.org/10.1111/spc3.12319

Schaller, M., Park, J., & Faulkner, J. (2003). Prehistoric dangers and contemporary prejudices. *European Review of Social Psychology, 14*(1), 105–137. https://doi.org/10.1080/10463280340000036

Schjoedt, U., Sørensen, J., Nielbo, K. L., Xygalatas, D., Mitkidis, P., & Bulbulia, J. (2013). Cognitive resource depletion in religious interactions. *Religion, Brain & Behavior, 3*(1), 39–55. https://doi.org/10.1080/2153599X.2012.736714

Smith, E. A., & Wishnie, M. (2000). Conservation and subsistence in small-scale societies. *Annual Review of Anthropology, 29*, 493–524.

Sommer, M., Rucht, D., Haunss, S., & Zajak, S. (2019). *Fridays for future: Profil, Entstehung und Perspektiven der Protestbewegung in Deutschland.* Institut für Protest- und Bewegungsforschung.

Stanley, S. K., Ng Tseung-Wong, C., & Leviston, Z. (2022). Welcoming climate refugees to the United States: Do attitudes depend on refugee origins, numbers, or permanence? *Journal of Environmental Psychology, 83*, 101874. https://doi.org/10.1016/j.jenvp.2022.101874

Stevenson, R. J. (2010). An initial evaluation of the functions of human olfaction. *Chemical Senses, 35*(1), 3–20. https://doi.org/10.1093/chemse/bjp083

Stouten, J., De Cremer, D., & van Dijk, E. (2005). I'm doing the best I can (for myself): Leadership and variance of harvesting in resource dilemmas. *Group Dynamics: Theory, Research, and Practice, 9*, 205–211. https://doi.org/10.1037/1089-2699.9.3.205

Tang, P., Deng, C., Shao, S., & Shen, G. Q. (2017). Leveraging intergovernmental and cross-sectoral networks to manage nuclear power plant accidents: A case study from China. *Journal of Cleaner Production, 162*, 1551–1566. https://doi.org/10.1016/j.jclepro.2017.06.144

Thomas, V. J., & Maine, E. (2019). Market entry strategies for electric vehicle start-ups in the automotive industry – Lessons from Tesla Motors. *Journal of Cleaner Production, 235*, 653–663. https://doi.org/10.1016/j.jclepro.2019.06.284

Treen, K. M. d'I, Williams, H. T., & O'Neill, S. J. (2020). Online misinformation about climate change. *WIRES: Climate Change, 11*(5), e665.

Tybur, J. M., Lieberman, D., Kurzban, R., & DeScioli, P. (2013). Disgust: Evolved function and structure. *Psychological Review, 120*, 65–84. https://doi.org/10.1037/a0030778

Tyler, T. R., & Degoey, P. (1995). Collective restraint in social dilemmas: Procedural justice and social identification effects on support for authorities. *Journal of Personality and Social Psychology, 69*(3), 482.

van der Linden, S. L., Leiserowitz, A. A., Feinberg, G. D., & Maibach, E. W. (2015). The scientific consensus on climate change as a gateway belief: Experimental evidence. *PLOS One, 10*(2), e0118489. https://doi.org/10.1371/journal.pone.0118489

van der Linden, S., Leiserowitz, A., Rosenthal, S., & Maibach, E. (2017). Inoculating the public against misinformation about climate change. *Global Challenges, 1*(2), 1600008. https://doi.org/10.1002/gch2.201600008

van Knippenberg, D., De Cremer, D., & van Knippenberg, B. (2007). Leadership and fairness: The state of the art. *European Journal of Work and Organizational Psychology, 16*(2), 113–140. https://doi.org/10.1080/13594320701275833

Van Veelen, B. (2018). Negotiating energy democracy in practice: Governance processes in community energy projects. *Environmental Politics, 27*(4), 644–665. https://doi.org/10.1080/09644016.2018.1427824

Van Vugt, M., Griskevicius, V., & Schultz, P. W. (2014). Naturally green: Harnessing stone age psychological biases to foster environmental behavior. *Social Issues and Policy Review, 8*(1), 1–32. https://doi.org/10.1111/sipr.12000

Van Vugt, M., Hogan, R., & Kaiser, R. B. (2008). Leadership, followership, and evolution: Some lessons from the past. *American Psychologist, 63*(3), 182–196. https://doi.org/10.1037/0003-066X.63.3.182

Van Vugt, M., & Ronay, R. (2014). The evolutionary psychology of leadership: Theory, review, and roadmap. *Organizational Psychology Review, 4*(1), 74–95. https://doi.org/10.1177/2041386613493635

Van Vugt, M., & Smith, J. E. (2019). A dual model of leadership and hierarchy: Evolutionary synthesis. *Trends in Cognitive Sciences, 23*(11), 952–967. https://doi.org/10.1016/j.tics.2019.09.004

Van Vugt, M., & Spisak, B. R. (2008). Sex differences in the emergence of leadership during competitions within and between groups. *Psychological Science, 19*(9), 854–858. https://doi.org/10.1111/j.1467-9280.2008.02168.x

Vogler, J., & Stephan, H. R. (2007). The European Union in global environmental governance: Leadership in the making? *International Environmental Agreements: Politics, Law and Economics, 7*(4), 389–413. https://doi.org/10.1007/s10784-007-9051-5

Wang, X., Van der Werff, E., Bouman, T., Harder, M. K., & Steg, L. (2021). I am vs. we are: How biospheric values and environmental identity of individuals and groups can influence pro-environmental behaviour. *Frontiers in Psychology, 12*. https://www.frontiersin.org/articles/10.3389/fpsyg.2021.618956

Wurzel, R. K. W., Liefferink, D., & Torney, D. (2019). Pioneers, leaders and followers in multilevel and polycentric climate governance. *Environmental Politics, 28*(1), 1–21. https://doi.org/10.1080/09644016.2019.1522033

Wüstenhagen, R., Wolsink, M., & Bürer, M. J. (2007). Social acceptance of renewable energy innovation: An introduction to the concept. *Energy Policy, 35*(5), 2683–2691. https://doi.org/10.1016/j.enpol.2006.12.001

Zahavi, A., & Zahavi, A. (1999). *The handicap principle: A missing piece of Darwin's puzzle*. Oxford University Press.

6

SUSTAINABILITY LEADERSHIP STARTS WITH OUR MINDSET

Isabel Rimanoczy and Beate Klingenberg

Chapter Summary

This chapter explores the unsustainability mindset that led us to the multiple and interconnected global crises shaping our context and challenges. It introduces the 12 sustainability mindset principles for how leaders can develop the key aspects for a new mindset that can best prepare them for resiliency, innovation and, most important, the imagination to shape a better world.

Introduction

Dean Cycon is the founder of Dean's Beans, a social enterprise that establishes long-term relationships with coffee growers in developing countries, buying their organic produce directly and then roasting and selling it in the United States. In a conversation about his business philosophy about a decade ago, he shared that he has frequently been asked what the next step

DOI: 10.4324/9781003343011-7

will be in his business, what his growth strategy is and how he plans to expand to be able to sell to a wider customer base, including supermarket chains. Why this expectation of growth?, he wondered. Why can a business not just stabilise, with a small market, and that be its goal? What is wrong with that?

What he was bringing up was not the simple answer to the question of his vision of business growth; rather, he was touching on the foundation of the global social and environmental challenges we are experiencing. He was hinting at assumptions related to the purpose of business. They form our globalised paradigm, cemented in values that associate economic growth with prosperity, wealth with happiness, innovation with progress. The conversation opened a path to reflect on the possible need to revisit those taken-for-granted aspects guiding our collective behaviours. Was prosperity perhaps not necessarily linked to growth? What if growth had a negative impact? Might there be a connection between those unquestioned values and the impact that the resulting behaviours were having on the environment and society? To this day, there is a corporate lentitude in proactively addressing climate change. Might this be linked to unexplored aspects of our shared paradigm, a worldview that includes values that have become the anchors of our personal identity and which we cannot let go?

This chapter explores the unsustainability mindset that led us to multiple and interconnected global crises, shaping our context and challenges. We need to develop a mindset for net positive businesses (Polman & Winston, 2021), sustainable prosperity (Elf et al., 2022) or sustainable hedonism (Lelkes, 2021). We propose that changing the mindset is the path for leadership transformation. We will introduce the 12 sustainability mindset principles (SMPs) as a model for leaders to develop and monitor the key aspects for a new mindset that enables them to become innovative change leaders for a long-overdue paradigm shift. What Dean was suggesting over a decade ago has become more than timely: it is now urgent.

Theory and Basic Concepts

In the year 2006, Al Gore's movie *An Inconvenient Truth* (Guggenheim & Gore, 2006) was one of the first attempts to wake up and educate the global general public about the climate change path we were on. The world was operating as usual, without noticing in the everyday how local events like droughts, unusual storms or floods were linked to a broader pattern of transformations that would change our lives forever. Some disregarded the information, arguing that the human contribution to climate was insufficiently supported by scientific evidence. God and the cyclical evolution of planet Earth were seen as the real causes. We humans were not that powerful (Brechin, 2003; Immerwahr, 1999; Malm & Hornborg, 2014).

Though scientists had been studying and warning about the trend for decades (Anderson et al., 2016; Carson, 1962/2015), their academic language had not reached the broader population or the corporate and political decision makers (Hoffman, 2005; Van den Hove et al., 2002; Wright & Nyberg, 2017). The idea that our use of fossil fuels might have a role to play was unthinkable for businesses and states anywhere on the planet. How could we even envision doing business without energy? The economic impact this supposed had all the characteristics of a potential global collapse, with serious and unthinkable social implications. Challenging consumption patterns, manufacturing practices, energy sources and global trade was a thought that no government or business was interested in entertaining. There had to be a flaw in the data, because our whole way of functioning could not simply be wrong. Or, if anything, history has demonstrated over millennia the brilliance of human imagination to solve and invent our way against the odds of nature. Unparalleled technology might produce solutions just in time (Hulme, 2014; Korpivaara, 2013).

In the early 2000s, media had little to no coverage suggesting that local climate phenomena might be related to a larger anthropogenic pattern (Bowden et al., 2021; Boykoff & Rajan, 2007), so It was difficult for the general public to see the systemic interconnections because events were reported in a compartmentalised way. Certainly, cyclones impacted the local economies, the livelihood and health of the population. Droughts affected specific communities, their food and employment. But what about the larger ripple effects? How was nutrition, education and health impacted? What about the consequences on poverty rates, violence, addictions and crime? How was the capacity to export and import been impacted, something core to the global economy? What about climate refugees and the challenges this posed on the larger system? The wider implications of climate-related events were rarely considered, disassociating them from decision making that focused on the here and now. Maintaining the status quo was our unspoken collective aim.

Furthermore, the attention on the debate about human-made climate change was leaving out the consideration of multiple other consequences of our civilisation's practices; for example, pollution of soil and underground waters resulting from pesticide and fertiliser use; microplastics in the oceans entering the food chain and impacting human and animal health; industrial monocultures of palm oil decimating the biodiversity of ancient rainforests; export of nuclear waste to the developing world; overfishing to meet consumption demands, creating dead zones in the oceans; and extinction of species at an average rate of 25% (Intergovernmental Science-Policy Platform on Biodiversity and Environmental Services, 2019).

With such a number of crises rising globally, a question became even more important: What was holding us back? What were the unseen anchors of our identity that we so unconsciously and fiercely defended? Furthermore, what motivated certain leaders to take the less traveled road and champion a transformation towards sustainability in their business? Could we learn something from them?

This last question thus became the focus of qualitative exploratory research aimed at identifying what elements leading to sustainability behaviours have the potential to be intentionally developed (Rimanoczy, 2010). The study showed several aspects that the studied leaders had in common and which played a role in the transformation of their worldview. The identified aspects were unrelated to personal circumstances that might have influenced the subjects in critically reflecting on their life's mission and behaviours. They related to how the leaders processed and analyzed information, how they revised their personal values and developed introspective habits as well as how they explored their personal purpose (Kassel et al., 2016). The sum of those aspects played a significant role in developing what was called a *sustainability mindset*, the platform for very different decision making (Rimanoczy, 2014). The term sustainability mindset includes the perspective of mindset theories by incorporating cognitive procedures (Keller et al., 2019), such as the implicit theories held by an individual which predict a variety of key outcomes in their achievement and interpersonal domain (Bernecker & Job, 2019). It also included the perspective of orders of making meaning (Merron et al., 1987), which are not necessarily conscious but of which individuals can become aware. A later study by Schein (2017) validated the findings on which the sustainability mindset framework was based.

The Sustainability Mindset Principles

The elements identified in the study became the foundation for the SMPs, which are organised into four content areas: ecological worldview, systems perspective, emotional intelligence and spiritual intelligence (Rimanoczy, 2020).

Ecological worldview is a particular way of looking at the world and making meaning of information and data. It notices the breadth of the planet's challenges, their complexity and interconnections, and acknowledges the feelings and emotions such information brings up in us (Brosch, 2021; Drengson, 1995; Glasser, 2011; Macy, 1995). Furthermore, this worldview includes the consideration of the personal role we individually play as part of the problems. Therefore, it allows the individual to move from being an overwhelmed and disempowered victim or witness of larger dramas to reclaiming the personal agency and ability to respond (*response-ability*). Ecological worldview thus transcends the mere intellectual understanding of our reality by integrating the emotions that function as intrinsic motivators to action. Two principles, *ecoliteracy* and *my contribution*, offer a guided path to develop our ecological worldview.

System thinking is a way of processing information, by noticing the mutual relationships among subsystems, their interdependencies and their feedback flows. It includes considerations about multicausality, paradoxes, non-dualistic thinking and complexity thinking. Rationalism has dominated our collective thinking processes for the last 500 years, allowing for an analytical approach to phenomena conducive to scientific exploration and important discoveries (Llamazares, 2013; Rimanoczy & Llamazares, 2021). Dissecting and deconstructing reality is instrumental to studying parts. At the same time, the fragmentation of our experience of social and environmental challenges is a major obstacle in understanding the anthropogenic characteristics of the problems. The general theory of systems and cybernetics (Clayton & Radcliffe, 2018; Frisk & Larson, 2011) provided a complementary approach, considering relationships, patterns and flows. In other words, a system's perspective allows us to see the larger picture, how we are impacting it and how we could act differently. The principles of *long-term thinking*, *both/and thinking*, *flow in cycles* and *interconnectedness* provide a guide to develop such a perspective.

Three elements identified in Rimanoczy's (2010) study fell into the content area of **emotional intelligence**. One is the ability to pause and reflect, which includes noticing our personal pace and intentionally slowing down before jumping into automatic reactions. This plays a key role in exploring potential unsustainable impacts of our daily decisions (principle of *reflection*). The second element is expanding self-awareness about the unsustainable anchors of our identity. What values are important for me? How are they guiding my behaviours and decisions? This element, represented by the principle of *self-awareness*, as mentioned before, scrutinises the collectively shared paradigms and beliefs. Is progress, wealth, growth, achievement, independence, speed, being in control, the right to have a family important for me? What do these values mean, in the everyday context? How sustainable (or not) are they? The third element in this content area is the principle of *creative innovation*, which calls for identifying our limiting beliefs about how creative we are. In a time when everything must be reinvented for sustainability, unleashing the maximum individual creativity becomes essential.

Lastly, engaging in sustainability actions calls for a holistic experience of self in relation to the world. Ecopsychology (Roszak et al., 1995), deep ecology (Sessions, 1987), quantum leadership (Laszlo, 2020) and spiritual leadership (Fry & Egel, 2017) are some of the approaches suggesting that the intrinsic motivation leading to sustainability actions is based on a personal experience of how we see ourselves, each other and the non-human world. Considered a deep transformational process, this journey can be supported by activities and exercises to develop a sense of *oneness with nature*, *mindfulness* practices and exploration of personal *purpose*. This is the content area of **spiritual intelligence**.

Table 6.1 illustrates the contributors to our unsustainability mindset and the aspects that an individual can develop for a sustainability mindset.

Mindset Assessment

The model of the sustainability mindset has been evolving since 2010, thanks to its application in higher education courses and scholarly work of over 230 academics, members of the Working Group on the Sustainability Mindset (LEAP, 2014), a network of the Principles of Responsible Management Education (PRME, 2023), the academic arm of the United Nations Global Compact (United Nations, 2000). These academics are teaching a variety of disciplines – business courses, urban planning, literature, liberal arts, religions of the

Contributors to Unsustainability Mindset	*Aspects for a Sustainability Mindset*	*Principles*	*Content Area*
Cognitive approach to facts: I know of something	Engage emotions	Ecoliteracy	Ecological worldview
Compartmentalised information (superficial or in depth)	Identify interdependencies, complexity		
Personal distance which leads to inaction. Blaming others, feeling helpless, a victim of larger powers. Defense mechanism to manage feelings of overwhelm, anxiety, despair	Identifying the personal part in the problems Connecting our unintentional contributions to the problems with alternative behaviours	My contribution	
Focus on here and now, short-term thinking	Develop long-term thinking habits (then and there) Expand the mental time frame, from ancestors to future generations	Long-term thinking	Systems perspective
Either–or thinking Polarised options; that is, either planet or profit; either my needs or yours	Develop both/and thinking Identification of stakeholders (including future generations and non-human beings) Develop social sensitivity to step into other shoes Inclusion and diversity practices	Both/and thinking	
Linear thinking models Linear growth models Unrestricted growth goals Growth as an undiscussed value Nature as a provider for resources for human needs Use of non-renewable or slow-renewable resources	Humans and human activities embedded in laws of nature: birth, growth, decay, death, new birth Cycles and feedback loops Alternatives to linear models: circular economy, de-growth	Flow in cycles	
Fragmentation for analysis Siloed information processing Focus on independent action, autonomy, self as a unit separate from the rest	Considering interconnections and interdependencies Development of social sensitivity, gratitude, compassion	Interconnectedness	
Fast action, speed as a value Automatic behaviours Adapting to surrounding pace	Noticing downsides of automatic behaviours, impact on unsustainable decisions Noticing the personal pace, learning to slow down intentionally to pause and reflect before acting automatically Becoming an example for others, influencing others' pace	Reflection	Emotional intelligence

(continued)

Contributors to Unsustainability Mindset	*Aspects for a Sustainability Mindset*	*Principles*	*Content Area*
Self-limiting thoughts about personal creativity potential Rational focus	Unleashing personal creativity Revisiting the self-image about creative potential Discovering ways to expand creativity to innovate processes for more sustainable impact Learning to incorporate non-verbal wisdom, listen to our intuition	Creative innovation	
Automatic behaviours based on (unconscious) unsustainable values; that is, to compete, be a winner; material wealth as a symbol of personal value and achievement; innovation=progress; do more, have more to be happy; be in control; be independent, be rational, etc.	Exploration of the personal anchors of identity: what are our priorities, our values driving our decisions and actions? How sustainable are they? What are our alternatives? Who would we want to be?	Self-awareness	
Instrumental use of nature, nature perceived as available resources for human consumption and needs Anthropocentrism Humans as top of the creation, in control and ownership	Develop a sense of oneness with nature. We are nature and are in it Soul experience of connectedness with all that is, leading to more compassionate and thoughtful actions, particularly relating to our consumption and manufacturing practices	Oneness with nature	Spiritual intelligence
Focus on doing and action Automatic responses to gain time and efficiency Repetition of previous behaviours without pondering impacts Disconnect between personal behaviours and unsustainable impacts Focus on the past and/or the future Disconnect from feelings and emotions	Noticing self: automatic responses, patterns of repetition, emotions as something ‘happening’ to us, not who we are Developing contemplative practices, experimenting with diverse ways to develop mindfulness Learn to be more (fully) present. Re-connect with our higher self	Mindfulness	
Focus on getting things done, on current demands, on expectations	Expand the horizon beyond the immediate Explore motives and question the personal purpose: What do you really want to do, to be? What is your purpose? What is the best thing you have to bring to the world? What is the difference you want to make?	Purpose	

world and tourism – and are working at universities in 57 countries, providing a diversity of context that enriches the whole. They have innovated, adapted and designed learning interventions and teaching materials that are reflected in their scholarly publications, conference proceedings, books and book chapters (see, for example, Arevalo et al., 2017; Burga et al., 2022; Ivanova & Rimanoczy, 2022; Lees, 2021; Lelkes, 2021; Mette, 2022; Onwuegbuzie & Ugwuanyi, 2018; Rimanoczy, 2013, 2016; Ritz & Rimanoczy, 2020; Schein, 2017; Sharma, 2018; Sunley & Leigh, 2017).

Over the past 10 years, scholars in this network have been seeking ways to assess the impact of their pedagogical interventions, specifically to establish whether their activities were leading to a more sustainable mindset of their students. Informal surveys, end-of-course questionnaires, pre–post surveys and quizzes were used to establish transformational impact. One such efforts has been the development of the Sustainability Mindset Indicator (SMI; Rimanoczy & Klingenberg, 2021), a tool to map and profile where an individual is on their journey of developing such a mindset. Structured as an online questionnaire, it uses the model of the SMPs to organise a variety of statements, inviting the individual to select those that best represent them. The indicator explores the mindset from three angles: the cognitive (what we know, how we think about a particular item), the affective (how we feel about it) and the behavioural (how we act about it). This allows for a more detailed picture of where the individual is on their journey, because the three perspectives do not necessarily develop at equal pace.

The development and validation of the SMI had three phases (Rimanoczy & Klingenberg, 2021):

1. After initial development, the statements were validated to ensure capturing the meaning of the SMPs.
2. Linguistic issues or logical inconsistencies were eliminated.
3. Iteratively, the improvements were validated against the meaning of the SMPs.

Practice: Methods, Techniques and Application

The SMI is an instrument that maps where an individual is on their journey towards a sustainability mindset. It is designed as a personal development tool for the individual; hence, it does not focus on scores and there are no right/wrong answers. Instead, it offers an appreciative, qualitative picture of where the individual feels more comfortable at the given time, with suggestions to explore the up- and downsides of that mindset in connection with social and environmental sustainability. The SMI generates a 33-page confidential personalised report, with questions to ponder and suggestions to consider. Underlying are opposite statement pairs for each of the SMPs a participant needs to choose, one representing the SMP, the other a more conventional mindset. The SMP statements were validated regarding the correctness of their meanings with a survey procedure that asked 21 participants with significant knowledge of the SMPs to rank four explanatory phrases to the statements. Of these explanatory phrases, one fully matched the SMP content, two matched it somewhat and one did not. This procedure allowed for the identification of statements that needed rephrasing, which were then re-validated. The use of the opposing statement follows the framework of intentional change theory (Boyatzis & Akrivou, 2006). In this framework, the consideration of the ideal self is seen as the starting point for the creation of emotions that may move individuals towards transformation. Besides using this approach in the personalised reports, the opposing statements point to a 'good' option, while also presenting the 'better' one that reflects the sustainability mindset.

The instructor (educator or coach) using the SMI with a group in turn receives an instructor report of approximately 30 pages, as the aggregate of the group, without identifying individual responses. This aggregate picture shows the strongest areas and those that may need development, also differentiating between the cognitive, affective and behavioural angles. The instructor can select which aspects are particularly relevant for that audience and tailor interventions to support the transformation of the more 'unsustainable' aspects. Instructors and coaches can find specific activities to each result constellation in a series of workbooks for educators and coaches in corporate settings (Rimanoczy, 2022a, 2022b). Trainings, certification and a community of practice are also available for further exploration and exchange experiences (see Klingenberg et al., 2021).

Researchers use the SMI as a tool to assess the impact of their teaching, as a pre–post instrument. Within the first 6 months after the launch of the indicator (January 2022), educators were using it with their audience in Australia, Canada, Germany, Indonesia, Italy, Mexico, Russia, Spain, the

UK and the United States. In a first publication documenting the SMI use, researchers present critical reflection essays of students in a collaborative online international learning project (Burga et al., 2022). Quantitative studies are ongoing (see, for example, Klingenberg et al., 2023). Institutions are considering the SMI as an entry tool for all incoming students, to provide them from the start with a personal development resource that can both support their journey and facilitate the educator's job, particularly in institutions strongly committed to developing conscious and responsible leaders and professionals. They form part of a network of system influencers, exchanging experiences, collaborating in their pioneering efforts of organisational transformation and learning together.

The model of the SMPs has been embedded into various contexts, showcasing its relevance across disciplines. Members of the PRME Working Group on the Sustainability Mindset are using it in their classes on accounting, entrepreneurship, finance, human resource management, leadership, operations management, strategic management, supply chain and sustainable business. Fairleigh Dickinson University has incorporated the sustainability mindset into their hospitality and tourism courses; Al-Akhawayn University, Morocco, has included it in their liberal arts education program; and the school of Architecture of the University of Lund has incorporated mindfulness and systems thinking. The principles have also been incorporated into a course on religions of the world (Lees, 2021).

It exists as a stand-alone course in the United States at Fordham University, New York; Fairleigh Dickinson, New Jersey; and Nova Southeastern University, Florida, and in Al-akhawayn University, Morocco, for graduates and undergraduate students.

In a coaching context, it is used by coaches focusing on diversity, inclusion mindfulness and sustainability.

The pedagogical approaches include the use of art (Yang et al., 2021), meditation (Wamsler et al., 2018), service learning (Hernández-Barco et al., 2020), experiences in nature (Ives et al., 2018), educational travel (Paul, 2020; Storksdieck, 2006) and special passion projects by students to make a difference as well as students teaching younger students.

Professors from Canada, Spain, and Indonesia conducted a cross-cultural team experience. The students worked on a project related to the United Nations Sustainable Development Goals (SDGs) using the platform Aim-2Flourish.[1] The SMI was used as a pre–post assessment tool to explore the impact of pedagogical activity on the development of their sustainability mindset. The course resulted in the creation of an open-source book with students' essays about their powerful experience of cross-cultural change for sustainability (Burga et al., 2022).

Some institutions are using the framework of the SMPs and the SMI to develop their faculty, to create a common language and provide a professional development opportunity to their educators (Excelia Business School, France; Bologna Business School, Italy; Dominican University, United States; TEC Monterrey, Mexico).

We see through these various applications that the SMPs offer a framework to design interventions in academic and corporate development settings. The assessment tool (SMI) in turn provides a foundation for further research to measure the impact of and tailor pedagogical and training approaches related to sustainability.

Concluding Remarks

We are living in a time of increasing awareness of social and environmental challenges; however, thanks to initiatives such as the SDGs, there are frameworks for action pertinent to any discipline, profession, or organisation. Principles for responsible investment, PRME, LEED (Leadership in Energy and Environmental Design) construction standards and even accreditation bodies such as the Association to Advance Collegiate Schools of Business, the Central and East European Management Development Association and Equis are inviting voluntary engagement in more sustainable actions. Unfortunately, regulations are still lagging, despite the agreement of the scientific community that there is no time to waste, as the last report of the Intergovernmental Panel for Climate Change (2022) indicates. The younger generation is raising their voice through grassroots movements like Fridays for Future and Extinction Rebellion, and entrepreneurs are leading start-ups under new business formats like B corporations. Yet this is far from sufficient. Decisions are made every day by leaders with an unsustainable mindset, and the consequences are not only ignoring climate change but worsening the unsustainability of the whole planet.

Discussions about the capabilities these leaders need to develop are urgent, and so is the deeper look into what can accelerate the transformation from the inside out. Resistance to change needs to be listened to, because it has information of what is at stake for the individual, what she orhe is trying to protect and defend. Our behaviours are the visible expression of an unconscious paradigm, and we now have the tools to address the values and beliefs at its roots. Expanding awareness of the unsustainable aspects of our mindset opens the path of transformation, particularly if we can re-connect our intellectual understanding with our feelings and our higher self. The SMPs are a model to address such a mindset, providing paths to its development. The SMI complements this effort, allowing a qualitative assessment and providing pedagogical guidance, a research instrument and personal development support for the journey of transformation and growth. Developing a sustainability mindset equips leaders of any profession with resiliency, innovation and, most important, the impetus to shape a better world.

Discussion Points

- Rationalism led to many inventions and innovations; however, it also resulted in a reductionist approach that often decontextualised science, neglecting systems perspectives. In your context, what are examples of this effect?
- In your perspective, what are unsustainable aspects of the current economic paradigm?
- What are alternatives?

Note

1 Aim2Flourish is an initiative of the Fowler Center for Business. It connects students with business innovators aligned with the UN SDGs (aim2flourish.com).

Suggested Reading

Rimanoczy, I. (2020). *The sustainability mindset principles: A guide to develop a mindset for a better world.* Routledge.

Rimanoczy, I. (2021). Anthropocene and the call for leaders with a new mindset. In A. A. Ritz & I. Rimanoczy (Eds.), *Sustainability mindset and transformative leadership* (pp. 117–139). Palgrave Macmillan.

Rimanoczy, I., & Llamazares, A. M. (2021). Twelve principles to guide a long-overdue paradigm shift. *Journal of Management, Spirituality & Religion, 18*(6), 54–76.

References

Anderson, T. R., Hawkins, E., & Jones, P. D. (2016). CO_2, the greenhouse effect and global warming: From the pioneering work of Arrhenius and Callendar to today's Earth system models. *Endeavour, 40*(3), 178–187.

Arevalo, J. A., Paterson, W., & Mitchell, S. F. (Eds.). (2017). *Handbook of sustainability in management education – In search of a multidisciplinary, innovative and integrated approach*. Edward Elgar.

Bernecker, K., & Job, V. (2019). Mindset theory. In K. Sassenberg & M. L. W. Vliek (Eds.), *Social psychology in action – Evidence-based interventions in theory and practice* (pp. 179–191). Springer.

Bowden, V., Nyberg, D., & Wright, C. (2021). 'We're going under': The role of local news media in dislocating climate change adaptation. *Environmental Communication, 15*(5), 625–640.

Boyatzis, R. E., & Akrivou, K. (2006). The ideal self as the driver of intentional change. *Journal of Management Development, 25*(7), 624–642.

Boykoff, M. T., & Rajan, S. R. (2007). Signals and noise: Mass-media coverage of climate change in the USA and the UK. *EMBO Reports, 8*(3), 207–211.

Brechin, S. R. (2003). Comparative public opinion and knowledge on global climatic change and the Kyoto Protocol: The U.S. versus the world? *International Journal of Sociology and Social Policy, 23*(10), 106–134.

Brosch, T. (2021). Affect and emotions as drivers of climate change perception and action: A review. *Current Opinion in Behavioral Sciences, 42*, 15–21.

Burga, R., Rodriguez-Tejedo, I., & Naim, A. (2022). *Critical reflections on innovative flourishing businesses in the context of the UN Sustainable Development Goals – A cross-cultural perspective*. University of Guelph. https://books.lib.uoguelph.ca/criticalreflectionsoninnovativeflourishingbusinesses/

Carson, R. (2015). *Silent spring*. Penguin Books. (Original work published 1962)

Clayton, T., & Radcliffe, N. (2018). *Sustainability: A systems approach*. Routledge.

Drengson, A. (1995). The deep ecology movement. *The Trumpeter, 12*(3).

Elf, P., Isham, A., & Jackson, T. (2022). *Self-transcendent experiences and sustainable prosperity*. Centre for the Understanding of Sustainable Prosperity. http://whel-primo.hosted.exlibrisgroup.com/openurl/44WHELF_NLW/44WHELF_NLW_services_page?u.ignore_date_coverage=true&rft.mms_id=993457683902419

Frisk, E., & Larson, K. L. (2011, March). Educating for sustainability: Competencies & practices for transformative action. *Journal of Sustainability Education, 2*, 1–20.

Fry, L. W. J., & Egel, E. (2017). Spiritual leadership. *Graziadio Business Review, 20*(3).

Glasser, H. (2011). Naess's deep ecology: Implications for the human prospect and challenges for the future. *Inquiry, 54*(1), 52–77.

Guggenheim, D. (Director), & Gore, A. (Writer). (2006). *An inconvenient truth: A global warning*. Paramount.

Hernández-Barco, M., Sánchez-Martín, J., Blanco-Salas, J., & Ruiz-Téllez, T. (2020). Teaching down to earth – Service-learning methodology for science education and sustainability at the university level: A practical approach. *Sustainability, 12*(2), 542.

Hoffman, A. J. (2005). Climate change strategy: The business logic behind voluntary greenhouse gas reductions. *California Management Review, 47*(3), 21–46.

Hulme, M. (2014). *Can science fix climate change? A case against climate engineering*. Polity Press.

Immerwahr, J. (1999). *Waiting for a signal: Public attitudes towards global warming, the environment and geophysical research*. American Geophysical Union. https://policycommons.net/artifacts/1175129/waiting-for-a-signal/1728258/

Intergovernmental Panel on Climate Change. (2022). *Climate change 2022: Mitigation of climate change. Contribution of Working Group III to the Sixth Assessment Report of the Intergovernmental Panel on Climate Change* [P. R. Shukla, J. Skea, R. Slade, A. Al Khourdajie, R. van Diemen, D. McCollum, M. Pathak, S. Some, P. Vyas, R. Fradera, M. Belkacemi, A. Hasija, G. Lisboa, S. Luz, J. Malley, (Eds.)]. Cambridge University Press. doi:10.1017/9781009157926

Intergovernmental Science-Policy Platform on Biodiversity and Environmental Services. (2019). *Global assessment report on biodiversity and ecosystem services of the Intergovernmental Science-Policy Platform on Biodiversity and Ecosystem Services* [E. S. Brondizio, J. Settele, S. Díaz, and H. T. Ngo (Eds.)]. IPBES Secretariat. https://doi.org/10.5281/zenodo.3831673

Ivanova, E., & Rimanoczy, I. (2022). *Revolutionizing sustainability education: Stories and tools of mindset transformation*. Routledge.

Ives, C. D., Abson, D. J., Von Wehrden, H., Dorninger, C., Klaniecki, K., & Fischer, J. (2018). Reconnecting with nature for sustainability. *Sustainability Science, 13*(5), 1389–1397.

Kassel, K., Rimanoczy, I., & Mitchell, S. F. (2016). The sustainable mindset: Connecting being, thinking, and doing in management education. *Academy of Management Proceedings, 2016*(1), 16659.

Keller, L., Bieleke, M., & Gollwitzer, P. M. (2019). Mindset theory of action phases and if–then planning. In K. Sassenberg & M. L. W. Vliek (Eds.), *Social psychology in action – Evidence-based interventions in theory and practice*. (pp. 23–37). Springer.

Klingenberg, B., Boffelli, A., & Madonna, A. (2023, March 20–23). *Experiential learning approaches and assessment for teaching sustainable supply chain management* [Paper presentation]. EurOMA Sustainability Forum [virtual].

Klingenberg, B., Koch, F., & Rimanoczy, I. (2021). Sustainability Mindset Indicator. www.smindicator.com

Korpivaara, S. (2013). *In technology we trust: Moral justifications in the climate change disputes in the United States.* University of Helsinki. http://urn.fi/URN:NBN:fi:hulib-201703272300

Laszlo, C. (2020). Quantum management: The practices and science of flourishing enterprise. *Journal of Management, Spirituality & Religion, 17*(4), 301–315.

LEAP. (2014). PRME Working Group on Sustainability Mindset. https://www.unprme.org/prme-working-group-on-sustainability-mindset

Lees, M. (2021). *Religions of the world: Spirituality & practice.* Kendall Hunt.

Lelkes, O. (2021). *Sustainable hedonism: A thriving life that does not cost the Earth.* Bristol University Press.

Llamazares, A. M. (2013). *Del reloj a la flor de loto: Crisis contemporánea y cambio de paradigmas* [From the clock to the lotus flower: contemporary crisis and paradigm shifts]. Del Nuevo Extremo.

Macy, J. (1995). Working through environmental despair. In T. Roszak, M. E. Gomes, & A. D. Kanner (Eds.), *Ecopsychology: Restoring the Earth, healing the mind* (pp. 240–259). Counterpoint.

Malm, A., & Hornborg, A. (2014). The geology of mankind? A critique of the Anthropocene narrative. *The Anthropocene Review, 1*(1), 62–69.

Merron, K., Fisher, D., & Torbert, W. R. (1987). Meaning making and management action. *Group & Organization Studies, 12*(3), 274–286.

Mette, M. (2022), *Responsible management education – The PRME global movement.* Taylor & Francis.

Onwuegbuzie, H., & Ugwuanyi, I. (2018). Experiential learning methods for teaching entrepreneurship with a sustainability mindset. In K. Kassel & I. Rimanoczy (Eds.), *Developing a sustainability mindset in management education* (pp. 161–185). Routledge.

Paul, L. (2020). *The flying classroom: Study trips in education for sustainable development.* Uppsala University. https://www.diva-portal.org/smash/record.jsf?pid=diva2%3A1438448&dswid=7473

Polman, P., & Winston, A. (2021). *Net positive: How courageous companies thrive by giving more than they take.* Harvard Business Review Press.

PRME. (2023). *Principles of responsible management education.* https://www.unprme.org/

Rimanoczy, I. (2010). *Business leaders committing to and fostering sustainability initiatives*. Teachers College, Columbia University.
Rimanoczy, I. (2013). *Big bang being – Developing a sustainability mindset*. Greenleaf.
Rimanoczy, I. (2014). A matter of being: Developing sustainability-minded leaders. *Journal of Management for Global Sustainability, 2*(1), 95–122.
Rimanoczy, I. (2016). *Stop teaching: Principles and practices for responsible management education*. Business Expert Press.
Rimanoczy, I. (2020). *The sustainability mindset principles: A guide to develop a mindset for a better world*. Routledge.
Rimanoczy, I. (2022a). *The resource workbook for coaches* (Vols. 1–4).
Rimanoczy, I. (2022b). *The resource workbook for educators* (Vols. 1–4).
Rimanoczy, I., & Klingenberg, B. (2021). The sustainability mindset indicator: A personal development tool. *Journal of Management for Global Sustainability, 9*(1), 43–79.
Rimanoczy, I., & Llamazares, A. M. (2021). Twelve principles to guide a long-overdue paradigm shift. *Journal of Management, Spirituality & Religion, 18*(6), 54–76.
Ritz, A., & Rimanoczy, I. (Eds.). (2020). *Sustainability mindset and transformative leadership – A multidisciplinary perspective*. Palgrave Macmillan.
Roszak, T. E., Gomes, M. E., & Kanner, A. D. (1995). *Ecopsychology: Restoring the Earth, healing the mind*. Sierra Club Books.
Schein, S. (2017). *A new psychology for sustainability leadership: The hidden power of ecological worldviews*. Taylor & Francis.
Sessions, G. (1987). The deep ecology movement: A review. *Environmental Review, 11*(2), 105–125.
Sharma, R. R. (2018). A value-centric approach to eudaimonia and sustainability. In K. Kassel & I. Rimanoczy (Eds.), *Developing a sustainability mindset in management education* (113–132). Routledge.
Storksdieck, M. (2006). *Field trips in environmental education*. BWV.
Sunley, R., & Leigh, J. (Eds.). (2017). *Educating for responsible management: Putting theory into practice*. Routledge.
United Nations. (2000). Take action 20th anniversary campaign. https://unglobalcompact.org/take-action/20th-anniversary-campaign#:~:text=Launched%20in%202000%20by%20former, face%20to%20the%20global%20market
Van den Hove, S., Le Menestrel, M., & De Bettignies, H. C. (2002). The oil industry and climate change: Strategies and ethical dilemmas. *Climate Policy, 2*(1), 3–18.

Wamsler, C., Brossmann, J., Hendersson, H., Kristjansdottir, R., McDonald, C., & Scarampi, P. (2018). Mindfulness in sustainability science, practice, and teaching. *Sustainability Science, 13*(1), 143–162.

Wright, C., & Nyberg, D. (2017). An inconvenient truth: How organizations translate climate change into business as usual. *Academy of Management Journal, 60*(5), 1633–1661.

Yang, C., Ivanova, E., & Hufnagel, J. (2021). Using contemplative photography in transformative sustainability management education: Pedagogical applications in the United States, Russia, and Germany. *The International Journal of Management Education, 19*(3), 100568.

7

ECOLOGICAL LEADERSHIP IN A PLANETARY EMERGENCY

Christopher D. Ives and Jenny Wilkinson

Chapter Summary

Human activities are leading to global environmental changes that threaten the stability and integrity of both human and natural systems globally. Environmental research has revealed that dramatic societal shifts are required to mitigate and adapt to anthropogenic climate change, biodiversity loss and other associated environmental changes. The scale, magnitude, complexity and urgency of environmental crises pose profound challenges for conceptions of leadership, within both organisations and societies at large. As a counterpoint to conventional leadership theories, this chapter presents 'ecological leadership' as a way forward. It presents a perspective on global ecological change and the failure of historical leadership to grapple adequately with the interdependency of humans and the natural world. Drawing on existing theories of ecological leadership, it highlights the importance of relational approaches by considering organisations' positionality with respect to socio-environmental realities. This chapter brings leadership studies

DOI: 10.4324/9781003343011-8

into conversation with fundamental principles of social–ecological systems and recent scholarship from sustainability science, emphasising the complexity of relationships, non-linear dynamics, and the normativity of transformative futures.

Introduction

Humanity is facing a nexus of unprecedented environmental crises. The volume and quality of scientific evidence available to support decision making for a sustainable future has never been greater, and yet the gap between aspirations and actions remains gapingly wide (Intergovernmental Panel on Climate Change, 2022; Obura et al., 2022; SEI & CEEW, 2022). The planetary emergency is therefore a crisis of leadership. The amplification of environmental messages is leading organisations across scales, sectors and societies to rethink their environmental impacts, social and economic influences and, ultimately, their concepts of leadership.

Climate change is the environmental issue most prominent in the minds of government policymakers, business leaders and the general public. A recent survey of 20 publics from around the world showed that the majority of people consider climate change to be a very serious problem (Pew Research Centre, 2020). Yet, often climate change is often separated from other environmental challenges, such as ecological degradation and the loss of biodiversity. There is a need for environmental issues to be addressed in an integrated manner and for climate change leadership to be expanded to leadership for the earth (cf. Manolopoulos, 2021). Numerous frameworks and models from sustainability science and practice have pointed to the interconnected nature of environmental and social issues. The planetary boundaries framework (Steffen, Richardson, et al., 2015) is one of these, which recognises nine biophysical 'limits' that human activities must not transgress in order to maintain safe conditions for humanity to thrive. These include climate change, along with changes in land systems, freshwater use and nutrient flows. Doughnut economics (Raworth, 2017) is another framework that builds on the biophysical limits of the planetary boundaries and incorporates a set of social foundations (e.g., housing, education, social equity) that define good conditions for humanity. Other scholars (Folke et al., 2016) have organised the UN Sustainable

Development Goals (SDGs) in a way that embeds economic and social goals within fundamental biosphere-focused ones (e.g., SDGs 6, 13, 14, 15).

The connection between climate and nature is becoming increasingly clear. This is due firstly to their biophysical relationship, whereby the terrestrial biosphere absorbs approximately 20% of fossil fuel CO_2 emissions through aboveground forest biomass and soil ecosystems (Arneth et al., 2017). Second, there is a large evidence base documenting the contribution of climate change to the loss of biodiversity (Bellard et al., 2012), with examples including the bleaching of coral reefs, ecological regime shifts from rainforest to savannah habitats and the movement of species' home ranges towards polar or higher altitude environments. Third, the role of 'nature-based solutions' has been highlighted in recent years as a counterpoint to engineered solutions because of their additional benefits for biodiversity and ability to enhance system resilience. Indeed, the COP27 agreement emphasised the 'importance of protecting, conserving and restoring nature and other terrestrial and marine ecosystems acting as sinks and reservoirs of greenhouse gases and by protecting biodiversity ecosystems to achieve the Paris Agreement temperature goal' (United Nations Framework Convention on Climate Change, 2022). Finally, it has become apparent that the underlying drivers of biodiversity loss and climate change are largely synonymous. Despite half of the world's gross domestic product depending on nature (United Nations Environment Programme [UNEP], 2022), economic models of unfettered growth that externalise environmental impacts underpin biodiversity loss and climate change, as do social values and behaviours that exploit the natural world (UNEP, 2021).

To advance an understanding of leadership for climate change, this chapter therefore takes an ecological approach. Firstly, it grounds leadership in a planetary context by looking at human activity and ecological change at the earth system scale. It then provides a summary of 'conventional' leadership theories and positions them in contrast to newer 'ecological' theories of leadership. Drawing on work by Simon Western and other leadership scholars, ecological leadership is characterised by its biophysical foundation, the role of nature in understanding dynamics of change, the centrality of an ethical commitment to sustainability, and an ambition for transformation. It therefore aims to offer leadership scholars and practitioners a radical new set of principles by which sustainable change can be mobilised in multiple organisational settings.

Theory and Key Concepts: Earth System Change

Since contemporary global environmental issues are unprecedented in their magnitude and scope (Steffen, Broadgate, et al., 2015), an understanding of the kind of leadership needed to address them must begin by looking at historical human activity at the same scale. Today, scientists recognise that humans are the dominant force of environmental change on Earth. The term given for this is the Anthropocene – the most recent epoch of geological time. The term has seen widespread adoption in scholarly and public settings, yet there remains much debate among geologists as to the point at which we entered this period. While it is beyond the scope of this chapter to explore the scientific arguments for different geological boundary events, considering some of the candidates provides insights into the nature of human-led environmental change and therefore the nature of such 'leadership' that underpins them.

Lewis and Maslin (2015) reviewed major events in human history and pre-history that offer possibilities for the beginning of the Anthropocene. The first is the use of fire by human populations and the extinction of megafauna that came from hunting between 50,000 and 10,000 years ago. During this time, about half of all large-bodied mammals were lost globally (Lewis & Maslin, 2015). The second event was the agricultural revolution, with farming practices originating independently in different parts of the world between 4,000 and 11,000 years ago. Agricultural activity led to large-scale clearing of vegetation and an increase in CO_2 concentrations, which raised temperatures around the world. The third possible event is the collision of Old and New Worlds, initiated by the arrival of Europeans in the Caribbean in 1492 fuelled by colonialism and imperial aspirations and resulting in extraction of resources for mercantile expansion. This collision led to the mixing of species across continents and the simplification of ecologies (biotic homogenisation; Crosby, 2003). It also resulted in a devastating loss of human life, through violence and disease. So pronounced was this impact that the reduction in human population in the Americas from 61 million in 1492 to 6 million in 1650 led to regeneration of forest and a temporary decline in CO_2 that is detectable in the geological record (Ahn et al., 2012).

The fourth event in human history that offers a candidate for the start of the Anthropocene is the Industrial Revolution, which began in the mid-18th century in Britain and rapidly spread around the world. It was characterised by a rapid increase in consumption of resources and CO_2 emissions and driven by entrenchment of capitalist ideology. The final possible marker is related to the 'great acceleration' of human activity in the post–World War II 20th century (Steffen, Broadgate, et al., 2015). This included rapid growth in human population, energy use and material consumption. The marker for the start of the period has been proposed as the first nuclear bomb tests, which left an isotopic fingerprint in global sediments.

It is evident from the above examples that global impacts of human activity are collectively associated with profound growth, exploitation of resources and domination of people and ecosystems. While some of these events may be celebrated as 'progress' (e.g., the expansion of agriculture or industry), in the 21st century it has become abundantly clear that these developments have come at enormous environmental cost. Even the remarkable and laudable reduction in global poverty that has taken place over the past few decades has not been accompanied by protection or restoration of natural systems and has resulted in accelerated consumption of natural resources, leading to an increasing number of countries finding themselves in an ecological poverty trap (Wackernagel et al., 2021). Consequently, any such 'leadership' that has enabled such human 'progress' needs to be fundamentally reconsidered. As Evans (2018, p. 63) proposed:

> Centuries of European colonization laid the foundations for modern capitalist opportunism to spread globally, creating persistent economic and political inequities between former imperialist colonizer nations and former colonies whose lands and peoples were the objects of conquest. ... Leadership for 'success' in such a system is not sustainable leadership; it is simply domination.

Indeed, literature on the evolutionary emergence of leadership finds no association between leadership and domination (Van Vugt, 2006), implying that the exploitation of ecologies and people groups should not be associated with leadership at all.

The ecological manifestation of the Anthropocene is stark. Scientists have identified a number of ecological tipping points whereby unabated climate change will result in runaway feedback loops that would lead to devastating outcomes for humanity (Lenton et al., 2019). These include the drying of the Amazon, leading to dramatic release of carbon, or the thawing of permafrost in the arctic tundra. Indicators of ecological health globally are showing profound declines, with the rates of species extinctions representing the Earth's sixth mass extinction event (Ceballos et al., 2015) and terrestrial ecological communities worldwide having lost 20% of their original biodiversity and population sizes of plants and animals dramatically declining (Díaz et al., 2019). The Intergovernmental Science-Policy Platform on Biodiversity and Ecosystem Services (IPBES) identified five key drivers of the nature crisis: changes in land and sea use (to enable expansion of agriculture and urban uses), climate change (stressing species and ecosystems), pollution (from chemicals such as insecticides and waste such as plastic), direct exploitation of natural resources (such as logging or overfishing) and invasive species (often facilitated by global trade and movement of goods and people; IPBES, 2019). Yet positive changes towards sustainability must be achieved at a time when extreme events such as storms, heatwaves, fires and floods are becoming more extreme and frequent and societal turbulence and upheaval more acute (Wiseman, 2021). This presents marked leadership challenges. Before we can outline the nature of 'ecological leadership', it is first necessary to summarise 'conventional' leadership approaches.

Theory and Key Concepts: History of Conventional Leadership

Promotion of an ecological leadership theory which combines relational leadership with a deep ethical commitment to a flourishing social–environmental future builds on and extends established leadership conceptualisations. Therefore, consideration must be given to both the limitations and best use of existing theories in developing and operationalising ecological leadership.

There are strengths in all of the above-mentioned leadership paradigms, and many areas overlap. The proliferation and overlapping nature of leadership models and theories provide for a confusing and sometimes contradictory landscape that can be challenging for practicing leaders wishing to identify clear guidance. Models differ in their limitations: some are too focused on the individual efforts of the leader and fail to recognise the value of networks and relationships, some pay little attention to values, whilst

Table 7.1 A Summary of Dominant Leadership Theories and Approaches

Theory/Approach	*Period*	*Theme and Advocates*	*Discourse*
Command and control	19th-century industrial era to 1940s	A rule-based, 'scientific management' approach, focusing on efficiency	Controller: Characterised by efficiency and productivity. Grounded in scientific rationalism and mechanistic assumptions of change. Associated with an emphasis on audits and targets
Trait theories	Up to the 1940s	Leadership ability is innate and linked to personal qualities	
Behavioural theories	1950s–1970s	Leadership is associated with personal behaviour and leadership style (Blake & McCanse, 1991; Likert, 1967; Mintzberg, 1973)	
Situational and Contingency models	Late 1960s onwards	Leadership is affected by context and situation. Situational leadership (Hersey & Blanchard, 1992): leader adapts their style according to the competence and commitment of the followers. Action-centred leadership (Adair, 1983): an adaptive leadership approach with a focus on task, team and/or individual	Therapist/human relations: Focused on relationships and motivations. Characterised by therapy culture and associated with the rise of human relations approaches to organisational management
Transactional leadership	1970s	Reinforcement of performance ("transactional" behaviour) Bass (1985) 'Full-range' model of transactional leadership consisted of three dimensions: Contingent reward, clarification of expectations and establishment of reward Management by exception, corrective action on the basis of results (active and passive)	
Charismatic leadership	1970s	Charismatic leaders articulate an inspirational vision and motivate others to follow them.	Messiah/transformational leadership: Focused on individual leaders who can provide vision and establish strong organisational cultures

(*continued*)

Theory/Approach	Period	Theme and Advocates	Discourse
Transformational leadership	1970/1980s	Understanding followers and building their self-worth and focus ('transformational' behaviours). Credibility, vision, values, competence, judgement, experimentation and engagement of staff are all emphasised. Bass (1985), building on the work of Burns (1978), developed a four dimensional model of leadership: *Charisma*, idealised influence, the extent to which the leader behaves in admirable ways to attract followers to identify with them *Inspirational motivation*, the ability to articulate a vision and communicate optimism *Intellectual stimulation*, the ability to challenge assumptions, take risks and encourage creativity in their followers *Individualised consideration*, attending to follower's needs, acting as mentor or coach and listening to their concerns and needs	
Servant leadership	1970s	Initially coined by Robert Greenleaf (1977). Servant leadership focuses on the growth of those who are being simultaneously led and served. Anderson and Sun (2017) synthesised a multitude of dimensions from various theorists into 12 conceptually distinct areas: *Altruistic calling*, a deep-rooted desire to make a positive different in the lives of others through service *Persuasive mapping*, sound reasoning and mental frameworks to map issues and conceptualise future possibilities *Courage*, seeing things differently and taking risks to find new solutions *Agapao love*, considering the whole person, not treating them as a means to an end *Emotional healing*, spiritual recovery from hardship and trauma *Forgiveness*, letting go of perceived wrong doings *Humility*, understanding own strengths and weaknesses in proper perspective *A covenantal relationship*, accepting others as they are and engaging as equals *Behaving ethically*, holding oneself to high moral standards and acting with integrity *Authenticity*, accurately reflecting the public and private self *Creating value for the community*, preparing organisations to contribute positively to society *Accountability*, holding followers accountable for what they can control	

Authentic leadership	1990–2000	Promoting positive psychological capacities and positive ethical climate. A four-dimensional model (Walumbwa et al., 2008): *Self-awareness*, insight into self through exposure to others and knowing one's impact on other people *Relational transparency*, presenting an authentic self *Balanced processing*, objectivity in analysis of information and soliciting views which challenge their own position *Internalised moral perspective*, internal and integrated self-regulation based on internal rather than group or organisational moral values and standards	
Ethical leadership	2000	Drawing on social learning theory, M. E. Brown et al. (2005) theorised that ethical leadership is a distinct leadership style based on three factors which state that an ethical leader is: *a moral person*, fair honest, trustworthy and principles; *a moral role model*, living as well as stating their moral code; *a moral manager*, making ethics an explicit part of their leadership agenda.	
Spiritual leadership	2000	The values, attitudes and behaviours of the leader creates a spiritual environment that helps followers to thrive. Fry's (2003) spiritual leadership framework is a key text.	

Western (2013) organised 'traditional' leadership theories into distinct phases or discourses, which are presented in the 'Discourse' column to demonstrate their intersection with established theories.
Adapted from McCaffery (2010) and Anderson and Sun (2017).

others have limited focus on output. In an increasingly globalised world, the vast majority of the literature on leadership is focused on Western ideologies. Empirical research regarding the impact of more recent models such as authentic and or spiritual leadership is limited: few studies have linked authentic leadership to outcomes, and there is disagreement in the literature regarding the level of analysis of spiritual theory (Anderson & Sun, 2017).

Nevertheless, in terms of advancing ecological leadership, the most pertinent weaknesses of traditional leadership theories have been summarized as being overly concerned with the individual ambition and personality of the leader (Wielkiewicz & Stelzner, 2010), too focused on industrial effectiveness (Rost, 1997) and lacking in values connected to the environment (Allen et al., 1998; Bendell et al., 2018). Western then presented a new paradigm – ecological leadership – which explicitly addresses these shortcomings. It is important to highlight that elements of each leadership style may overlap and that, in practice, multiple leadership discourses are present concurrently in particular contexts. Building on Western's work and other related scholars, the following section outlines foundational principles of ecological leadership (also referred to as eco-leadership) as they are required in contemporary society.

Theory and Key Concepts: Ecological Leadership in a Planetary Emergency

The complexity of global challenges has become starkly evident in recent years. The COVID-19 pandemic revealed the interconnected nature of human and environmental systems and the challenge of leadership under uncertainty. The science of ecology developed in the 20th century through studying the dynamics of natural systems: flows of energy and nutrients, relationships among species and individual organisms and interactions between biotic and abiotic elements (Begon & Townsend, 2020). It therefore offers a useful foundation for understanding leadership under uncertainty and in the context of complexity. We are not suggesting that forms or structures that resemble nature are innately better or morally superior, because this would be at risk of committing the naturalistic fallacy (Moore & Baldwin, 1993). Rather, it recognises that adopting a systems perspective (foundational to ecology) is a powerful starting point for understanding and delivering change for environmental sustainability (Ison, 2010; Voulvoulis et al., 2022). Ecological leadership is explored here firstly by describing key ecological features that act as a foundation to the concept, second by presenting key leadership principles that characterise ecological leadership, third by exploring the normative motivations behind this approach and finally by advocating for transformative leadership practice.

Ecology as a Foundation and a Model

At the beginning of the 21st century, leadership scholars began extrapolating principles from ecology to social and organisational leadership. A landmark publication was Allen et al. (1998; later build on by Wielkiewicz & Stelzner, 2010), who identified fundamental ecological processes pertinent to leadership. The *interdependence* of natural systems – seen, for example, in food webs – emphasises that 'leadership is relational' (Allen et al., 1998, p. 69) and that context is critical. The importance of *feedback loops* that characterise complex adaptive systems and define ecosystem resilience (Folke, 2006) recognises how the interplay of organisational and environmental variables can give rise to non-linear change or provide capacities to reorganise in response to shocks. An understanding of *cycling of resources* in ecosystems, whereby resources move fluidly in and out, emphasises the need for leadership that recognises and utilises people and capabilities wherever present and promotes possibilities for leadership in particular contexts and times. Finally, just as ecosystems *adapt* to stress and change, there is recognition that leadership is needed to enable sharing of knowledge and facilitate processes of continual learning (Allen et al., 1998).

The following sections outline existing key principles of ecological leadership and extend thinking on this topic by incorporating thinking from current sustainability science. The first three sections focus on how an ecological leadership paradigm recasts an understanding of the nature of organisations, the nature of leadership and the nature of change. This is followed by exploration of the normative foundation of ecological leadership and the necessity for transformative action.

The Nature of Organisations

Ecological leadership starts from a systems view of the world. The fields of complexity science and systems theory have developed over the past decades and understand phenomena as emerging from complex interactions among sets of variables, whether that be in the context of business, environmental management, social welfare, health or technology (Ison, 2010; Stroh, 2015). This perspective has begun to transform leadership and management fields of research and practice (Jackson, 2016; Kellerman, 2016; Satterwhite, 2010; Senge, 1990; Stroh, 2015). From an ecological leadership perspective, organisations are not to be viewed as stable, predictable, controllable or independent entities. They exist within a landscape of influence both internally and externally. The performance of a business can be impacted by unexpected events beyond its control, such as extreme weather events or social upheaval. Similarly, 'solutions' employed by an organisation can have perverse and unintentional knock-on impacts, such as accelerated deforestation following more stringent legal controls (Lim et al., 2017) or expansion of agricultural land use alongside intensification (Phelps et al., 2013). Further, the internal workings of an organisation must be understood as being impacted by external pressures, with the COVID-19 pandemic a stark example of this. The social or ecological consequences of actions taken by an organisation may also only be evident over longer timescales and beyond traditional monitoring procedures (Western, 2013). Ultimately, adopting the view of organisations as themselves complex adaptive systems is foundational for a renewed perspective on leadership itself.

The Nature of Leadership

The ecological leadership paradigm has developed as an alternative to hierarchical, individualist, positional models of leadership (Western, 2013). Rather than leadership being understood as the qualities or actions of a single positional leader, it understands leadership as an emergent phenomenon within an organisation (Cletzer & Kaufman, 2018), with individuals able to exercise leadership from anywhere within an organisation as the need arises. Western (2018, p. 58) framed individual leaders as 'one part of an array of actors that comprise a distributed leadership approach within the networks of activity made up of human and non-humans'. This aligns with Bendell et al. (2018, p. 26), who defined sustainable leadership (analogous ecological leadership) as 'any ethical behaviour that has the intention and effect of helping groups of people addressed shared dilemmas in significant ways not otherwise achieved'. Similarly, Goldstein et al. (2010) advanced an idea of distributed leadership that decouples leaders (individuals) from leadership (process), in recognition that change occurs systemically through relationships. Such perspectives resonate with Indigenous notions of leadership, which often integrate individual and collective understandings of change and agency(Gram-Hanssen, 2021).

The Nature of Change

Given that leadership is understood as a process occurring in a distributed way at a particular time for particular outcomes, the process of change that leadership facilitates is therefore relational. Western (2018) presented this concept as follows: 'Eco-leadership...begins deep within each individual, works through relationships, through to how Eco-leaders influence wider networks, and how they form strategies to deliver change' (p. 55). In this way, outcomes should be understood as an 'emergent phenomenon' (Cletzer & Kaufman, 2018, p. 81) stemming from interactions among individuals (Wielkiewicz & Stelzner, 2010). This is in contrast to command-and-control concepts of change that characterise many traditional leadership paradigms.

If ecological leadership is about relationships, then the quality and nature of such relationships is key. Although not explicitly related to leadership for environmental sustainability, Erwin Friedman's theory of self-differentiated leadership offers a useful perspective on how relationships can be managed in leadership processes (Friedman, 2007). As a student of Murray Bowen, founder of family systems theory, Friedman emphasised the tendency for people to be drawn into unhealthy, anxiety-prone relationships with others, especially in contexts of tension or stress. The solution is to maintain 'differentiation of self', which Bowen defined as 'the ability to be in emotional contact with others yet still autonomous in one's own emotional functioning' (Kerr & Bowen, 1988, p. 145). Effective leadership therefore requires individuals to simultaneously maintain strong connections with others while maintaining a degree of self-differentiation, thereby avoid becoming 'fused' with others. The result is leadership that can 'maintain a modifying, non-anxious, and sometimes challenging presence' (Friedman, 2007, p. 16). This perspective resonates strongly with other established literature on acceptance and commitment therapy (Hayes et al., 2011) and adult development theories, which emphasise the importance of perspective taking and understanding oneself as a discrete individual with desires and agency yet formed by interpersonal and contextual interactions (Kegan, 1982; Levinson, 1986). Given growing uncertainty and turbulence as a result of environmental change both within organisations and across society at large, the need for leadership that maintains a non-anxious presence is needed more than ever.

A focus on the quality of relationships therefore raises new challenges in terms of the skills and capabilities required of leaders. Attention to the 'inner' dimensions of leadership, including personal strengths, is critical here (Ives et al., 2020; MacKie, 2021). This includes 'horizontal' skills of relational competence, as well as vertical learning related to mindset transformation (B. Brown, 2013). An encouraging initiative that is advancing this agenda is the 'Inner Development Goals': those capacities needed for bringing change for sustainability. These include a sense of connectedness and empathy towards other people and the natural world, social skills of collaboration, communication, maintaining trusting relationships and the creativity and courage to drive forward change (IDG Initiative, 2021). The kind of sustainable leadership being considered in this context therefore is one that is both strong (ensuring social and economic outcomes are embedded within ecological realities) and deep (identifying the underlying drivers of unsustainability, rather than superficial solutions).

The Normative Foundation of Ecological Leadership

Ecological leadership is not value neutral or purpose agnostic. Given its grounding in environmental realities, it upholds a commitment to environmental care and an ecological ethic. Western's presentation of the eco-leader discourse grounds it in ideas from deep ecology and therefore advances an ethics that represents an ecocentric worldview (Western, 2013). Ecological leadership is therefore not a framework that can be readily picked up and applied to various other human endeavours that are driven by ideas of unfettered growth or narrow measures of success such as profits.

In essence, ecological leadership must have a strong moral foundation. Vinkhuyzen and Karlsson-Vinkhuyzen (2014) explored concepts of morality and leadership in the context of sustainability. They held that the *intent* of leadership must not be separated from the process of leadership and contended that 'a true service oriented leader is not motivated by a desire for personal gain, but by love' (p. 107). In a similar vein, Evans (2018, p. 62) highlighted the ultimate purpose of sustainability as central, namely, to 'enhance the long-term health, integrity, and resilience of the community and natural systems of which it is a part'. This normative foundation for action has become explicitly recognised in biodiversity conservation. The IPBES values assessment (2022) identified a set of 'sustainability-aligned values' that underpin effective nature conservation and ought to be emphasised in policy and practice. These include values of care (love, solidarity, responsibility), unity (sense of 'we', empathy), equity and justice and participation and democracy. Such values should therefore be central to processes of ecological leadership across all organisational contexts.

Measurement and Assessment

Measurement and assessment tools for assessing the efficacy of ecological leadership approaches are limited. However, Allen et al. (1998) presented a set of characteristics or indicators of 'open leadership' (synonymous in this context with ecological leadership). While more recent commentary on ecological leadership exists (as reviewed above), these indicators remain useful for guiding individuals and groups towards ecological leadership paradigms, processes and principles. It could also form the basis of a more structured assessment tool for organisations.

The foundations of ecological leadership – an ethical commitment to environmental sustainability, appreciation of context and complexity and emphasis on relationality – do not, however, sit well with quantitative measurements or universal assessment tools. Most conventional measurement inventories of leadership are better suited to analysis of simple rather than complex systems. Consequently, qualitative understandings of ecological leadership, including the stories of delivering change and the motivations and personal commitments of individuals, can be more powerful in illuminating the degree to which a culture of ecological leadership is present in an organisation. Some self-assessment tools to help leaders reflect on their own practice have been developed (see, for example, Allen, 2019), yet the value of this measurement approach is the formation of the leader themselves and an aid to understand their leadership context, rather than informing a process of externally validated professional development. Indeed, we argue that fixation on professional improvement in leadership

Table 7.2 Characteristics of Organisations Employing Ecological Leadership Approaches Compared With Traditional Forms of Leadership

Ecological (Open) Leadership	*Traditional (Closed) Leadership*
Information flow is unrestricted and free.	Decisions are made behind closed doors.
Individuals are rewarded for voicing issues, positions and concerns that cause the direction of the organisation to be reconsidered, especially those related to environmental sustainability.	The organisation has an established culture and history that discourages innovative thinking.
The structure and functions of the organisation are flexible.	The organisation has a hierarchical structure.
The speciality of an individual does not restrict with whom they interact.	Individuals tend to communicate with a restricted group of people with similar job titles.
Reward systems recognise and value the contribution of all members of the organisation.	Upper-level managers receive the credit and rewards for the organisation's success.
The organisation and its members have a shared standard of ethical conduct.	Conduct is judged by its benefit to the organisation.
Organisational success is regarded as a team effort.	There is competition within the organisation to be 'the best' or 'most successful'.
The core values and purpose of the organisation are clear and aligned with environmental sustainability. Members are committed to these values, challenging the process when these core values are ignored.	The purpose and core values of the organisation are unclear and/or members are not committed to these values.
Development and personal growth are highly valued and supported in the organisation.	Personnel changes such as hiring new individuals, firing others and transfers are used to make changes in the organisation.

Adapted from Allen et al. (1998).

can lead to an over-inflated sense of individual agency at the expense of a deep and reflexive understanding of one's context and relational possibilities. Thus, an ecological approach to leadership calls for a 'deepening' of leadership understanding rather than 'raising the bar' of one's ability to individually achieve outcomes.

Conventional leadership practices, such as those represented in the Institute of Leadership and Management (ILM) *Dimensions of Leadership* (ILM,

2023a) are yet to fully embrace true ecological leadership practices as outlined by Western and others. Whilst there are some existing overlaps in themes such as employee engagement, vision, future readiness and adaptability, there is more to be done on mapping Western's ideas to existing language and mainstream concepts. Current leadership priorities are focused on a post-COVID world which is facing financial crisis and political instability. Individual positional leaders are challenged to support their workforce in navigating an uncertain future through significant and continuous change. Indeed, themes identified for discussion at the 2023 ILM International Leadership Week include managing remote teams, future-readiness and business agility and emotional intelligence (ILM, 2023b). Workplace practices such as hybrid working and the need to support the mental health and well-being of groups and individuals is a prominent feature of leadership discussion in 2023. Whilst eco-leadership practices such as relational leadership and ethical commitments to social–environmental flourishing are valued, these ideas are fighting for attention in a congested landscape of leadership concerns. Leadership that grapples with the current environmental emergency and the deep interconnections between global environmental, social and economic systems remains marginal to mainstream discourse. The culture and norms of the leadership 'industry', with its emphasis on measurement and evidence-based practice, may unfortunately be precluding ecological leadership principles from being adopted since the relationality and complexity of ecological leadership does not lend itself to quantitative assessment.

Application: Leadership for Social–Ecological Transformation

Much of the literature on ecological leadership literature has focused on the adaptability of organisations to changing contexts (e.g., Allen et al., 1998). While this is essential, it has become especially evident in recent years that progress towards a sustainable planetary future is grossly inadequate and that transformational change of structures, systems and societies is necessary. We advance this discourse by recognising the importance of leadership for transformation. Transformation has been defined as 'profound and enduring non-linear systemic changes, typically involving social, cultural, technological, political, economic, and/or environmental processes'

(Linnér & Wilbeck, 2019, p. 4). Along with the UN Agenda 2030 being known as the 'transformative agenda', scholars of climate change, biodiversity and sustainability more broadly have increasingly highlighted the necessity of societal transformation in recognition of the yawning gap between environmental ambition and reality (Abson et al., 2017; Chan et al., 2020; O'Brien, 2012). The UNEP report *Making Peace With Nature* (UNEP, 2021) set out six areas for system transformation: economy and finance; food and water; energy; human settlements; health, equity and peace; and environment. In each of these settings there is a need for leadership that enables such transformation to occur. Such leadership must necessarily adopt principles of ecological leadership, as outlined in this chapter, given a focus on system change rather than individually initiated and predictable outcomes.

The conflation of leadership with individualised, top-down, positional forms of change has led many environmental scholars to reject the term leadership altogether in recognition of broader, systemic processes of change. Alternatives include 'transformative agency' (Westley et al., 2013), 'change agency' (van Poeck et al., 2017), or 'organisational entrepreneurs' (Hahn et al., 2006). Westley et al.'s (2013) theory of transformative agency for example recognises particular places and times within the adaptive cycle of systems (Walker et al., 2004), where different actions can be deployed by agents of change to bring about transformation. This incudes the importance of building networks, trust and capacity during times of stability and seizing windows of opportunity when a system has experienced shock or destabilisation. This perspective on change resonates with the concept of 'dancing with systems' proposed by Meadows (2002).

Literature on ecological leadership has not sufficiently engaged with this need for transformation. Here we proposed a structure for considering ecological leadership for sustainability transformation, based on ideas introduced by philosopher and theologian Dallas Willard's V-I-M model of personal spiritual formation (Willard, 2002). Willard understood personal formation as requiring a *Vision* of desirable change, an *Intention* to bring about change, and the *Means* to enable it. When applied to ecological leadership for sustainability transformation, such a model could be developed as follows:

1. Vision = Transforming *goals*. Here, leaders carry an ethically informed vision of a just, sustainable and ecologically flourishing future. This vision should be held at multiple scales: both that of the organisation and that of the wider societal and ecological context.

2. Intention = Transforming *processes*. This dimension of leadership consists of understanding and committing to processes of transformative change within systems. This may include working with theories of systemic resilience, assemblages of actors or multi-level governance.
3. Means = Transforming *people*. This consists of the formation of personal qualities that are needed to mobilise action in complex systems. Examples include ecocentric ethical orientation, sustainability-aligned values and interpersonal capacities for leadership.

Conclusions

Climate change is a symptom of a fractured relationship between humanity and the planet. As such, leadership responses to climate change need to be couched within a broader suite of environmental challenges, including the degradation of the natural world. With biodiversity conservation practice having entered a paradigm of relational interactions between people and nature (Mace, 2014), it is fruitful to advance leadership theory and practice by grounding it in an understanding of ecological principles. Externally, leaders (those facilitating change) should begin from a clear understanding of the relationship between humanity and the natural world and the urgent imperative to move towards a more harmonious relationship with it. Leadership should also be understood as an open process, whereby change occurs through complex relationships among people and structures and entities rather than via predictable pathways and control mechanisms. Internally, leaders need to be grounded in strong normative goals of care and responsibility for people and planet and cultivate the personal character strengths needed to authentically act in accordance with their deep values. Such internal and external leadership characteristics are required for societal transformation towards ecological sustainability. There is a need now for leaders across all sectors and organisational contexts to pursue models of change based on distributed, relational and systemic realities and to work for a safe and just climate future and a flourishing biosphere.

Discussion Points

- Given the importance of relationships and distributed processes of change emphasised by ecological leadership, is the title of 'leader' now unhelpful?

- What practices or habits could be developed to allow for regular reflection on the vision of leadership, intention of change processes and means (ethical commitment) individuals have for driving change for sustainability?
- With greater recognition of the biodiversity crisis have come proposals for new paradigms for policy and industry that can safeguard nature; for example, 'nature positive' approaches (Narain et al., 2022). What new paradigms could be proposed for other organisational settings?
- How can leaders and organisations recognise and leverage connections between inner qualities, such as empathy, creativity and courage, and external measures of system change, such as reduction in carbon emissions, sustainability of supply chains or stewardship of biodiversity? How might these opportunities for influence vary across different types of organisational settings?

Suggested Reading

Redekop, B. W., Gallagher, D. R., & Satterwhite, R. (Eds.). (2018). *Innovation in environmental leadership: Critical perspectives.* Routledge.

Western, S. (2013). *Leadership: A critical text.* Sage.

Westley, F. R., Tjornbo, O., Schultz, L., Olsson, P., Folke, C., Crona, B., & Bodin, Ö. (2013). A theory of transformative agency in linked social–ecological systems. *Ecology and Society, 18*(3). https://doi.org/10.5751/ES-05072-180327

References

Abson, D. J., Fischer, J., Leventon, J., Newig, J., Schomerus, T., Vilsmaier, U., von Wehrden, H., Abernethy, P., Ives, C. D., Jager, N. W., & Lang, D. J. (2017). Leverage points for sustainability transformation. *Ambio, 46*(1), 30–39. https://doi.org/10.1007/s13280-016-0800-y

Adair, J. (1983). *Effective leadership.* Pan Books.

Ahn, J., Brook, E. J., Mitchell, L., Rosen, J., McConnell, J. R., Taylor, K., Etheridge, D., & Rubino, M. (2012). Atmospheric CO_2 over the last 1000 years: A high-resolution record from the West Antarctic Ice Sheet (WAIS) Divide ice core. *Global Biogeochemical Cycles, 26*(2). https://doi.org/10.1029/2011GB004247

Allen, K. E. (2019). *Leading from the roots: Nature inspired leadership lessons for today's world.* Morgan James.

Allen, K. E., Stelzner, S. P., & Wielkiewicz, R. M. (1998). The ecology of leadership: Adapting to the challenges of a changing world. *The Journal of Leadership Studies, 5*(2), 62–82.

Anderson, M. H., & Sun, P. Y. T. (2017). Reviewing leadership styles: Overlaps and the need for a new 'full-range' theory. *International Journal of Management Reviews, 19*(1), 76–96. https://doi.org/10.1111/ijmr.12082

Arneth, A., Sitch, S., Pongratz, J., Stocker, B. D., Ciais, P., Poulter, B., Bayer, A. D., Bondeau, A., Calle, L., Chini, L. P., Gasser, T., Fader, M., Friedlingstein, P., Kato, E., Li, W., Lindeskog, M., Nabel, J. E. M. S., Pugh, T. A. M., Robertson, E., ... Zaehle, S. (2017). Historical carbon dioxide emissions caused by land-use changes are possibly larger than assumed. *Nature Geoscience, 10*(2), 79–84. https://doi.org/10.1038/ngeo2882

Bass, B. M. (1985). *Leadership and performance beyond expectations.* Free.

Begon, M., & Townsend, C. R. (2020). *Ecology: From individuals to ecosystems.* John Wiley & Sons.

Bellard, C., Bertelsmeier, C., Leadley, P., Thuiller, W., & Courchamp, F. (2012). Impacts of climate change on the future of biodiversity. *Ecology Letters, 15*(4), 365–377. https://doi.org/10.1111/j.1461-0248.2011.01736.x

Bendell, J., Little, R., & Sutherland, N. (2018). The seven unsustainabilities of mainstream leadership. In B. W. Redokop, D. R. Gallagher, & R. Satterwhite (Eds.), *Innovation in environmental leadership: Critical perspectives* (pp. 13–31). Routledge. http://ebookcentral.proquest.com/lib/nottingham/detail.action?docID=5229009

Blake, R. R., & McCanse, A. A. (1991). *Leadership dilemmas: Grid solution.* Butterworth-Heinemann.

Brown, B. (2013). The future of leadership for conscious capitalism. *Journey of Integral Theory and Practice, 5*, 1–22.

Brown, M. E., Treviño, L. K., & Harrison, D. A. (2005). Ethical leadership: A social learning perspective for construct development and testing. *Organizational Behavior and Human Decision Processes, 97*(2), 117–134. https://doi.org/10.1016/j.obhdp.2005.03.002

Burns, J. (1978). *Leadership.* Harper & Row.

Ceballos, G., Ehrlich, P. R., Barnosky, A. D., García, A., Pringle, R. M., & Palmer, T. M. (2015). Accelerated modern human–induced species losses: Entering the sixth mass extinction. *Science Advances, 1*(5). https://doi.org/10.1126/sciadv.1400253

Chan, K. M. A., Boyd, D. R., Gould, R. K., Jetzkowitz, J., Liu, J., Muraca, B., Naidoo, R., Olmsted, P., Satterfield, T., Selomane, O., Singh, G. G., Sumaila, R., Ngo, H. T., Klintuni, A., John, B., Ana, A., Aguiar, P. D. de, Armenteras, D., Balint, L., ... Gregr, E. J. (2020, June). Levers and leverage points for pathways to sustainability. *People and Nature*, 1–25. https://doi.org/10.1002/pan3.10124

Cletzer, D. A., & Kaufman, E. K. (2018). Eco-leadership, complexity science, and 21st century organisations. In B. W. Redekop, G. D. Rigling, &

R. Satterwhite (Eds.), *Innovation in environmental leadership: Critical perspectives* (pp. 80–96). Routledge.

Crosby, A. W. (2003). *The Columbian exchange: Biological and cultural consequences of 1492*. Greenwood.

Díaz, S., Settele, J., Brondízio, E. S., Ngo, H. T., Agard, J., Arneth, A., Balvanera, P., Brauman, K. A., Butchart, S. H. M., Chan, K. M. A., Garibaldi, L. A., Ichii, K., Liu, J., Subramanian, S. M., Midgley, G. F., Miloslavich, P., Molnár, Z., Obura, D., Pfaff, A., ... Zayas, C. N. (2019). Pervasive human-driven decline of life on Earth points to the need for transformative change. *Science, 366*(1327). https://doi.org/10.1126/science.aaw3100

Evans, T. L. (2018). Sustainable leadership toward restoring the human and natural worlds. In B. W. Redekop, G. D. Rigling, & R. Satterwhite (Eds.), *Innovation in environmental leadership: Critical perspectives* (pp. 61–79). Taylor & Francis.

Folke, C. (2006). Resilience: The emergence of a perspective for social–ecological systems analyses. *Global Environmental Change, 16*(3), 253–267. https://doi.org/10.1016/j.gloenvcha.2006.04.002

Folke, C., Biggs, R., Norström, A. v., Reyers, B., & Rockström, J. (2016). Social–ecological resilience and biosphere-based sustainability science. *Ecology and Society, 21*(3), 41. https://doi.org/10.5751/ES-08748-210341

Friedman, E. H. (2007). *A failure of nerve: Leadership in the age of the quick fix*. Church Publishing.

Fry, L. W. (2003, September). Toward a theory of spiritual leadership. *The Leadership Quarterly, 14*, 693–727. https://doi.org/10.1016/j.leaqua.2003.09.001

Goldstein, J., Hazy, K. J., & Lichtenstein, B. B. (2010). *Complexity and the nexus of leadership: Leveraging nonlinear science to create ecologies of innovation*. Palgrave Macmillan.

Gram-Hanssen, I. (2021). Individual and collective leadership for deliberate transformations: Insights from Indigenous leadership. *Leadership, 17*(5), 519–541. https://doi.org/10.1177/1742715021996486

Greenleaf, R. K. (1977). *Servant leadership: A journey into the nature of legitimate power and greatness*. Paulist Press.

Hahn, T., Olsson, P., Folke, C., & Johansson, K. (2006). Trust-building, knowledge generation and organizational innovations: The role of a bridging organization for adaptive comanagement of a wetland landscape around Kristianstad, Sweden. *Human Ecology, 34*(4), 573–592. https://doi.org/10.1007/s10745-006-9035-z

Hayes, S. C., Kirk, D. S., & Wilson, K. G. (2011). *Acceptance and commitment therapy: The process and practice of mindful change*. Guilford.

Hersey, P., & Blanchard, K. H. (1992). *Management of organizational behavior* (6th ed.). Prentice-Hall.

IDG Initiative. (2021). *Inner development goals (IDG): Background, method and the IDG framework.* https://static1.squarespace.com/static/600d80b3387b98582a60354a/t/616eb1adbee9380a25085e35/1634644401138/211019_IDG_Report.pdf

Institute of Leadership and Management. (2023a). *Dimensions of leadership.* https://www.institutelm.com/learning/leadership-framework.html

Institute of Leadership and Management. (2023b). *International Leadership Week 2023.* https://www.institutelm.com/whats-on/international-leadership-week.html

Intergovernmental Panel on Climate Change. (2022). *Climate change 2022: Mitigation of climate change.* https://www.ipcc.ch/working-group/wg3/

Intergovernmental Science-Policy Platform on Biodiversity and Ecosystem Services. (2019). *Global assessment report on biodiversity and ecosystem services of the Intergovernmental Science-Policy Platform on Biodiversity and Ecosystem Services.*

Intergovernmental Science-Policy Platform on Biodiversity and Ecosystem Services. (2022). *Summary for policymakers of the methodological assessment of the diverse values and valuation of nature of the Intergovernmental Science-Policy Platform on Biodiversity and Ecosystem Services.*

Ison, R. (2010). *Systems practice: How to act in a climate change world.* Springer.

Ives, C. D., Freeth, R., & Fischer, J. (2020). Inside-out sustainability: The neglect of inner worlds. *Ambio, 49*(1), 208–217. https://doi.org/https://doi.org/10.1007/s13280-019-01187-w

Jackson, M. C. (2016). *Systems thinking: Creative holism for managers.* John Wiley & Sons.

Kegan, R. (1982). *The evolving self: Problem and process in human development.* Harvard University Press.

Kellerman, B. (2016). Leadership – It's a system, not a person! *Daedalus, 145*(3), 83–94. https://doi.org/10.1162/DAED_a_00399

Kerr, M. E., & Bowen, M. (1988). *Family evaluation.* W.W. Norton.

Lenton, T. M., Rockström, J., Gaffney, O., Rahmstorf, S., Richardson, K., Steffen, W., & Schellnhuber, H. J. (2019). Climate tipping points – Too risky to bet against. *Nature, 575*, 592–595.

Levinson, D. J. (1986). A conception of adult development. *American Psychologist, 41*(1), 3–13. https://doi.org/10.1037/0003-066X.41.1.3

Lewis, S. L., & Maslin, M. A. (2015). Defining the Anthropocene. *Nature, 519*(7542), 171–180. https://doi.org/10.1038/nature14258

Likert, R. (1967). *New patterns of management.* McGraw-Hill.

Lim, F. K. S., Carrasco, L. R., McHardy, J., & Edwards, D. P. (2017). Perverse market outcomes from biodiversity conservation interventions. *Conservation Letters, 10*(5), 506–516. https://doi.org/10.1111/conl.12332

Linnér, B.-O., & Wilbeck, V. (2019). *Sustainability transformations: Agents and drivers across societies.* Cambridge University Press.

Mace, G. M. (2014). Whose conservation? *Science, 345*(6204), 1558–1560. https://doi.org/10.1126/science.1254704

MacKie, D. (2021). Strength-based coaching and sustainability leadership. In W. Smith, I. Boniwell, & S. Green (Eds.), *Positive psychology coaching in the workplace* (pp. 375–396). Springer. https://doi.org/10.1007/978-3-030-79952-6_20

Manolopoulos, M. (2021). *A theory of environmental leadership.* Routledge. https://doi.org/10.4324/9781003035350

McCaffery, P. (2010). *The higher education manager's handbook: Effective leadership and management in universities and colleges* (2nd ed.). Routledge.

Meadows, D. (2002). Dancing with systems. *Systems Thinker, 13*, 2–6.

Mintzberg, H. (1973). *The nature of management work.* Harper and Row.

Moore, G. E., & Baldwin, T. (1993). *Principia ethica.* Cambridge University Press.

Narain, D., Bull, J. W., Alikhanova, S., Evans, M. C., Markham, R., & Maron, M. (2022). A step change needed to secure a nature-positive future – Is it in reach? *One Earth, 5*(6), 589–592.

O'Brien, K. (2012). Global environmental change II: From adaptation to deliberate transformation. *Progress in Human Geography, 36*(5), 667–676. https://doi.org/10.1177/0309132511425767

Obura, D. O., DeClerck, F., Verburg, P. H., Gupta, J., Abrams, J. F., Bai, X., Bunn, S., Ebi, K. L., Gifford, L., Gordon, C., Jacobson, L., Lenton, T. M., Liverman, D., Mohamed, A., Prodani, K., Rocha, J. C., Rockström, J., Sakschewski, B., Stewart-Koster, B., ... Zimm, C. (2022). Achieving a nature- and people-positive future. *One Earth, 6*(2), 105–117. https://doi.org/10.1016/j.oneear.2022.11.013

Pew Research Centre. (2020, September 29). *Concern over climate and the environment predominates among these publics.* https://www.pewresearch.org/science/2020/09/29/concern-over-climate-and-the-environment-predominates-among-these-publics/

Phelps, J., Carrasco, L. R., Webb, E. L., Koh, L. P., & Pascual, U. (2013). Agricultural intensification escalates future conservation costs. *Proceedings of the National Academy of Sciences, 110*(19), 7601–7606. https://doi.org/10.1073/pnas.1220070110

Raworth, K. (2017). *Doughnut economics: Seven ways to think like a 21st-century economist.* Chelsea Green.

Rost, J. C. (1997). Moving from individual to relationship: A postindustrial paradigm of leadership. *Journal of Leadership Studies, 4*(4), 3–16. https://doi.org/10.1177/107179199700400402

Satterwhite, R. (2010). Deep systems leadership: A model for the 21st century. In B. W. Redekop & S. Olson (Eds.), *Leadership for environmental sustainability* (pp. 230–242). Routledge.

SEI & CEEW. (2022). *Stockholm+50: Unlocking a better future.* https://doi.org/10.51414/sei2022.011

Senge, P. (1990). *The fifth discipline: The art and practice of the learning organization.* Random House.

Steffen, W., Broadgate, W., Deutsch, L., Gaffney, O., & Ludwig, C. (2015). The trajectory of the Anthropocene: The Great Acceleration. *The Anthropocene Review, 2*(1), 81–98. https://doi.org/10.1177/2053019614564785

Steffen, W., Richardson, K., Rockström, J., Cornell, S., Fetzer, I., Bennett, E., Biggs, R., Carpenter, S. R., de Wit, C. a., Folke, C., Mace, G., Persson, L. M., Veerabhadran, R., Reyers, B., & Sörlin, S. (2015). Planetary boundaries: Guiding human development on a changing planet. *Science, 347*(6223), 1259855. https://doi.org/10.1126/science.1259855

Stroh, D. P. (2015). *Systems thinking for social change: A practical guide to solving complex problems, avoiding unintended consequences, and achieving lasting results.* Chelsea Green.

United Nations Environment Programme. (2021). *Making peace with nature: A scientific blueprint to tackle the climate, biodiversity and pollution emergencies.*

United Nations Environment Programme. (2022). *Beyond GDP: Making nature count in the shift to sustainability.* https://www.unep.org/news-and-stories/story/beyond-gdp-making-nature-count-shift-sustainability

United Nations Framework Convention on Climate Change. (2022). *COP27 Sharm el-Sheikh implementation plan.* https://unfccc.int/sites/default/files/resource/cop27_auv_2_cover%20decision.pdf

van Poeck, K., Læssøe, J., & Block, T. (2017). An exploration of sustainability change agents as facilitators of nonformal learning: Mapping a moving and intertwined landscape. *Ecology and Society, 22*(2). https://doi.org/10.5751/ES-09308-220233

Van Vugt, M. (2006). Evolutionary origins of leadership and followership. *Personality and Social Psychology Review, 10*(4), 354–371.

Vinkhuyzen, O. M., & Karlsson-Vinkhuyzen, S. I. (2014). The role of moral leadership for sustainable production and consumption. *Journal of Cleaner Production, 63*, 102–113. https://doi.org/10.1016/j.jclepro.2013.06.045

Voulvoulis, N., Giakoumis, T., Hunt, C., Kioupi, V., Petrou, N., Souliotis, I., Vaghela, C., & binti Wan Rosely, W. I. H. (2022). Systems thinking as a paradigm shift for sustainability transformation. *Global Environmental Change, 75*, 102544. https://doi.org/10.1016/j.gloenvcha.2022.102544

Wackernagel, M., Hanscom, L., Jayasinghe, P., Lin, D., Murthy, A., Neill, E., & Raven, P. (2021). The importance of resource security for poverty eradication. *Nature Sustainability, 4*(8), 731–738. https://doi.org/10.1038/s41893-021-00708-4

Walker, B., Holling, C. S., Carpenter, S. R., & Kinzig, A. (2004). Resilience, adaptability and transformability in social–ecological systems. *Ecology and Society, 9*(2), 5. https://doi.org/10.1103/PhysRevLett.95.258101

Walumbwa, F. O., Avolio, B. J., Gardner, W. L., Wernsing, T. S., & Peterson, S. J. (2008). Authentic leadership: Development and validation of a theory-based measure. *Journal of Management, 34*(1), 89–126. https://doi.org/10.1177/0149206307308913

Western, S. (2013). *Leadership: A critical text*. Sage.

Western, S. (2018). The eco-leadership paradox. In B. W. Redekop, G. D. Rigling, & R. Satterwhite (Eds.), *Innovation in environmental leadership: Critical perspectives* (pp. 48–60). Routledge.

Westley, F. R., Tjornbo, O., Schultz, L., Olsson, P., Folke, C., Crona, B., & Bodin, Ö. (2013). A theory of transformative agency in linked social–ecological systems. *Ecology and Society, 18*(3). https://doi.org/10.5751/ES-05072-180327

Wielkiewicz, R. M., & Stelzner, S. P. (2010). An ecological perspective on leadership theory, research, and practice. In B. W. Redekop & S. Olson (Eds.), *Leadership for environmental sustainability* (pp. 17–35). Taylor & Francis.

Willard, D. (2002). *Renovation of the heart*. NavPress.

Wiseman, J. (2021). *Hope and courage in the climate crisis*. Springer. https://doi.org/10.1007/978-3-030-70743-9

8

ENVIRONMENTAL LEADERSHIP IS CONTEMPORARY LEADERSHIP

STATE OF THE LITERATURE AND RECOMMENDATIONS

Rian Satterwhite

Chapter Summary

This chapter chronicles the last 20 years of environmental and sustainable leadership thinking to identify trends and future directions. The author uses this literature review to make six recommendations for organisational leadership practice: centring nature as the context and consequence of contemporary leadership, consuming less and more ethically, shifting our frameworks of organisational power, centring collective leadership and indigenous wisdom, clearly articulating the difference between leadership and management and fostering systems literacy.

Introduction

I will treat the terms *sustainability leadership* and *environmental leadership* as the same, though elsewhere in the literature distinctions may be drawn. My

DOI: 10.4324/9781003343011-9

interest is in clarifying how leadership theory and practice changes as we increasingly recognise (a) the ways in which it has been complicit in reinforcing systems of inequality, (b) the fact that the Earth's biosphere serves as the universal context in which all leadership occurs, and (c) that we have a broad responsibility to and dependency upon natural systems, which require care and a fundamental reorientation to time.

Assessing Our Shared Leadership Context

Leadership is a socially constructed phenomenon (Grint, 2005), shaped and defined by the context and environment in which it is enacted. This means that leadership does not exist in any objective sense, but the study of it should be 'concerned instead with how people characterise, negotiate and enact what they call "leadership"' (Liu, 2021, p. 8). It is my goal to situate 'good leadership' in the shared environmental contexts in which we all now find ourselves and explore the implications of this context for organisational leadership theory and practice. What follows is consistent with Raelin's (2016) call for a more collective understanding of leadership, an approach that is itself in line with the lessons we learn from sustainability practices and principles, as will be highlighted later.

Through times of uncertainty and challenge, good or effective leadership should move us forward, creating new and needed capacity and insight; good leadership must invite us into the difficult work of navigating the ambiguity of fundamental change. Indeed, Heifetz (2006) argued that in the long term, 'leadership generates new cultural norms that enable people to meet an ongoing stream of adaptive challenges, realities, and pressures likely to come' (p. 76). Yet the field, discipline or industry of leadership, depending on how one chooses to frame it, is not yielding the results that we require right now or in the future. Whether one's focus lies with the 'industry' of leadership consultants and coaches (Kellerman, 2012, 2018) or within higher education, which Kolditz et al. (2021) argued operates with the implicit presumption that leadership development is a natural outcome of the collegiate experience and not worth broadly and strategically investing in, there is an undeniable gap between what is espoused and the real and systemic leadership failures – conflict, corruption, assaults on democratic norms, inequality – we are seeing day to day.

The current global context of leadership in which we all operate is characterised by volatility, environmental destruction, ecosystem collapse and a deep questioning of prevailing social, economic and organisational systems. Leadership theory and practice has been part of the problem, largely reflecting these issues rather than helping to steer our way through them. Kellerman (2012) concluded her scathing analysis of the leadership industry with these words: leadership 'must reflect the object of its affection – change with the changing times' (p. 200). The dominant discourse of leadership is a product of – and therefore largely serves to uphold – the dominant social norms of capitalism, consumption and Whiteness, among others that could be named (see Bendell & Little, 2015; Evans, 2011; Guthrie & Chunoo, 2018; Liu, 2021; Western, 2019). This is not to say that the discourse of leadership has remained static, because it certainly has not, but rather that the changes which *have* occurred have largely been those permitted by or consistent with dominant paradigms and structures; evolutionary changes, not revolutionary. In other words, dominant narratives and discourses of leadership most often serve to reproduce the unequal power structures that already exist.

One of the crucial lessons from both critical and systems thinking which are core to my argument here is the realisation that the systems we have today are perfectly suited to produce the outcomes that we see (see Meadows, 2008). The negative outcomes that we see (e.g., rising inequality, authoritarian challenges to democracy, environmental degradation and ecosystem collapse) are not externalities of systems helping us achieve other more positive ends but from a systems lens are the very purposes the systems are presently designed to achieve. To change these outcomes, we need to change the systems that produce them (see Capra & Luisi, 2014). The tower of expertise that built these systems has collapsed, and in the aftermath we find ourselves in a fundamentally new context. Our thinking and enactment of leadership must be as different as this new context that we find ourselves practicing it in.

Feedback Loops Are Shouting at Us

Feedback loops are telling us that the fundamental contexts of leadership have changed. Are we willing to listen? Earth's species have, on average, experienced a 69% population decline in the last 50 years (World Wildlife

Fund, 2022). Amidst this accelerated recent decline, evidence suggests that as many as 7.5% to 13% of all 2 million known species have gone extinct since 1500 (Cowie et al., 2022). This precipitous decline indicates that we are likely living through just the sixth mass extinction on Earth, only this time it is driven not by natural processes or external forces but by the systematic actions of one species. Experts believe that this will lead to loss of food security as pollinators decline, habitat changes, soil fertility deteriorates and water shortages occur as natural disasters become more regular and extreme. Additional pandemics are likely to emerge as humans and animals come into closer contact through habitat fragmentation and displacement. Without concerted effort, our ecological degradation will continue to worsen and intensify a range of social challenges including malnutrition, forced migration, illness and conflict (Institute for Economics and Peace, 2022). Further, a recent assessment of the economic impact of extreme heat – just one of many foreseen trends of climate change – found the cumulative economic losses between 1992 and 2013 to be between $5 trillion and $29.3 trillion globally (Callahan & Mankin, 2022).

These are amongst the most pressing leadership challenges of our time, and they are with us today, not lurking in a forecast of an uncertain statistical future. We must listen to these feedback loops that are demanding not only our attention but a reorientation to what good and effective leadership is.

Nurturing Critical Hope

There is a more effective way to mobilise action, though, than rehashing a list of fears, however real. Hope is a more reliable motivator, one that can and must be sustained through action. When it comes to sustainability, our challenges are informed and tempered by hope for greater justice, equity and sustainability. Freire (1994) declared that 'as an ontological need, hope needs practice in order to become historical concreteness … without a minimum of hope, we cannot so much as start the struggle' (p. 2). Preskill and Brookfield (2009) argued that 'hope begins with an effective critique of the present and is sustained by a powerful, unifying vision for the future' (p. 173). Environmental leadership is no different. It requires an effective and piercing critique of the present, coupled with an inspiring and shared vision of the future. We have real challenges, and the road will not be easy, nor will it be fair, because the systems in which we operate do not yet create the equity that we seek. But maintaining a critical hope for the future is essential, lest despair set in and sabotage the work that must be done.

Clarifying the Orienting Purpose of Leadership: Identifying a Direction Through a Literature Review

What, precisely, is our orienting purpose of organisational leadership if not to more effectively address, mitigate and adapt to the challenges that are experienced by every person and organisation on this planet? To craft the aforementioned 'powerful, unifying vision for the future'? And if we can agree on an organising purpose of leadership that centres our environment as both a context and metric of success, how must our practices change to effectively prepare leaders, systems and organisational cultures for these challenges? Despite the fact that environmental leadership is still a marginalised and emergent framing, some authors outlined below have attempted to answer this question and, indeed, the pace has quickened in recent years as broader awareness spreads about the impacts that we are seeing daily of climate change and habitat loss. It is useful, then, to briefly review findings from environmental leadership literature to attempt to identify points of consensus.

What I include here are only those that clearly and explicitly connect their work, research or theorising to some notion of sustainability or environmental leadership, and even then it is incomplete. It should be noted as well that there are many 'sustainability-adjacent' concepts such as systems thinking, social theory and adaptive leadership that much of the environmental leadership theory draws from, which are beyond the scope of this chapter.

In 1992, Wheatley published the first edition of *Leadership and the New Science*, with revelatory impact on the field (and this author). Drawing lessons and exploring application from developments in science and observations of nature, Wheatley writes in the second edition of the text that 'being out in the world with new eyes and a willingness to be taught, I have found that nature and people provide more hopeful examples of self-organisation than I can possibly comprehend' (1999, p. 168). While Wheatley does not explicitly engage with terminology such as environmental or sustainability leadership – and her focus is on translating lessons from nature to organisational settings rather than transforming organisations to better support a sustainable and healthy natural environment – the impact of the book is lasting and worthy of inclusion as a starting point here.

In 1994, Egri and Frost edited a special issue of the journal *Leadership Quarterly*, with a theme of 'the nature of leadership needed to bring about progressive changes in humankind's relationships with the natural environment and with social environments' (p. 195). They argued that the different voices and research represented within the special issue 'display a remarkable convergence on the environmentalist values of egalitarianism, holism, self-actualisation, environmental sustainability, and participative involvement' (p. 199). This is one of the earliest examples of environmental leadership in Western leadership studies literature, and while these themes evolve in some ways with subsequent research and thinking, we will see that they also hold relatively steady throughout.

In 1999, Allen et al. proposed a systems understanding of leadership with principles derived from principles of ecology (interdependence, open systems and feedback loops, cycling of resources and adaptation) and called for a 'radical shift in our perspectives of leadership' that is rooted in an expanded understanding of our place within natural systems (p. 62). This article is a remarkably prescient – and still relevant – foundation upon which many subsequent voices in the field have built their work.

In 2005, Wielkiewicz and Stelzner published a seminal paper in the *Review of General Psychology*, in which they put forth an ecological theory of leadership that makes four assertions, of which two are

> (a) effective leadership processes involve temporary resolution of a tension between the traditional industrial approach and the neglected ecological approach, (b) specific leaders are less important than they appear because the ecological context is more important than what leaders decide to do. (p. 326)

This paper was also later reprinted as a chapter in Redekop's edited text (2010), discussed subsequently.

In 2007, Ferdig argued that sustainability leaders 'lead "with" rather than "over" others in ways that account for the long-term viability of complex, interconnected living systems' (p. 25). She also suggested that 'sustainability leaders embrace the inevitability of continually changing dynamics in everyday life, while developing reasonable actions with others in an integrated framework that provides coherent direction, clear accountability, *and* enough flexibility to allow for mid-course corrections' (Ferdig, 2007, p. 32).

In 2008, the book *The Necessary Revolution: How Individuals and Organizations Are Working Together to Create a Sustainable World* was published, in which Senge et al. suggested that seeing systems, collaborating across boundaries and creating desired futures are the core learning capabilities necessary for systemic change in light of global complex challenges such as climate change. Additionally, Western (2008) employed critical theory to identify four active discourses of leadership: controller, therapist, messiah and, most recently, the emergence of eco-leadership, which in this framework also serves as a metadiscourse to guide the use of the other three more effectively.

In 2009, Middlebrooks et al. reported on results from an academic course designed to foster a sustainability leadership mindset shift, resulting in 'increased awareness, importance, and commitment to sustainability' as well as conceptual shifts in their understanding of the topic (p. 31). In it, they summarised sustainability leadership as (a) 'the ability to see organizational culture', (b) the knowledge and awareness of 'balances and interconnections between bottom lines in the pursuit of sustainable ends', (c) 'a desire to make a positive difference, big picture and long term', (d) 'the ability to influence in a socially just manner' and (e) 'the ability to manage behavior and systems change' (p. 42).

In 2010, Redekop edited the first volume focused on leadership for environmental sustainability and found adaptive leadership, systems thinking and complexity approaches as emergent and shared foundations for much of the contributed content. Redekop concluded with the statement that 'the greatest leaders are those who ... have a vision that is both cosmic and individual, universal and yet pragmatic, highly spiritual but rooted in time and place' (p. 247), suggesting that environmental leadership is precisely the organising principle necessary for such practice.

In 2011, Evans called for sustainable leadership, asserting that leadership is only as good as the purpose it serves and that it should 'specifically aim to create and nurture reciprocal, sustaining relationships among people and between humans and nature. Such leadership would expose the contradictions of exploitative leadership that is ultimately self destructive'

(p. 13). Here, Evans used the term *exploitative leadership* to characterise the extractive nature of modern capitalistic leadership and its extreme and harmful impact on the natural world upon which we all depend.

In 2012, Gallagher edited a prodigious multi-part volume, *Environmental Leadership: A Reference Handbook*, in which Shriberg (2012) convincingly makes the case that sustainability leadership *is* 21st-century leadership. The handbook contains approximately 100 contributions and is far too large to cover effectively here, though far too important to not include.

In 2013, Scharmer and Kaufer argued that we are living in a period of death and rebirth – death of an old system and the messy birth of a new one. To effectively navigate this, they suggested that we need to move 'from an ego-system awareness that cares about the wellbeing of oneself to an *eco*-system awareness that cares about the well-being of all, including oneself' (Scharmer & Kaufer, 2013, p. 2).

In 2015, Bendell & Little made the case that traditional leadership theory is in fact problematic for the pursuit of sustainability and employ a critical approach – using insights from social theory, critical discourse analysis and psychology – to deconstruct and reconstruct leadership into a more useful framework for sustainability. Case et al. (2015) critically examined 'the centrality and importance of environmental science's construction and mobilisation of leadership discourse' (p. 396), ultimately expanding on Grint's work to call for a 'more critically oriented leadership research aligned with an understanding of environmental crises from a political ecology perspective' (p. 413).

Additionally, Schein (2015) helped to fill a gap by asserting that leadership literature would do well to more directly engage with and incorporate the interdisciplinary work of what he calls the ecological worldview literature (inclusive of eco-psychology, deep ecology, environmental psychology, social psychology, ecological economics, integral ecology, indigenous studies and developmental psychology and sustainability). Further, Schein identified five ways in which post-conventional worldviews may be expressed:

1. A greater awareness of context and diversity of worldviews
2. Holding longer historical and future time horizons
3. An enhanced systems consciousness
4. A widening circle of identity and care
5. A consistent capacity for inquiry

Taken together, these indicators help point the way towards the capacities that a developmental approach to environmental leadership should foster.

In 2016, Kuenkel offered a compelling vision for the ways in which collaboration and a collective orientation to leadership both arise from and serve as an effective response to the complex global challenges of our time including climate change.

In 2018, Redekop et al. returned with a follow-up volume to the 2010 text, this time employing a critical lens to analyze dominant narratives, normative assumptions and power relations in leadership, arguing that 'leadership both functions within the natural world and is regulated by it – a critical perspective far outside of traditional theories that are anchored in charisma and power' (p. 243). They continued, concluding that

> The existential challenges of environmental leadership ... call on us to critically revise theory and update our practice. We must move away from leadership theory and practice that operate in myopic ignorance of the larger natural and social systems of which we are a part; that disrupt communities, celebrate position over impact, and serve harmful power dynamics by generating limited narratives of heroism and charisma. Instead, we must commit to developing critical, reflective, and connective practices with one another. The theories that guide us should be grounded in empiricism and intuition, in pragmatism and justice, in lived and inherited wisdom. As responsible inhabitants of the biosphere, we must relentlessly pursue connectedness, collaboration, and justice; in doing so, we will develop leadership practices that better serve people *and* the planet. (p. 244)

Rather than revising leadership theory, in 2019 Allen constructed a set of frameworks and principles derived from observations of natural systems that build upon one another: organisations can evolve, nature has lessons to inspire and help us think differently about our leadership and our organisations and, finally, working with the dynamics of living systems enables us to lead in ways that are more effective for the complex challenges we face today. Principles derived from 'leading from a living systems mindset' include centring interdependence, the crucial value of diversity, the constancy of change, a call to both listen to and intentionally build feedback loops and the concept that living systems only accept solutions that the system helped to build.

Also in 2019, an edited book in the International Leadership Association's Building Leadership Bridges series was published, titled *Evolving Leadership for Collective Wellbeing: Lessons for Implementing the United Nations Sustainable Development Goals* (Steffen et al., 2019), which offers one of the first clear uses of the United Nation Sustainable Development Goals as a framework for effective leadership (see also Satterwhite et al., in press).

Building upon these sources and others, in 2020 the fifth priority of the 2020–2025 *National Leadership Education Research Agenda* was identified as 'contextualizing our leadership education approach to complex problem solving', and the authors (Satterwhite et al., 2020) outlined 10 interrelated learning areas that emerge from reviewing the sustainability leadership literature. They asserted that these learning areas should be the focus of leadership education and development to better prepare leaders and leaderful systems for the complex challenges of today and tomorrow (Satterwhite et al., 2020, p. 65):

1. Centring the biosphere as a fundamental context of leadership (integrating/reconciling anthropocentric and ecocentric ethics)
2. Collaborating across boundaries
3. Developing systems literacy (and by extension understanding leadership to be the capacity of a system or community)
4. Employing critical social theory
5. Expanding our time horizons
6. Increasing comfort with uncertainty and shifting contexts
7. Learning from nature
8. Moving from reactive problem solving to co-creating a desired future
9. Nurturing adaptive capacity in our systems and communities
10. Revisiting, centring and learning from indigenous and non-Western traditions

In 2021, the International Leadership Association released its *General Principles for Leadership Programs* paper, which included a prompt that programs should account for the social contexts and issues in which teaching and learning is taking place, a reference to the United Nations Sustainable Development Goals as a viable framework for leadership education and development and an explicit call that leadership learning should 'create conditions for people and organizations to thrive by addressing equity, justice, and sustainability across diverse populations and contexts' (p. 10).

In this same year, Manolopoulos (2021) called for Earth-centred leadership and extended the famous quip from Burns, saying, 'If leadership remains the most observed and least understood phenomenon on Earth, then environmental leadership remains both the least observed and least understood' (p. 153). Manolopoulos offered a critique of early environmental leadership scholarship, saying that 'what often passes for environmental leadership is actually human-centered-environmental management' (2021, p. 15). He offered, instead, an interesting conception of leadership that balances the traditional focus on 'change-making' with a necessary and equal focus on maintenance, depending on the situation.

Additionally, Kempster and Jackson (2021) called for a shift away from the leader/follower dyadic focus to a leader/stakeholder focus in leadership studies, which has the opportunity to foster 'responsible leadership to enable business to generate value for all stakeholders: shareholders, employees, supply chains, communities, the environment and indeed humanity' (p. 62). Finally, Appelbaum et al. (2021) provided an exploration of both organisational implications and the changes in psychology, consciousness, culture and worldview that are required in a sustainability leadership framework.

In 2022, Satterwhite et al. published a tensions model (see Figure 8.1) that centres the biosphere as a fundamental context of all leadership activities and acknowledged that while some paradigm shifts are underway (and are necessary), other changes that we are either seeking or experiencing are less a shift from one state to another and are instead more about rebalancing between two ever present poles. These pairs of poles include anthropocentric and ecocentric values, long and short timescales, abundance and scarcity, mechanistic and living systems and individual and collective capacity building in the practice of effective leadership.

Stepping back and examining this body of literature together, themes begin to emerge and we can identify the start of a road map to use in reconstructing organisational leadership theory and practice in ways that are bookended by natural systems as both the governing context and sustaining purpose of leadership. Many of these themes are not easy; they fly in the face of conventional practice and philosophy and steer us in new directions that require unlearning much of what we think we know. In the process, we have the opportunity to radically transform our communities and organisations not just for a more sustainable future for but a more just

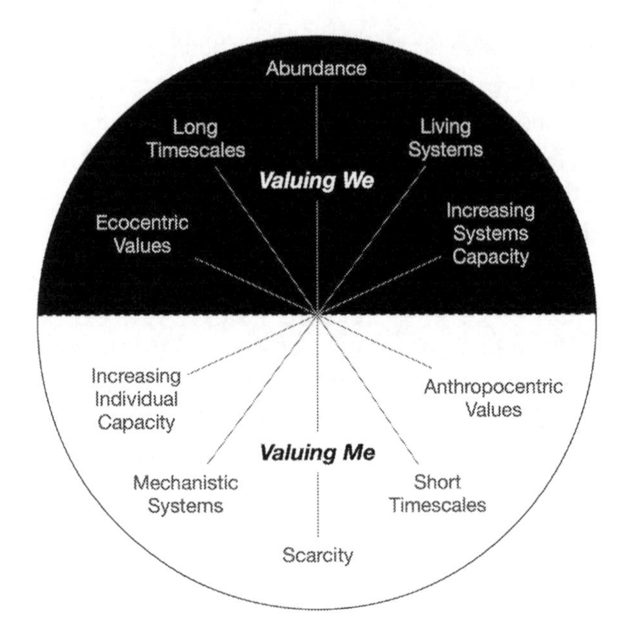

Figure 8.1 Tensions Model

From Satterwhite, Sheridan, & McIntyre Miller (2022). Reprinted with permission.

one. After all, one of the lessons learned is this: we cannot fix our problems with the same tools that created them, nor can we artificially separate the pursuit of a sustainable environment from a socially just one. What follows is an attempt to synthesise these themes into practical recommendations for organisational culture and practice.

Methods, Techniques and Actions: Recommendations From Themes in the Literature

Calls for tending to context as an important factor in leadership theory and practice are not new, but few leadership theories have expanded so far as to include the natural environment. And yet it is inescapable that we all operate within the constraints of the natural world. Its apparent, though false, limitless abundance has in part kept us from appreciating the value of scarcity in fostering creativity and value. As the concept of the Anthropocene becomes more common, the 'responsibility towards otherness' that it brings can become an organising force (Preiser et al., 2017, p. 86).

Environmental leadership requires an expansion of our spheres of concern, care and responsibility to extend to the natural world of which we sometimes must remind ourselves that we are a part. Learning to effectively balance and navigate anthropocentric values and ecocentric values (there is a continuum here; it is not an either/or proposition) is one of the primary individual and organisational tasks. What follows is a set of recommendations for organisations, derived from synthesising some of the previously discussed writing and thinking.

Recommendation #1: Centring the Natural Environment as a Context and Consequence of Contemporary Leadership

Strive for developing metrics, strategic plans and an organisational culture that centres the natural environment as context, constraint and goal. This may start with the triple bottom line but goes well beyond it to centre the natural environment and unborn generations in organisational decisions. Consider, too, place-based practices and extending timelines that you currently make decisions based on. Intentionally investing in sustainability values development must be a high priority for organisations, and building a culture that fosters engagement, transparency and decision making regarding the short- and long-term impacts on the natural world is key.

We should follow the call of Redekop at el. (2018) and critically revise our theory and update our practice to reflect the biosphere *as both context and consequence of leadership*. Unlearning will be an important part of this process, as we have much to deconstruct on our path to effectively reconstructing and reinventing a more effective and contemporary understanding of leadership. Such leadership begins with the environment as a foundational context, focuses on cultivating restorative practices as a fundamental operating principle, and takes a long-term perspective that is uncommon in most of our present practices (Satterwhite et al., 2016).

Recommendation #2: Consuming Less and More Ethically

Seek to better understand, identify and map the consumption habits of your organisation. Critically examine the ethical implications of these trends and identify ways to both reduce overall and improve ethically.

As much as we each carry some personal responsibility for the consumption habits that we maintain, organisations are responsible for a large part of greenhouse gas emissions, with some accounting individually for more than 1% of all U.S. emissions (Political Economy Research Institute, 2021). Our organisations have a responsibility to radically overhaul consumption and waste habits to effectively meet the adaptation needs of our present and future. In addition to reducing our consumption, there is an ethical aspect that we rarely grapple with. Kimmerer (2013) posed a powerful question: 'Whether we are digging wild leaks or going to the mall, how do we consume in a way that does justice to the lives we take?' (p. 177).

Going one step further, restorative leadership is an emerging concept in leadership that goes beyond reducing harm to actively improving the environment and righting the wrongs of the past (see Steffen, 2019).

Recommendation #3: Shifting Our Frameworks of Organisational Power

Right now leadership is conceptually tightly bundled with hierarchy for most people, but that is not going to work moving forward. Hierarchy is not going away. When done well and the true purpose of the system is not lost or co-opted, systems thinking tells us that there are great efficiencies to be had from hierarchical structures. But falsely equating hierarchy with leadership limits our understanding of and conceptual access to leadership practice at a time when we need to be unleashing the full creativity and collective capacity of humanity. Power should be acknowledged and distributed; it is ever-present anyway – a culture of not speaking about it only serves to further shelter and privilege those in power. Bringing it out into the light normalises the conversations that must be had about and accountability that must be built at all levels of an organisation.

Recommendation #4: Centring Collective Leadership and Indigenous Wisdom

Related to shifting our frameworks of power and moving towards a more collective orientation, rigid hierarchy vs. a nonhierarchical approach is the first of 35 contrasts between the common dominant worldview manifestation and common indigenous worldview manifestations presented by Four Arrows (2020, as cited in Four Arrows & Narvaez, 2022). Other contrasts presented in this source that align with and predate the argument I am making here include a focus on self and personal gain vs. emphasis on community welfare, anthropocentric vs. animistic and biocentric, rigid boundaries and fragmented systems vs. flexible boundaries and interconnected systems and learning is fragmented and theoretical vs. learning is holistic and place based. Much of the learning to be done related to environmental leadership is already known and modelled by indigenous traditions and cultures. Yunkaporta (2020) established the universal wisdom that we all have at least a partial claim to far more powerfully than I am capable of:

> All humans evolved within complex, land-based cultures over deep time to develop a brain with the capacity for over one hundred trillion neural connections, of which we now use only a tiny fraction. Most of us have been displaced from those cultures of origin, a global diaspora or refugees severed not only from land but from the sheer genius that comes from belonging in symbiotic relation to it. (p. 2)

Recommendation #5: Clearly Articulating the Differences Between Leadership and Management

Organisations should clearly delineate between management (which is hierarchical) and leadership (which is not). Both are valuable and must be invested in, but professional development initiatives too often conflate the two. Unlocking the full potential of leadership behaviour within an organisation requires that everyone understand that they have access to it and ensuring that the organisational culture and structure is built around this belief as opposed to paying lip service to it. This requires several things to occur. First, it is important to be consistent in differentiating between leadership and management. Second, leadership should be clearly communicated to be something that anyone within an organisation can enact – it occurs whenever someone invests meaningful effort in making a substantial change in the spirit of justice and sustainability. Third, leadership professional development must be a strategic investment and not just for senior or middle management.

Recommendation #6: Fostering Systems Literacy

Identify ways in which your organisation can learn from, be advised by and incorporate wisdom from Indigenous traditions. Caution: this runs the risk of following an all-too-familiar extractive and exploitative tradition, so think carefully about meaningful, authentic ways of doing this.

Systems literacy is not a foreign concept for many organisations, but often the powerful insights that can be achieved are only applied towards the ends of profit and efficiency, not the moral quandaries of our responsibility to each other, to other living organisms and to the unborn generations of the future. Systems thinking can, and should, also lead us down a moral path. Meadows (2008) reminded us that

> Living successfully in a world of complex systems means expanding not only time horizons and thought horizons; above all it means expanding the horizons of caring. There are moral reasons for doing that, of course. And if moral arguments are not sufficient, then systems thinking provides the practical reasons to back up the moral ones... As with everything else about systems, most people already know about the interconnection that make moral and practical rules turn out to be the same rules. They just have to bring themselves to believe that which they know. (p. 184)

Invest in building systems literacy at all levels of an organisation. This may be a risky project for those in power because, equipped with this way of seeing the whole, employees or community members may call for changes in an organisation. But its promise of this practice is transformational and has the potential to transform.

Conclusion

These recommendations may be seen as a simplified – but hopefully useful – distillation of an array of work that has emerged as the field of leadership wrestles with ontological dilemmas related to the domain of leadership. In the dominant Western paradigm, the phenomenon of leadership was originally conceived of as the domain of the few (White men). It was then expanded to be the purview of those with formal positional authority within hierarchical structures. We must continue to push on this boundary so that leadership is democratised and accessible, rooted in a collective and critical hope for the future.

Leadership is, of course, a socially constructed and therefore human endeavour (at least as conceived here), but we do not operate separately from the world, and our leadership behaviours and decisions impact that world in deep and profound ways. We are not just a part of the Earth but are *of the Earth*. 'Our' systems – food systems, economic systems, governing systems – are intertwined with and intimately connected to natural, living systems that we are actively and severely disrupting. Leadership – good, effective leadership – has an important role to play in correcting this and preparing a more sustainable, livable, equitable and just world for our grandchildren and their grandchildren and their grandchildren to live in. It will require a multiplicity of individual, organisational, governmental and metalevel changes, but this work is already underway. My hope is that this chapter helps contribute towards some of that work by offering an imperfect summary of where we are and where we should be heading.

Discussion Points

- What meaningful changes that advance an environmental mindset have you seen recently in your organisational setting?
- What resistance have you seen recently in your organisational setting to meaningful changes in this same direction?
- What changes are possible within your sphere of influence in the near term that would be consistent with the recommendations in this chapter?
- What would it mean for your organisation to genuinely factor the natural environment as a core stakeholder? As a fundamental context and consequence of its operations?
- What would it look like for your organisation to embrace a 'leaderful' orientation, where leadership is actively encouraged at all levels of the organisation?
- What would that look like to embrace a longer-term perspective in the day-to-day operations of your organisation?

Suggested Reading

Allen, K. (2019). *Leading from the roots: Nature-inspired leadership lessons for today's world.* Morgan James.

Kuenkel, P. (2016). *The Art of leading collectively: Co-creating a sustainable, socially just future.* Chelsea Green.

Redekop, B., Gallagher, D., & Satterwhite, R. (Eds.). (2018). *Innovation in environmental leadership: Critical perspectives.* Routledge.

References

Allen, K. (2019). *Leading from the roots: Nature-inspired leadership lessons for today's world.* Morgan James.

Allen, K., Stelzner, S., & Wielkiewicz, R. (1999). The ecology of leadership: Adapting to the challenges of a changing world. *Journal of Leadership & Organizational Studies, 5*(2), 62–82. https://journals.sagepub.com/doi/pdf/10.1177/107179199900500207

Appelbaum, R. P., Steiner, F., Stillman, P., & Willis, D. B. (2021). *Leadership in sustainability: Perspectives on research, policy, and practice.* Fielding University Press.

Bendell, J., & Little, R. (2015). Seeking sustainability leadership. *The Journal of Corporate Citizenship, 60,* 13–66. https://www.jstor.org/stable/10.2307/jcorpciti.60.13

Callahan, C. W., & Mankin, J. S. (2022). Globally unequal effect of extreme heat on economic growth. *Science Advances, 8,* 1–22. https://doi.org/10.1126/sciadv.add3726

Capra, F., & Luisi, P. L. (2014). *The systems view of life: A unifying vision.* Cambridge University Press.

Case, P., Evans, L. S., Fabinyi, M., Cohen, P. J., Hicks, C. C., Prideaux, M., & Mills, D. J. (2015). Rethinking environmental leadership: The social construction of leaders and leadership in discourses of ecological crisis, development, and conservation. *Leadership, 11*(4), 396–423. https://doi.org/10.1177/1742715015577887

Cowie, R. H., Bouchet, P., & Fontaine, B. (2022). The sixth mass extinction: Fact, fiction, or speculation? *Biological Reviews, 97,* 640–663. https://doi.org/10.1111/brv.12816

Egri, C. P., & Frost, P. J. (1994). Leadership for environmental and social change. *Leadership Quarterly, 5*(3/4), 195–200. https://doi.org/10.1016/1048-9843(94)90011-6

Evans, T. (2011, March). Leadership without domination? Toward restoring the human and natural world. *Journal of Sustainability Education, 2,* 1–16. http://www.jsedimensions.org/wordpress/wp-content/uploads/2011/03/Evans2011.pdf

Ferdig, M. A. (2007). Sustainability leadership: Co-creating a sustainable future. *Journal of Change Management, 7*(1), 25–35. https://doi.org/10.1080/14697010701233809

Freire, P. (1994). *Pedagogy of hope: Reliving pedagogy of the oppressed.* Continuum.

Four Arrows, & Narvaez, D. (2022). *Restoring the kinship worldview: Indigenous voices introduce 28 precepts for rebalancing life on planet Earth.* North Atlantic Books.

Gallagher, D. R. (Ed.). (2012). *Environmental leadership: A reference handbook.* Sage.

Grint, K. (2005). Problems, problems, problems: The social construction of 'leadership'. *Human Relations, 58*(11), 1467–1494. doi: 10.1177/0018726705061314

Guthrie, K., & Chunoo, V. S. (Eds.). (2018). *Changing the narrative: Socially just leadership education.* Information Age.

Heifetz, R. (2006). Anchoring leadership in the work of adaptive progress. In F. Hesselbein & M. Goldsmith (Eds.), *The leader of the future 2: Visions, strategies, and practices for the new era* (pp. 73–84). Jossey-Bass.

Institute for Economics and Peace. (2022). *Ecological threat report 2022: Analysing ecological threats, resilience, and peace.* https://www.economicsandpeace.org

International Leadership Association. (2021). *General principles for leadership programs, concept paper 2021.* https://ilaglobalnetwork.org/wp-content/uploads/2021/02/Feb-8-2021_-ILA-General-Principles-Concept-Paper.pdf

Kellerman, B. (2012). *The end of leadership.* HarperCollins.

Kellerman, B. (2018). *Professionalizing leadership.* Oxford University Press.

Kempster, S., & Jackson, B. (2021). Leadership for what, why, for whom and where? A responsibility perspective. *Journal of Change Management, 21*(2), 45–65. https://doi.org/10.1080/14697017.2021.1861721

Kimmerer, R. W. (2013). *Braiding sweetgrass: Indigenous wisdom, scientific knowledge, and the teachings of the plants.* Milkweed Editions.

Kolditz, T., Gill, L., & Brown, R. P. (2021). *Leadership reckoning: Can higher education develop the leaders we need?* Monocle Press.

Kuenkel, P. (2016). *The Art of leading collectively: Co-creating a sustainable, socially just future.* Chelsea Green.

Liu, H. (2021). *Redeeming leadership: An anti-racist feminist intervention.* Bristol University Press.

Manolopoulos, M. (2021). *A theory of environmental leadership: Leading for the Earth.* Routledge.

Meadows, D. (2008). *Thinking in systems: A primer.* Chelsea Green.

Middlebrooks, A., Miltenberger, L., Tweedy, J., Newman, G., & Follman, J. (2009). Developing a sustainability ethic in leaders. *Journal of Leadership Studies, 3*(2), 31–43. https://doi.org/10.1002/jls.20106

Political Economy Research Institute. (2021). Greenhouse 100 Polluters Index. https://peri.umass.edu/greenhouse-100-polluters-index-current

Preiser, R., Pereira, L. M., & Biggs, R. (2017). Navigating alternative framings of human–environment interactions: Variations on the theme of 'Finding Nemo'. *Anthropocene, 20*, 83–87. https://doi.org/10.1016/j.ancene.2017.10.003

Preskill, S. & Brookfield, S. D. (2009). *Learning as a way of leading: Lessons from the struggle for social justice.* Jossey-Bass.

Raelin, J. A. (2016). Imagine there are no leaders: Reframing leadership as collaborative agency. *Leadership, 12*(2), 131–158.

Redekop, B. (Ed.). (2010). *Leadership for environmental sustainability*. Routledge.

Redekop, B., Gallagher, D., & Satterwhite, R. (Eds.). (2018). *Innovation in environmental leadership: Critical perspectives*. Routledge.

Satterwhite, R., Sarid, A., Cunningham, C. M., Goryunova, E., Crandall, H. M., Morrison, J. L., Sheridan, K., & McIntyre Miller, W. (2020). Contextualizing our leadership education approach to complex problem solving: Shifting paradigms and evolving knowledge – Priority 5 of the National Leadership Education Research Agenda 2020–2025. *Journal of Leadership Studies, 14*(3), 63–71. https://doi.org/10.1002/jls.21717

Satterwhite, R., Sheridan, K., & McIntyre Miller, W. (2016). Rediscovering deep time: Sustainability and the need to re-engage with multiple dimensions of time in leadership studies. *Journal of Leadership Studies, 9*(4), 47–53. https://doi.org/10.1002/jls.21426

Satterwhite, R., Sheridan, K., & McIntyre Miller, W. (2022). Tensions in sustainability leadership. In K. Guthrie & K. Priest (Eds.), *Navigating complexities in leadership: Moving towards critical hope* (pp. 27–38). Information Age.

Satterwhite, R., Sheridan, K., & McIntyre Miller, W. (in press). Introduction to leadership for complex problems and the United Nations Sustainable Development Goals. *New Directions for Student Leadership.*

Scharmer, O., & Kaufer, K. (2013). *Leading from the emerging future: From ego-system to eco-system economies.* Berrett-Koehler.

Schein, S. (2015). *A new psychology for sustainability leadership: The hidden power of ecological worldviews.* Greenleaf.

Senge, P., Smith, B., Kruschwitz, N., Laur, J., & Schley, L. (2008). *The necessary revolution: How individuals and organizations are working together to create a sustainable world.* Doubleday.

Shriberg, M. (2012). Sustainability leadership as 21st century leadership. In D. Gallagher (Ed.), *Environmental leadership: A reference handbook* (pp. 469–478). Sage.

Steffen, S. L. (2019). The emergence of restorative leadership. In S. L. Steffen, J. Rezmovits, S. Trevenna, & S. Rappaport (Eds.), *Evolving leadership for collective wellbeing: Lessons for implementing the United Nations Sustainable Development Goals.* Emerald.

Steffen, S. L., Rezmovits, J., Trevenna., S., & Rappaport, S. (Eds). (2019). *Evolving leadership for collective wellbeing: Lessons for implementing the United Nations Sustainable Development Goals.* Emerald.

Western, S. (2008). *Leadership: A critical text* (1st ed.). Sage.
Western, S. (2019). *Leadership: A critical text* (3rd ed.). Sage.
Wheatley, M. (1992). *Leadership and the new science* (1st ed.). Berrett-Koehler.
Wheatley, M. (1999). *Leadership and the new science* (2nd ed.). Berrett-Koehler.
Wielkiewicz, R. M., & Stelzner, S. P. (2005). An ecological perspective on leadership theory, research, and practice. *Review of General Psychology, 9*(4), 326–341. https://doi.org/10.1037/1089-2680.9.4.326
World Wildlife Fund. (2022). *Living planet report 2022*. https://livingplanet.panda.org/en-US/
Yunkaporta, T. (2020). *Sand talk: How indigenous thinking can save the world.* HarperCollins.

Part II

TRANSITIONS

9

GREEN LEADERSHIP

Talib Karamally and Jennifer L. Robertson

Chapter Summary

As we move into the third decade of the new millennium, academic and practitioner interest in corporate environmental responsibility has become widespread. The implementation and subsequent success of any environmental responsibility activity is largely dependent on organisational leaders who exhibit environmental leadership. Several leadership styles have been linked to environmental responsibility, with environmentally specific transformational leadership (ETFL) being the dominant style shown to have a significant impact. This chapter starts by reviewing conceptualisations and frameworks of environmental leadership. We then review the definition of ETFL and explicate its primary dimensions. Additionally, we discuss the relevant theories surrounding ETFL and describe the measurement of this form of environmental leadership. To better understand how such leadership manifests in the workplace, this chapter outlines outcomes of ETFL, including its impact on subordinates, while also discussing some potential predictors of this

DOI: 10.4324/9781003343011-11

leadership style. Finally, to provide an example of how ETFL can be applied within an organisational setting, this chapter presents a case study detailing an instance in which this leadership style has been successfully leveraged in a private sector company. The chapter ends with recommendations for future research and suggests ways in which ETFL can be cultivated in organisations.

Green Leadership

The results from the Intergovernmental Panel on Climate Change are alarming: climate change is widespread and escalating rapidly (Masson-Delmotte et al., 2021). *Climate change* refers to any enduring changes in average temperature or weather patterns that may result in storms, heat waves, changing sea levels, shifts in precipitation patterns and the acidification of oceans (Intergovernmental Panel on Climate Change, 2021). Scientists have concluded that accelerated changes in climate patterns since the 1950s are human induced (Intergovernmental Panel on Climate Change, 2021; Zalasiewicz et al., 2011) and driven primarily by burning fossil fuels such as coal, gas and oil (National Research Council, 2010), which in turn leads to large volumes of greenhouse gases in the atmosphere. Other behaviours, such as overconsumption, littering and polluting the environment, also contribute to environmental degradation (Gifford, 2011; National Research Council, 2010; Swim et al., 2011).

Corporations have been identified as some of the primary emitters of greenhouse gases (Sakhel, 2017). As such, political, social and economic pressures have been placed on corporations to become more environmentally responsible (Babiak & Trendafilova, 2011; Wu et al., 2022). Given that leaders have a high degree of decision-making power within the corporate sphere (Mazutis & Zintel, 2015), the role of leaders is relevant to resolving environmental problems proliferated by organisations. Indeed, scholars have suggested that it is important to focus on the psychological factors driving leader behaviour (e.g., Robertson & Barling, 2015). Psychological interventions can be utilised to develop leaders' motivational states to make them more effective at directing a pro-environmental paradigm. Thus, organisational scholarship is increasingly focused on environmental leadership.

By drawing upon academic research and a case example of environmental leadership at a Canadian organisation, this chapter outlines the role of leaders in positively influencing their organisation's environmental responsibility. To do so, this chapter first provides an overview of environmental leadership by discussing the differences in various conceptualisations and frameworks as well as by demonstrating how it differs from traditional leadership. We then turn our attention to focus on ETFL, a style of environmental leadership that has been dominant in the literature. Thereafter, we consider the recent development of environmentally specific servant leadership as an alternative style of environmental leadership. To highlight ETFL within practice, we discuss how the leadership at Tentree, a Canadian tree-planting company, can be characterised as ETFL. Finally, the chapter closes by making recommendations for future research, highlighting how environmental leadership may be cultivated in organisational settings.

Environmental Leadership: Conceptualisations and Frameworks

Environmental leadership can be understood in different ways. For example, there are person-based, outcome-based, process-based, position-based and purpose-based conceptualisations of leadership (Grint et al., 2016). While researchers may assume one or another of these constructions in their definitions, we will not critique or analyze the theoretical basis of such conceptualisations because it is beyond the scope of this chapter. Rather, this chapter is concerned with the practical definitions, associated models and frameworks of environmental leadership proposed as organisational solutions for addressing the empirical problems of climate change.

While there are different definitions of environmental leadership in the literature, most emphasise the necessity of moving away from traditional leadership by putting the environment at the centre of organisational concerns. Berry and Gordon (1993) proposed one of the earliest definitions of environmental leadership: 'the ability of an individual or a group to guide positive change toward a vision of an environmentally better future' (p. 3). Berry and Gordon emphasised that this change must happen owing to the unique difficulties environmental challenges present. Given the long-term, complex, multidisciplinary and emotion-charged nature of environmental concerns, these authors stressed the need for a new leadership style that is radically distinct from traditional leadership.

Shrivastava (1994) also advocated for a new leadership style and focused on the concept of eco-centric management, which 'places ecology at the center of corporate and management concerns, rather than at their periphery' (p. 224). Shrivastava stated that the goal of eco-centric management is to improve the circumstances of organisational stakeholders while increasing growth and profits in ethical and environmentally sustainable ways. Egri and Herman (2000) developed this way of thinking about environmental leadership but emphasised leaders' embodiment of ecocentric values. They defined environmental leadership as 'the ability to influence individuals and mobilize organizations to realize a vision of long-term ecological sustainability' (Egri & Herman, 2000, p. 572).

Portugal and Yukl (1994) also focused on the role of leader influence, particularly as it relates to influencing external stakeholders such as the environment. This framework recognises two *levels* of influence: individual and organisational. Individual-level influence focuses on interactions between individuals or small groups (e.g., subordinates and managers). Organisational-level influence focuses on influencing many people simultaneously by analyzing aspects, such as organisational policies, structures and culture. Furthermore, the framework recognises two *types* of influence: internal and external. Internal influence focuses on influence among members of the same organisation. External influence focuses on influencing those outside the organisation (e.g., suppliers and government entities). For example, individual-level influence may involve a manager persuading subordinates to recycle used paper, while organisational-level influence may involve implementing a company-wide environmental policy. Internal influence, on the other hand, may involve leaders meeting with subordinates to determine ways to reduce waste produced by the organisation, while external leadership may involve forming relationships with outside organisations to solve environmental issues.

More recent definitions of environmental leadership, like that of Gallagher's (2012), underscore the urgency of environmental concerns and the collective action required to address them promptly. Thus, she argued that everyone should be encouraged to become environmental leaders. Given these ideas, Gallagher's definition of environmental leadership includes not just leaders but all humans. She stressed the need for leaders to regard their environmental mission as extending beyond the organisation by acknowledging the interests of a broad network of stakeholders that includes not only humans but all living entities. Consequently, Gallagher defined environmental leadership as 'a process by which Earth's inhabitants apply interpersonal influence and engage in collective action to protect the planet's natural resources and its inhabitants from further harm' (2012, p. 5). Although Gallagher's definition evokes a broad framework designed to apply to all organisations, government bodies, private enterprise and individuals, she noted that '[t]he private sector is increasingly the setting for acts of environmental leadership' (Gallagher, 2012, p. 8). Accordingly, we believe her model is appropriate for the corporate context as leaders can use a process of collective action and interpersonal influence to advance environmental goals while stimulating innovation and prosperity.

More recently, Robertson and Barling (2015) presented an environmental leadership framework that emphasises leaders' personal values, attitudes and perceptions. They argued that environmental leadership involves a shared vision of environmental sustainability that motivates individuals to build sustainable organisations in a socially just manner while respecting the environment. In addition, Robertson and Barling defined environmental leadership as 'a process in which, inspired by their own personal values, leaders strive to influence others at all levels of the organization ... to benefit the natural environment' (2015, p. 166). In this chapter, we adopt the definition of Robertson and Barling as we believe it is the one of the more comprehensive definitions given its focuses on the role of leaders' values, attitudes and perceptions in influencing their organisations to achieve environmental outcomes.

Contrasting Environmental Leadership With Traditional Leadership

To comprehend the novel features of environmental leadership, it is helpful to clarify how environmental leadership is distinguished from traditional forms of leadership. We see three main ways in which these types of leadership differ. First, traditional leadership prioritises the bottom line, whereas environmental leaders prioritise nature and humans' interdependence with the natural world, incorporating these latter factors into corporate goals (Egri & Herman, 2000; Hart, 1995; Johnson, 1998; Shrivastava, 1995).

Gallagher (2012) stated that environmental leaders follow the New Environmental Paradigm (NEP), which highlights that much human activity has devastating consequences for the planet upon which humans depend (Dunlap & Van Liere, 1978; Dunlap et al., 2000). Recent developments in the NEP attempt to integrate the value of the natural world into the corporate sphere by widening the definition of organisational success.[1] For example, Elkington's triple bottom line introduced a shift in traditional financial accounting by moving away from a single bottom line (i.e., profit) to a triple bottom line, which not only calculates profit but also measures social and environmental impacts (Elkington, 2004). Traditional leadership has been more focused on the single bottom line, whereas environmental leadership, rooted in the more recent applications of the NEP, prioritises Elkington's triple bottom line. Second, traditional leadership styles assume that nature exists to serve humans, whereas environmental leadership advocates that humans should identify with and value nature (Egri, 1997; Shrivastava, 1994). Third, traditional and environmental leadership styles view stakeholders differently. Environmental leadership recognises a broader network of stakeholders external to the traditional organisation, including non-human stakeholders (Gallagher, 2012). As a result, environmental leadership pushes traditional boundaries by not strictly focusing on the narrow scope of internal financial interests. This idea is part of a larger expansion of stakeholder perspectives, from the focus on private profits to public good (Dietz et al., 2002; Egri & Herman, 2000; Johnson, 1998). Unlike traditional leaders, environmental leaders navigate the challenge of carefully balancing economic prosperity and environmental sustainability (Gallagher, 2012).

The Relevance of Transformational Leadership

Although there have been many leadership styles applied to the environmental context (e.g., laissez-faire, transactional: Graves & Sarkis, 2012; ethical: Metcalf & Benn, 2013; participatory: Siebenhüner & Arnold, 2007; servant: Mughal et al., 2022), transformational leadership remains the dominant theory used to understand environmental leadership (Robertson & Barling, 2015). Transformational leadership comprises a cluster of qualities and behaviours, including encouraging and inspiring followers to exceed their expectations and goals, helping followers grow and develop into leaders themselves and ensuring that the goals of followers and the organisation are aligned (Bass & Bass, 2008; Bass & Riggio, 2006). Specifically, transformational leadership comprises four behaviours: idealised influence, inspirational motivation, intellectual stimulation and individualised consideration (Bass & Riggio, 2006). Idealised influence constitutes behaviours that confidently communicate purpose and value and help leaders gain respect from followers who view their leaders as worth emulating. Inspirational motivation refers to how much a leader fosters follower motivation by expressing enthusiasm for organisational goals while articulating a compelling vision of the future that reveals their values. Intellectual stimulation involves stimulating followers to think in creative and innovative ways. Finally, individualised consideration involves developing and mentoring individual followers (Bass & Riggio, 2006).

According to Gladwin (1993), transformational leadership is needed to inspire and guide the 'fundamental transformations of mission, structure, and political, cultural, and technical systems' (p. 53) required for environmental sustainability. Accordingly, Portugal and Yukl (1994) were among the first to apply transformational theory to environmental leadership, delineating how transformational leadership could be expressed in ways that seek to positively impact corporate environmental responsibility. Specifically, these authors demonstrated how environmental inspirational motivation could manifest as expressing an engaging vision of environmental sustainability, while environmental intellectual stimulation could be expressed by challenging subordinates' ways of thinking about the environment. Environmental expressions of individualised influence can surface as role-modelling behaviours to show leaders' devotion to nature (Portugal & Yukl, 1994). The remaining dimension of transformational leadership (i.e., individualised consideration) was later applied to environmental concerns by Graves and Sarkis (2012), who defined it as a leader's willingness to gauge each employee's ability to attend to environmental concerns while providing customised developmental opportunities.

Environmentally Specific Transformational Leadership

These different attempts to apply transformational leadership behaviours to environmental problems inspired the development of a target-specific transformational leadership style, namely, ETFL. The idea of target-specific transformational leadership is illustrated when the behaviours that comprise transformational leadership are targeted to influence specific outcomes (Robertson, 2018). Over the years, this idea has percolated in the literature, and scholars have demonstrated that target-specific transformational leadership is a predictor of specific targeted behaviours. For example, Barling et al. (2002) invoked the concept of safety-specific transformational leadership. Beauchamp et al. (2011) extended the focus of target-specific transformational leadership to teaching. Finally, Robertson and Barling (2013) leveraged the notion of target-specific transformational leadership to formalise the idea of ETFL, defining it as 'a manifestation of transformational leadership in which the content of the leadership behaviors are all focused on encouraging pro-environmental initiatives' (p. 177).

Extending the work of Portugal and Yukl (1994) and Graves and Sarkis (2012), Robertson and Barling (2013, 2015) applied the four behaviours that comprise transformational leadership to the environmental context by outlining how these behaviours can manifest as an expression of environmental leadership. Through environmental idealised influence, leaders show how highly they value nature and behave as environmental role models. By expressing environmental inspirational motivation, leaders encourage environmentally friendly behaviours and demonstrate passion and optimism for improving the environment. Environmental intellectual stimulation involves focusing on encouraging others to think creatively and innovatively about environmental problems. Finally, environmental individualised consideration is displayed by leaders who recognise others' abilities to improve an organisation's environmental performance, help others develop these capacities and acknowledge their environmental contributions. Based on this conceptualisation, we and others began to empirically demonstrate how ETFL can successfully affect corporate environmental responsibility.

Notable Empirical Findings of ETFL

Since ETFL is focused on influencing environmental initiatives, researchers began to demonstrate how ETFL both directly and indirectly affects employees' pro-environmental behaviours. In terms of the direct effects, several studies have consistently shown leaders who exhibit ETFL can directly affect employees' pro-environmental behaviours (e.g., Graves et al., 2019; Robertson & Barling, 2017; Robertson & Carleton, 2018). A notable study by Robertson and Barling (2017) demonstrated that compared to general transformational leadership, participants exposed to ETFL engaged in higher levels of pro-environmental behaviours. In doing so, this research provided some evidence for the construct and predictive validity of ETFL over general transformational leadership.

With respect to indirect effects, researchers have examined several individual and contextual factors that mediate the relationship between ETFL and employees' environmental performance. Graves et al. (2013) demonstrated that ETFL was associated with higher levels of employees' autonomous and external motivation. Additionally, they found that employees' autonomous motivation was positively related to pro-environmental behaviours. Turning to emotive mediators, Robertson and Barling (2013) showed that ETFL affects employees' pro-environmental behaviours by first invoking passion for environmental concerns. Robertson and Barling also found that leaders' environmental descriptive norms are an antecedent to ETFL. More recently, research has shown that ETFL can indirectly predict employees' pro-environmental behaviours by impacting employees' environmental concern (Kura, 2016), motivation (Graves & Sarkis, 2018; Graves et al., 2019) and their beliefs in their ability to propel environmental initiatives (W. Kim et al., 2020). Robertson and Carleton (2018) focused on a contextual variable, examining how ETFL fosters a climate in which employees' co-workers support environmental initiatives, which in turn influences employees' environmentally responsible behaviours. At the group level, Peng et al. (2021) demonstrated that ETFL can indirectly predict team pro-environmental behaviours by cultivating team environmental harmonious passion and team pro-environmental goal clarity.

Within several of these studies, the researchers also examined whether any variables strengthened or weakened (i.e., moderating variables) the effects of ETFL. For example, Robertson and Carleton (2018) explored the moderating effects of internal environmental locus of control (i.e., the extent to which one feels responsible for and able to positively affect environmental outcomes; Cleveland & Kalamas, 2015). In doing so, they found that the indirect relationship between ETFL and employees' pro-environmental behaviours through organisational climate perceptions was only significant for employees who were moderate, high or very high in internal environmental locus of control. Graves and Sarkis (2018) found that employees' values moderated the relationship between environmental leadership and employees' internal motivation. Specifically, their findings demonstrated that environmental leadership had the strongest positive association with internal motivation when employees had strong environmental values. Graves and colleagues (2019) subsequently examined ETFL as a moderator itself, finding that employees' external motivation and workplace pro-environmental behaviours were positively correlated only when ETFL was high and negatively correlated when ETFL was low. Finally, the study conducted by Peng et al. (2021) examined the moderating effect of power distance and found that the environmental outcomes of ETFL (i.e., pro-environmental goal clarity, pro-environmental harmonious passion and subsequent pro-environmental behaviours) were stronger in groups with high power distance, as such groups are more likely to behave according to the requests of their leaders.

More recently, research has moved beyond pro-environmental behaviour to examine the effects of ETFL on other relevant variables. For example, a study by Al-Ghazali et al. (2022) demonstrated that green transformational leadership predicted employees' green creativity (i.e., the development of new and valuable environmentally sustainable products, methods, and practices). The study's results also demonstrated that green organisational identity (i.e., an organisation's central, distinctive and enduring characteristic from an environmental standpoint) and green thinking (i.e., individuals' concern for and awareness of environmental issues) mediated this relationship.

Many of the aforementioned studies used modified scales of transformational leadership (e.g., the Multifactor Leadership Questionnaire and the Transformational Teaching Questionnaire) to measure ETFL (e.g., Graves et al., 2013; Robertson & Barling, 2013, 2017). While it is not uncommon to use modified scales to measure a new construct, doing so can raise concerns regarding the validity and reliability of findings. Robertson (2018) highlighted these concerns, noting that deleting and modifying a questionnaire's items can damage its psychometric properties, thereby raising questions as to whether the construct was measured correctly. Thus, Robertson developed a psychometrically valid and reliable scale of ETFL that contains 12 items and four subscales that measures the four dimensions of ETFL. The conceptualisation of ETFL and the definitions of its four dimensions were used to create the relevant items for each dimension. To enhance its usability both in practice and research, Robertson also created an abbreviated version of this scale by selecting the item with the highest factor loading on its target dimension from the four subscales. Each of these scales demonstrated good reliability (i.e., overall ETFL scale, α =.93; abbreviated scale, α =.82) as well as good convergent, divergent, concurrent and nomological validity. Since its development, this scale has been utilised and adapted in recent research (e.g., Peng et al., 2020, 2021), providing greater confidence in the findings between ETFL and environmental outcomes.

Environmentally Specific Servant Leadership

Scholars have recognised that the literature on environmental leadership disproportionately focuses on transformational leadership (e.g., Roberston & Barling, 2015). Parallel research examining the effect of other types of leadership styles on corporate environmental responsibility is lacking. Consequently, Robertson and Barling (2017) put forth a call for researchers to move beyond the transformational leadership paradigm and focus on other forms of leadership, such as servant leadership. The notion of servant leadership was introduced by Greenleaf (1977) and defined by Spears (1996) as 'a new kind of leadership model … which puts serving others as the number one priority. Servant-leadership emphasizes increased service to others; a holistic approach to work; promoting a sense of community; and the sharing of power in decision making' (p. 33). Christensen et al. (2014) argued that servant leadership's concern for others is important for predicting environmental sustainability.

Given the relevance of servant leadership to environmental outcomes, scholars have proposed environmentally specific servant leadership as a style of leadership in which leaders cater to followers' environmental interests (Tuan, 2020). Similar to ETFL, environmentally specific servant leadership predicts a variety of pro-environmental outcomes such as employees' pro-environmental behaviours (Faraz et al., 2021; Fatoki, 2021; Mughal et al., 2022), environmental innovation (Tuan, 2020), organisational environmental citizenship behaviour (Islam et al., 2022) and employee workplace in-role and extra-role green behaviours (Gu & Liu, 2022). A 16-item scale, which Luu (2018) adapted from Liden et al.'s (2008) servant leadership measure, is commonly used to assess environmentally specific servant leadership. Luu chose items from Liden et al.'s scale that could be altered so that they are relevant in the context of influencing environmental outcomes. The scale has been used by researchers (e.g., Afsar et al., 2018) and has demonstrated acceptable reliability (Siddiquei et al., 2021).

Why Should Organisations Strive for Environmental Leadership?

There are numerous reasons why environmental leadership is beneficial for organisations beyond the ethical goal of mitigating environmental damage. First, environmental leadership is associated with not only an organisation's environmental performance but also its financial performance (Su et al., 2020). In fact, companies that adopt environmental leadership financially outperform comparable companies in the same industry and sector that do not adopt environmental leadership (DiSegni et al., 2015). Thus, environmental responsibility is a worthwhile pursuit as it may lead to better financial performance through cost reduction as evidenced by lower material and energy consumption and reduced environmental liabilities (Graafland & Mazereeuw-Van der Duijn Schouten, 2012). An organisational example of these findings can be seen in Autosmart, a used car dealership company. Autosmart benefited from improved sales and reduced inefficiencies by participating in a British environmental management program (Robinson & Clegg, 1998). Second, there are various employee-related benefits to environmental leadership. For example, an organisation's engagement in corporate environmental responsibility is positively associated with employee commitment (Choongo, 2017) and job satisfaction (Krémer, 2019). Third, companies that strive for environmental leadership are more likely than those that do not to maintain their social license and improve their social reputation by being more likely to be perceived as environmentally responsible by the community (Melo & Garrido-Morgado, 2012). Taken together, the research clearly demonstrates the benefits of environmental leadership and should be used as evidence to persuade more organisations to cultivate environmental leadership styles among their leaders within their organisational hierarchies.

Case Example of ETFL: Tentree

Having outlined the research on the positive effects of ETFL on corporate environmental responsibility and the benefits of cultivating environmental leadership more generally, we now turn our attention to what ETFL looks like in an organisation. To do so, we provide a case example of ETFL that is exhibited by Tentree, [2] a Canadian tree-planting company that sells apparel for carbon footprint offsetting purposes. *Tentree's The Environmentor* blog provides an overview of the company's history (Henczel, n.d.). According to the blog, in 2011, Derrick and Kalen Emsley implemented a business model that involved planting trees for every clothing item purchased by a customer. Tentree was subsequently founded in 2012 with Derrick assuming the role of CEO. The business grew, and the brothers committed to creating the most environmentally progressive clothing possible, recognising the opportunity to challenge the clothing industry, which has created much environmental damage. According to the company's blog, the company hit a milestone in 2014 by planting 1 million trees, thereby creating 160,000 h of work for individuals in developing countries. Tentree also introduced the Impact Wallet tree registry app in 2014, which visually depicts where customers' trees are planted. In 2016, Tentree's environmental commitment and accountability were validated by a B Corp certification, which is only given to businesses that meet rigorous standards of transparency, accountability and social and environmental responsibility. In 2020, the company started the Climate+ program, which offers tree-planting packages that help consumers offset the environmental damage associated with their lifestyles. That same year, the company planted 50 million trees, accomplishing a major milestone (Henczel, n.d.).

We assert that these environmental achievements and accolades were obtained through Tentree's environmental leadership. More specifically, we believe that Tentree's top leadership team exhibits the four primary dimensions of ETFL. Through environmental idealised influence, Derrick demonstrated a strong value for the natural environment by emphasising that the organisation 'exist[s] to plant trees' (Emsley & Becker, 2021, para. 4). Tentree's focus on planting trees helps to offset carbon dioxide being released into the atmosphere to help restore the environmental imbalance causing climate change (Cluff, 2022). According to Derrick, 'While tree planting is not a silver bullet, it can be an incredibly important part of the climate crisis solution if done correctly' (Cluff, 2022, para. 11). Further exhibiting environmental idealised influence, Tentree's leadership has demonstrated effective environmental role modelling behaviours by, for example, getting their suppliers to sign a code of conduct that obliges them to be transparent about their environmental footprint, mitigate their environmental damage and make efforts to improve their environmental performance (Tentree, n.d.b). Tentree's leadership embodies environmental inspirational motivation by motivating environmentally friendly behaviours. They do this by encouraging other businesses to integrate the Veritree platform into their business models to incentivise their customers to plant trees and track their environmental impact (Cluff, 2022). Moreover, Tentree's leadership expresses optimism about Veritree's influence on other businesses' abilities to positively impact the environment. Derrick stated, 'Veritree exists as a separate entity that enables businesses – and their consumers – to move towards a restorative business model where they can do "more good" for the environment, rather than "less harm"' (Cluff, 2022, para. 14). By encouraging other businesses to adopt Veritree and emphasising its ability to change the way organisations do business, Tentree's leadership inspires and motivates other businesses to adopt corporate environmental responsibility practices and demonstrates optimism about a future in which organisations do not contribute to climate change but rather are key players in helping to restore the planet (Emsley & Becker, 2021). The leadership at Tentree also embodies environmental intellectual stimulation. For instance, Tentree leaders demonstrate a willingness to implement novel and creative metrics of success (i.e., number of trees planted instead of profits earned), demonstrating leadership that inspires others to think of success in terms of environmental sustainability (Emsley & Becker, 2021). Moreover, by describing Tentree as 'a tree-planting company that sells apparel, not an apparel company that plants trees' (Emsley & Becker, 2021, para. 1), Emsley gets people to think of his company in an unconventional way by putting trees instead of apparel at the centre of the business. Finally, Tentree's leadership demonstrates environmental individualised consideration. By tracking and publishing the number of trees planted on behalf of each customer (Tentree, n.d.a), Tentree's leadership recognises individuals' contributions to environmental sustainability. By exhibiting the four dimensions of ETFL, followers are often consumers engaged in the common pursuit of eco-values. This active customer followership suggests that the influence of Tentree's leadership expands beyond the traditional leader–follower relationship.

Directions for Future Research

Although research on ETFL has moved passed its infancy stage, we see ample opportunities for future research on this style of environmental leadership. First, given that most research on ETFL has focused on its consequences (Robertson & Barling, 2013), we believe it will be fruitful for future studies to focus on how ETFL can be developed. There exists ample empirical evidence demonstrating that characteristics of transformational leadership can be developed using different approaches, such as role-playing exercises and self-awareness training (e.g., Barling et al., 1996; Vella et al., 2013). Extending these findings, we believe it is plausible that such developmental approaches can be leveraged and enriched to develop ETFL. For example, such approaches may include information sessions to make leaders aware of issues related to climate change or training programs that teach leaders how to connect with nature and behave pro-environmentally. Second, drawing from research that has linked mindfulness to transformational leadership (e.g., Lange et al., 2018) and higher levels of pro-environmental behaviour (e.g., Ray et al., 2021), we suggest that ETFL may be cultivated through nature-based mindfulness interventions within which individuals are instructed to stay in the present moment by focusing on nature-based cues (e.g., trees, rivers, lakes, etc.; Nisbet et al., 2019). Third, future research should compare the effects of ETFL in different organisations, industries and cultural milieus to see how ETFL manifests in diverse contexts. Finally, future research should identify more moderators to the effects of ETFL. For example, scholars can investigate whether employees' involvement in the development of corporate environmental responsibility initiatives (i.e., co-creation; Simpson et al., 2020) moderates the effects of ETFL. According to H.-R. Kim et al. (2010), when employees have the chance to suggest the nature of corporate social responsibility initiatives, they are more likely to identify with their organisation and exhibit a commitment to organisational goals. If those goals have an environmental orientation and employees have the opportunity to contribute to corporate environmental responsibility initiatives, it seems plausible that employees are more likely to be receptive to environmental goals put forth by an environmental leader, which, in turn, could enhance the relationship between ETFL and environmental outcomes. Exploring these and other avenues in future studies will enrich our knowledge about the importance of ETFL, while also providing organisations with important information not only as to why they should cultivate ETFL but also how they can do so.

Conclusion

As the climate crisis continues to accelerate, now more than ever, environmental leadership is needed so that some of the largest greenhouse gas emitters – organisations – can begin to reduce their environmental impact. The purpose of this chapter was to describe the conceptualisation of environmental leadership, the significance of the most dominant type (i.e., ETFL), as well as an emerging type (environmentally specific servant leadership), and propose directions for future research so that this information can be used by organisations to help slow down the climate crisis. Derrick Emsley stated that 'we believe in a world where businesses can be pacesetters, where companies are no longer looked at as the problem and, instead, can lead the conversation on restoring our planet' (Emsley & Becker, 2021, para. 14). As such, environmental leaders can become players in facilitating a paradigm shift in which organisations are drivers of positive environmental change.

Discussion Questions

- Given that there are so many definitions of environmental leadership, which do you feel is the strongest, and why? Would you make any modifications? Why or why not?
- In which contexts (e.g., cultural and organisational) would ETFL and environmentally specific servant leadership be optimal environmental leadership styles? Explain.
- Can you think of any organisations that have reaped both environmental and non-environmental benefits due to implementing environmental leadership?
- What other avenues for future research would you propose for ETFL research, and why?

Notes

1 Other approaches call for a radical shift away from capitalism. For example, Hickel (2021) advocated for degrowth, an economic model focusing on radical abundance that opposes capitalist policies of austerity while emphasizing the planned reduction of energy and resource use. Hickel asserted that this model is designed to balance the economy with the environment to reduce inequality and improve human well-being. Similarly, Jackson (2021) advocated for a post-growth economy in which capitalist values of excessive consumption are replaced with values highlighting balance, growth limits and an economy of care and sustainability.

2 Although no interviews were conducted with the company's leadership, Tentree was chosen as a case study for ETFL as its leadership served as a noteworthy example of ETFL qualities and characteristics. All information was obtained using the company's website and online news sites and interpreted by the authors as examples of ETFL behaviours.

Suggested Reading

Bratton, A., Robertson, J., & Paulet, R. (2023). Leading pro-environmental change. In J. Bratton (Ed.), *Organizational leadership* (2nd ed., pp. 313–332). SAGE.

Robertson, J. L., & Barling, J. (2013). Greening organizations through leaders' influence on employees' pro-environmental behaviors. *Journal of Organizational Behavior, 34*(2), 176–194. https://doi.org/10.1002/job.1820

Robertson, J. L., & Barling J. (2015). The role of leadership in promoting workplace pro-environmental behaviors. In J. L. Robertson & J. Barling (Eds.), *The psychology of green organizations* (pp. 164–186). Oxford University Press.

Zacher, H., Rudolph, C. W., & Katz, I. M. (in press). Employee green behavior as the core of environmentally sustainable organizations. *Annual Review of Organizational Psychology and Organizational Behavior.*

References

Afsar, B., Cheema, S., & Javed, F. (2018). Activating employee's pro-environmental behaviors: The role of CSR, organizational identification, and environmentally specific servant leadership. *Corporate Social Responsibility and Environmental Management, 25*(5), 904–911. https://doi.org/10.1002/csr.1506

Al-Ghazali, B. M., Gelaidan, H. M., Ali Shah, S. H., & Amjad, R. (2022). Green transformational leadership and green creativity? The mediating role of green thinking and green organizational identity in SMEs. *Frontiers in Psychology, 13*. https://doi.org/10.3389/fpsyg.2022.977998

Babiak, K., & Trendafilova, S. (2011). CSR and environmental responsibility: Motives and pressures to adopt green management practices. *Corporate Social Responsibility and Environmental Management, 18*(1), 11–24. https://doi.org/10.1002/csr.229

Barling, J., Loughlin, C., & Kelloway, E. K. (2002). Development and test of a model linking safety-specific transformational leadership and occupational safety. *Journal of Applied Psychology, 87*, 488–496. https://doi.org/10.1037/0021-9010.87.3.488

Barling, J., Weber, T., & Kelloway, E. K. (1996). Effects of transformational leadership training on attitudinal and financial outcomes: A field experiment. *Journal of Applied Psychology, 81*(6), 827–832. https://doi.org/10.1037/0021-9010.81.6.827

Bass, B. M., & Bass, R. (2008). *The Bass handbook of leadership: Theory, research, and managerial applications*. Free Press.

Bass, B. M., & Riggio, R. E. (2006). *Transformational leadership*. Erlbaum.

Beauchamp, M. R., Barling, J., & Morton, K. (2011). Transformational teaching and adolescent self-determined motivation, self-efficacy, and intentions to engage in leisure time physical activity: A randomized controlled pilot trial. *Applied Psychology: Health and Well-Being, 3*(2), 127–150. https://doi.org/10.1111/j.1758-0854.2011.01048.x

Berry, J. K., & Gordon, J. C. (1993). *Environmental leadership: Developing effective skills and styles*. Island Press.

Choongo, P. (2017). A longitudinal study of the impact of corporate social responsibility on firm performance in SMEs in Zambia. *Sustainability (Basel, Switzerland), 9*(8), 1300. https://doi.org/10.3390/su9081300

Christensen, L. J., Mackey, A., & Whetten, D. (2014). Taking responsibility for corporate social responsibility: The role of leaders in creating, implementing, sustaining, or avoiding socially responsible firm behaviors. *The Academy of Management Perspectives, 28*(2), 164–178. https://doi.org/10.5465/amp.2012.0047

Cleveland, M., & Kalamas, M. (2015). Environmental locus of control. In J. Robertson & J. Barling (Eds.), *The psychology of green organizations* (pp. 187–212). Oxford University Press.

Cluff, J. (2022, April 25). *Where are all the planted trees? Tentree founders launch blockchain 'Veritree' to keep track*. https://gearjunkie.com/news/veritree-reforestation-blockchain-platform

Dietz, T., Dolšak, N., Ostrom, E., & Stern, P. C. (2002). The drama of the commons. In E. Ostom, T. Dietz, N. Dulsak, P. Stern, & S. Stonich (Eds.), *The drama of the commons* (pp. 3–34). National Academy Press.

DiSegni, D. M., Huly, M., & Akron, S. (2015). Corporate social responsibility, environmental leadership and financial performance. *Social Responsibility Journal, 11*(1), 131–148. https://doi.org/10.1108/SRJ-02-2013-0024

Dunlap, R. E., & Van Liere, K. D. (1978). The new environmental paradigm. *Journal of Environmental Education, 9*, 10–19. https://doi.org/10.3200/JOEE.40.1.19-28

Dunlap, R. E., Van Liere, K. D., Mertig, A., & Jones, R. E. (2000). Measuring endorsement of the new ecological paradigm: A revised NEP scale. *Journal of Social Issues, 56*(3), 425–442. https://doi.org/10.1111/0022-4537.00176

Egri, C. P. (1997). Spiritual connections with the natural environment. *Organization & Environment, 10*(4), 407–431. https://doi.org/10.1177/192181069701000405

Egri, C. P., & Herman, S. (2000). Leadership in the North American environmental sector: Values, leadership styles, and contexts of environmental leaders and their organizations. *Academy of Management Journal, 43*(4), 571–604. https://doi.org/10.5465/1556356

Elkington, J. (2004). Enter the triple bottom line. In A. Henriques & J. Richardson (Eds.), *The triple bottom line: Does it all add up?* (pp. 1–16). Earthscan.

Emsley, D., & Becker, M. S. (2021, January 22). How one business plans to grow one billion trees in 10 years. *Forbes.* https://www.forbes.com/sites/worldeconomicforum/2021/01/22/how-one-business-plans-to-restore-conserve-and-grow-one-billion-trees-in-10-years/?sh=1fcbeb1b5a3e

Faraz, N. A., Ahmed, F., Ying, M., & Mehmood, S. A. (2021). The interplay of green servant leadership, self-efficacy, and intrinsic motivation in predicting employees' pro-environmental behavior. *Corporate Social Responsibility and Environmental Management, 28*(4), 1171–1184. https://doi.org/10.1002/csr.2115

Fatoki, O. (2021). Environmentally specific servant leadership and employees' pro-environmental behaviour in hospitality firms in South Africa. *Geo Journal of Tourism and Geosites, 37*(3), 943–950. https://doi.org/10.30892/gtg.37328-730

Gallagher, D. L. (2012). Why environmental leadership? In D. R. Gallagher (Ed.), *Environmental leadership: A reference handbook* (pp. 3–10). Sage.

Gifford, R. (2011). The dragons of inaction: Psychological barriers that limit climate change mitigation and adaptation. *American Psychologist, 66*(4), 290–302. https://doi.org/10.1037/a0023566

Gladwin, T. N. (1993). The meaning of greening: A plea for organizational theory. In K. Fischer & J. Schot (Eds.), *Environmental strategies for industry: International perspectives on research needs and policy implications* (pp. 37–62). Island Press.

Graafland, J., & Mazereeuw-Van der Duijn Schouten, C. (2012). Motives for corporate social responsibility. *De Economist, 160*(4), 377–396. https://doi.org/10.1007/s10645-012-9198-5

Graves, L. M., & Sarkis, J. (2012). Fostering employees pro-environmental behaviour: The impact of leadership and motivation. In D. R. Gallagher (Ed.), *Environmental leadership: A reference handbook* (pp. 161–171). Sage.

Graves, L. M., & Sarkis, J. (2018). The role of employees' leadership perceptions, values, and motivation in employees' pro-environmental behaviors. *Journal of Cleaner Production, 196*, 576–587. https://doi.org/10.1016/j.jclepro.2018.06.013

Graves, L. M., Sarkis, J., & Gold, N. (2019). Employee proenvironmental behavior in Russia: The roles of top management commitment, managerial leadership, and employee motives. *Resources, Conservation and Recycling, 140*, 54–64. https://doi.org/10.1016/j.resconrec.2018.09.007

Graves, L. M., Sarkis, J., & Zhu, Q. (2013). How transformational leadership and employee motivation combine to predict employee proenvironmental behaviors in China. *Journal of Environmental Psychology, 35*, 81–91. https://doi.org/10.1016/j.jenvp.2013.05.002

Greenleaf, R. K. (1977). *Servant leadership*. Paulist Press.

Grint, K., Jones, O. S., & Holt, C. (2016). What is leadership? In J. Storey, J. Hartley, J.-L. Denis, P. Hart, & D. Ulrich (Eds.), *The Routledge companion to leadership* (pp. 3–20). Routledge.

Gu, F., & Liu, J. (2022). Environmentally specific servant leadership and employee workplace green behavior: Moderated mediation model of green role modeling and employees' perceived CSR. *Sustainability, 14*(19), 1–18. https://doi.org/10.3390/su141911965

Hart, S. L. (1995). A natural-resource-based view of the firm. *Academy of Management Review, 20*(4), 986–1014. https://doi.org/10.2307/258963

Henczel, T. (n.d.). The story of Tentree. *The Environmentor.* https://blog.tentree.com/the-story-of-tentree/

Hickel, J. (2021). What does degrowth mean? A few points of clarification. *Globalizations, 18*(7), 1105–1111. https://doi.org/10.1080/14747731.2020.1812222

Intergovernmental Panel on Climate Change. (2021). *Climate change 2021: The physical science basis*. Cambridge University Press. https://www.ipcc.ch/report/sixth-assessment-report-working-group-i/

Islam, T., Ahmad, S., & Ahmed, I. (2022). Linking environment specific servant leadership with organizational environmental citizenship behavior: The roles of CSR and attachment anxiety. *Review of Managerial Science, 17*, 855–879. https://doi.org/10.1007/s11846-022-00547-3

Jackson, T. (2021). *Post growth: Life after capitalism*. Polity.

Johnson, D. B. (1998). Green businesses: Perspectives from management and business ethics. *Society and Natural Resources, 11*(3), 259–266. https://doi.org/10.1080/08941929809381078

Kim, H.-R., Lee, M., Lee, H.-T., & Kim, N.-M. (2010). Corporate social responsibility and employee–company identification. *Journal of Business Ethics, 95*(4), 557–569. https://doi.org/10.1007/s10551-010-0440-2

Kim, W., McGinley, S., Choi, H.-M., & Agmapisarn, C. (2020). Hotels' environmental leadership and employees' organizational citizenship behavior. *International Journal of Hospitality Management, 87*, 102375. https://doi.org/10.1016/j.ijhm.2019.102375

Krémer, V. (2019). The impact of CSR on job satisfaction and employee retention in Hungarian hotels. In R. Schmidpeter, N. Capaldi, S. Idowu, & A. Stürenberg Herrera (Eds.), *International dimensions of sustainable management. CSR, sustainability, ethics & governance* (pp. 307–327). Springer. https://doi.org/10.1007/978-3-030-04819-8_19

Kura, K. M. (2016). Linking environmentally specific transformational leadership and environmental concern to green behaviour at work. *Global Business Review, 17*(3), 1S-14S. https://doi.org/10.1177/0972150916631069

Lange, S., Bormann, K. C., & Rowold, J. (2018). Mindful leadership: Mindfulness as a new antecedent of destructive and transformational leadership behavior. *Gruppe. Interaktion. Organisation. Zeitschrift für Angewandte Organisationspsychologie (GIO), 49*, 139–147. https://doi.org/10.1007/s11612-018-0413-y

Liden, R. C., Wayne, S. J., Zhao, H., & Henderson, D. (2008). Servant leadership: Development of a multidimensional measure and multi-level assessment. *The Leadership Quarterly, 19*(2), 161–177. https://doi.org/10.1016/j.leaqua.2008.01.006

Luu, T. T. (2018). Activating tourists' citizenship behavior for the environment: The roles of CSR and frontline employees' citizenship behavior for the environment. *Journal of Sustainable Tourism, 26*(7), 1178–1203. https://doi.org/10.1080/09669582.2017.1330337

Masson-Delmotte, V., Zhai, P., Pirani, A., Connors, S. L., Péan, C., Berger, S., Caud, N., Chen, Y., Goldfarb, L., Gomis, M. I., Huang, M., Leitzell, K., Lonnoy, E., Matthews, J. B. R., Maycock, T. K., Waterfield, T., Yelekçi, O., Yu, R., & Zhou, B. (2021). *Climate change 2021: The physical science basis. Contribution of Working Group I to the Sixth Assessment Report of the Intergovernmental Panel on Climate Change*. Intergovernmental Panel on Climate Change. https://report.ipcc.ch/ar6/wg1/IPCC_AR6_WGI_FullReport.pdf

Mazutis, D., & Zintel, C. (2015). Leadership and corporate responsibility: A review of the empirical evidence. *Annals in Social Responsibility, 1*(1), 76–107. https://doi.org/10.1108/ASR-12-2014-0001

Melo, T., & Garrido-Morgado, A. (2012). Corporate reputation: A combination of social responsibility and industry. *Corporate Social Responsibility and Environmental Management, 19*(1), 11–31. https://doi.org/10.1002/csr.260

Metcalf, L., & Benn, S. (2013). Leadership for sustainability: An evolution of leadership ability. *Journal of Business Ethics, 112*, 369–384. https://doi.org/10.1007/s10551-012-1278-6

Mughal, M. F., Cai, S. L., Faraz, N. A., & Ahmed, F. (2022). Environmentally specific servant leadership and employees' pro-environmental behavior: Mediating role of green self-efficacy. *Psychology Research and Behavior Management, 15*, 305–316. https://doi.org/10.2147/PRBM.S328776

National Research Council. (2010). *Advancing the science of climate change.* National Academies Press.

Nisbet, E., Zelenski, J. M., & Grandpierre, Z. (2019). Mindfulness in nature enhances connectedness and mood. *Ecopsychology, 11*(2), 81–91. https://doi.org/10.1089/eco.2018.0061

Peng, J., Chen, X., Zou, Y., & Nie, Q. (2021). Environmentally specific transformational leadership and team pro-environmental behaviors: The roles of pro-environmental goal clarity, pro-environmental harmonious passion, and power distance. *Human Relations, 74*(11), 1864–1888. https://doi.org/10.1177/0018726720942306

Peng, J., Yin, K., Hou, N., Zou, Y., & Nie, Q. (2020). How to facilitate employee green behavior: The joint role of green transformational leadership and green human resource management practice. *Acta Psychologica Sinica, 52*(9), 1105–1120. https://dx.doi.org/10.3724/SP.J.1041.2020.01105

Portugal, E., & Yukl, G. (1994). Perspectives on environmental leadership. *The Leadership Quarterly, 5*(3), 271–276. https://doi.org/10.1016/1048-9843(94)90017-5

Ray, T. N., Franz, S. A., Jarrett, N. L., & Pickett, S. M. (2021). Nature enhanced meditation: Effects on mindfulness, connectedness to nature, and pro-environmental behavior. *Environment and Behavior, 53*(8), 864–890.https://doi.org/10.1177/0013916520952452

Robertson, J. L. (2018). The nature, measurement and nomological network of environmentally specific transformational leadership. *Journal of Business Ethics, 151*(4), 961–975. https://doi.org/10.1007/s10551-017-3569-4

Robertson, J. L., & Barling, J. (2013). Greening organizations through leaders' influence on employees' pro-environmental behaviors. *Journal of Organizational Behavior, 34*(2), 176–194. https://doi.org/10.1002/job.1820

Robertson, J. L., & Barling J. (2015). The role of leadership in promoting workplace pro-environmental behaviors. In J. L. Robertson & J. Barling (Eds.), *The psychology of green organizations* (pp. 164–186). Oxford University Press.

Robertson, J. L., & Barling, J. (2017). Contrasting the nature and effects of environmentally specific and general transformational leadership. *Leadership & Organization Development Journal, 38*(1), 22–41. https://doi.org/10.1108/LODJ-05-2015-0100

Robertson, J. L., & Carleton, E. (2018). Uncovering how and when environmental leadership affects employees' voluntary pro-environmental behavior. *Journal of Leadership & Organizational Studies, 25*(2), 197–210. https://doi.org/10.1177/1548051817738940

Robinson, D., & Clegg, A. (1998). Environmental leadership and competitive advantage through environmental management system standards. *Eco-Management and Auditing, 5*(1), 6–14. https://doi.org/10.1002/(SICI)1099-0925(199803)5:1<6::AID-EMA74>3.0.CO;2-I

Sakhel, A. (2017). Corporate climate risk management: Are European companies prepared? *Journal of Cleaner Production, 165*, 103–118. https://doi.org/10.1016/j.jclepro.2017.07.056

Shrivastava, P. (1994). Ecocentric leadership in the 21st century. *The Leadership Quarterly, 5*(3), 223–226. https://doi.org/10.1016/1048-9843(94)90013-2

Shrivastava, P. (1995). Ecocentric management for a risk society. *Academy of Management Review,* 20(1), 118–137. https://doi.org/10.5465/amr.1995.9503271996

Siddiquei, A., Asmi, F., Asadullah, M. A., & Mir, F. (2021). Environmental-specific servant leadership as a strategic tool to accomplish environmental performance: A case of China. *International Journal of Manpower, 42*(7), 1161–1182. https://doi.org/10.1108/IJM-07-2020-0350

Siebenhüner, B., & Arnold, M. (2007). Organizational learning to manage sustainable development. *Business Strategy and the Environment, 16*(5), 339–353. https://doi.org/10.1002/bse.579

Simpson, B., Robertson, J. L., & White, K. (2020). How co-creation increases employee corporate social responsibility and organizational engagement: The moderating role of self-construal. *Journal of Business Ethics, 166*, 331–350.

Spears, L. (1996). Reflections on Robert K. Greenleaf and servant-leadership. *Leadership & Organization Development Journal,* 17(7), 33–35. https://doi.org/10.1108/01437739610148367

Su, X., Xu, A., Lin, W., Chen, Y., Liu, S., & Xu, W. (2020). Environmental leadership, green innovation practices, environmental knowledge learning, and firm performance. *SAGE Open, 10*(2). https://doi.org/10.1177/2158244020922909

Swim, J. K., Clayton, S., & Howard, G. S. (2011). Human behavioral contributions to climate change: Psychological and contextual drivers. *American Psychologist, 66*(4), 251–264. https://doi.org/10.1037/a0023472

Tentree. (n.d.a). Let's track your impact. https://impact.tentree.com/welcome

Tentree. (n.d.b). Supplier code of conduct.https://cdn.shopify.com/s/files/1/2404/6643/t/465/assets/Code_of_Conduct_2020.pdf?v=166082809401424354751637179840

Tuan, L. T. (2020). Environmentally-specific servant leadership and green creativity among tourism employees: Dual mediation paths. *Journal of Sustainable Tourism, 28*(1), 86–109. https://doi.org/10.1080/09669582.2019.1675674

Vella, S. A., Oades, L. G., & Crowe, T. P. (2013). A pilot test of transformational leadership training for sports coaches: Impact on the developmental experiences of adolescent athletes. *International Journal of Sports Science & Coaching, 8*(3), 513–530. https://doi.org/10.1260/1747-9541.8.3.513

Wu, B., Fang, H., Jacoby, G., Li, G., & Wu, Z. (2022). Environmental regulations and innovation for sustainability? Moderating effect of political connections. *Emerging Markets Review, 50*, 1–12. https://doi.org/10.1016/j.ememar.2021.100835

Zalasiewicz, J., Williams, M., Haywood, A., & Ellis, M. (2011). The Anthropocene: A new epoch of geological time? *The Royal Society, 369*(1938), 835–841. https://doi.org/10.1098/rsta.2010.0339

10

RESPONSIBLE LEADERSHIP IN THE GOVERNANCE OF MANAGED RETREAT

A PLACE-BASED APPROACH TO CLIMATE CHANGE ADAPTATION

Sasha Maher, Brad Jackson, Jonathan Boston and Steve Kempster

Chapter Summary

Climate change presents unprecedented leadership and governance challenges (Boston & Lawrence, 2018). *Managed retreat*, defined as the strategic withdrawal of people, assets and activities to reduce risk to place-based climate change harm, will be one of the most vexing. This is because of the deep uncertainty and profound social, environmental, economic and cultural disruption(s) that will be caused by relocating communities. Our chapter sets out to better understand and promote the leadership and governance practices that need to be developed for individuals, businesses, communities, regions and governments to proactively respond to climate change in a responsible, integrated and

DOI: 10.4324/9781003343011-12

sustainable way. Some attention has been given to developing governance frameworks that lay out roles, responsibilities and accountabilities. However, we argue that the specific leadership and governance practices that are required for proactive, pre-emptive retreat have been largely ignored. Such practices require urgent attention as they will take considerable time to identify, develop and refine at the local, national and international levels. In this chapter, we argue that to achieve positive leadership for managed retreat, we must take a place-based, long-term stakeholder perspective that is focused on cross-sectoral collaboration.

Introduction

The science is unequivocal that human-induced climate change causes widespread adverse impacts to nature and people, at magnitudes and frequencies beyond natural climate variability (Intergovernmental Panel on Climate Change [IPCC], 2021, 2022). The report of Working Group II of the Intergovernmental Panel on Climate Change (IPCC, 2022) made a bold call for action now to lessen the worst effects: any further delays in effective measures to reduce greenhouse gas emissions will close the window of opportunity to protect a healthy liveable planet (IPCC, 2022). A corollary to limited action on mitigation is the current slow rates of adaptation, planning and implementation that will severely limit our options (Lawrence et al., 2020).

Our research sets out to better understand and promote the interrelated leadership and governance practices that need to be developed for individuals, businesses, communities, regions and governments to proactively respond to climate change in a responsible, integrated and sustained way (Cikaliuk et al., 2022). Some attention has been given to developing governance frameworks that lay out roles, responsibilities and accountabilities. However, we shall argue in this chapter that the specific leadership and governance practices that are required (i.e., how will we *collectively* make this work?) have been largely ignored. Such practices require urgent attention as they will take considerable time to identify, develop and refine on local and international scales. We therefore welcome the publication of this handbook because it can help us begin to address the inadequacy of leadership and governance practices that we believe have been one of the important reasons for the failure to mitigate climate change (i.e., reduce emissions) and to undertake effective adaptation. Our specific contribution to this handbook is to argue that to achieve effective and responsible leadership for managed retreat, we must take a place-based, long-term stakeholder perspective that is focused on cross-sectoral collaboration. Such an approach seeks to bring together business, public, community and Indigenous leaders who are driven by a mutual and lasting commitment to collectively protect and enhance the place in which we live, work and create value (Kempster & Jackson, 2021).

In Chapter 15 of the Handbook, Johanna Nalau notes that, while most organisation have understandably been pre-occupied by the challenge of reducing emissions, leadership in adaptation remains an unexplored yet crucial area in climate risk management. She provides an excellent overview of the qualities and capabilities that can support climate change adaptation at different levels within organisations as well some of the steps that are already being taken by various organisations to adapt. Adaptation is the process of reducing exposure and vulnerability to climate change. In human systems this is a process of anticipatory or reactive adjustment, whereas in ecological systems it is the autonomous adjustment through ecological and evolutionary processes (IPCC, 2022). There is a range of adaptation approaches for humans, from avoiding the risk of hazards to accommodating and protecting from the impacts by using soft and hard engineering solutions. These defensive options often create moral hazard issues where people behave in ways that can increase future risks. At the other end of the adaptation spectrum is moving people and property out of harm's way, variously known as *managed retreat* or *planned relocation.*

The common definition of managed retreat is the strategic withdrawal of people, assets and activities to reduce risk to climate change harm and other hazardous phenomena such as earthquakes, volcanic eruptions and landslides (Hanna et al., 2021). This option is increasingly being viewed as not only inevitable because of the risk of coastal flooding, fire and other hazard-related harm but also transformative. The transformative potential with managed retreat is to fundamentally change and challenge existing patterns of social inequality; that is, to view the opportunity to integrate within the moving of vulnerable populations a broader engagement with systemic aspects of inequality. Without this type of engagement, research suggests that climate change adaptation options, including an unplanned managed retreat or 'unmanaged retreat' (Hanna et al., 2021, p. 8), could intensify socio-economic inequalities (Siders et al., 2021).

We build on this notion of transformation to posit that the purpose of managed retreat should be to not only relocate 'people, assets and activities' and address social inequalities (Siders et al., 2021) but also to enhance and restore ecosystems (O'Donnell, 2022), reduce inequalities and strengthen democracy (Habermas, 1984; Sancino, 2022). As Dundon and Abkowitz (2021) noted, there are positive co-benefits that can be realised through managed retreat, such as restoring fragile coastal ecosystems; additionally, it can provide an opportunity to put in place mechanism to establish a well-being economy.

In addition, we support the growing international consensus that climate change is interconnected with biodiversity loss and that adaptative responses, such as managed retreat, must consider how best to address both crises. Along with climate change scholars, we also recognise that new forms of collaborative governance that listen to, and share power with, local communities are urgently needed to promote proactive and responsible adaptation (Hanna et al., 2021; Lawrence et al., 2021). In this regard, we are guided by Elinor Ostrom's call to govern the commons (Ostrom, 2015) and are inspired by her challenge to seek out examples of collaborative governance that work, on the assumption that 'an arrangement that works in practice can work in theory' (Fennel, 2011, p. 11).

However, despite this recognition, the interdisciplinary literature on climate leadership predominately remains theory driven and is focused on leadership geared inwards towards the organisation and/or elides the specific context from which leadership emerges (Gupta & Grubb, 2000; Meijerink & Stiller, 2013). This includes work that seeks to move beyond leadership as a leader. Instead, leadership approaches draw on multiple strands of leadership, including complexity theory (Uhl-Bien et al., 2007) and collaborative forms of leadership (Imperial et al., 2016; Ospina & Foldy, 2010), to solve adaptation issues (Meijerink & Stiller, 2013). So, while calls increase in volume for governance that is inclusive and connected to local communities, most proposed adaptation approaches predominantly draw on leadership theories that are disconnected from practice. In most instances, these are disconnected from place.

In contrast, we argue that managed retreat, which is a response to the perceived risk or real physical manifestation of the impacts of climate change, must be firmly grounded in place. It thus seems axiomatic that political, business, public and community leadership is embedded in place (Harrison et al., 2019). The intimate attachment to place provides an opportunity for policy engagement that is very real, emotive, fraught with anxiety and conflictual. Such policy needs to recognise that, fundamentally, people and businesses will ultimately need to move from a place that is significant to them and to select and create a new place that needs to become important to them. The power of place has been recognised as the basis for place-based initiatives (PBIs) in a number of Western democracies to tackle social and economic inequity but, to our knowledge, only on a limited basis for environmental initiatives, most especially climate change. Moreover, the focus of these efforts has been on enhancing a place in situ as opposed to an ex situ place.

We argue that to achieve positive managed retreat, leadership must take a place-based, long-term stakeholder perspective that is focused on promoting cross-sectoral collaboration between business, public, community and Indigenous organisation leaders (Kempster & Jackson, 2021). Place is critical to managed retreat as it is the physical manifestation of intolerable impacts, but it also provides the opportunity to galvanise and strengthen deliberative democracy by creating a space from which to enact collective, shared leadership (Sotarauta & Beer, 2017). We explore both of these angles and propose that we should promote responsible leadership-in-governance practices that are broad and encompassing in terms of stakeholder inclusion to be collective, participatory and place based (Jackson, 2019). We also recognise the potential paradox posed by emphasising the importance of place-based leadership and orchestrating the retreat away from places in which people and businesses have such a strong attachment and deep affinity. We argue that place-based leadership not only serves to make the case for managed retreat but also serves to identify, transition and create *new* places in which even stronger attachments and affinities might be forged through a powerful 're-placement' process.

Fundamental to the success of place-based leadership is the need to ground responsible leadership practices that can genuinely address the full gamut of social, economic, environmental and cultural challenges we all share in common. Jackson et al. (2023) have recently argued for a series of five re-orientations that responsible leaders need to embrace: from focusing on leadership behaviour towards studying decisions, actions and outcomes;

from a preoccupation with leader(s) and followers towards leader(s) and stakeholders; from a short-term focus towards a long-term focus; from a place-agnostic approach towards a place-centric approach; from individualistic (and heroic) approaches to leading towards collaborative approaches with a strong emphasis placed upon stewardship.

Theory and Basic Concepts: The Challenge of Managed Retreat(s)

Managed retreat is arguably the most vexing and contentious of climate adaptation options. As the IPCC and other science bodies have made clear, over the coming century, more physical assets, places, ecosystems and species will be vulnerable to the impacts of climate change, especially sea level rise. The impacts will include more severe riverine, pluvial and lake flooding as well as coastal erosion and inundation. In some cases, measures to accommodate the impacts may be technically possible, but in other cases they will be extremely costly to maintain and/or not adequately protect people or the environment. In these cases, managed retreat will be the preferred policy solution.

Managed retreat captures and highlights the multiple trade-offs and difficult decision making at the centre of climate change. Key questions that must be addressed are the following: Where should managed retreat occur? Who should be relocated? Who should make the decisions? Who should bear the costs? And when and how relocations should be carried out? As Lawrence et al. (2020) and others noted (e.g., Hanna et al., 2021), complications range from public opposition to equity concerns to loss of property, landscapes and ecosystems; to asset value reduction; and to erosion of cultural and spiritual identity and livelihoods. The ramifications flow outwards to connect localities to regions and others seemingly unperturbed by the physical impacts of climate change.

First, the terminology of managed retreat itself is routinely debated. Broadly defined, as noted earlier, it is the relocation of people, assets and activities from a vulnerable location (Dundon & Abkowitz, 2021). This conceptualisation is agreed on by climate change scholars, but issues arise in the connotations it has with defeat, failure and, most problematic, colonial or forced relocations of discriminated groups and people. Carey (2020) noted that because of its association with force and failure, to consider managed retreat as an option is politically perilous.

In view of these concerns, alternative descriptors have been advanced. These include the more neutral 'planned relocation' (to avoid the 'manage' and 'control' references), 'strategic retreat', as well as 'transformative adaptation' which is an attempt to highlight the potentially positive co-benefits to movement. Examples of such benefits reflect opening up space for public recreation or the enhancement of ecosystems (Dundon & Abkowitz, 2021). Countering these concerns about the negative associations, Koslov (2016) suggested that managed retreat could be reframed as a genuinely restorative process that provides the opportunity to re-group and heal in a safe location. Moreover, the term does indeed succinctly convey the essence of the challenge that needs to be addressed.

We are cautioned by these critiques, in particular the trauma of forced relocation. We wish to broaden the definition to signal the transformative potential of managed retreat. Managed retreat can be done either well or poorly, in an inclusive or exclusive manner, for the common or for individual good. This is why we advocate a climate leadership lens versus a climate management lens. As such, we choose to use the term managed retreat, but to acknowledge the multiple contextualised experiences, we agree with Hanna et al. (2021) that it is useful to think of a managed retreat as in fact comprising of multiple managed retreats. This slight but significant turn of phrase also flags that managed retreat should not be applied top-down in a homogenous one-size-fits-all manner. Rather, managed retreat should be co-designed in a genuinely participatory manner to speak to the specificities of each place in which it enfolds and takes place (Susskind & Kim, 2022). Ensuring widespread ownership of the managed retreat process is vital to ensuring its long-term success and acceptability. Managed retreat interventions should therefore actively engage with individual citizens as well as the private, public and community sector organisations that have a stake in the place that has been identified as the key focus for the intervention. They should actively consider both public and private goods. However, as Simon Winchester (2021) provocatively concluded in his comprehensive investigation of the history of land ownership:

> Might the very fact of land's newly realised impermanence not suggest to some that this could be the time to consider what has so for very long been well beyond consideration – the notion of sharing land, rather than merely owning it, outright? (p. 402)

Winchester rightly pointed out that shared land ownership has always been an integral feature of Indigenous societies around the world, so this is by no means a novel or untested approach.

Although presented as a distinct and discrete event, managed retreat is better thought of as a long-term evolving process. The actual staging and timing will differ according to the particular geographical, social–cultural and political–economic dynamics of the place. In many cases, managed retreat will be ongoing for generations; it will be iterative and interactive; clean-ups will be happening next door to new community initiatives for the next set of residents and businesses that will need to move. This process can be mapped over the following five phases (Olufson, 2019):

1. **Community engagement:** to enable co-production and design of managed retreat, collaborative governance and buy-in of the solution
2. **Planning and preparation:** risk assessments and identification of options including rezoning and restricting further development often undertaken in parallel with community engagement
3. **Investment:** funding of relocation (people, property, infrastructure) via compensation typically for acquisitions by a public authority and limitations on financing improvements to at-risk property, infrastructure
4. **Active retreat:** the physical movement of people and the removal or abandonment of public and private property, infrastructure, and services
5. **Clean-up, repurposing**: demolition and/or repurposing of land and buildings

As well as being long term, most managed retreats must be anticipatory to minimize the costs of climate change–related impacts. However, because science is still evolving, the timing and scale of such impacts is deeply uncertain. This makes decision making particularly challenging and underscores the need for leadership that is focused on risk management, cross-sectoral solutions and local engagement. Whereas mitigation is primarily conceived of as a 'global' issue, adaptation is primarily conceived as being location based, even though they are clearly interdependent. This fundamental but frequently forgotten point leads us to seek out leadership frameworks and practices that are explicitly place based. It is to this body of literature that we now turn.

Methods, Techniques and Application: Place-Based Leadership

Although managed retreat scholars frequently mention place and the significance of location or context, there is a narrow framing of the concept. Often place is referred to in the negative sense as either a hazardous location, a site of problematic 'place attachments' or an empty space (or a specific community) in which individuals or communities are 'received'. Place attachment is characterised as a psychological 'barrier' that must be addressed through 'more effective communication' (Hanna et al., 2021, p. 7).

This rendering of place as a problem (Foucault, 1991) elides the potential for place to not only heal (Hanna et al., 2021) but also provide the common basis for the co-creation of public value through responsible leadership (Kempster & Jackson, 2021). Place can act as both an important strategic resource for leadership in building collective identity, purpose and direction (Jackson & Parry, 2018) and a significant constraint. As such, places provide important bases for political, economic, social and organisational action at many levels (Gibney & Collinge, 2015; Ropo et al., 2015; Sotarauta & Beer, 2017). Most significant, places can transcend personality- or positionally driven leadership to focus on longer-term and more enduring goals that are multi-generational, such as climate change adaptation. The threat of losing an existing place due to repetitive flooding or submersion must be compellingly countered with the prospective promise of creating a new and better place through a responsibly led relocation of existing communities.

Since the original enactment of place-based leadership by First Nations peoples to care for country and culture (Yunkaporta, 2019), there has been a rich and evolving history of local place actors working within and across sectors to address local sustainability and other complex challenges such as climate change readiness and response. Diverse methods have been deployed in recent times to advance these place-based ambitions, including community development (Cavaye, 2001), asset-based community development (Kretzmann & McKnight, 1993), doughnut economics in action (Raworth, 2022), local government-led approaches and various environmental management campaigns (e.g. Australian Conservation Foundation, 2022).

PBIs are defined as 'programmes designed and delivered with the intention of targeting a specific geographical location(s) and particular population groups in order to respond to complex social problems' (Wilks et al., 2016, p. 3). In Australia, PBIs have ebbed and flowed with political cycles and typically focus on areas of, and communities experiencing, entrenched disadvantage. They attempt to integrate responses to issues such as health, education, child development, family well-being, housing, urban regeneration, crime reduction, employment, economic development and social inclusion. Within New Zealand, the most celebrated PBI is the Southern Initiative, which has been based in South Auckland over the past 10 years (www.tsi.nz). The Logan Together PBI based in Queensland (www.logan-together.org.au) provides a useful Australian comparison. As yet, we are unaware of any explicit PBI aimed at ameliorating climate change though the promotion of managed retreat, although we note that initiatives are underway to move villages and even larger communities in many parts of the world. As of around 2015, some 1.3 million people globally had been affected by managed retreat/relocation (Hino et al., 2017).

The important role that leadership plays in determining the success or failure of PBIs has only recently been given due recognition. Sotarauta and Beer (2017, p. 211) noted firstly,

> The increasing interest in place-based leadership represents a growing recognition of the need to reinsert questions of agency in accounts of regional performance, as attention has focused almost exclusively on structural factors at the expense of understanding the human drives of change.

In advancing the increased prominence that is being given to place-based leadership in PBIs, Sotarauta et al. (2017) also noted that place-based leadership recognises the salience of fragmented or shared actions across organisations and/or leaders rather than top-down intra-organisational leadership processes. Place-based leadership also recognises the importance of multi-scalar, dynamic and interactive governance processes between national, local and regional government actors, firms, universities, research institutions and public and/or semi-public development agencies (Budd & Sancino, 2016; Crosby & Bryson, 2005; Hambleton, 2015; Sotarauta & Beer, 2017). A key task moving forward is to find novel and sustainable ways to develop place-based leadership capability and capacity. The focus of such leadership capability and capacity is on engendering collaboration, power and trust in the formation of horizontally based leadership coalitions that are anchored in a meaningful way with specific places (Beer & Clower, 2014; Worrall & Kjaerulf, 2019).

The potential advantages of policy responses which feature PBIs (Hambleton & Howard, 2013; Leech & Worrall, 2018; Office of Information Commissioner, 2016; Taylor & Buckly, 2016; Wilks et al., 2016) can be summarised as follows: policy interventions can be better targeted based on local evidence, there is potential for communities to have a greater say in how issues are identified and services are provided and innovative service delivery that might lead to increased effectiveness and efficiency can be fostered. In contributing to these outcomes, there is a general aspiration that PBIs might lead to improved social cohesion and resilience which, in the longer term, might lead to improved trust and engagement with government – a priority for most Western democracies.

While the advantages of PBIs are generally well recognised, the risks also need to be acknowledged and considered (Hambleton & Howard, 2013; Leech & Worrall, 2018; Office of Information Commissioner, 2016; Taylor & Buckly, 2016; Wilks et al., 2016). First, there is the potential for duplication of effort and inefficient allocation of resources as the PBI overlays and occasionally competes with existing public and community initiatives. Second, there is a risk that PBIs could be launched to create an immediate response to a crisis to satisfy media pressure rather than to commit to long-term change. Third, PBIs can be derailed by inadequate or confused resourcing, platforming and coordination between central, state and local governments. Fourth, there can be a temptation to address this problem by adding extra layers of governance, which can dissipate effort, resources and support. Fifth, while it is relatively straightforward to launch PBIs, it is considerably more difficult to ensure effective operationalisation and transition from the PBI to a new but different 'business as usual' situation. Finally, there is the reverse 'NIMBY' syndrome in which cities and regions may feel aggrieved if they are not the focus of a PBI. It is an intriguing exercise to contemplate the day when communities might fight to become the focus of managed retreat PBIs!

Despite considerable efforts and investment in programme monitoring and evaluation, PBIs have yet to demonstrate their impact in a fully convincing and unqualified manner. They have, however, continued to receive community and political support. Boorman et al. (2023) have recently argued that PBI impact can be strengthened by leveraging and learning from collective impact and mission-oriented innovation methodologies to tackle specific United Nations Sustainable Development Goals. We argue that PBIs are ideally suited to climate change adaptation initiatives such as managed retreat because of the readily appreciable recognition that land and ecosystems are centrally important in terms of defining the challenge as well as the response. Moreover, PBIs tend to work more effectively when a longer-term approach can be taken. It will be very important to draw on what we have already learned from our work with PBIs in tackling an array of other societal and community issues beyond the realm of climate change. At the core of the future impact of PBIs is the better understanding and development of governance and leadership practices in ensuring that place-based managed retreat initiatives are effectively executed and sustained (Jackson, 2019).

We next outline three case vignettes to illustrate the direction of our argument. Please note that these cases are not offered as evidence or explanatory insight into what occurred, why and how but rather as practical illustrations in support of our argument. We recognise that this work is at a very early stage of development and that significantly deeper theoretical and wider empirical work needs to be undertaken. Hence, this work is presented by way of invitation to climate change leadership researchers.

Three Managed Retreat Case Studies

The three case studies presented here have been selected because they exhibit one or more features of responsible leadership in governance and they take a strong place-based stakeholder approach. These aspects have all served to create high-levels of community buy-in, which we anticipate has contributed to the success of the managed retreat initiative. By analysing these examples, we note the absence of the private sector and suggest that there is a role for the private sector to also work alongside civil society and Indigenous groups and the government. In recent work, Kempster et al. (2019) argued that for businesses, community-based activity is more than a responsibility and duty. They articulated that investment into a community generates a series of dividends for the business in terms of multiple sources of value. So, it is in this context that we suggest that business can and should add value. Significant value can be added by supporting conversations with customers, employees and investors; providing local data and information; and help in financing programmes but most especially in playing an active role in co-leading the transition. In turn, the private sector can broaden their understanding and appreciation of stakeholders beyond a shareholder perspective and strengthen their standing in the community they are a part of (Kempster et al., 2019).

The first case study focusses on the formation of a managed retreat strategy in Hawkes Bay, New Zealand. This strategy emerged from over 18 months of sustained interaction among local government, communities and Māori representatives. A premium was placed n listening and engaging with local leadership. The second case study highlights the role of cluster property buy-outs in managed retreat work within New Jersey, United States. The third case study illustrates how policy experiments guided by placed-based governance in Lacanau, France, led to increased acceptability support from residents who were previously strongly opposed to managed retreat. The common element in all three of these examples is the way in which they highlight the critical interface between local leadership, governance and co-design. These case studies show that, in addition to the provision of public funding/compensation, managed retreat requires significant local buy-in and common ownership of both the problem and the solution and that local, place-based leadership approaches are an important prerequisite for this.

The Clifton and Tangoio Coastal Hazards Strategy 2120, Hawkes Bay, New Zealand

The Hawke's Bay region is located on the east coast of the North Island, New Zealand. The 353-km coastline is geologically active and supports a diversity of species and habitats. The region has a population of 176,110 (2021), who are mostly located in the centres of Napier and Hastings. Hawkes Bay is exposed to tsunami and significant earthquake risk. The main city, Napier, was built on reclaimed land following the 1931 earthquake, and approximately 8,000 houses are less than 150 cm above spring high tide mark. The population centres also lie in the Heretaunga Plains and are highly vulnerable to flooding owing to the high water table. Exacerbating these underlying hazards is climate change. Climate change will increase coastal erosion and lead to more frequent and extensive coastal flooding. Higher storm surges lead to saltwater intrusion into coastal aquifers and further inland in estuaries. Further consequential impact are changes in surface water quality, groundwater characteristics and sedimentation.

The Clifton and Tangoio Coastal Hazards Strategy 2120 is a 100-year strategy that was co-designed by multiple stakeholders to respond to the region's specific climate change risks (Organisation for Economic Co-operation and Development, 2019; Schneider et al., 2020). Governance was highly collaborative and comprised private and public sector stakeholders with decision making via an elected joint committee. Membership of the committee included not only local and central government officials but the local Māori iwi. Early in the process stakeholders agreed to take a long-term, anticipatory view and applied a pre-emptive risk assessment tool called the DAAP (Dynamic Adaptive Policy Pathways) framework. The framework helped stakeholders decide on the tipping points which would trigger a managed retreat. The strategy is now in the implementation phase. The case study illustrates how success rested on broad community buy-in and was achieved by local collaboration with central authorities (Schneider et al., 2020).

Blue Acres Programme, New Jersey, United States

New Jersey is a state in the northeastern United States with a total area of 22,590 km^2 and 2,900 km of tidally influenced shoreline by the Atlantic Ocean. New Jersey is the most densely populated state in the United States, with 7 million of the total 8.9 million people living on the coast. Residential and commercial development has often been built on fragile ecosystems such as barrier islands or filled wetlands. There are over 230 coastal communities. These are mostly located in low-lying areas that are made up of residential and holiday housing, commercial development, agriculture, industry, critical infrastructure and cultural and historical facilities. Due to the density and proximity to other major centres, New Jersey has high coastal property values, which poses a challenge to property buyouts during managed retreat.

Blue Acres (New Jersey Department of Environmental Protection, 2022) is a managed retreat programme in the northeastern coastal state of New Jersey. Blue acres is an example of a state-run programme that works collaboratively with local government and communities to identify and purchase privately owned properties. This is undertaken both proactively and post-disaster in places that are routinely threatened or flooded due to sea level rise or significant weather events (Lakhwala, 2022). The programme is unique in that it is focused on the voluntary buyouts of neighbourhoods or property clusters instead of individual properties. The cluster approach creates large, interconnected spaces, rather than patchy areas within privately held land. The large, connected spaces increase the potential for large-scale environmental restoration for both anthropogenic ecosystem services (flood protection, local parks, etc.) and/or purely biodiversity- and environmentally focused projects. The success of the programme has been identified as being due to the local-level leadership from residents to educate and engage their neighbours to form clusters (Freudenberg et al., 2016; Spidalieri & Smith, 2020).

Experimental Governance, Lacanau, Nouvelle-Aquitaine, France

Lacanau is a coastal district in the Nouvelle-Aquitaine region. With a population of approximately 4,500, the region relies heavily on its natural amenities of the ocean, beach and forest for its tourism, which has become significant to the local economy. However, the 1 to 3 m per year of coastal retreat is threatening private and public property and infrastructure. By 2040, a forecasted 1,200 homes, 100 businesses and many roads and car parks will be affected by coastal erosion, and some may require relocation (André, 2019).

In 2012, the French Ministry for the Environment selected Lacanau as a site of experimental place-based governance (André, 2019). The main objective was to actively engage with local residents in strategy and scenario testing to (a) increase knowledge about current and future coastal dynamics, (b) problematise future coastal issues and (c) analyse the technical and social feasibility of planned retreat. Alongside forums and workshops, local residents undertook scenario back-casting whereby participants imagined a future state back towards the present, identifying what policy tools would need to be in place to reach that future state.

The experiment led to increased awareness of coastal risks and increased cooperation between actors to act on climate adaptation (Rocle et al., 2021; Rocle & Salles, 2018). A majority of the actors no longer considered managed retreat as being taboo, and the concept stopped being a divisive device within the community. The experiment worked to break down barriers between institutions and political actors, as well as build trust across these relationships and with local communities. Learnings from this localised approach informed the national adaption policy, and some recommendations were included in the Climate and Resilience Law adopted in August 2021 (Rocle et al., 2021).

Discussion and Conclusion

This chapter has highlighted a very particular climate change challenge that focuses on climate adaptation. Most of the work that is included in this volume is understandably and rightly concerned with the leadership of climate mitigation policy and interventions which have historically received the dominant larger share of media, political and policy attention. We have built on Meijerink and Stiller (2013) to argue that leadership researchers should also strive to recognise, understand and develop interventions to address the unprecedented leadership and governance challenges posed by climate adaptation. We believe that managed retreat, defined as the strategic withdrawal of people, assets and activities to reduce risk to place-based climate change harm will be one of the most crucial challenges to address. This is because of the deep uncertainty and profound social, environmental, economic and cultural disruption that will be caused by relocating communities. In short, places matter to people, most especially when they are taken away from them. They cannot simply be re-placed.

Our endeavour here is to stimulate interest among leadership researchers to better understand and promote the leadership and governance practices that will be needed for individuals, businesses, communities, regions and governments to proactively respond to climate change in a responsible, integrated and sustained way. While some attention has been given to developing governance frameworks that lay out roles, responsibilities and accountabilities, we believe that the specific leadership and governance practices that are required have been largely ignored. The leadership and governance practices require urgent attention. They will take considerable time to identify, develop and refine on local and international scales. In applying a responsible leadership lens to managed retreat, we highlight the transformational potential of managed retreat that counterweighs the primarily transactional approach that privileges the financial calculus that centres on who ultimately pays and how they pay and who ultimately wins and who loses.

To achieve positive leadership for managed retreat, we must take a responsible, long-term, place-based stakeholder perspective that is focused on cross-sectoral collaboration. Associated with this, we have highlighted the crucial role of business leadership in promoting climate adaptation as well mitigation. We are concerned that most of the focus to date by climate change researchers has been exclusively on the role of government, at the national and local levels, as well as the role of nongovernmental organisations. Thus, the critical resource of business leadership and expertise has been overlooked and the outcomes of managed retreat are compromised as a consequence. It is strikingly clear that business leadership is not widely recognised and certainly under-valued in adaptation responses. Viewing managed retreat as collective responsibility of all affected communities similarly embraces the important contribution of indigenous leadership.

This Handbook has highlighted the need for contemporary leadership models to be re-purposed for the age of the Anthropocene (Crutzen, 2006) to stimulate the development of effective and capable climate change leaders. As things stand, the qualities and capabilities of leaders who successfully orchestrate the development and implementation of climate change policies and interventions within private, public and not-for-profit organisations remain unclear. This chapter has suggested that a promising line of inquiry for the development of climate leadership can be found through the hybridisation of responsible leadership and governance and place-based leadership theory and practice. We have highlighted the potential of this hybridised approach with respect to one facet of climate adaptation; that is, managed retreat. However, we suggest that this hybridised approach is equally important for developing climate mitigation leadership and encourage leaders and scholars who are focused on this goal to begin to pursue this line of inquiry.

Discussion Points

- Managed retreat initiatives will likely generate considerable sustained resistance on the part of residents, property owners, community groups and businesses. How might place-based leadership initiatives anticipate and work with this resistance to develop the best new place outcomes?

- Businesses are critical stakeholders of place. What roles do you think business leaders, from both corporations and small and medium-sized enterprises, can and should play in placed-based leadership initiatives aimed at promoting responsible managed retreat?
- More often than not, we value what we measure often trumps what we measure is what we value. What metrics might be used to monitor and evaluate the success of placed-based managed retreat initiatives?
- We have argued in this chapter that collaboration is key to embracing all stakeholder voices, talents, insights, experiences, networks and contributions. But there are downsides to collaboration in the context of managed retreat. What do you see as the potential disadvantages, limitations and risks associated with a place-based leadership approach to managed retreat? How might these potential risks be mitigated?

Suggested Reading

Dryzek, J., & Pickering, J. (2019). *The Politics of the Anthropocene.* Oxford University Press.

Lofthouse, J.K. & Herzberg, R.Q. The Continuing case for a polycentric approach for coping with climate change. *Sustainability* 2023, 15, 3770.

Siders, A.R., Ajibade, I., & Casagrande, C. (2021). Transformative potential of managed retreat as climate adaptation. *Current Opinion in Environmental Sustainability*, 50, 272–280.

References

André, C. (2019). Management of coastal erosion on the Aquitaine coast – Strategic approaches and governance implemented by GIP littoral. *Coastal Management 2019*, 407–418. https://www.icevirtuallibrary.com/doi/10.1680/cm.65147.407

Australian Conservation Foundation. (2022). Together we can ramp up climate solutions. https://www.acf.org.au/

Beer, A., & Clower, T. (2014). Mobilizing leadership in cities and regions. *Regional Studies, 48*(1), 5–20. https://doi.org/10.1080/21681376.2013.869428

Boorman, C., Jackson, B., & Burkett, I. (2023). SDG localization: Mobilizing the potential of place leadership through collective impact and mission-oriented innovation methodologies. *Journal of Change Management, 23*(1), 53–71. https://doi.org/10.1080/14697017.2023.2167226

Boston, J., & Lawrence, J. (2018). Funding climate change adaptation. *Policy Quarterly*, 14(2), 40–49. https://doi.org/10.26686/pq.v14i2.5093

Budd, L., & Sancino, A. (2016). A framework for city leadership in multilevel governance settings: The comparative contexts of Italy and the UK. *Regional Studies, 3*(1), 129–145.

Carey, J. (2020). Managed retreat increasingly seen as necessary in response to climate change's fury. *Proceedings of the National Academy of Sciences, 117*(24), 13182–13185. https://doi.org/10.1073/pnas.2008198117

Cavaye, J. (2001). Rural community development – New challenges and enduring dilemmas. *Regional Analysis and Policy, 31*(2), 109–124.

Cikaliuk, M., Erakovic, E., Jackson, B., Noonan, C., & Watson, S. (2022). *Responsible leadership in corporate governance: An integrative approach*. Routledge. https://doi.org/10.4324/9781003054191

Crosby, B., & Bryson, J. (2005). A leadership framework for cross-sector collaboration. *Public Management Review, 2*(2), 177–201. https://doi.org/10.1080/14719030500090519

Crutzen, P. J. (2006). The Anthropocene. In E. Ehlers & T. Krafft (Eds.), *Earth system science in the Anthropocene*. Springer, 13–18. https://doi.org/10.1007/3-540-26590-2_3

Dundon, L. A., & Abkowitz, M. (2021). Climate-induced managed retreat in the U.S.: A review of current research. *Climate Risk Management, 33*, 100337. https://doi.org/10.1016/j.crm.2021.100337

Fennel, L. (2011). Ostrom's law: Property rights in the commons. *International Journal of the Commons, 5*(1), 9–27.

Foucault, M. (1991). *Discipline and Punish: The Birth of a Prison*. London: Penguin.

Freudenberg, R., Calvin, E., Tolkoff, L., & Brawley, D. (2016). *Buy-in for buyouts: The case for managed retreat from flood zones*. Lincoln Institute of Land Policy. https://www.lincolninst.edu/sites/default/files/pubfiles/buy-in-for-buyouts-full.pdf

Gibney, J., & Collinge, C. (2015). *Leadership and place*. Routledge.

Gupta, J., & Grubb, M. (Eds.). (2000). *Climate Change: A Sustainable Role for Europe?*. Kluwer Academic Publishers.

Habermas, J. (1984). *The Theory of Communicative Action*. Boston: Beacon Press.Hambleton, R. (2015), *Leading the Inclusive City: Place-based Innovation for a Bounded Planet*, Policy Press, Bristol.

Hambleton, R., & Howard, J. (2013). Place based leadership and public service innovation. *Local Government Studies, 39*(1), 1–24. https://doi.org/10.1080/03003930.2012.693076

Hanna, C., White, I., & Glavovic, B. C. (2021). Managed retreats by whom and how? Identifying and delineating governance modalities. *Climate Risk Management, 31*, 100278. https://doi.org/10.1016/j.crm.2021.100278

Harrison, R. T., Kaesehage, K., & Leyshon, C. (2019). Special issue of leadership: Leadership and climate change: Authority, legitimacy and the 'crisis of governance'. *Leadership, 15*(6), 768–773. https://doi-org.ezproxy.auckland.ac.nz/10.1177/1742715019870385

Hino, M., Field, C., & Mach, K. J. (2017). Managed retreat as a response to natural hazard risk. *Nature Climate Change, 7*, 364–370. https://doi.org/10.1038/nclimate3252

Imperial, M. T., Ospina, S., Johnston, E., O'Leary, R., Thomsen, J., Williams, P., & Johnson, S. (2016). Understanding leadership in a world of shared problems: Advancing network governance in large landscape conservation. *Frontiers in Ecology and the Environment, 14*(3), 126–134. doi:10.1002/fee.1248

Intergovernmental Panel on Climate Change. (2021). *Climate change 2021: The physical science basis. Contribution of Working Group I to the Sixth Assessment Report of the Intergovernmental Panel on Climate Change* [V. Masson-Delmotte et al. (Eds.)]. Cambridge University Press.

Intergovernmental Panel on Climate Change. (2022). *Climate change 2022: Impacts, adaptation, and vulnerability. Contribution of Working Group II to the Sixth Assessment Report of the Intergovernmental Panel on Climate Change* [H.-O. Pörtner et al. (Eds.)]. Cambridge University Press.

Jackson, B. (2019). The power of place in public leadership research and development. *International Journal of Public Leadership, 15*(4), 209–223. https://doi.org/10.1108/ijpl-09-2019-0059

Jackson, B., Kempster, S., Liyanage, C., Shang, S., & Sun, P. (2023). 'Responsible leadership: Theory building or re-orientation mobilisation?' In D. Schedlitzki, M. Larsson, B. Carroll, & M. Bligh (Eds.), *Sage handbook of leadership* (2nd ed., pp. 212–226). Sage.

Jackson, B., & Parry, K. (2018). *A very short, fairly interesting and reasonably cheap book about studying leadership.* Sage.

Kempster, S., & Jackson, B. (2021). Leadership for what, why, for whom and where?: A responsibility perspective. *Journal of Change Management, 21*(1), 45–65. https://doi.org/10.1080/14697017.2021.1861721

Kempster, S., Maak, T., & Parry, K. (2019). *Good dividends: Responsible leadership of business purpose.* Routledgosle.

Koslov, L. (2016). The case for retreat. Public Culture, *28*(2), 359–387.

Kretzmann, J. P., & McKnight, J. (1993). *Building communities from the inside out: A path toward finding and mobilising a communities' assets.* The Asset-based Community Development Institute, Northwestern University.

Lakhwala, L. F. (2022). *Blue displacement: Environmental displacement and the Blue Acres Buyout program.* Rutgers The State University of New Jersey, School of Graduate Studies ProQuest Dissertations Publishing.

Lawrence, J., Allan, S., & Clarke, L. (2021, November). Inadequacy revealed and the transition to adaptation as risk management in New Zealand. *Policy and Practice Reviews, 3*, Article 734726.

Lawrence, J., Boston, J., Bell, R., Olufson, S., Kool, R., Hardcastle, M., & Stroombergen, A. (2020). Implementing pre-emptive managed retreat: constraints and novel insights. *Current Climate Change Reports, 6*, 66–80. https://doi.org/10.1007/s40641-020-00161-z

Leech, D., & Worrall, R. (2018, March/April). Place-based leadership: Both opportunity and challenge. *National Health Executive Newsletter*, 40–41.

Meijerink, S., & Stiller, S. (2013). What kind of leadership do we need for climate adaptation? A framework for analyzing leadership objectives, functions, and tasks in climate change adaptation. *Environment and Planning C: Government and Policy, 31*(2), 240–256. https://doi-org.ezproxy.auckland.ac.nz/10.1068/c11129

New Jersey Department of Environmental Protection. (2022). Blue Acres. https://www.nj.gov/dep/blueacres/

O'Donnell, T. (2022). Managed retreat and planned retreat: A systematic literature review. *Philosophical Transactions of the Royal Society B: Biological Sciences, 377*(1854), 1–11. https://doi.org/10.1098/rstb.2021.0129

Office of Information Commissioner. (2016). Transcript: Solomon Lecture, 28 September 2016. https://www.oic.qld.gov.au/__data/assets/pdf_file/0007/31687/Transcript_RTI-Day-Solomon-Lecture-2016.pdf

Olufson, S. (2019). *Managed retreat components and costing in a coastal setting* [Unpublished doctoral thesis]. Victoria University of Wellington. http://researcharchive.vuw.ac.nz/handle/10063/8359

Organisation for Economic Co-operation and Development. (2019). *Responding to rising seas: OECD country approaches to tackling coastal risks*. OECD Publishing. https://doi.org/10.1787/9789264312487-en

Ospina, S., & Foldy, E. (2010). Building bridges from the margins: The work of leadership in social change organizations. *The Leadership Quarterly, 21*(2), 292–307.

Ostrom, E. (2015). *Governing the commons: The evolution of institutions for collective action*. Cambridge University Press.

Raworth, K. (2022). *Doughnut economics: Seven ways to think like a 21st-century economist*. Penguin Random House.

Rocle, N., Dachary-Bernard, J., & Rey-Valette, H. (2021). Moving towards multi-level governance of coastal managed retreat: Insights and prospects from France. *Ocean & Coastal, 213, 227–293*. https://www.sciencedirect.com/science/article/abs/pii/S0964569121003756?via%3Dihub https://doi.org/10.1016/j.ocecoaman.2021.105892

Rocle, N., & Salles, D. (2018). 'Pioneers but not guinea pigs': Experimenting with climate change adaptation in French coastal areas. *Policy Sciences, 51*, 231–247. https://doi.org/10.1007/s11077-017-9279-z

Ropo, A., Salovaara, P., Sauer, E., & De Paoli, D. (2015). *Leadership in spaces and places*. Edward Elgar.

Sancino, A. (2022). *Public value co-creation: A multi-actor and multi-sector perspective*. Emerald.

Schneider, P., Lawrence, J., Glavovic, B., Ryan, E., & Blackett, P. (2020). A rising tide of adaptation action: Comparing two coastal regions of Aotearoa-New Zealand. *Climate Risk Management, 30*, 100244. https://doi.org/10.1016/j.crm.2020.100244

Siders, A. R., Ajibade, I., & Casagrande, D. (2021). Transformative potential of managed retreat as climate adaptation. *Current Opinion Environmental Sustainability, 50*, 272–280. https://doi.org/10.1016/j.cosust.2021.06.007

Sotarauta, M., & Beer, A. (2017). Governance, agency and place leadership: Lessons from a cross-national analysis. *Regional Studies, 51*(2), 210–223. https://doi.org/10.1080/00343404.2015.1119265

Spidalieri, K., & Smith, I. (2020). *Managing the retreat from rising seas. Woodbridge Township, New Jersey: Post–Hurricane Sandy buyouts*. Georgetown Climate Center. https://www.georgetownclimate.org/files/MRT/GCC_20_Woodbridge-4web.pdf

Susskind, L., & Kim, A. (2022). Building local capacity to adapt to climate change. *Climate Policy, 22*(5), 593–606. https://doi-org.ezproxy.auckland.ac.nz/10.1080/14693062.2021.1874860

Taylor, M., & Buckly, E. (2016). *Historical review of place-based approaches*. Institute of Voluntary Action Research.

Uhl-Bien, M., Marion, R., & McKelvey, B. (2007). Complexity leadership theory: shifting leadership from the industrial age to the knowledge era. *The Leadership Quarterly, 18*, 298–318.

Wilks, S., Lahausse, J., & Edwards, B. (2016). Commonwealth place-based service delivery initiatives: Key learnings project (Research Report No. 32). Australian Institute of Family Studies.

Winchester, S. (2021). *Land: How the hunger for ownership shaped the modern world*. William Collins.

Worrall, R., & Kjaerulf, F. (2019). Transforming minds, people and places: Leadership coalition building as catalyst for intersectoral collaboratives in urban violence prevention. *Aggression and Violent Behaviour, 47*, 282–292. https://doi.org/10.1016/j.avb.2019.02.012

Yunkaporta, T. (2019). *Sand talk: How Indigenous thinking can save the world*. The Text Publishing Company.

11

THE INTERSECTION BETWEEN ENVIRONMENTAL ETHICS AND LEADERSHIP

David J. Brown and Robert M. McManus

Chapter Summary

This chapter examines the intersection between environmental ethics and leadership using McManus and Perruci's five components of leadership model. The chapter defines the terms *leadership*, *ethical leadership* and *environmental ethics* before it explores four major approaches to environmental ethics: anthropocentricism, sentientism, biocentrism and ecocentrism. The authors then examine three of the major concepts of environmental ethics including a limitation of freedoms, the ethical standing of the environment and the responsibility to future generations. The authors close by proposing that environmental ethics demands that the natural world be considered as a superlayer encompassing the leadership process.

Leadership and ethics have been studied in tandem for millennia. Early thinkers such as Plato, Aristotle and Confucius are just a few examples of

DOI: 10.4324/9781003343011-13

history's luminaries to consider the intersection of these disciplines. In his *Republic*, Plato (375 B.C.E./2007) held that leaders should know the 'true, good, and beautiful' to be able to lead followers wisely. In his *Nicomachean Ethics*, Aristotle (ca. 340 B.C.E./2009) maintained that leaders should create circumstances that promoted their followers' flourishing. In his *Analects*, Confucius (ca. 330 B.C.E./2002) identified a long list of virtues that leaders should nurture and embody to be able to be worthy of leading their followers. Likewise, in contemporary history, the field of leadership has seen a growing interest in the intersection of leadership and ethics. Leadership programmes and leadership textbooks often include lessons or chapters on ethics, with the assumption that to practice good leadership, one must behave ethically (Ciulla, 2014; Johnson, 2020; Northouse, 2022).

The specific connection between *environmental ethics* and leadership has also been studied more recently. It is often implicitly assumed in the area of environmental leadership (Gallagher, 2012; Redekop, 2010; Redekop et al., 2018). Likewise, environmental ethics is often identified under the umbrella of corporate social responsibility and environment, social and corporate governance (Carroll et al., 2017). This increased interest in the intersection between environmental ethics and leadership is undoubtedly due to the present crises the Earth is facing such as global climate change, species loss and the overall deterioration of the natural world.

In this chapter, we will draw an explicit connection between environmental ethics and leadership to highlight how these two fields inform each other in both theory and practice. The basic question this chapter asks and attempts to answer is 'What is the place of the natural world in the leadership process?' In answering this question, we will first define our terms; then, we will highlight some of the major concepts of environmental ethics; finally, we will close with a way to conceive of environmental ethics that explicitly informs the leadership process.

Definition of Terms

To help focus our discussion, we will use the five components of leadership model proposed by McManus and Perruci (2020). The authors presented leadership as a *process* and offered that leadership should be viewed as 'purposeful interaction' (McManus & Perruci, 2020, p. 19). They argued that leadership exists wherever and whenever two or more people work towards a goal. The authors then presented the various components of the leadership process, including the leader, the followers, the goal, the context and the cultural values and norms that encompass the process.

Let us briefly consider each of these components. A leader can be a single person, a group of people or even an organisation. Essentially, the leader provides the legitimate authority or holds the power or influence to set the direction and motivate followers towards the goal. The followers are an integral part of the leadership equation. They may not have as much authority, power or influence as the leader, but they are instrumental in helping to achieve the goal. The third component in McManus and Perruci's model is the goal. The goal is the motivating factor or purpose that drives the leader and followers' interactions. As we will see later in this chapter, environmental ethics specifically speaks to the ways in which leaders and followers go about attempting to achieve their goal. The practice of leaders and followers working together to achieve their goals takes place in a particular context. This context also profoundly impacts the leadership process. What might be considered ethical in one context, such as war, might be utterly unethical in another, such as day-to-day business. Finally, we must consider the culture in which the leadership process is embedded. The values and norms of a particular culture may have weighty implications for what is considered appropriate or even ethical. Culture may determine what is moral regarding how leaders and followers interact, how they accomplish the goal or even the goal itself. Given these five components, we set forth the definition of leadership that we will use in this chapter.

Leadership

'Leadership is the process by which leaders and followers work together towards a goal (or goals) within a context shaped by cultural values and norms' (McManus & Perruci, 2020, p. 17).

Figure 11.1 depicts McManus and Perruci's definition of leadership and the five components of leadership model. Throughout our discussion, we will return to this definition of leadership and its five components.

Ethical Leadership

Before we move forward, we also need to define what we mean by *ethical leadership*. For this definition, we turn to the work of McManus et al. (2023), in which they propose a twofold meaning of ethical leadership. Ethical

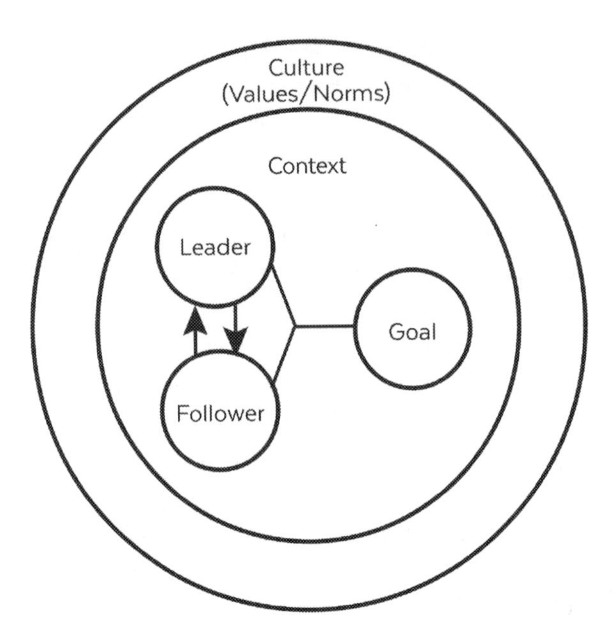

Figure 11.1 The Five Components of Leadership Model (© 2015, 2022 by Robert M. McManus and Gama Perruci. Used by permission of Routledge. All rights reserved.)

leadership is (a) the practice of leaders using various approaches of ethics to make ethically sound decisions and (b) using one's position of leadership position to bring about positive change (McManus et al., 2023).

It is worth taking time to unpack each of these statements. First, the authors' focus on understanding approaches to ethics implies that leaders must be able to *think* ethically before they can *act* ethically. As leadership scholar John Gardner (1993) said, 'The first step is not action; the first step is understanding. The first step is how to think about leadership' (p. xiv). The first step in acting ethically is understanding the ethical ideas that may inform leadership practice. Leaders and followers need at least a *basic* understanding of ethics to make ethically informed decisions. Later in this chapter, we will explore some fundamental concepts of environmental ethics and their relation to leadership. This exploration will help fulfill the first portion of McManus et al.'s definition of ethical leadership. Second, the authors' emphasis on using one's leadership position to bring about positive change implies that leaders and followers are responsible for transferring their thinking into action. Both leaders and followers are responsible not only for achieving the goal but also for achieving the goal in an ethical way using ethical means. Again, we will return to this idea later in our chapter.

Now that we have a clearer understanding of the terms leadership and ethical leadership, we must define the term *environmental ethics*. After that, we can more closely examine how environmental ethics inform the leadership process.

Environmental Ethics

Applied ethics is the process of evaluating a situation and using ethical theories and principles to determine the right or good decision regarding how to respond to that situation. This process can provide the reasoning for acting in one way as opposed to another way. The environment is defined as the surroundings or conditions and in the natural world; the term *environment* refers to the systems of nature. Environmental ethics is a subdiscipline of ethics used to make sense of humans' relationship to the environment and their impacts on the environment. It is a process that can decide how the environment and natural resources should be used by considering what our obligations are to others and to ourselves and also considering whether humans have obligations to non-human animals, plants and ecosystems.

History

To examine how leadership interacts with and is impacted by environmental ethics, it is essential to understand the historical major approaches to the field. As we progress, we will examine four basic lines of thought including anthropocentrism, sentientism, biocentrism and ecocentrism.

Anthropocentrism

In general, a Western valuation of environmental resources is seen to be human-centred or anthropocentric.[1] In this view, only humans are viewed as having moral standing, and value is primarily determined by the usefulness of an environmental component to contribute to human well-being. This approach can be used to evaluate resources like trees for lumber or minerals for computer chips. However, it could also be used to ascribe value more generally to the environment. In addition to the instrumental value of resources, humans can ascribe value to the environment for other reasons, such as aesthetics, as a reservoir of knowledge that humans could learn from or recreational opportunities and the impact of those activities on humans. However, ascribing an intrinsic value to natural areas can be more challenging since not all people value these areas the same. Some place a high value on them and are renewed by visiting these areas; some people do not visit natural areas but find it reassuring that natural areas still exist and therefore value their existence. Still other people may argue that maintaining the natural areas is not valuable and that extracting the resources they contain would be more useful. Another challenge associated with placing values on environmental components is that some species (e.g., mosquitos) or areas could be considered either not beneficial to humans or even harmful. To address these challenges, it is necessary to consider the foundations of Western thoughts on the environment.

Two parts of the foundation of Western civilisation will be examined here, the first being Greek philosophy and then religious texts. In both cases, they present a human-centred approach, and ethical value or standing is only ascribed to humans. For example, Aristotle proposed a hierarchy of species based on their ability to reason (Aristotle, ca. 350 BCE/1916). Those organisms lower in the hierarchy were there to be used by higher species. Humans were at the top, and all of the lower organisms were there to provide for humans. In this perspective, the natural world exists for humans' benefit and has become incorporated into Christianity. Thomas Aquinas (1225–1274), an Italian philosopher and theologian, embraced this idea expressed by Aristotle and related this and other Aristotelian ideas to the principles of Christianity. Aristotle's view of nature as a hierarchy matched well with Christianity's view of humanity having a special position relative to nature with 'dominion over the fish of the sea and over the fowl of the air, and over every living thing that moveth upon the earth' (*King James Bible*, Gen. 1:28). In his major unfinished work, the *Summa Theologica*, Thomas Aquinas (ca. 1265/2006) indirectly expanded upon this relationship with nature in his classification of different types of sins. The possibility of sinning against non-human animals or nature was not included. Essentially this implies that non-human animals and nature do not have ethical standing and their destruction is not a sin unless it harms humans.

Working from this foundation provides one way of valuing environmental components based on the instrumental value those resources have in supporting humans. However, the environment and non-human animals do not intrinsically have ethical standing or value based on this foundation. However, these perceptions began to be questioned in the 20th century. As the human population continued to increase and human impacts on the environment became more apparent, there were calls to reassess the relationship between humans and the environment. Events like the smog episodes in London in 1952 and New York City in 1966 and the multiple fires on the Cuyahoga River in Ohio in the 1960s captured the general population's attention. They made them think about the relationship between humans and nature and what responsibilities humans had to protect nature.

Similarly, the publication of *Silent Spring* by Rachel Carson in 1962 (Carson 1962/2022) introduced a broad audience to the impacts of the use of pesticides on the environment. It promoted the view that humans should not consider themselves separate from nature. This interest in how humans relate to nature led to environmental ethics and several philosophies defining the human–nature relationship. These philosophies go beyond the anthropocentric philosophy and extend intrinsic value to environmental components other than just humans. We will look at these philosophies beginning with the more narrowly focused (sentientism) and moving to the more broadly encompassing ecocentrism.

Sentientism

Arguments have been made that we should move beyond these anthropocentric foundations and consider the possibility that at least some components of the environment should have ethical standing. Ethicist Peter Singer (2002) developed his argument by explaining that Aristotle had also used his hierarchy as justification for slavery. In Aristotle's hierarchy, captured non-Greeks were considered less rational and to not have intrinsic value but served a higher purpose by their service to their Greek captors (Aristotle, ca. 350 B.C.E./2016). Similarly, the Bible has also been used to justify slavery in the past (Cheever, 1857; Harris, 1788; McKivigan & Snay, 1998; Singer, 2002; Stringfellow, 1856). We now reject these arguments in support of slavery, mainly because we accept that enslaved individuals also have interests and their enslavement devalues or reduces their ability to pursue those interests. Even if we accept that these non-Greeks were less rational, they can still enjoy life, feel pain and value their relationships with family and friends. Singer showed how this argument against slavery can also be used to justify extending ethical value to non-human animals. Many non-human animals can feel pain, they can enjoy life and they can suffer if they are separated from their family. Singer argued that because sentient non-human animals have interests, they should have some standing, which should be considered in decisions. The life of an animal might not be given the same value as the life of a human, but the death of that animal does inflict a loss on that animal that cannot be ignored. If we accept this argument, it is possible to place a value on at least sentient components of the environment beyond just what their value is to support humans. Singer could not come up with a justification for placing an ethical value on non-sentient beings; for example, plants. However, suppose we accept that non-human animals have some level of standing to be allowed to survive. In that case, this provides secondary protection to other non-sentient components of the environment because non-human animals need that habitat to survive. This line of thinking allows us to move beyond the human-centred value system that only ascribes value based on whether something is useful to humans.

Biocentrism

However, some people consider anthropocentrism and sentientism too narrow to define moral standing and intrinsic value when considering the environment. Biocentrism is a broader theory that goes beyond ascribing moral standing to sentient organisms and claims *that all living organisms should be considered when making decisions.* To support this argument, Routley (1973) proposed a thought experiment called the 'Last Man'. In this thought experiment, the premise is that a single human has survived a global catastrophe. This simplifies the problem since the individual's actions will not harm other humans and there isn't the possibility of future humans that might be affected. The question is then posed, if this individual aimlessly destroys the plants and animals around him, would this be acceptable? Routley proposed that most people would condemn this destruction. Further, he argued that the good of plants and animals leads to an environmental ethic where humans have an obligation not to aimlessly destroy living things. The argument is that even non-sentient organisms like plants have a good of their own and goals. The argument is further made that this good is not dependent on sentience or having feelings, and the ability of the organism to reach those goals is intrinsically valuable. Therefore, it would be wrong to do something that harms even an insentient organism. This argument does not rely on ascribing ethical standing to all living organisms but rather is based on the idea that humans have an obligation not to destroy these organisms without cause because these organisms have a good of their own.

Ecocentrism

Biocentrism focuses on the value of individual organisms, whether sentient or insentient. Ecocentrism is an even broader theory in that it also recognises that systems like ecosystems and the non-living components of these systems also have value. Ecocentrists argue that the value of the ecosystem goes beyond its ability to support the lives of living components of that ecosystem, whether sentient or insentient. Therefore, the ecosystem has a value of its own that goes beyond the value of the organisms it supports. One of the first proponents of this theory was Aldo Leopold. In his essays published posthumously (Leopold, 1949/2020), he combined his observations of nature while presenting a philosophy that placed an intrinsic value on nature. He was making the argument that nature was good or desirable in itself and did not only have instrumental value. He argued that humans needed to recognise that they were a part of nature and the ecosystem could be thought of as a community. Humans are members of this community, but they are not dominators or owners of the system; rather, the success of the system is based on the competition and cooperation of the individuals in the community. Therefore, there needed to be a change in how humans value environmental components and systems. He called this new values system a 'land ethic' that focuses on the ecosystem's long-term health (Leopold, 1949/2020). The idea was summarised in one of his most well-known quotes: 'A thing is right when it tends to promote the integrity, stability, and beauty of the biotic community. It is wrong when it tends otherwise' (Leopold, 1949/2020, p. 242. Note that in this passage, Leopold is referring to the 'community' and not to individuals.)

Major Concepts in Environmental Ethics

Now that we have a basic understanding of the historical approaches to the study of environmental ethics, we can more precisely identify some of the specific ethical implications and major concepts highlighted in the field.

Limitation of Freedoms

At its basis, ethics is a process that is used to make decisions that involve value judgements. Faced with a problem, someone might use ethics to decide by considering what rules were in place that are relevant to the problem, considering what options were available and considering how those options would affect themselves as well as how the decision would potentially impact others. If we agree to use ethics to address problems like this, we must recognise that this limits our freedoms. Instead of making a decision based on what is best for us, ethics asks that we also consider the impacts on others and consideration of any rules that have been adopted by society that are relevant to the problem being addressed. In general, these limitations are viewed as acceptable because humans are interdependent in social settings and using ethics to address problems helps limit conflicts.

To illustrate the concept of interdependence, Garret Hardin (1968) created a thought experiment that asks us to consider a pasture shared by 10 ranchers. The pasture can accommodate 10 cows; thus, each rancher can allow 1 cow to graze on the pasture. However, what if 1 rancher decides to place 2 cows on the pasture? In this instance, the other ranchers would see a 10% decrease in their production, but the rancher placing 2 cows on the pasture would receive almost a 90% increase in benefit. If all the ranchers were to do this, the pasture would be unable to sustain any cattle in a short amount of time. Hardin introduced the concept of the tragedy of the commons to explain the problem when environmental resources that are considered common are used by individuals making decisions based on their own good. In that situation, each individual benefits if they maximise their use of the resource, but this leads to depletion of the resource and, eventually, a tragedy for all of the individuals using it. Hardin claimed that the community could not rely on the conscientiousness of individuals to do what was best for the community as a way to solve this problem. He argued that individuals who limited their resource use based on conscientiousness would gain less. However, not all individuals would be conscientious since they would benefit if they ignored the good of the community. Several possible solutions have been suggested to the tragedy of the commons. One possible solution is to move from a commons to private ownership of portions of the resource. This limitation places more of a direct responsibility on the individual owners to decide how to use the resource. Hopefully, they will be more concerned about the sustainability of the resource. However, this is less applicable to some resources, such as water or air, and not all owners will make decisions that contribute to the resource's long-term sustainability. Hardin also proposed the idea of 'mutually agreed upon coercion'; basically, the community agrees upon a penalty or cost for using the resource, which becomes incorporated into the decision-making process and can be used to regulate the use of the resource. Each of these solutions has some weaknesses, and environmental ethics is another possible solution to the tragedy of common resources that could provide a more rational justification for limiting resource use.

The Value and Ethical Standing of the Environment

When we specifically focus on environmental ethics, we use ethics to make decisions about how we interact with the environment and, particularly, how environmental or natural resources are used. To make these value-based judgements, we need to address two main points. First, how do we place values on environmental resources or entities and, in particular, do non-human components of the environment have ethical standing that should be considered? The second question relates to the stakeholders in an environmental issue and their rights and responsibilities. We will begin by looking at the value question and then consider who has a stake in different environmental issues.

We can then move on to the second question: Who are the stakeholders in environmental issues? In some cases, it seems like the stakeholders should be easy to identify – just identify individuals with a right or responsibility related to the evaluation of the resource or environmental component. For example, if we go back to the common pasture that Hardin (1968) discussed in 'The Tragedy of the Commons', the chief stakeholders would be the people in the community who had a right to graze their livestock on that land. However, other individuals have a potential stake in this issue. For example, are there individuals in the community who do not have livestock and are limited in their use of this land because it is being used as pasture?

Additionally, suppose we accept that non-human sentient animals also have a standing in this issue. In that case, we should also consider the livestock and other non-human animals in the area affected by how the pasture resource is used. In this example, not all of the potential stakeholders' interests in this issue would be considered equivalent. Some stakeholders, such as the individuals who graze their livestock on the pasture, would have a more significant stake in the use of this resource, and their interests would be weighted accordingly.

When we consider the potential stakeholders who have an interest in an issue as simple as Hardin's common pasture, we start to recognise how complex ethical decisions can end up being. However, it is possible to predict the impact on different stakeholder populations and determine the overall impact of each possible solution for an environmental problem. Understandably, this becomes more complex for some environmental issues. For example, if the issue were waste being disposed of into a river, the stakeholders would include the community disposing of their waste. They would also include all downstream stakeholders impacted by the decreased water quality. Some environmental issues are even more complex, such as threats to biodiversity and climate change. These are issues in which all human and sentient non-human animals have a stake.

The Responsibility for Future Generations

Finally, one more issue needs to be considered concerning stakeholders in environmental issues. Ideally, the goal of decisions about an environmental issue is for that environmental resource to be used in a sustainable way in which it is not depleted and will continue to exist into the future. Essentially, this means that we are also considering future generations as having a stake in the issue; therefore, their interests should also be considered. The United Nations specifically identified this aspect of environmental ethics in its Brundtland Commission report titled *Our Common Future* (World Commission on Environment and Development, 1987). In this seminal work, the authors of the report defined 'sustainable development' as 'development that meets the needs of the present without compromising the ability of future generations to meet their own needs' (World Commission on Environment and Development, 1987, p. 43). This definition of sustainable development places an ethical responsibility to consider the stakeholders who are not yet able to advocate for themselves – in most cases, generations who are not even born. Note, however, that the report implicates only human stakeholders and, therefore, an anthropocentric view of environmental ethics. Given the other approaches to environmental ethics highlighted in this chapter, this definition of sustainable development may also apply to sentient beings, insentient beings and ecosystems. Thus, environmental ethics also forces leaders and followers to consider the implications of their actions not only on present stakeholders but on future stakeholders as well.

Conclusion

We began this chapter by asking the question, 'What is the place of the natural world in the leadership process?' In attempting to answer this question, we defined leadership and, specifically, ethical leadership. We also presented some of the major lines of historical thinking surrounding environmental ethics, as well as three of the major concepts in the field.

Turning back to the five components of leadership model introduced earlier in this chapter, we can begin to see environmental ethics fit into the leadership process. As we have seen from our brief summary of environmental ethics, the natural world encompasses all parts of the leadership process – the leader, follower, goal, context and culture. The process of leadership is enabled and constrained by the limits of the natural world. Thus, we propose the natural world is a super layer encompassing the leadership process (McManus, 2018). This superlayer of the natural world is the crucial variable of the leadership process as it relates to answering the question that motivates this chapter. This is depicted in Figure 11.2.

In theory, leaders and followers must realise that their ability to reach their goal is both enabled and constrained by the resources provided by the natural world. The goal must be one that meets the needs of both current generations while allowing future generations to meet their needs as well. Allowing future generations to meet their needs must be considered as part of the context. Although cultural values and norms may vary, the natural world acts outside cultural values and norms and enables and constrains them as well.

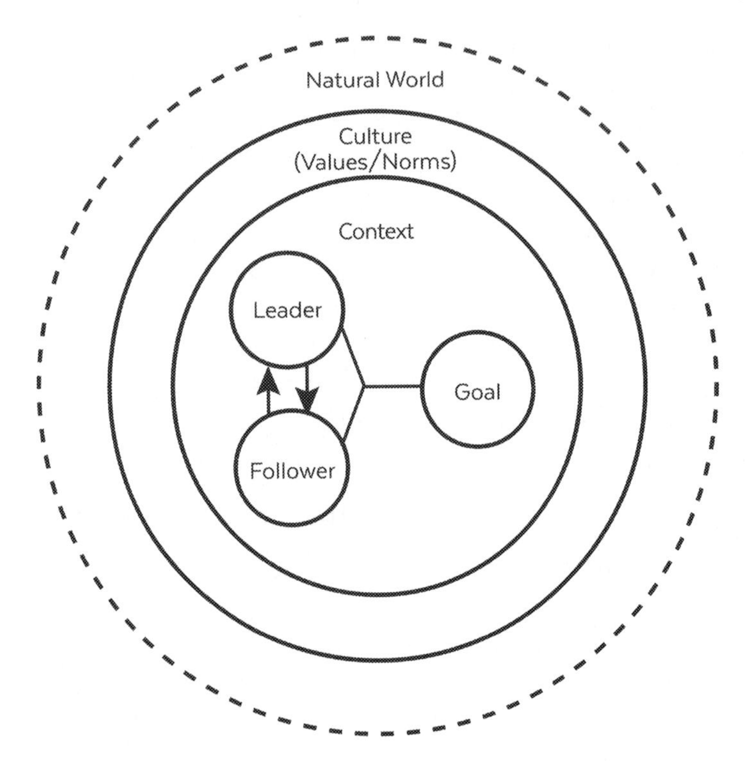

Figure 11.2 The Five Components of Leadership Model Set Within the Natural World (© 2015, 2022 by Robert M. McManus and Gama Perruci. Used by permission of Routledge. All rights reserved. Alteration made with permission by the authors.)

In practice, environmental ethics demands that leaders and followers consider the implications of their actions not only on other human beings or even sentient beings but on all living organisms and ecosystems. These creatures and systems all have moral standing and must be considered when leaders and followers go about pursuing their goal and the means they use to achieve their goals. This means that leaders and followers must be willing to limit their freedoms to protect the natural world. They must also acknowledge the intrinsic value and moral standing of the natural world and not only value the environment for its instrumental value to helping them pursue their goals. Finally, leaders and followers must also work to ensure the protection of future generations, sentient and insentient organisms, biosystems and ecosystems, allowing all of these stakeholders the ability to flourish.

Discussion points

- An argument could be made that the eco-centric approach is the most compelling theory of environmental ethics. Why might it be useful to apply the other environmental ethical theories covered in this chapter?
- Make an ethical argument for preserving the Amazon rainforest using each of the ethical theories covered in this chapter.
- Which of the ethical theories proposed in this chapter most closely comports with your approach to environmental ethics. Why?

Notes

1 We will be approaching the question of the ethical value of environmental resources primarily from a Western cultural perspective. This focus on Western values and norms is partly a result of the authors' cultural upbringing, but we recognise that culture will impact how environmental ethics are approached. However, approaching environmental ethics from a Western perspective could be more challenging. Therefore, many of the arguments that will be considered will be applicable in other cultural contexts.

Suggested Reading

Attfield, R. (2018). *Environmental ethics: A very short introduction.* Oxford.
Leopold, A. (1986). *A Sand County almanac.* Ballantine.

References

Aquinas, Saint Thomas. (2006). *Summa theologica.* (Fathers of the English Dominican Province, Trans.) The Project Gutenberg eBook of Summa Theologica, Part I (Prima Pars). (Original work published ca. 1265). https://www.gutenberg.org/cache/epub/17611/pg17611-images.html

Aristotle. (2009). *Nicomachean ethics* (D. Ross & L. Brown, Trans.). Oxford. (Original work published ca. 340 B.C.E.)

Aristotle. (2016). *Politics* (W. Ellis, Trans). J.M. Dent and Sons. (Original work published ca. 350 B.C.E.)

Carroll, A. B., Brown, J., & Buschholtz, A. K. (2017). *Business & society: Ethics, sustainability & stakeholder management* (10th ed.). Cengage Learning.

Carson, R. (2022). *Silent spring.* Mariner. (Original work published 1962)

Cheever, G. B. (1857). *God against slavery.* Reform Tract and Book Society.

Ciulla, J. (2014). *Ethics: The heart of leadership* (3rd ed.). Praeger.
Confucius. (2002). *Analects*. Project Gutenberg of the Chinese Classics by James Legee. (Original work published ca. 330 B.C.E.). https://www.gutenberg.org/cache/epub/3100/pg3100-images.html
Gallagher, D. R. (2012). *Environmental leadership: A reference handbook*. Sage.
Gardner, J. (1993). *On leadership*. Free Press.
Hardin, G. (1968). The tragedy of the commons. *Science, 162*(3859), 1243–1248.
Harris, R. (1788). *Scriptural researches on the licitness of the slave-trade*. Hodgson.
Johnson, C. E. (2020). *Meeting the ethical challenges of leadership: Casting light or shadow*. Sage.
King James Bible. (2017). King James Bible Online. https://www.kingjamesbibleonline.org/ (Original work published 1769)
Leopold, A. (2020). *A Sand County almanac*. Oxford. (Original work published 1949)
McKivigan, J. R., & Snay, M. (1998). *Religion and the Antebellum debate over slavery*. University of Georgia Press.
McManus, R. M. (2018). Toward an understanding of the relationship between the study of leadership and the natural world. In B. Redekop, D. R. Gallagher, & R. Satterwhite (Eds.), *Innovation in environmental leadership: Critical perspectives* (97–115). Routledge.
McManus, R. M., & Perruci, G. (2020). *Understanding leadership: An arts and humanities perspective*. Routledge.
McManus, R. M., Ward, S. J., & Perry, S. K. (2023). *Ethical leadership: A primer* (2nd ed.). Edward Elgar.
Northouse, P. G. (2022). *Leadership: Theory and practice* (9th ed.). Sage.
Plato. (2007). The republic (D. Lee, Trans). Penguin. (Original work published 375 B.C.E.)
Redekop, B. (Ed.). (2010). *Leadership for environmental sustainability*. Routledge.
Redekop, B., Gallagher, D. R., & Satterwhite, R. (Eds.). (2018). *Innovations in environmental leadership: Critical perspectives*. Routledge.
Routley, R. (1973). Is there a need for a new, an environmental, ethic? *Proceedings of the XVth World Congress of Philosophy*, 1, 205–210.
Singer, P. (2002). *Writings on an ethical life*. Ecco.
Stringfellow, T. (1856). *A Scriptural and statistical views in defense of slavery*. J.W. Randolph.
World Commission on Environment and Development. (1987). *Our common future*. Oxford University Press.

Part III

PROGRESSIONS

12

WE ARE PROLONGING UNSUSTAINABILITY. SHOULDN'T WE SAVE HUMANITY INSTEAD?

Nancy E. Landrum

Chapter Summary

Corporate sustainability has not produced the expected results to address the climate crisis and, in fact, carbon emissions and other greenhouse gases continue to accumulate in the atmosphere. Earth's average global temperature has already increased by nearly 1°, and research suggests that we are on track for a total increase between 2.5° (United Nations Environment Programme, 2022; United Nations Framework Convention on Climate Change, 2022) to 3.2°C (Intergovernmental Panel on Climate Change [IPCC], 2022), well beyond the 1.5°C increase by 2030 goal that scientists set as the threshold to avert severe consequences. Businesses have used economic science to guide sustainability decision making and have become mired in business-centred sustainability, or business as usual with incremental improvements, a form of weak sustainability. But weak business-centred 'sustainability' is a misnomer and is not sustainable at all. Weak business-centred sustainability only

DOI: 10.4324/9781003343011-15

masks and prolongs unsustainability. The only solution to the climate crisis and to save humanity is to move business, industry and society towards strong sustainability.

Introduction

How long have we known that humans are negatively impacting the environment or that burning fossil fuels would lead to a warming planet? Twenty-five years? Fifty years? It's been much longer. Approximately 225 years ago, Thomas Malthus (1798) told us that humans are negatively impacting the environment when he warned us that, over time, population growth would outstrip the Earth's resources and lead to ecological and social collapse. It's been more than 165 years since Eunice Foote (1856) told us that trapped carbon dioxide would lead to changing planetary temperatures, Nearly 160 years ago, George Perkins Marsh (1864) observed that humans were destroying the environment through greed of the technological enterprise. And it's been more than 125 years since Svante Arrhenius (1896) told us that emissions from industrial activity would lead to climate change. Yet here we are, amid the converging problems of a climate crisis, the sixth mass extinction of biodiversity loss, exceeding planetary boundaries and facing pandemics and social upheaval (Dixson-Decleve et al., 2022) – many of these interconnected problems are because we have chosen to ignore science. Together, these problems comprise the concerns of sustainability science.

Theory and Basic Concepts

There is a rhetorical push for sustainability in our personal lives and in business and industry. Yet there is a lot of confusion and debate over sustainability, its meaning and how to enact it. Some argue that sustainability, historically, only encompasses environmental concerns (Åkerman, 2003; Mebratu, 1998), while others argue that it encompasses environmental, social and economic concerns (World Commission on Environment and Development, 1987). Similarly, while one company promotes its sustainability activities or its sustainable product, others accuse the company of greenwashing.

For clarification, sustainability encompasses environmental, social and economic concerns and their current and future impacts (Brundtland, 1987). Environmental concerns are issues that impact our life-supporting systems, such as oxygen, water and biodiversity. Social concerns are issues that impact people's quality of life, such as health, family and relationships, education, work–life balance, diversity, equity and inclusion. Economic concerns are issues that impact sustainable economic development, such as production and consumption and the just distribution of resources. Each of these three entrails of sustainability are necessary yet insufficient alone. Together, they create an integrated and holistic concept; the aspects are not separate and equal as we have been led to believe and as commonly depicted in Venn diagrams, pillars, or stools (Dawe & Ryan, 2003; Lehtonen, 2004).

It is useful to think of sustainability along a continuum of varying degrees ranging from a very weak sustainability orientation to a very strong sustainability orientation (Pearce, 1993). Using this continuum, five stages of sustainability (Table 12.1) have been identified (Landrum, 2018). Companies can have sustainability initiatives in several stages, but most of a company's sustainability efforts will align with one of the following stages.

1. *Compliance.* Companies engaged in compliance sustainability adopt actions that are required and enforced by external bodies, such as regulatory standards.
2. *Business-Centred* (or self-centred). Companies engaged in business-centred sustainability adopt actions for self-benefit (or for the benefit of immediate stakeholders), such as reduced costs, increased profits, improved image and reputation or increased market share.
3. *Systemic.* Companies engaged in systemic sustainability work with others to adopt or promote actions that seek to change systems and that will benefit others beyond the company and its immediate stakeholders, such as improved labour practices, stricter industry regulations or supporting the wide-scale adoption of renewable energy.
4. *Regenerative.* Companies engaged in regenerative sustainability work to repair the social, environmental and economic damage caused by past industrial activities, such as through regenerative agriculture, reparations or wealth redistribution.
5. *Coevolutionary.* Companies engaged in coevolutionary sustainability work to control company and industry activities to operate in balance with other social, environmental and economic systems, such as self-control of organisational impacts to maintain balance with systems rather than authoritative control over others to meet the needs of the organisation.

Table 12.1 Stages of Corporate Sustainability

	Compliance	Business-centered	Systemic	Regenerative	Coevolutionary
Sustainability spectrum position	Very weak	Weak	Intermediate	Strong	Very strong
Orientation	Economic science-oriented Business-oriented	Economic science-oriented Business-oriented	Economic science-oriented Business-oriented	Ecological science-oriented Ecology-oriented	Ecological science-oriented Ecology-oriented
Understanding of sustainability	Meet compliance requirements Internal firm-centric view	"Do less bad" Internal firm-centric view	"Do more good" Begins to look externally in defining sustainability Business is part of a larger industry and community working together toward systemic change	Repair damage to systems	Humans and all earth's beings are in a mutually enhancing and beneficial relationship
Relationship to natural world	To be managed and controlled anthropocentric Resource exploitation	To be managed and controlled anthropocentric Resource exploitation Eco-efficiency	To be managed and controlled; anthropocentric Resource exploitation Eco-efficiency	Part of the natural world Operate within planetary boundaries Manage and repair	Self-management as part of the natural world Participate in cooperative symbiotic relationship with the natural world
Economic growth	Pursuit of production, consumption and growth	Pursuit of production, consumption and growth	Pursuit of production, consumption and growth	Qualitative development without production, consumption and growth Steady-state growth	No growth in production or consumption Qualitative improvements
Sustainability concerns	Externally enforced or regulated activities Defensive actions with regard to economic, environmental or social concerns	"Business case" is the motivation and measure of success Adoption and internal enforcement of activities Incremental improvements to business-as-usual May focus on one or more realms of sustainability (economic, environmental, social)	Integrates three realms of sustainability (economic, environmental, social) Work with other human systems	Integrates three realms of sustainability (economic, environmental, social) Work with human and non-human systems	Work in balance with other systems Contribute to flourishing of other systems

Source: Landrum (2018). Reproduced with permission.

Of the five stages, the first three stages (compliance, business-centred and systemic) represent varying degrees of *weak* sustainability. But weak sustainability is a misnomer in that these stages are not sustainable at all; they simply slow human destruction and prolong unsustainability. The last two stages (regenerative and coevolutionary) represent varying degrees of *strong* sustainability. Strong sustainability is the only option that is sustainable and that can achieve a flourishing future. Uleander and Eriksson (2022) presented this dichotomy as shown in Figure 12.1.

Because strong sustainability (regenerative sustainability and coevolutionary sustainability) is the only path to achieving sustainability, it necessitates further elaboration. Regenerative sustainability gestures restore, regenerate and repair; they follow nature's circular model wherein waste

	weak sustainability	**strong sustainability**
Primary motivation for sustainability	Business case (profit, growth reputation, competition, retention)	Ecological & social (planetary health, and wellbeing of humans, animals & plants)
Openness to comprimise sustainability values	Higher	Lower
Common solutions	Technological improvements. Consumers should make better choices.	Changes in behavior and mindsets. Nature based solutions coexist with technology. Integrating with ecosystems. Systems thinking.
Relation to nature	Business often contributes to extracting, polluting, and degrading the environment. Limited awareness and knowledge.	Respect ecosystems and boundaries. Equality of all. Awareness and knowledge about e.g., ecology.
Economy	Pursuit of consumption, production, profit and growth.	Pursuit of quality of life, balance and appropriate size. Services and sharing.
Life style	Commonly resource intensive, high consumption, fast living.	Facilitate a sustainable lifestyle for clients and customer. Rethinking sourcing, production, consumption, distribution and packaging.
Change	Incremental improvements towards sustainability. Greening.	Rapid transformation, solutions that align with the size of challenges.
Responsibility	Sees responsibility as limited (scoping).	Full responsibility. Focus on collaboration.
Communication	Selective communication. Lack of transparency and information on total impact.	Honest, self-critical and transparent communication.
Justice	Justice?	Fair distribution of benefits and risks (between generations, global & local). Participation, recognition, capacity.
Result		

Figure 12.1 Weak vs. Strong Sustainability

Source: Uleander and Eriksson (2022). Reproduced with permission.

becomes food for another process. In today's circular economy model, the process seeks to regenerate natural systems. This contrasts with the earlier stage of systemic sustainability gestures that often involve actions that recapture, recycle, reuse or reduce, demonstrating that there is an alternative to wasteful standard industry practices and seeking to disrupt the industry and showcase better methods. While there are many examples of companies restoring, regenerating and repairing resources, ironically, it is the regenerative side of the equation that is often overlooked in today's discourse on regenerative sustainability. The 'regenerative element … is left out when resources are not replaced at the rate that they are taken' (Tazawa, 2021). Regenerative sustainability can easily be demonstrated by companies whose core business is to restore the environment or by the philanthropic efforts of businesses that donate to environmental protection and restoration. However, these efforts can be greenwashing if they are used as an offset to camouflage business as usual that continues to degrade the environment. Furthermore, research shows that tree planting projects are often ineffective and sometimes cause more harm (Lewis et al., 2019; Luthy, 2022). Therefore, caution is urged with these types of regenerative and restorative practices. Fortunately, companies don't need to be biologically based to be regenerative. The separation of the biological (businesses based on nature) and technical (businesses based on man-made products) spheres of the circular economy leads us to believe that regeneration only happens on the biological side of the equation. This is a critical point to note: businesses on the technical side of the economy can and should engage in regenerative practices, too. The challenge is to identify how to apply principles of restoration ecology and regenerative agriculture to the functioning of technically based business, industry and the economy. Virtually every business relies on natural resources. Regenerating nature in a strategic manner would have businesses regenerating the natural resources upon which it relies rather than randomly selecting environmental philanthropy efforts – this is the difference between checkbook philanthropy and strategic philanthropy (Porter & Kramer, 2002, 2006).

Coevolutionary sustainability embraces the goal of human and nonhuman systems coexisting together in synergy, without conflict between the systems and functioning in a symbiotic relationship with the business as an active participant in nature's ecological systems and cycles. Of distinction in this stage is that humans do not control nature; rather, they control themselves to exist in balance with nature. Rachel Carson (Golds et al., 2007) summed up this stage when she stated, 'We in this generation must come to terms with nature, and I think we're challenged as mankind has never been challenged before to prove our maturity and our mastery, not of nature, but of ourselves' (44:25).

Both strong sustainability approaches (regenerative and coevolutionary) employ nature-based solutions. Nature-based solutions are strategies and tactics to work in partnership with nature to address a sustainability challenge. Regenerative and coevolutionary sustainability's nature-based solutions have different goals/outcomes: one to restore and improve functioning of a damaged system and one to integrate with the system in a long-term symbiotic relationship.

Measurement – Reliable and Valid Assessment

Current business practices towards sustainability do not fare well. Research on readings assigned in U.S. business schools (Landrum & Ohsowski, 2017), sustainability reports by global companies (Landrum & Ohsowski, 2018) and sustainability schemes used by U.S. companies (Demastus & Landrum, 2023) all share similar findings. First, there is a strong presence of compliance sustainability; companies are following regulatory compliant activities but touting the activities as proof of green credentials. Second, business-centred (or self-centred) sustainability is the dominant approach; companies are only engaging in incremental change without substantive change to current practices. Third, there is minor movement towards systemic sustainability; relatively few companies are taking the next step to work with others to change systems beyond those that are self-serving. And fourth, there is a noticeable absence of regenerative sustainability and coevolutionary sustainability; even fewer companies have adopted the levels of sustainability required for a flourishing future.

These findings are troublesome because, as noted earlier, compliance, business-centred and systemic sustainability are variations of weak sustainability and only seek to *prolong unsustainability*; they will never help us achieve our sustainability goals. Yet this is where research shows that businesses are firmly rooted; approximately 71% of Landrum and Ohsowski's (2017) sample were aligned with a variation of weak sustainability. Businesses have attempted to deflect blame and shift responsibility to consumers while continuing business as usual with incremental changes (Landrum, 2020; Park, 2022). For example, we know that businesses and industries, particularly the highly polluting fossil fuel and cement industries (Climate Accountability Institute, 2020), have invested a significant number of resources in climate change denial and have sown public doubt and confusion (Brigham, 2020; Halttunen et al., 2022; InfluenceMap, 2022; Kaganovsky, 2021; McGreal, 2021; Mills, 2019), similar to the corporate history attempting to obfuscate the relationship between nicotine and cancer (Proctor, 2011). Deflecting responsibility has long been a favoured, and even predictable, corporate response to taking responsibility for its actions.

There are several theories that attempt to explain why businesses are failing to enact the transformational change that is needed to address our multiple social, environmental and economic crises and are thus stuck in weak sustainability. For example, virtually every report identifies climate change as one of the most critical issues facing humanity, yet little is done to address the problem. Some blame government inaction fuelled by industry lobbyists and a short-term lens (Paulson, 2015). Others point to the perceived cost to address the issue when, in fact, research shows that the sooner it is addressed, the cheaper it will be (Calel et al., 2020; Glanemann et al., 2020; IPCC, 2022). Demastus and Landrum (2023) indicated that sustainability schemes are complicit and have failed to challenge current practices or guide companies towards significant change and instead have reinforced business as usual with incremental change. It has also been suggested that individual leaders are the problem; they must be skilled in a variety of leadership types (Goleman, 2000), and leaders who have not mastered these styles then fail to adopt an adequate leadership style to spur corporate action (Vignola et al., 2017). Similarly, Miller and Serafeim (2015) showed that the role of the corporate sustainability officer changes, particularly in the degree of authority to create change, as organisations become more committed to sustainability and progress through stages. It has also been suggested that individual leaders experience tension between the need for companies to change and the need to continue business as usual (Halttunen et al., 2022), yet cognitive biases prevent decision makers and companies from acting (Mazutis & Eckardt, 2017). Whatever the cause for inaction and given the limited response of government, business and industry, it is no wonder that social, environmental and economic conditions are worsening (Dyllick & Muff, 2016; IPCC, 2022).

It is only through regenerative and coevolutionary sustainability, both variations of strong sustainability, that we can meet Paris Agreement goals and provide hope in tackling our environmental, social and economic crises. Yet research shows that these levels of sustainability are absent in practice (Demastus & Landrum, 2023; Landrum & Ohsowski, 2017, 2018).

Practice: Methods, Techniques and Application

The question now becomes how to move out of weak sustainability and into the realm of strong sustainability. Strong sustainability includes regenerative sustainability and coevolutionary sustainability; however, there is little guidance from academia or practice on specific actions necessary for companies to achieve strong sustainability (de Oliveira Neto et al., 2018; Özkaynak et al., 2004). In fact, de Oliveira Neto et al. (2018) found that only 5% of the academic literature in their study discussed strong sustainability.

Awareness of regenerative sustainability has been growing since Lyle's (1994) seminal book on regenerative design and the subsequent work to apply these ideals to business and industry (cf. Hahn & Tampe, 2021). Regenerative sustainability is rooted in an ecological worldview, following principles of restoration ecology (Landrum, 2018). A. Kim et al. (2021, p. 2) described it as 'healing nature that has been damaged by humans' and 'surgery and treatment for the natural environment, that treats and restores the diseased nature to the intact one'.

Despite the progress made in defining regenerative and restorative approaches, we lack operationalisation of regenerative sustainability for businesses. However, the United Nations Environment Programme has sought to integrate a variety of principles for restorative activities into one set of principles that underpin all restorative activities and which are applicable to all (Food and Agriculture Organization, 2021). These principles of restoration can serve as a high-level guide for regenerative sustainability (Food and Agriculture Organization, 2021):

- Contributes to the Sustainable Development Goals and the Rio Conventions Goals
- Promotes inclusive and participatory governance, social fairness and equity
- Includes a continuum of restorative activities

- Aims to achieve the highest level of recovery for biodiversity, ecosystem health and integrity and human well-being
- Addresses direct and indirect causes of degradation
- Incorporates all types of knowledge and promotes their exchange and integration
- Based on well-defined short, medium- and long-term ecological, cultural and socio-economic goals and objectives
- Tailored to the local ecological, cultural and socio-economic contexts while considering the larger context within which it is embedded
- Includes monitoring, evaluation and adaptive management throughout and beyond the lifetime of the project or program
- Enabled by policies and measures that promote long-term progress, fostering replication and scaling up

Beyond regenerative sustainability, there is even less awareness of the next stage, coevolutionary sustainability. Coevolutionary sustainability is based on the principles of reconciliation ecology that promote co-existence of multiple human and non-human spaces, reduction and elimination of conflict between these spaces, maximisation of benefit for those in each space, promotion of biodiversity and capping human activities and impacts wherein humans balance their needs with those of other species (Rosenzweig, 2003). Coevolutionary sustainability also aligns with convivial conservation (Buscher & Fletcher, 2019), an integrated whole earth vision in which the goal is to practice conservation of balance and mutually beneficial relationships between human needs and nature's needs without human dominance over nature but also to find synergy and balance in social and economic systems. Similar to regenerative sustainability, there is lack of operationalisation of coevolutionary sustainability and how to enact it.

Companies do not know how to move out of weak sustainability and into strong sustainability. To address this void in operationalising both variations of strong sustainability (regenerative and coevolutionary), de Oliveira Neto et al. (2018) identified eight actions that companies can take to promote strong sustainability:

1. Increase resource consumption efficiency
2. Limit consumption of renewable resources and their renewal rate
3. Reduce greenhouse gas emissions

4. Reuse waste as inputs
5. Replace toxic inputs with organic products
6. Replace non-renewable energy resources by renewable energy resources
7. Increase affordability
8. Increase sustainability manufacturing.

Brozovic's (2019) research focused on business models that support strong sustainability. He identified four common themes that strong sustainability business models share:

1. Preserve, regenerate or benefit nature
2. Center nature as the primary stakeholder
3. Increase resilience of local systems
4. Limit growth to stay within planetary boundaries

In yet another attempt to fill the gap between theory and practice, Uleander and Eriksson (2022) used design science research to help practitioners visualise the five stages of corporate sustainability. These visualisations can help translate theoretical concepts, such as strong sustainability, into engaging and understandable images for practitioners (Figure 12.2).

Given the limited concrete and research-based evidence on how to adopt strong sustainability, it can be helpful to look at case examples. For illustration, I will provide a brief example of company sustainability activities at each stage of sustainability.

Case Examples

For the sake of comparison, I will provide examples of sustainability activities in each stage of sustainability. Examples of weak sustainability (compliance, business-centred and systemic) are abundant, while examples of strong sustainability (regenerative, coevolutionary) are less common; therefore, I will provide additional examples of strong sustainability. Two examples of regenerative sustainability are provided (one government and one technically based business) and four examples of coevolutionary sustainability are provided (two biologically based businesses and two technically based businesses, to demonstrate that a business does not have to be biologically based to be coevolutionary). These two strong sustainability

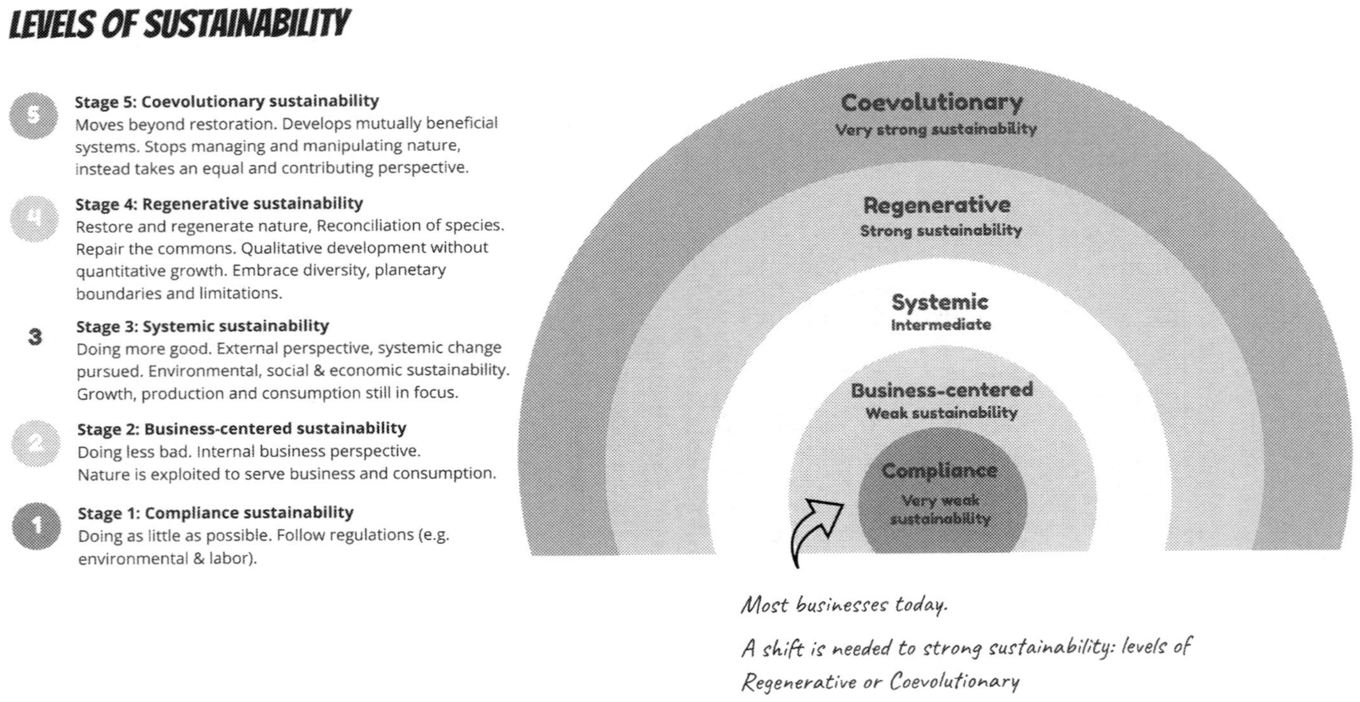

LEVELS OF SUSTAINABILITY

5 **Stage 5: Coevolutionary sustainability**
Moves beyond restoration. Develops mutually beneficial systems. Stops managing and manipulating nature, instead takes an equal and contributing perspective.

4 **Stage 4: Regenerative sustainability**
Restore and regenerate nature, Reconciliation of species. Repair the commons. Qualitative development without quantitative growth. Embrace diversity, planetary boundaries and limitations.

3 **Stage 3: Systemic sustainability**
Doing more good. External perspective, systemic change pursued. Environmental, social & economic sustainability. Growth, production and consumption still in focus.

2 **Stage 2: Business-centered sustainability**
Doing less bad. Internal business perspective.
Nature is exploited to serve business and consumption.

1 **Stage 1: Compliance sustainability**
Doing as little as possible. Follow regulations (e.g. environmental & labor).

Coevolutionary
Very strong sustainability
Regenerative
Strong sustainability
Systemic
Intermediate
Business-centered
Weak sustainability
Compliance
Very weak sustainability

Most businesses today.

A shift is needed to strong sustainability: levels of Regenerative or Coevolutionary

Figure 12.2 Levels of Sustainability (the Rainbow)

Source: Uleander and Eriksson (2022). Reproduced with permission.

orientations (regenerative and coevolutionary) represent the blue ocean (W. Kim & Mauborgne, 2004) of uncontested market space since relatively few companies adopt a strong sustainability orientation, thus presenting opportunities for competitive advantage.

The two strong sustainability approaches (regenerative and coevolutionary) should be emphasised if we are to achieve a level of sustainability that addresses climate change and a flourishing future. While companies often have activities in all five stages, if we list each sustainability activity of the company, it will be noted that at least one stage has more activities than the others. As companies develop sustainability activities, such as those listed below, companies should focus on the adoption of more regenerative and coevolutionary activities.

Compliance

Nestle, a U.S.-based company, is the world's largest food and beverage company. A plastic waste audit by volunteers around the world found that Nestle is also one of the world's top plastic polluters (Break Free From Plastic, 2020) despite the company's website claims of commitment to reduce plastic usage. Nestle is also one of the world's top producers of chocolate candy. The company has a decades-long history of child and slave labour in its cocoa supply chain. The company voluntarily signed on to the Harkin-Engel Protocol in 2001 (alongside other major chocolate manufacturers) to eliminate some child labour in the supply chain by 2005. However, the goals were not achieved by the 2005 deadline and the chocolate companies' deadline was extended to 2008, then to 2010, and then again to 2020 (Whoriskey & Siegel, 2019). Because there is no enforcement or consequence for failing to meet the goals, companies, such as Nestle, primarily focus on what is legally required (Whoriskey & Siegel, 2019) while simultaneously claiming to address issues on company websites, such as plastic reduction or the elimination of child and slave labour.

Business-Centred

Walmart, a U.S.-based retail company, used its massive power and influence to move sustainability from a niche strategy to a mainstream strategy. Walmart is also a champion of the business case for sustainability.

The company gets approximately 46% of its energy from renewable energy sources, pursues a 100% renewable energy strategy, aggressively works across its supply chain to reduce greenhouse gas emissions, invests in one acre of habitat preservation for every acre of land developed in the United States, diverts 78% of global waste from landfills and donates 696 million pounds of food in the United States (Walmart, 2022). Research shows that these types of initiatives are associated with great cost savings, which, in turn, can contribute to improved profits as well as improved image and reputation (Whelen & Fink, 2016). These types of sustainability activities align with Walmart's cost leadership strategy.

Systemic

Nucao is a German chocolate company. The company's chocolate products are made with sustainably cultivated 100% organic fair-trade cocoa that is vegan with lower sugar content and no palm oil (Nucao, 2022). The company pays fair wages to cacao suppliers in Peru, does not use child or slave labour, uses recyclable and compostable packaging (over 19 tons of plastic saved) and is working to improve industry carbon labelling and awareness of sustainable consumption (Nucao, 2022). Nucao donates 3% of sales to reforestation projects to fight climate change (a regenerative activity) and has planted over 13 million trees to date. Most of the company's activities reflect a company that is bucking standard industry practice while setting an example with more ethical and responsible alternatives (Nucao, 2022).

Regenerative

One of the best examples of regenerative sustainability is found in New York City. The city's water source comprises reservoirs and lakes between 75 and 125 miles north of the city that travel through aqueducts and tunnels; the water is so clean it does not require further filtration (Appleton, 2002; Heller & Salzman, 2021). However, with a growing population, urban sprawl, changing land use and pollution degrading the quality of the watershed in the early 1990s, the city faced a decision of whether to invest $4 to $6 billion and annual operating costs of $250 million to build a water filtration plant (Appleton, 2002; Heller & Salzman, 2021). Instead, the city chose to spend approximately $1.5 billion to restore surrounding land

and forests within the watershed to help naturally purify the city's water (Appleton, 2002; Heller & Salzman, 2021). By strategically regenerating a natural system on which it relied for inputs, not only were the financial benefits obvious and significant but the environmental restoration project also contributed to reduced greenhouse gas emissions, improved biodiversity and created a healthier ecosystem.

The MAINE New England Brasserie Company is a bar and grill in Dubai, United Arab Emirates. The company partnered with Emirates Marine Environmental Group, an environmental non-profit, and The Arbor School, a local school with an environmentally based curriculum, to collaboratively restore local coral reef systems. The restaurant discards over 500,000 oyster shells annually but now saves its oyster shells, and the school integrates the shells into its curriculum on marine ecosystems (The Million Oyster Project, 2022). The students place the shells in discarded fish traps and return the shell-filled traps to the sea, where they create reefs and grow new oysters. Oysters can filter up to 50 gallons of seawater each day, and the goal is to return 1 million oyster shells to the sea annually. The project's result is diversion of oyster shell food waste (approximately 250,000 shells collected in the project's first 6 months), beach clean-up of discarded fish traps, improved water quality, renewed habitat for hundreds of species (including the oysters upon which the MAINE relies as a critical supply), creation of a breeding ground for the endangered hawksbill turtle and increased biodiversity of the ecosystem (The Million Oyster Project, 2022). While similar projects exist around the world, they are projects of non-profit organisations. This project is differentiated by the fact that it is an initiative launched by a for-profit company to restore one of its critical supply chain inputs (oysters).

Coevolutionary

Veta la Palma is a fish farm in southern Spain. When acquired, the land had been drained to raise cattle. The company restored the land by allowing water back into the wetlands to recreate the natural wetland estuary ecosystem; this created a 27,000-acre fish farm (Barber, 2010). As a result, over 250 species of birds returned and created the largest bird sanctuary in the country. In this restored and healthy ecosystem, birds consume 50% of the shrimp and 20% of the fish produced at the farm, similar to ratios found in nature, and this allows the ecosystem to operate according to nature's principles. The birds, fish and shrimp feed on the phytoplankton and microalgae in this natural ecosystem, and the water that flows through this ecosystem is cleaner when it exits to the Atlantic Ocean than it was when it entered the ecosystem from the canals, creating self-cleaning and self-renewing water cycles. The only inputs to this system are energy and fish feed for the hatchery. The outputs are approximately 2,000 tons of fish and shrimp per year (Barber, 2010). Following the early restoration work, the company transitioned to coevolutionary sustainability as it learned to operate in balance with the surrounding systems.

Paicines Ranch is a polyculture ranch in the United States, producing food, fuel and fibre. When the family purchased the ranch in 2001, they immediately began restoring the land by working with natural systems to regenerate the ranch ecosystem's plants, water and wildlife (Paicines Ranch, 2022). Using holistic planned grazing, the cattle and sheep are moved frequently to allow plants to recover and to contribute to a healthy and productive ecosystem. Sheep also graze in the vineyard, which eliminates tillage, mowing, weeding and the need for fertilisers and herbicides and results in very little human labour since the sheep both weed and fertilise the area. Approximately 60% of the ranch is used for organic minimum till cropland to improve soil health. The result has been a four to five times increase in biomass, cattle reaching goal weight in a shorter time (California State University Chico, 2022), a 66% increase in soil organic matter, 10% more soil microbes, over five times greater beneficial insect abundance with no change in pest insect abundance, an increase in native perennial grasses, increased soil and ecosystem biodiversity (Paicines Ranch, 2022), 90% reduction in irrigation and increased crop yield (American Farmland Trust, 2017). This unconventional farming system modeled after principles of nature allows Paicines Ranch to operate in balance with its surrounding ecosystem.

Interface is a carpet manufacturer in the United States. The company was a first mover in adopting sustainability and has a long history of forward-thinking sustainability initiatives. Interface built a factory in New South Wales, Australia, following biomimicry and circular economy principles for land and building use. The company identified a referent ecosystem and quantified the ecosystem services provided by nature's water, oxygen, carbon, nitrogen and phosphorous cycles (Biomimicry 3.8, 2016; King, 2015).

The company then identified the disruptive gap created by the factory's presence and developed biomimicry design strategies to replicate the referent ecosystem services (Biomimicry 3.8, 2016; King, 2015). Through implementation of these design strategies, the factory became an active participant in a healthy functioning ecosystem, creating biodiversity, habitat, water filtration, carbon sequestration and other ecosystem services like the referent ecosystem after which it was modelled. This is a prime example of coevolutionary sustainability in which the company manages and controls its own activities and impacts to operate in balance with surrounding systems rather than manipulating systems for its own benefit.

ECOSTP is an Indian company providing eco-friendly sewage treatment solutions. The company's 'Zero Power Zero Chemical' technology uses biomimicry design principles modelled after a cow's digestive system. The low-cost, low-tech eco-friendly sewage treatment plant can treat wastewater without energy, moving parts and chemicals and uses only gravity and anaerobic bacteria to produce clean recycled water that is suitable for flushing toilets and gardening. This system can save up to 90% on operating costs (JCN Newswire, 2020). In the company's first 3 years of existence, it is estimated to have treated 59 million liters of sewage and saved 96 megawatts of energy (Karelia, 2020). This innovation contributes to a business's ability to live in balance with its surrounding ecosystem, reduce its greenhouse gas emissions, filter water, return clean water to the ecosystem and divert human waste from alternative energy- and chemical-intensive processes or from untreated release into the environment and provides environmentally friendly solutions in the face of India's sanitation, water and energy crises. The system is also being used in the Kham River basin to help clean and restore the area by keeping raw sewage from entering the river. In its first year in the Kham River basin, the system helped restore 11.9 km upstream and 7.6 km where the river passes through the city of Aurangabad, Maharashtra (Singhal, 2022). The Living Machine (United States) is another sewage treatment solution that uses a different eco-friendly technology than ECOSTP. The Living Machine uses bioremediation, or the use of organisms, such as fungi and plants, to detoxify and eliminate pollution. Using plants and bacteria to treat and reuse wastewater, the Living Machine mimics the ecosystem services provided by wetlands.

As companies seek to adopt more strong (regenerative and coevolutionary) sustainability activities, it is worth repeating the differentiating factors that will help move companies towards strong sustainability leadership.

- *Regenerative*: What is needed to restore this ecosystem to health? The common theme we see in exemplars of regenerative sustainability activities is the repair and restoration of environmental damage caused by human activities. This is still anthropocentric because humans are seen as separate from nature and seek to dominate, control and manipulate natural systems, yet restoration is critical to a healthy planet.
- *Coevolutionary*: How does nature already do this activity, and how can we mimic nature's activities? The common theme we see in exemplars of coevolutionary sustainability activities is the imitation of nature for better integration with nature in a symbiotic relationship. This is no longer anthropocentric but becomes more eco-centric because humans are seen as part of nature and the emphasis of control is on the benign integration of self into the natural environment.

These two stages of strong sustainability and associated activities that match these themes should be the priority of any company that wishes to be a sustainability leader; anything less simply prolongs unsustainability.

Conclusion

The converging environmental, social and economic crises make it clear that change is needed. After hundreds of years of failing to heed science, the dire situation we face demands action, particularly regarding the climate crisis. We are facing a global polycrisis in which the sum of the parts is greater than the individual crises. Collectively, we have been following weak sustainability, only doing what is required, that which benefits us or that which allows us to continue the status quo with minor adjustments. Governments and companies have started taking some climate action in recent decades, but research shows it is insufficient and is still firmly grounded in weak sustainability that allows us to continue business as usual and to prolong unsustainability. If it is our intent to save our habitat for human survival, we must move into strong sustainability. There is little to guide corporate action on the path to strong sustainability. The brief case examples here seek to highlight the differences in each of the stages of sustainability to demonstrate the chasm between what we currently call sustainability (but which is actually weak sustainability or 'unsustainability prolonged') and the radical shifts that are required to achieve strong sustainability for a flourishing future. Adoption of regenerative and coevolutionary practices is critical for sustainability leadership.

Discussion Points

- Explain the five stages of sustainability.
- Differentiate between regenerative and coevolutionary sustainability.
- Compare and contrast weak sustainability with strong sustainability.
- Identify a business in each stage of sustainability. Explain and defend your positioning of the company within the five stages.
- Why do you think there has been and continues to be limited government and business action regarding climate change (for the past 100–200 years)?
- How can we both educate and motivate business, government and society to act on the converging environmental, social and economic polycrisis?

Suggested Reading

Polman, P., & Winston, A. (2021). *Net positive: How courageous companies thrive by giving more than they take.* Harvard Business Review Press.

References

Åkerman, M. (2003). What does 'natural capital' do? The role of metaphor in economic understanding of the environment. *Environmental Values, 12*, 431–448.

American Farmland Trust. (2017). *Paicines Ranch.* http://stewards.farmland.org/wp-content/uploads/2017/04/Paicines-Ranch-Profile.pdf

Appleton, A. (2002). *How New York City used an ecosystem services strategy carried out through an urban–rural partnership to preserve the pristine quality of its drinking water and save billions of dollars and what lessons it teaches about using ecosystem services.* Convention on Biological Diversity. https://www.cbd.int/financial/pes/usa-pesnewyork.pdf

Arrhenius, S. (1896). On the influence of carbonic acid in the air upon the temperature of the ground. *London, Edinburgh, and Dublin Philosophical Magazine and Journal of Science: Series 5, 41*, 237–275. https://www.rsc.org/images/Arrhenius1896_tcm18-173546.pdf

Barber, D. (2010). *Dan Barber: How I fell in love with a fish* [Video]. TED Conferences. https://www.ted.com/talks/dan_barber_how_i_fell_in_love_with_a_fish/up-next

Biomimicry 3.8. (2016). *A carpet factory that functions like a forest.* https://biomimicry.net/our-work/factory-forest/

Break Free From Plastic. (2020). *Branded vol. III: Demanding corporate accountability for plastic pollution*. https://www.breakfreefromplastic.org/wp-content/uploads/2020/12/BFFP-2020-Brand-Audit-Report.pdf

Brigham, K. (2020). *The money funding climate change denial*. CNBC. https://www.cnbc.com/2020/12/20/the-big-business-of-climate-change-denial-.html

Brozovic, D. (2019). Business model based on strong sustainability: Insights from an empirical study. *Business Strategy and the Environment, 29*(2), 763–778.

Brundtland, G. H. (1987). *Our common future: Report of the World Commission on Environment and Development* (UN-Dokument A/42/427). United Nations.

Buscher, B., & Fletcher, R. (2019). Towards convivial conservation. *Conservation and Society, 17*(3), 283–296.

Calel, R., Chapman, S., Stainforth, D., & Watkins, N. (2020). Temperature variability implies greater economic damages from climate change. *Nature Communications, 11*, 5028. https://www.nature.com/articles/s41467-020-18797-8/

California State University Chico. (2022). *Paicines Ranch*. Center for Regenerative Agriculture and Resilient Systems. https://www.csuchico.edu/regenerativeagriculture/demos/paicines-ranch.shtml

Climate Accountability Institute. (2020). *Carbon majors*. https://climateaccountability.org/carbonmajors.html

Dawe, N., & Ryan, K. (2003). The faulty three-legged-stool model of sustainable development. *Conservation Biology, 17*(5), 1458–1460.

Demastus, J., & Landrum, N. (2023). Organizational sustainability schemes align with weak sustainability. *Business Strategy and the Environment*. https://doi.org/10.1002/bse.3511

de Oliveira Neto, G., Pinto, L., Amorim, M., Giannetti, B., & Almeida, C. (2018). A framework of actions for strong sustainability. *Journal of Cleaner Production, 196*(20), 1629–1643.

Dixson-Decleve, S., Gaffney, O., Ghosh, J., Randers, J., Rockstrom, J., & Stocknes, P. (2022). *Earth for all: A survival guide for humanity. A report to the Club of Rome*. New Society Publishers.

Dyllick, T., & Muff, K. (2016). Clarifying the meaning of sustainable business: Introducing a typology from business-as-usual to true business sustainability. *Organization & Environment, 29*, 156–174.

Food and Agriculture Organization. (2021). *Principles for ecosystem restoration to guide the United Nations decade 2021–2030*. https://www.fao.org/3/cb6591en/cb6591en.pdf

Foote, E. (1856). Circumstances affecting the heat of the sun's rays. *The American Journal of Science and Arts, 22*(66), 382–383. https://static1.squarespace.com/static/5a2614102278e77e59a04f26/t/5aa1c3cf419202b500c3b388/1520550865302/foote_circumstances-affecting-heat-suns-rays_1856.pdf

Glanemann, N., Willner, S., & Levermann, A. (2020). Paris Climate Agreement passes the cost–benefit test. *Nature Communications, 11*, 110. https://www.nature.com/articles/s41467-019-13961-1

Golds, A. (Producer), Osgood, C., & Assuras, T. (Directors). (2007). *Silent spring* [Video/DVD].

Goleman, D. (2000). Leadership that gets results. *Harvard Business Review, 78*(2), 78–90.

Hahn, T., & Tampe, M. (2021). Strategies for regenerative business. *Strategic Organization, 19*(3), 456–477.

Halttunen, K., Slade, R., & Staffell, I. (2022). 'We don't want to be the bad guys': Oil industry's sensemaking of the sustainability transition paradox. *Energy Research & Social Science, 92*, 1–13. https://doi.org/10.1016/j.erss.2022.102800

Heller, M., & Salzman, J. (2021). *How the salvation of New York City drinking water can be a model for saving the planet*. Literary Hub. https://lithub.com/how-innovative-ownership-design-can-save-the-planet-from-ruin/

InfluenceMap. (2022). *Big oil's real agenda on climate change 2022: An InfluenceMap report*. https://influencemap.org/report/Big-Oil-s-Agenda-on-Climate-Change-2022-19585

Intergovernmental Panel on Climate Change. (2022). *Climate change 2022: Impacts, adaptation and vulnerability. Working Group II contribution to the Sixth Assessment Report of the Intergovernmental Panel on Climate Change*. Cambridge University Press. https://www.ipcc.ch/report/ar6/wg2/downloads/report/IPCC_AR6_WGII_FullReport.pdf

JCN Newswire. (2020). *ECOSTP secures funding from Habitat for Humanity's Shelter Venture Fund to improve access to sanitation across India*. FinanzNachrichten. https://www.finanznachrichten.de/nachrichten-2020-09/50837852-ecostp-secures-funding-from-habitat-for-humanity-s-shelter-venture-fund-to-improve-access-to-sanitation-across-india-011.htm

Kaganovsky, M. (2021). *How corporations profit off of climate change denial*. The Leaflet. https://theleaflet.org/home-1/corporations-climate-denial

Karelia, G. (2020). *Startup-s zero-power tech converts 59 million litres of sewage into reusable water*. The Better India. https://www.thebetterindia.com/224824/bengaluru-startup-innovation-technology-convert-sewage-to-reusable-water-sustainable-india-gop94/

Kim, A., Lim, B., Seol, J., & Lee, C. (2021). Principle of restoration ecology reflected in the process creating the National Institute of Ecology. *Journal of Ecology and Environment, 45*(12), 2. https://jecoenv.biomedcentral.com/articles/10.1186/s41610-021-00187-w

Kim, W., & Mauborgne, R. (2004). *Blue ocean strategy: How to create uncontested market space and make the competition irrelevant.* Harvard Business Review Press.

King, B. (2015). *Can a carpet factory run like a forest?* Greenbiz. https://www.greenbiz.com/article/can-carpet-factory-run-forest

Landrum, N. (2018). Stages of corporate sustainability: Integrating the strong sustainability worldview. *Organization & Environment, 31*(4), 287–313. http://journals.sagepub.com/doi/full/10.1177/1086026617717456

Landrum, N. (2020, April). *Fifty years of Earth Day. Where did we go wrong?* The Hill. https://thehill.com/opinion/energy-environment/494129-fifty-years-of-earth-day-where-did-we-go-wrong

Landrum, N., & Ohsowski, B. (2017). Content trends in sustainable business education: An analysis of introductory courses in the U.S. *International Journal of Sustainability in Higher Education, 18*(3), 385–414. https://doi.org/10.1108/ijshe-07-2016-0135

Landrum, N., & Ohsowski, B. (2018). Identifying worldviews on corporate sustainability: A content analysis of corporate sustainability reports. *Business Strategy and the Environment, 27*(1), 128–151. https://onlinelibrary.wiley.com/doi/abs/10.1002/bse.1989

Lehtonen, M. (2004). The environmental–social interface of sustainable development: Capabilities, social capital, institutions. *Ecological Economics, 49*, 199–214.

Lewis, S., Wheeler, C., Mitchard, E., & Koch, A. (2019). Restoring natural forests is the best way to remove atmospheric carbon. *Nature, 568*, 25–28. https://doi.org/10.1038/d41586-019-01026-8

Luthy, Q. (2022). *Reconsidering reforestation and tree planting projects.* Earth.org. https://earth.org/reforestation-projects/

Lyle, J. (1994). *Regenerative design for sustainable development.* John Wiley & Sons.

Malthus, T. (1798). *An essay on the principle of population.* J. Johnson. http://www.esp.org/books/malthus/population/malthus.pdf

Marsh, G. (1864). *Man and nature: Or, physical geography as modified by human action.* S. Low, Son and Marston.

Mazutis, D., & Eckardt, A. (2017). Sleepwalking into catastrophe: Cognitive biases and corporate climate change inertia. *California Management Review, 59*(3), 74–108.

McGreal, C. (2021, June 30). Big oil and gas kept a dirty secret for decades. Now they may pay the price. *The Guardian*. https://www.theguardian.com/environment/2021/jun/30/climate-crimes-oil-and-gas-environment

Mebratu, D. (1998). Sustainability and sustainable development: Historical and conceptual review. *Environmental Impact Assessment Review, 18*(6), 493–520.

Miller, K., & Serafeim, G. (2015). Chief sustainability officers: Who are they and what do they do? In R. Henderson, R. Gulati, & M. Tushman (Eds.), *Leading sustainable change: An organizational perspective* (pp. 196–224). Oxford University Press.

The Million Oyster Project. (2022). *About*. https://themillionoysterproject.com/

Mills, V. (2019, July 18). Risky business: When corporations fund climate denial. *Forbes*. https://www.forbes.com/sites/edfenergyexchange/2019/07/18/risky-business-when-corporations-fund-climate-denial/?sh=449643a582c0

Nucao. (2022). *About us*. https://www.the-nu-company.com/

Özkaynak, B., Devine, P., & Rigby, D. (2004). Operationalising strong sustainability: Definitions, methodologies and outcomes. *Environmental Values, 13*(3), 279–303.

Paicines Ranch. (2022). *Our work*. https://paicinesranch.com/our-work/

Park, W. (2022). *How companies blame you for climate change*. BBC Future. https://www.bbc.com/future/article/20220504-why-the-wrong-people-are-blamed-for-climate-change

Paulson, H. (2015). *Short-termism and the threat from climate change*. McKinsey & Company. https://www.mckinsey.com/capabilities/strategy-and-corporate-finance/our-insights/short-termism-and-the-threat-from-climate-change

Pearce, D. (1993). *Blueprint 3: Measuring sustainable development*. Earthscan.

Porter, M., & Kramer, M. (2002). The competitive advantage of corporate philanthropy. *Harvard Business Review, 80*(12), 56–68.

Porter, M., & Kramer, M. (2006). Strategy and society: The link between competitive advantage and corporate social responsibility. *Harvard Business Review, 84*(12), 78–92.

Proctor, R. (2011). The history of the discovery of the cigarette–lung cancer link: Evidentiary traditions, corporate denial, global toll. *Tobacco Control, 21*, 87–91. https://tobaccocontrol.bmj.com/content/tobaccocontrol/21/2/87.full.pdf

Rosenzweig, M. (2003). *Win–win ecology: How the Earth's species can survive in the midst of human enterprise*. Oxford University Press.

Singhal, S. (2022). *CSE alumnus impact: How a green entrepreneur helped restore Kham River.* Down to Earth. https://www.downtoearth.org.in/blog/water/cse-alumnus-impact-how-a-green-entrepreneur-helped-restore-kham-river-81760

Tazawa, M. (2021). *Regenerative thinking meets circular economy in the bioeconomy.* GreenBiz. https://www.greenbiz.com/article/regenerative-thinking-meets-circular-economy-bioeconomy

Uleander, A., & Eriksson, C. (2022). *Reimagine corporate sustainability* [Master's thesis, Uppsala Universitet, Uppsala, Sweden]. http://urn.kb.se/resolve?urn=urn:nbn:se:uu:diva-480707

United Nations Environment Programme. (2022). *The closing window: Climate crisis calls for rapid transformation of societies.*

United Nations Framework Convention on Climate Change. (2022). *Nationally determined contributions under the Paris Agreement. Synthesis report by the Secretariat.* https://unfccc.int/sites/default/files/resource/cma2022_04.pdf

Vignola, R., Leclerc, G., Morales, M., & Gonzalez, J. (2017). Leadership for moving the climate adaptation agenda from planning to action. *Current Opinion in Environmental Sustainability, 26–27*, 84–89.

Walmart. (2022). *Sustainability.* https://corporate.walmart.com/purpose/sustainability#:~:text=As%20of%202021%2C%20we've, partnership%20with%20Acres%20for%20America.&text=Private%2Dbrand%20packaging%20by%202025

Whelan, T., & Fink, C. (2016). The comprehensive business case for sustainability. *Harvard Business Review, 21*, 2–8. https://hbr.org/2016/10/the-comprehensive-business-case-for-sustainability

Whoriskey, P., & Siegel, R. (2019, June 5). Cocoa's child laborers. *The Washington Post.* https://www.washingtonpost.com/graphics/2019/business/hershey-nestle-mars-chocolate-child-labor-west-africa/

World Commission on Environment and Development. (1987). *Our common future.* Oxford University Press.

13

A SYSTEMS PERSPECTIVE ON ORGANISATIONAL LEADERSHIP FOR CLIMATE CHANGE

IMPLICATIONS OF VIEWING ORGANISATIONS AS COMPLEX ADAPTIVE SOCIO-TECHNICAL SYSTEMS

William Donaldson and Benjamin W. Redekop

Chapter Summary

This chapter suggests that to understand how individuals can help their organisation productively respond to the daunting challenges posed by climate change, one needs to view the organisation as a complex adaptive socio-technical system (CAST). We explain what a CAST is and explore the climate leadership implications of a systems view for organisations, advancing in the process a set of practical insights and action steps that can be taken by organisational actors interested in showing leadership on this issue. An important starting point is to help everyone in the organisation understand the systems of which they are a part and the goals and purposes of their organisation within that system. In addition, organisational climate leaders must help to align sub-systems with

DOI: 10.4324/9781003343011-16

the goals of the organisation and, by extension, the larger systems of which it is a part and understand that doing so may necessitate the sub-optimisation of certain parts of the organisational system. To achieve this difficult task, organisational climate leaders will need to demonstrate how aligning the organisation with the larger natural systems it depends on creates value for the organisation and its constituents.

Introduction

Dennis Bushnell (2010), the chief scientist at NASA, Langley, wrote that humankind's voracious appetite and corresponding carbon footprint currently leave us one-third of a planet shy of providing basic needs to all humankind – shelter, water, electricity, etc. – and faced with rising seas and temperatures which are unsustainable. He continued that if we bring all global citizens up to a Western standard of living using our current approaches, we will be two whole planets shy. He ended with an observation that humankind has found extra planets in short supply and very hard to access (Bushnell, 2010). Viewed in this light, the threats of climate change and sustainability loom large for all of us.

Many of humankind's most vexing challenges result from reductionist thinking and polarising distinctions that lead individuals and groups to believe that their point of view is the only valid frame of reference and that there is no consequence to such polarisation (Meadows, 2008). Systems thinking was, and is, a response to this reductionist thinking. In the system where we are all inexorably connected – our planet – no distinctions hold up. The system does not care about our human-made distinctions or boundaries (Donaldson, 2021a). Global warming does not and will not stop at convenient geopolitical boundaries. In nature, and in the overarching systems in which we humans share a place, there are no boundaries. There are only human-made political, racial, religious, economic and similar boundaries designed to help us understand and organise our complex world.

Humankind faces what systems thinkers call 'wicked' problems, which derive from our inter-connected nature and shared resources. Climate change is one such wicked problem. Wicked systems problems are often described using the acronym VUCA, for they are volatile, uncertain, complex and ambiguous (Bennis & Nanus, 1985). While the basic problem of global warming is crystal clear (human-emitted greenhouse gases are warming the planet far too rapidly, leading to dislocation and disruption of both human and non-human communities), there is no simple 'solution' to the problem, as the climate is connected to every living system, including a rather complex fossil fuel energy system that we humans currently rely on. Such complexity can be vexing for both leaders and followers, yet this is precisely the context under which they must operate.

Theory and Basic Concepts

One of the most powerful techniques espoused by systems thinking is the ability to view the system seamlessly at multiple scales, from its most granular components to the large systems the system of record is enmeshed in, a technique referred to as *in-scoping and out-scoping*, or what Senge (2006) called 'systems intelligence'. One of the dimensions to be included is temporal. Most leaders are far too focused short term and downward and inward on their organisations and view them only as a mechanistic collection of parts. One might argue that environmental problems' complex, interrelated nature should bring forth a more dispersed, systems, process view of leadership (Middlebrooks et al., 2009; Western, 2019). Systems thinking encourages leaders to view their organisations as constantly evolving, dynamic, interconnected entities and to further extend the view to all of the greater systems and dynamics that shape the context for the system of record.

Quinn and Dalton (2009, p. 34) highlighted this fundamental capability when they suggested that

> leaders not only recognise the interconnections between their business operations, the natural environment, and society; they actively pursue strategies to respect and honor these connections. Their efforts to integrate a societal need into the business are not tacked on to an existing operation. Rather, the very nature of how business is conducted has been changed, to include broader and more interdependent views of strategy and planning, stakeholder engagement, and employee involvement.

Middlebrooks et al. (2009) suggested that a sustainability leader's mindset must include the ability to see and manage at a meta or systems level (see also Rimanoczy et al., this volume). For his part, Simon Western (2019) has branded the emerging systems view of leadership the 'eco-leadership discourse' (p. 256) – arguing that organisations are ecosystems within ecosystems connected to wider natural and social systems. Eco-leaders are those individuals who design and facilitate ethical organisational systems that are able to adapt to changing circumstances via empowerment of all members of the organisation to exercise influence, on the model of natural systems in which power and influence is dispersed throughout the biological community.

Such networked communities are able to flourish and adapt much better than top-down, hierarchical organisations, since no one person or group is able to fully understand and successfully direct the systems of which they are a part (Western, 2019). This does not mean there are no positional leaders; rather, such individuals recognise and act upon the systemic nature of their organisations and the inherent connections between them and the extra-organisational systems that surround them. Doing so often includes decentralisation of power and the strengthening of networks within and between organisations and other relevant systems, including the natural environment. What this means in practice, from a systems perspective, is that leaders are no longer the sole actor or decision maker in the system and enabled followers become critical participants in the leadership process.

Complex Adaptive Socio-Technical Systems and Systems Thinking

As Kellerman and others have pointed out, all leadership occurs within a context, and that context shapes and informs the leadership that inevitably emerges to adapt to that context (Kellerman, 2016). Given the context for leadership is a CAST, systems thinking becomes an essential skill for leaders. ('Socio-technical' highlights the degree to which human social systems are enmeshed in and conditioned by technology.) The World Economic Forum has deemed systems thinking one of the most critical skills for leaders and followers to develop to tackle humankind's wicked problems (Gafni, 2019). For this chapter, the authors will use Donella Meadows' sparse, simple, yet robust definition of a system (Meadows, 2008, p. 11):

> *A set of elements or parts that is coherently organized and inter-connected in a pattern or structure that produces a characteristic set of behaviors, often classified as its 'purpose'.*

This definition – elements interacting with a purpose – encompasses almost all human activities. We create a communications system, an interstate highway system, a weapons system or a school system for a purpose. We develop political parties and nations for a purpose. We interact with the economies and the environment on purpose. People are purposeful, and we seek to align with systems that align with our purpose. Because ascribing or eliciting purpose – having a vision – is such a critical role for leadership, this chapter will concentrate on purpose and the purpose of the system and how that context shapes leadership in the individual and within the system. Alignment around purpose provides capacity to collaborate across boundaries in solving complex problems.

CASTs are notoriously hard to understand, lead and manage. As Mobus and Kalton (2015) have indicated, this is because the CAST elements are characterised by networks of relationships that emerge and develop complex dynamics that are not always obvious as to source and raison d'etre. Secondly, CASTs are constantly adapting through the interactions of intelligent agents. People within the CAST are adapting, but the level of intelligence can vary dramatically. Each agent can, and will, develop its perspective on the system, and the collective view may be very different, leading to elements of the CAST being at cross-purposes (see next section). This intelligence variability means that the CAST elements evolve and develop at different rates and scales, leading to potential friction and turbulence. A second-order effect of this phenomenon is that transfers of information among and within the CAST and the encoding of knowledge occur at different rates and times, further complexifying the dynamics. Finally, these differing dynamics drive different levels of energy and passion within the CAST, leading to variable emotional states – all of which point to the salience of the acronym VUCA.

Implications for Leadership

Leaders must be acutely aware of these CAST dynamics and sensitive to potential and actual misalignments of information, knowledge and action within the CAST. Mark Wade, writing in *Responsible Leadership*, cautioned about the need for consistency of language and presentation essential to avoid confusion and get the story straight at all levels (Wade, 2006). The CAST is always developing, gathering information and making determinations.

Leadership must ensure that this information and knowledge is consistent and ubiquitous. As Interface CEO Ray Anderson (2009, p. 52) memorably put it in regards to remaking a company into a truly sustainable enterprise:

> A leader must articulate the vision[,] set the right example, and keep pounding on the drum. ... A good leader will keep up that drumbeat, consistently and persistently, because some folks are going to figure that if they hide their heads long enough this program will eventually go away. Everyone must have impressed upon them – over and over – that this is real and is *not* going away. Not tomorrow. Not next month. Not *ever.*

Leaders must constantly be breaking down the barriers that inhibit connectivity between systems of all kinds. Also clear from this depiction of CASTs is that clarity of purpose becomes one of the critical responsibilities of leadership. Leadership must mediate inevitable tensions between social, corporate, governmental, functional and ethical challenges to purpose. Absent clear purpose and alignment to the same, coherent direction and action become difficult or, worse, muddled.

Purpose and Governance

Michael Jackson, a British systems scientist, provides a useful distinction concerning systems that will be used to highlight key steps leaders can take in aligning their organisation(s) for sustainability. Jackson classified systems as bounded – unitary, pluralist, coercive and unbounded – human-made and natural (Jackson, 2003). To clarify Jackson's distinctions, here are examples of the system types and comments on each.

- Bounded unitary – In these types of systems, the enterprise is the system of interest and has clear, unitary governance that establishes a coherent purpose. Note: In all cases, clear governance may or may not imply good governance. The leader's challenge here is to ensure that the governance structure is aligned with sustainability as a central tenet of the purpose of the system. This may prove to be a more difficult task in for-profit entities, especially publicly traded and private equity–backed enterprises. In these entities, the profit motive and time pressure often conspire against undertaking the investments needed to achieve sustainability. Often, sustainability is viewed as an expense rather than an opportunity. Further compounding this problem is that many of these entities are engaged in activities where the economic costs to the environment and communal well-being are not accounted for, leading to profitability being privatised but the resulting damage to the community and environment being borne by the public. Aligning the entity with sustainability is easier with privately held entities, non-profits, and government agencies. Still, the governance function must embrace sustainability and charge leadership with pursuing sustainability as a central activity within the overall purpose. It is the job of leadership to make the connection between pursuing sustainability at the organisational level and the well-being not only of the planet but of the organisation itself and its stakeholders, who are *also* members of the larger biotic community.

- Bounded pluralist – Examples of these systems are partnerships, joint ventures, HMOs, associations, communications networks, etc., where there are multiple governance inputs but a generally aligned purpose. Again, the leader's challenge is to ensure that the governance structure is aligned with sustainability as a central tenet of the purpose of the system. The further challenge becomes alignment within and through the various players involved in the aligned entities. Leadership and the governance structure must be vigilant to shifting alignments within the aligned entities and the emergence of cross-purposes. The complex and difficult task of collaborating across boundaries must be undertaken (Williams, 2010).
- Bounded coercive – Examples of these systems include treaty organisations, political blocs, international agencies, etc. These systems are characterised by governance inputs bound together but not necessarily coherently governed and often at cross-purposes. Their relationship with each other is essentially coercive, particularly when interests conflict. As witnessed by the United Nations, the World Health Organisation, the Paris Accords and other iconic global accords, these systems are particularly hard to gain sufficient alignment with which to address global issues such as sustainability and climate change. Yet, they are precisely the mechanisms that are crucial for success. Leadership's challenge then becomes aligning entities that may be operating at cross-purposes. The most significant leverage in these

cases will be the education of the electorate/constituents as to the shared interests and needs across national and other boundaries and how cooperation rather than conflict will lead to better outcomes for all. In a networked, interconnected world, it is becoming increasingly difficult to 'go it alone', as is currently being demonstrated by Russia in its war against Ukraine.

- Unbounded, human-made – Social movements, the economy, drug epidemics, poverty, etc. No governance construct can span the entire system; leaders can only hope to align the system of system responses and create mutually enforcing dynamics to manage the dynamics and impacts of the greater, unbounded system. In short, leaders can only engage with the other systems involved in the dynamics at issue to coordinate a response.
- Unbounded natural – the environment, weather, biological and ecological systems. No governance can steer these systems; we can only hope to coordinate our joint response to such system dynamics.

Implications for Profit-Driven, Not-for-Profit and Governmental Entities

The critical insight for bounded and unbounded systems is that governance becomes the dominant determining input. Whether one is looking for leadership in the system of record or outward to cope with unbounded systems dynamics, or looking to align disparate systems to address an unbounded natural system occurrence such as global warming, governance becomes the primary defining interaction, and leadership is the crucial dynamic of governance, often setting or heavily influencing governance. The leadership of Ray Anderson of Interface, Inc. offers a compelling example of how a publicly traded company can pursue sustainability as a central part of their purpose and still be financially successful (Anderson, 2009; Stubbs, 2012). Here we can recommend Anderson's 2009 memoir and call to action, *Confessions of a Radical Industrialist: Profits, People, Purpose – Doing Business by Respecting the Earth*. Readers who are interested in fostering sustainability in their organisations but who may be sceptical of the business case for doing so will find much food for thought in Anderson's story. Anderson provides an illuminating case study of how one individual with power and influence can – with the help of willing followers – completely realign an organisation to become sustainable while maintaining profitability. Anderson spent years consulting with leading thinkers on sustainability and developed a comprehensive and systemic approach to the problem that is worthy of detailed analysis.[1]

Implications for Leadership

The critical insight for leaders is that alignment around sustainability becomes a key responsibility for both leaders *and* followers. Bartlett and Ghoshal (1994) argued for getting beyond just numbers and action plans in strategy and building a rich, engaging purpose that all constituents can connect with and commit to. Waldman et al. (2006) wrote that the leader's role is to capture the foresight that often exists throughout an organisation and harness it for sustainability. Portugal and Yukl (1994) advised that 'efforts to introduce environmental reforms are more likely to be successful if the leader builds a broad coalition of supporters both within and outside the organization' (p. 273).

In the case of bounded coercive and unbounded systems, leadership can look to build coalitions of the willing and like-minded to spur progress and engage the reluctant. In the case of for-profit entities engaged in destructive industries, leaders must be aware that the incentives to maintain the existing structure are normally robust and be prepared to offer alternative paths to alignment beyond mere shaming and stridency. Paradoxically, partnering with these entities and helping them find a sustainable approach rather than treating them like pariahs offers more significant potential for success than merely opposing their activities. Paul Hawken suggested that 'we need to imagine a prosperous commercial culture so intelligently designed and constructed that it mimics nature at every step, a symbiosis of company and customer and ecology' (Hawken, 2010). Wendy Stubbs (2012), writing about Interface, echoed much of the above, suggesting that leadership is critical and there must be a burning passion for sustainability from the top, including collaboration with all stakeholders. Managers and staff must believe in sustainability and its alignment with the profit motive (Stubbs, 2012).

Thus, while it is clear that grassroots leadership is crucial for achieving environmental sustainability and, in particular, effective climate action, we acknowledge that the other side of the coin is that top organisational leaders are also crucial drivers of change, particularly given the quasi-feudal power structures of many modern corporations and the generally hierarchical arrangement of most modern organisations. While change normally starts at the grassroots level, it usually doesn't tend to happen unless and until positional leaders engage the issue, as was the case with civil rights in the 1960s and environmental legislation in the 1970s. And although it is true to say that young people are often key drivers of grassroots environmental action, survey data indicate that older generations – typically holding more position power than youth – are also concerned about environmental issues like climate change (Redekop & Thomas, 2018). There is thus a dialectical relationship between grassroots and positional leadership on issues like climate change that is built partly on generational interactions (e.g.; Ray Anderson was clearly motivated by concern for his children and future generations or what he called 'tomorrow's child'; see TED, 2009).

Once a leader has attained a clear mandate for embedding sustainability in the organisation's purpose, the next task is to ensure that all of the other elements and the interactions of the CAST are aligned with this purpose.

Elements and Interactions

It should be clear to the reader that a critical leadership focus in the context of a system must be on the specific elements that make up the system and the resulting interactions. Elements – people, processes, inputs, outputs, etc. – must be assiduously chosen and constantly assessed for alignment with the purpose and sustainability as a critical consideration. Similarly, the emergent interactions must be monitored continuously for alignment and systemicity. All of this must be done with the whole system in mind. Ray Anderson made sustainability into an all-encompassing conceptual, practical and ethical framework for Interface. Anderson (and willing staff) aligned everything they did around sustainability, which in the end became a higher-order term encompassing efficiency, ecology, financial success, meaning and purpose (Anderson, 2009). Shriberg (2012) made a compelling case for sustainability as 'a bridging concept beneficial to both the corporate-dominated leadership theory and the emerging field of environmental leadership' (p. 469). Sustainability supplies a useful framework for leadership on environmental issues, as it recognises 'the long-term, complex, and interconnected nature of environmental and interrelated social problems and solutions' (Shriberg, 2012, p. 471). As such, sustainability 'has great potential as a leadership concept because it crosses disciplinary, organizational, and cultural boundaries...it is not an incremental or piecemeal strategy for environmental and social change ... [it] represents bold vision and potential' (Shriberg, 2012, p. 472). Thus, a strength of the concept of sustainable leadership is its depth, breadth and wide applicability; as such, it supports and empowers systems thinking and action.

Paradoxically, in accomplishing the above, leaders and managers must be trained to work against a basic management urge to optimise every system element individually, especially the one for which they are responsible. Herbert Simon (1972) powerfully argued against this practice he called 'bounded rationality'. Systems thinking reveals that the only effective way to optimise throughput is to optimise the whole system. This may mean sub-optimising individual elements of the system, which is anathema to most managers and leaders of individual sub-systems (Donaldson, 2017). When it comes to the question of optimisation vs. sub-optimisation of subsystems, this question is the starting point, forcing continual analysis of the place and role of each part in the whole. The difference is that the equation now includes a much wider set of variables and stakeholders with a systems view. This point reveals why the skill of in-scoping and out-scoping becomes so important and powerful.

A larger issue in this context is the reigning assumption of modern capitalism that 'bigger is better' and 'growth is (always) good'. But from a global sustainability perspective, this simply cannot be true, since (as we have noted) we are already exceeding the carrying capacity of our one and only habitable planet. It is also untrue from an evolutionary perspective: while researchers continue to find evidence for 'Cope's rule' that organisms such as mammals and marine animals have tended to evolve to become larger over time, for various adaptive reasons, a significant proportion (one-third or more) have also evolved to become *smaller*, to better fit into the changing niches which they inhabit. And this latter trend has been accelerating due to the rise of predatory hominids (us) and, most recently, global warming ('Animals Tend to Evolve Toward Larger Sizes Over Time', 2015; Baker, et al., 2015; Bittel, 2018; Nicholls, 2013; Parry, 2012; University of Chicago, 1997). The canny organisational leader will be able to recognise if and when sub-units need to become smaller for the overall health of the organisation and when the organisation itself may also need to adapt by becoming smaller. This latter trend is currently happening in higher education, as some colleges have downsized in response to a dwindling pool of students and the rise of mega-universities with large online programs.[2]

Implications for Leadership

With that in mind, the question for the systems leader to ingrain in their local organisation, radiating both inwardly and outwardly, is, 'Does doing X contribute to, or detract from, a holistic version of sustainability?' The point is not that the leader figures out what that is in every case but empowers and directs the whole organisation to continually engage with the question and act on it as appropriate. Thinking about the question gets everyone thinking in systems terms. Wade (2006) pointed out that it is not enough for the leader to merely align elements and tend to interactions; they must win hearts and minds; they must create a culture of supporting and advancing sustainability. This can be difficult since culture does not have any direct connections or controls. Culture is an emergent property of the system of record (Donaldson, 2017). Culture emerges from the system and derives from leaders' actions, not words and platitudes. Therefore, leaders must embrace sustainability and model those actions that reflect a commitment to sustainability. Leadership drives culture; Quinn and Dalton (2009) pointed out that sustainability 'leaders not only recognise the interconnections between their business operations, the natural environment, and society; they actively pursue strategies to respect and honor these connections' (p. 34). Doing so may include 'right-sizing' sub-units or the organisation as a whole, easier said than done to be sure, but consequential, ethical leadership is rarely easy.

Putting It All Together: Leverage in the System

Meadows (1997) pointed out that the most significant points of leverage in systems are centred in what are termed human and values-based regions, the axiological realm. Perceptions, mental models, viewpoints and what we subsequently value and how we value those things become the areas of most significant leverage. Therefore, the greatest leverage comes from changing minds and perspectives, changing what we value. This can take the concrete form of policy changes that force a shift in behaviours or, more broadly, changes in individual and group mindsets and perspectives. Of course, this is why gaining consensus around sustainability and humankind's acceptance of it is so very hard. Charles Sanders Peirce and others warned about man's intractability of beliefs and adherence to outdated mental models (Peirce, 1877). Elevate individual beliefs and values to the level of governments, religions, industries, economic sectors and nations and the problem only gets more difficult. In the end, what is needed is a transition from an anthropocentric value system to an ecocentric one that includes human ethical systems within it as sub-systems of the larger whole (Curry, 2011). It is thus crucially important for leaders of CAST systems to understand, embrace and champion an ecocentric mindset.

Climate change has often been referred to in the context of an infinite game (Donaldson, 2021b), where there are no winners and losers, just a constant playing of the ever-changing game. Game theory teaches us that there are certain keys to success in infinite games (Sinek, 2019). These are as follows (Donaldson, 2021b):

- A just cause – Surely, preserving our only livable planet is a just cause. Leaders will have to rally their organisations, employees, customers and constituents around the purpose of sustaining our shared planet.
- Courageous leadership – Narrowly focused, insular leadership cannot lead to success in an infinite game. Instead, it must be inclusive and far-reaching.
- Trust among the leaders, followers, and organisations enmeshed in the game – Without mutual trust, there can be no progress.
- A flexible playbook based on agreed-upon values – The axiological component is the most important. Absent agreement on values, trust cannot be built.

Implications for Leadership

Leaders will have to work towards aligning hearts and minds with a clear purpose incorporating sustainability. This work will have to be done both internally, to inspire the minds and hearts of all constituents, and externally, to align large-scale coalitions to address wicked problems. An 'infinite growth' mindset will need to be replaced with a 'infinitely sustainable' mindset. In practical terms, organisational leaders must ensure that those who are (initially) negatively impacted by sustainability efforts do not pay the price for the organisation as a whole. If individual safety and security is threatened, sustainability goes out the window. 'First, do no harm' must be the mantra of sustainability leaders, or else they risk damaging the very culture of sustainability they are trying to create. Every effort must be made to make the transition to sustainability work for all stakeholders, starting with those who are most immediately impacted – employees and colleagues. This will require creativity and some risk taking; but the nimble leader will find ways to repurpose and redirect organisational resources, rather than simply eliminating them.

Discussion Points

- Importance of governance – implications for leadership
- Clarity and alignment around purpose – obstacles and strategies for achieving it
- Sustainability as a central purposeful driver throughout the enterprise – what that means in practice
- Optimisation of the system – strategies and consequences, including for subsystems
- Trust – how to build within an organisation

Notes

1 See chapter 5 of Redekop (forthcoming) for a deep dive into the contours and dimensions of Anderson's environmental leadership.

2 One of the authors, Redekop, experienced this phenomenon at a small university at which he was a faculty member. It was a difficult process, but the school has continued to flourish even though it is now smaller (in terms of enrolment) than it once was. The school was lucky to have found a president who was willing to lead the way toward 'right-sizing' the institution around its core strengths and mission rather than blindly holding onto the past. In regard to the fact that some schools continue to grow while others shrink, here, too, there is an evolutionary precedent: as some mammalian species became larger, others became smaller, exploiting new niches that emerged in the wake of the enlargement of other species (Baker et al., 2015).

Suggested Reading

Anderson, R. (with White, R.). (2009). *Confessions of a radical industrialist: Profits, people, purpose – Doing business by respecting the Earth.* St. Martin's Press.

Donaldson, W. M. (2017). *Simple_Complexity: A management book for the rest of us. A guide to systems thinking.* Morgan James.

Meadows, D. H. (2008). *Thinking in systems: A primer.* Sustainability Institute.

Redekop, B., & Thomas, M. (2018). Climate change leadership: From tragic to comic discourse. In B. Redekop, D. Gallagher, & R. Satterwhite (Eds.), *Innovation in environmental leadership: Critical perspectives* (pp. 145–166). Routledge.

Shriberg, M. (2012). Sustainability leadership as 21st century leadership. In D. R. Gallagher (Ed.), *Environmental leadership: A reference handbook* (pp. 469–478). Sage.

TED. (2009). The business logic of sustainability [Video]. YouTube. https://www.youtube.com/watch?v=iP9QF_lBOyA

Wade, M. (2006). Developing leaders for sustainable business. In T. Maak & N. M. Pless (Eds.), *Responsible leadership* (pp. 227–244). Routledge.

Western, S. (2019). *Leadership: A critical text.* Sage.

References

Anderson, R. (with White, R.). (2009). *Confessions of a radical industrialist: Profits, people, purpose – Doing business by respecting the Earth.* St. Martin's Press.

Animals tend to evolve toward larger sizes over time, Stanford study finds. (2015, February 19). *Stanford Earth Matters.* https://news.stanford.edu/2015/02/19/body-size-evolution-021915/#:~:text=New%20Stanford%20research%20shows%20that, animals%20has%20increased%20150%2Dfold

Baker, J., Meade, A, Pagel, M., & Venditti, C. (2015). Adaptive evolution toward larger size in mammals. *Proceedings of the National Academies of Science, 112*(16), 5093–5098.

Bartlett, C. A., & Ghoshal, S. (1994). Beyond strategy to purpose. *Harvard Business Review, 72*(6), 79–88.

Bennis, W., & Nanus, B. (1985). *Leaders: The strategies for taking charge.* Harper & Row.

Bittel, J. (2018, April 19). Earth's mammals have shrunk dramatically, and humans are to blame. *The Washington Post.* https://www.washingtonpost.com/news/animalia/wp/2018/04/19/earths-mammals-have-shrunk-dramatically-and-humans-are-to-blame/

Bushnell, D. (2010). *Conquering climate change*. The Futurist. https://issuu.com/worldfuturesociety/docs/the_futurist_2011_jan-feb

Curry, P. (2011). *Ecological ethics: An introduction*. Polity Press.

Donaldson, W. (2017). *Simple_Complexity: A management book for the rest of us. A guide to systems thinking*. Morgan James.

Donaldson, W. (2021a). Humankind as a series of nested systems: The search for leadership in us and around us. *Journal of Leadership Studies, 15*(2), 33–35. https://doi.org/10.1002/jls.21775

Donaldson, W. (2021b). Postface – Introduction to issue 2. *Journal of Leadership Studies, 15*(2), 67–69. https://doi.org/10.1002/jls.21776

Gafni, N. (2019, December 20). *Why we need to redefine trust for the Fourth Industrial Revolution*. World Economic Forum. https://www.weforum.org/agenda/2019/12/trust-and-values-of-the-fourth-industrial-revolution/?utm_source=sfmc&utm_medium=email&utm_campaign=2709001_Agenda_weekly-FinalTemplate-3January2020-20200101_090548&utm_term=&emailType=Newsletter

Hawken, P. (2010). *The ecology of commerce revised edition: A declaration of sustainability*. HarperCollins. https://books.google.com/books?id=E1oiU1OWh2kC

Jackson, M. C. (2003). *Systems thinking – Creative holism for managers*. John Wiley & Sons.

Kellerman, B. (2016). Leadership – It's a system, not a person! *Daedalus, 145*(3), 83–94. https://doi.org/10.1162/DAED_a_00399

Meadows, D. H. (1997). Places to intervene in a system. *Whole Earth, 91.1*, 78–84.

Meadows, D. H. (2008). *Thinking in systems: A primer*. Sustainability Institute.

Middlebrooks, A., Miltenberger, L., Tweedy, J., Newman, G., & Follman, J. (2009). Developing a sustainability ethic in leaders. *Journal of Leadership Studies, 3*(2), 31–43.

Mobus, G. E., & Kalton, M. C. (2015). *Principles of systems science*. Springer.

Nicholls, H. (2013, February 6). Withering heights: Why animals are shrinking. *NewScientist*. https://www.newscientist.com/article/mg21729032-500-withering-heights-why-animals-are-shrinking/

Parry, W. (2012). *Evolution shrinks mammals quickly, but they're slow to grow*. Live Science. https://www.livescience.com/18201

Peirce, C. S. (1877). The fixation of beliefs. *Popular Science Monthly*, 12(1), 1–15.

Portugal, E., & Yukl, G. (1994). Perspectives on environmental leadership. *The Leadership Quarterly*, 5(3–4), 271–276. https://doi.org/10.1016/1048-9843(94)90017-5

Quinn, L., & Dalton, M. (2009). Leading for sustainability: Implementing the tasks of leadership. *Corporate Governance: The International Journal of Effective Board Performance, 9*(1), 21–38.

Redekop, B. (forthcoming). *Environmentally sustainable leadership: Past, present, and future*. Edward Elgar.

Redekop, B., & Thomas, M. (2018). Climate change leadership: From tragic to comic discourse. In B. Redekop, D. Gallagher, & R. Satterwhite (Eds.), *Innovation in environmental leadership: Critical perspectives* (pp. 145–66). Routledge.

Senge, P. (2006). Systems Citizenship: The Leadership Mandate for this Millenium. In F. Hesselbein and M. Goldsmith (Eds.), The Leader of the Future 2: Visions, Strategies, and Practices for the New Era (pp. 31–46). San Francisco: Jossey Bass.

Shriberg, M. (2012). Sustainability leadership as 21st century leadership. In D. R. Gallagher (Ed.), *Environmental leadership: A reference handbook* (pp. 469–478). Sage.

Simon, H. (1972). *Theories of bounded rationality* (R. Radner, Ed.). North-Holland.

Sinek, S. (2019). *The infinite game*. Penguin.

Stubbs, W. (2012). Interface's approach to sustainability leadership. In D. R. Gallagher (Ed.), *Environmental leadership: A reference handbook* (1st ed., pp. 191–200). Sage.

University of Chicago. (1997, January 23). As species evolve they get bigger – Or smaller. *The University of Chicago Chronicle, 16*(9). https://chronicle.uchicago.edu/970123/jablonski.shtml

Wade, M. (2006). Developing leaders for sustainable business. In T. Maak & N. M. Pless (Eds.), *Responsible leadership* (pp. 227–244). Routledge.

Waldman, D. A., Siegel, D. S., & Javidan, M. (2006). Components of CEO transformational leadership corporate social responsibility. *Journal of Management Studies (Wiley-Blackwell), 43*(8), 1703–1725.

Western, S. (2019). *Leadership: A critical text*. Sage.

Williams, R. (2010). Leadership and the dynamics of collaboration: Averting the tragedy of the commons. In B. Redekop (Ed.), *Leadership for environmental sustainability* (pp. 67–92). Routledge.

14

SYSTEM LEADERSHIP AND CLIMATE CHANGE MITIGATION

Christopher Beehner

Chapter Summary

Climate change, driven by dramatically increasing levels of greenhouse gas (GHG) emissions, is the most significant challenge humankind faces in the 21st century. Although businesses comprise the largest GHG-contributing collective, meaningful and effective business leadership in climate change mitigation has been lacking. To quickly and effectively respond to this global challenge, a paradigm shift in contemporary business leadership behaviour and action is necessary. System leadership is defined as the ability to see and comprehend larger systems and catalyse collective leadership to proactively co-create the future. System leaders are characterised by their ability to 'see the big picture' and transcend and influence across boundaries. System leadership has been advocated as an effective model for achieving sustainability and economic circularity. In this chapter, system leadership will be described and prescribed as an innovative model for achieving one of the goals related to sustainability and circularity – climate change mitigation.

DOI: 10.4324/9781003343011-17

Introduction

Climate change, driven by dramatically increasing levels of GHG emissions, is the most significant challenge humankind faces in the 21st century. While modest efforts have been made to mitigate climate change, contemporary leadership has largely failed in attempts to make meaningful progress in this area. Leaders from numerous organisations have accepted the challenge of reducing GHG emissions and increasing sustainability activities and programmes. However, any significant climate change impact requires a paradigm shift in corporate leadership policy and action. Corporate leaders must transform their thinking from a short-term profit focus to a long-term strategic focus to ensure that the post-Anthropocene era will be favourable for the planet's inhabitants. How corporations respond to the climate change threat will determine the likelihood of our existence in the post–climate change era.

Decision makers and society face a world that is becoming increasingly volatile, uncertain, complex and ambiguous (VUCA; Ross et al., 2022). Existing leadership models are becoming obsolete and must be repurposed to successfully confront the climate change threat. Leaders increasingly recognise that existing management structures and leadership styles are inadequate for successfully leading organisations in a VUCA world – a condition which climate change guarantees will persist for the foreseeable future (Ross et al., 2022). Responding to the VUCA world of climate change requires a different form of leadership that is more agile, ambidextrous and flexible (Ross et al., 2022). Harris and Jones (2015) suggested that climate change leaders must preserve the respected attributes of the existing ideas and practices, while introducing and demonstrating the benefits of new ones. However, existing ideas and practices have contributed to the current problem and must be replaced with restorative, rehabilitative ideas and practices. Identification and implementation of the ideas and practices necessary to mitigate climate change requires a new leadership model.

In this chapter, system leadership will be explored and proposed as a novel and emerging leadership model to expedite the development of influential and talented climate change leaders. Climate change mitigation requires leaders who can transcend physical, political and ideological boundaries and barriers to influence a variety of diverse stakeholders to collaborate and cooperate. This chapter will explore the theory, basic concepts, measurement and practice of system leadership within the context of corporate climate change action.

Theory and Basic Concepts

There are numerous definitions for leadership, describing the concept as a trait, skill, quality or process. For this chapter, we will consider leadership as a process, best defined by Northouse (2018) as the process of influencing a group of individuals to accomplish a common goal. While the focus of early leadership was with traits and qualities of leaders, subsequent researchers examined leadership behaviour and skills, with a worldview that leadership could be taught and mastered. More recently, leadership researchers have focused on the role of and interaction with followers. Leadership scholars and practitioners now recognise that demonstrating leadership does not require a formal position of authority, with individuals often unaware that they are demonstrating leadership.

System leadership is a leadership model in which an individual exercises influence outside of their prescribed sphere of influence, extending influence across entire systems (Ghate, 2015; Senge et al., 2015; Timmins, 2015). A system leader can see and understand the larger system and catalyse collective leadership to proactively co-create the future (Senge et al., 2015). Therefore, system leaders can influence stakeholders across boundaries that are inside and outside of their organisations, industries, sectors and nations. The system leadership experience has been described 'as a collective "journey" of discovery that evolves over time … which often crystallize in an "Aha! Moment" – a new insight that describes the dynamics at a given moment in the journey' (Dreier et al., 2019, p. 5).

System leadership has been examined as a model for achieving sustainability of academic achievements in primary and secondary school education (Hopkins & Higham, 2007). According to Senge and colleagues (2015), system leadership will be essential for overcoming society's most impossible problems. It has been proposed as an effective means for achieving sustainability (Beehner, 2020) and for overcoming the impossibilities of the circular economy (Beehner, 2022) and is introduced in this chapter as a model for achieving climate change mitigation.

Although system leadership is in the developmental stage and has not been broadly implemented, it offers a promising model for addressing the complexity, dynamism and scale of the multi-dimensional challenges facing local and global communities (Dreier et al., 2019). The global challenge of climate change affects most aspects of human life and requires coordination among numerous stakeholders, because no single organisation can address these complex challenges alone (Dreier et al., 2019). Although individuals can be motivating, system-level change cannot be sustained solely through individual efforts (Harris & Jones, 2015).

System leaders function well across sectors and organisations, particularly in complex situations, because they succeed by 'being comfortable with chaos' (Timmins, 2015, p. 4). They can transcend organisational boundaries (Fullan, 2004, 2005) because they understand entire systems and can achieve collective leadership for synergistic outcomes (Senge et al., 2015). System leaders influence stakeholders across internal and external systems at the organisational, industry and national levels. Although alliances, partnerships, leaders and followers may come and go, systemic challenges will continue, because issues such as climate change, hunger, poverty and resource scarcity are multi-generational, and no single coalition or movement can completely resolve them (Dreier et al., 2019). Because the interdependent nature of existing climate change inaction indicates that collaborative effort is necessary to achieve impactful mitigation action (Rickards et al., 2014), system leadership is an appropriate model for climate change mitigation.

Successful climate change mitigation requires systemic change. Lasting systemic change demands comprehensive, diligent, long-term effort, best achieved through the organisation, vision, trust building and innovation skills of system leadership (Dreier et al., 2019). Effective system leaders possess the ability to comprehend systems, sub-systems and interrelationships, which necessitates an understanding of systems thinking. Systems thinking is a holistic analytical approach for examining how a system's components interrelate and operate over time and within the context of larger systems (Ambler, 2013). A systems perspective is essential for leaders to understand the fundamental structures, perspectives and beliefs that define their organisations (Ambler, 2013). This systems perspective is also necessary to understand the structures, perspectives and beliefs that define the greater systems that influence and are influenced by climate change.

Measurement

There is currently no established system leadership assessment or measurement tool. However, there are various skills, elements, themes, characteristics, traits and competences of system leaders, which will be identified and discussed in this section. Because these attributes were derived from multiple sources, there is some overlap in their descriptions. Leaders who possess and demonstrate many of these skills, characteristics and traits can be classified as system leaders.

Several common skills and qualities have been identified among system leaders in the field of education. According to Hannon (2014), system leaders are

- System oriented
- Inclusive, recognising that contributors may come from a diversity of backgrounds and possess multiple skills
- Design thinkers who can conceive and develop new processes
- Entrepreneurial, able to combine and disseminate new ideas in creative ways
- Strategic and able to see the big picture instead of becoming lost in the detail
- Grounded in the realities of what is needed and what has been accomplished

In addition, the following leadership behaviours have been noted as lacking among conventional leaders (Hannon, 2014):

- Knowledge diffusion – outward looking in terms of intellectual curiosity and idea promotion
- Social networking – across sectors and geographical boundaries, building relationships, partnerships and alliances to transform systems and acquire a variety of ideas, expertise, and experience
- Cultural competence – easily step beyond comfort zones to share and learn across contexts, develop cross-cultural literacy and develop a range of resources, perspectives and skills
- Technology brokerage – apply skills in new technologies and assemble a full range of social media to collect and share their vision and experience
- Political activism – recognise the need to participate in 'movement making' to effectively create and defend need for change
- Experimentalism – willingness to engage in a vision of a system that does not yet exist and develop conditions necessary for the system to grow while mitigating risks

System leadership requires achieving collective leadership across and between organisations, systems and sub-systems. The three core capabilities for achieving collective leadership are the abilities to observe the overall system, stimulate reflection and innovative conversations and redirect the collective focus from reactive problem solving to co-creating the future (Senge et al., 2015). Other system leadership skills include accomplishing major achievements without taking credit and emotional intelligence (Timmins, 2015).

In an ongoing project at the James Irvine Foundation's Linked Learning Regional Hubs of Excellence, Equal Measure and Harder+Company (2107) identified nine themes that describe effective systems leaders:

1. Thinking systemically
2. Having an open mindset
3. Pressing for an unwavering attention to diversity, equity and inclusion
4. Building relationships and trust
5. Practicing effective communication
6. Focusing on results
7. Co-creating support structures
8. Empowering the collective, rather than the individual
9. Creating opportunities for individuals to see the benefits of their participation

While many of these traits are common to other forms of leadership, the overarching theme of these traits reflects an open, collective, systemic focus.

Thinking systemically requires the ability to see the whole picture as a living system of inter-woven causality and detect patterns and relationships that can be leveraged or disrupted to realise positive systemic change (Equal Measure & Harder+Company, 2017). System leaders must have an open mindset because attempting systemic change action is frequently innovative, risky and speculative, requiring leaders embrace learning, uncertainty and experimentation. Systems leaders apply a diversity, equity and inclusive approach, creating constructive tension around inequity to galvanise action (Equal Measure & Harder+Company, 2017).

Because relationships and trust form the basis for growth and change, systems leaders are committed to achieving meaningful change and capable of building relations and trust (Equal Measure & Harder+Company, 2017). Practicing effective communication is critical because system leaders must be able to listen to points of view that differ from their own. Therefore, system leaders must be able to communicate across multiple sectors to develop the levels of trust necessary for collaboration (Equal Measure & Harder+Company, 2017).

Focusing on results increases the likelihood that the numerous members of a collective integrate towards common aspirations rather than disjointed programmatic or sector goals. Goals should therefore be selected collectively so that all stakeholders can agree on and celebrate victories and milestones (Equal Measure & Harder+Company, 2017). A significant role of system leadership is to interpret and balance stakeholder tensions by focusing on the benefits that materialise throughout the process (Harris & Jones, 2015).

Research suggests that complex problems, such as climate change, are best addressed through co-creation, wherein public and private stakeholders are engaged in collaborative processes that define problems and introduce and implement innovative, beneficial solutions (Sørensen & Torfing, 2022). These stakeholders should include citizens, neighbourhoods, civil society organisations (Sørensen & Torfing, 2022) and business and industry representatives. Co-creating support structures improves idea exchange among stakeholders impacted by the change process. This can be accomplished through data sharing, group decision making, codifying stakeholders' commitments and agile governance frameworks. Empowering the collective involves recognition of the multiple actors at various levels who must lead change within their respective circumstances. Distributed leadership and power increases both capacity and power sharing (Equal Measure & Harder+Company, 2017).

System leaders create opportunities for individuals to see the benefits of participation, especially when participation requires extending their resources to accomplish more. However, because achieving systems change requires time, system leaders must help stakeholders recognise interim improvements that are directly beneficial to them by continuously reinvigorating the individual value proposition to maintain stakeholder engagement (Equal Measure & Harder+Company, 2017).

Because the previously described skills and abilities are common among multiple leadership styles and models, a model of system leadership for

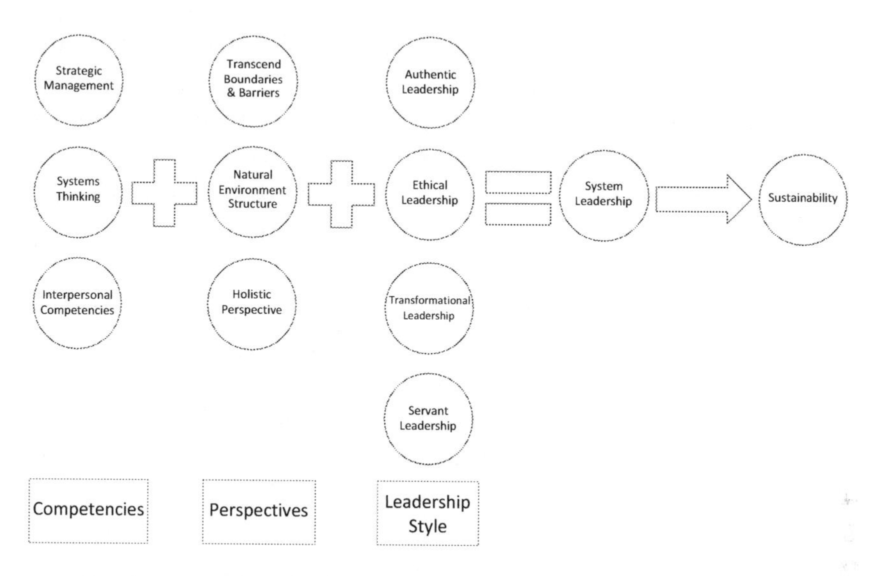

Figure 14.1 System Leadership for Sustainability Model
Source: Beehner (2020).

achieving climate change mitigation would be useful. Such a model has been previously developed for achieving sustainability through system leadership (Beehner, 2020). Because of the similarities and overlap of sustainability and climate change mitigation actions, this model is transferable between both concepts and is included in Figure 14.1.

In this model, when the three competencies of strategic management, systems thinking and interpersonal competencies are combined with the transcending boundaries and barriers, thinking in terms of the natural environment structure and a holistic perspective, any of four leadership styles complement the model, resulting in system leadership that is appropriate for achieving sustainability. In the next section we will explore methods, techniques and application of these competencies in the development and practice of system leadership.

Practice: Methods, Techniques and Application

In this section, we explore how to develop system leadership and apply system leadership in practice within the context of climate change mitigation. Most system leaders have never heard about system leadership, although they have mastered and apply many of the system leadership competencies. The three competencies of system leadership have been previously identified as systems thinking, strategic management and interpersonal competencies. These competencies enable system leaders to overcome artificial boundaries and barriers, have a worldview based on the natural environmental structure, see the big picture and influence entire systems (Beehner, 2020).

Because climate change mitigation requires broad and extensive systemic change, systems thinking must be understood and applied in all actions. Systems thinking requires knowledge of basic system characteristics: the role and function of inputs and outputs, energy creation requires energy, goods and services creation requires energy, preservation of life requires preservation of a healthy natural environment and politics matters (Siebert, 2018). However, the mental model of systems thinking is incomplete if the emotional, physical and spiritual elements are excluded (Stroh, 2015). To understand social, economic and environmental systems, it is necessary to recognise the emotional attachments to assumptions about those systems and how those attachments influence and impede perspectives and objectivity. Management of the emotional and mental elements takes place in the physical element. The spiritual element encourages system thinkers to recognise interconnectedness and opportunities for positive and negative alternatives and develop the necessary integrity and behaviours to make appropriate decisions (Stroh, 2015). 'Systems thinking is a team sport' (Stroh, 2015, p. 207) because stakeholders with diverse perspectives can work collectively to develop a plan for collective action.

Wicked problems such as climate change do not respect artificial or natural boundaries. Therefore, climate change mitigation requires leaders who can influence across geopolitical and socioeconomic boundaries (Beehner, 2020). Becoming a boundaryless leader requires understanding every stakeholder's interests and perspectives. Boundaryless leadership requires acknowledging and respecting cultural, national, religious and political differences while simultaneously engaging all stakeholders through recognised common interests. System leaders do not easily conform to traditional, hierarchical or bureaucratic structures (Beehner, 2020).

Strategic management requires decision making with a timeline of greater than 1 week, month, fiscal quarter, or year. Strategic thinkers consider the impacts of decisions and actions beyond their current and future jobs, timelines and organisations. Developing this ability requires the ability to see and understand the broader picture, including sub-systems, components, and actors which may be obscured (Beehner, 2022). Strategic managers develop this ability by asking probing questions about how and why an activity, event or process occurred or a task was accomplished.

Interpersonal competencies describe the skills and abilities that enable individuals to interact with others both individually and collectively. These competencies are necessary for negotiation, communication, establishing relationships and developing and leading teams. The European Academy for Executive Education (n.d.) identified the following essential interpersonal competencies: emotional intelligence, valuing people, empowering others and teaming skills, which are cultivated by improving communication skills, learning to manage diversity and upholding personal integrity. While these interpersonal competencies require time and patience to develop, many leaders already possess one or more of these attributes to some extent.

Developing system leadership is a dynamic, continuous process because the circumstances in which we lead are constantly changing (Beehner, 2022). However, system leadership can be developed by learning systems thinking, strategic management and interpersonal competencies. The systemic actions required to mitigate climate change require individuals, organisations, sectors and societies develop and embrace a new vision for our collective future. System leaders can create and share a vision through which all stakeholders can collaboratively work to mitigate climate change (Beehner, 2022).

System leadership is appropriate for complex situations that require collective action, especially when no single party is in control. However, the system leadership process is challenging and often involves high transaction costs, unclear outcomes and long timespans. System leadership is most suitable for complex problems that cannot be solved through more direct methods (Dreier et al., 2019).

Dreier et al. (2019) developed the 'CLEAR' framework for leading systems change based on five essential stages of the systems change process:

1. Convene and commit.
2. Look and learn.
3. Engage and energise.
4. Act with accountability.
5. Review and revise.

The five stages are not sequential and may overlap or reoccur throughout the systems change process. The *convene and commit* stage involves engaging key stakeholders in moderated discussions to focus on a complicated, shared problem or issue; define common interests and goals; and commit to collaboration for systemic transformation (Dreier et al., 2019). In the *look and learn* stage, stakeholders employ system mapping to construct a shared model of the elements, actors, dynamics and influences that occur in the system and their existing outcomes and generate new ideas and awareness (Dreier et al., 2019). During the *engage and energise* stage, formidable stakeholder engagement is established through regular communication to instil trust, commitment, innovation and collaboration and maintain improvement and momentum (Dreier et al., 2019). In the *act with accountability* stage, mutual goals and standards provide direction, while measurement frameworks assist with monitoring progress (Dreier et al., 2019). Finally, stakeholders periodically review progress and adapt their strategies in the *review and revise* stage. Throughout the process, maintaining an agile, responsive, innovative and learning-focused approach encourages meaningful transformation and innovation (Dreier et al., 2019). Although the CLEAR framework appears to be highly structured, the systems transformation process is frequently vague and unstructured.

Researchers with the Cambridge Institute for Sustainability Leadership developed a sustainability leadership model based on seven fundamental characteristics identified in individuals engaged in sustainability (Visser & Courtice, 2011). The characteristics are 'systemic, interdisciplinary understanding; emotional intelligence; values orientation; compelling vision; inclusive style; innovative approach; and, long-term perspective' (Peirce, 2011, p. 7). The components of the model are internal and external leadership; individual leader traits, styles, abilities and knowledge; and leadership actions. The combined model provides a unique combination of characteristics and actions for responding to sustainability challenges (Visser & Courtice, 2011). The researchers also identified several traits significantly related to sustainability leadership: being caring and ethical, systemic/holistic thinking, being inquisitive and open-minded, self-awareness and empathy and being both idealistic and courageous (Visser & Courtice, 2011).

Other techniques useful for developing and applying system leadership include life cycle thinking (LCT) and biomimicry. LCT is a whole systems approach to the production and consumption of products and services. Life cycle analysis, or life cycle assessment (LCA), is an LCT tool used to identify, measure and evaluate the environmental impacts of a product, service, activity or process from 'cradle to grave' (Srinivas, 2015). The use of LCA provides a preventative and proactive alternative to reactive and responsive environmental management. The LCA process consists of the following steps (Srinivas, 2015):

- Goal and scope definition: the purpose of the assessment is defined, assumptions and boundaries are determined and the scope is delineated.
- Analysis: the impacts of energy, materials, emissions and other characteristics of the product, service or process are identified, classified and measured.
- Assessment: the environmental impact(s) of the product, process or activity are determined.
- Interpretation/evaluation: the results are interpreted or evaluated to identify opportunities for environmental improvement and value determination.

Biomimicry is an innovative science in which best practices from nature are adapted for human use (Benyus, 1997). The goal of biomimicry is to design products and processes suitable for long-term life on Earth, based on recognition that nature has already solved many of the significant problems vexing humankind (Biomimicry Institute, 2019). From an evolutionary perspective, business systems mimic natural systems on several levels: on a business level as a social group and system and on a broader level as a participant in an economic system and the economic system as a subsystem of both social and environmental systems (Kassel, 2014).

Proposed solutions for incorporating biomimicry into climate change mitigation include energy effectiveness and energy efficiency, energy generation and carbon sequestration and storage (Aanuoluwapo & Ohis, 2017). While energy generation by humankind has significantly contributed to the current climate crisis, natural organisms are capable of successful and sustainable energy generation. By emulating the effectiveness of living organisms and systems producing renewable, less resource-intensive energy, humankind can dramatically improve energy efficiency without dependence on fossil fuels. It is noteworthy that natural organisms and systems obtain and produce all required energy from renewable sources and not fossil fuels (Aanuoluwapo & Ohis, 2017).

BioPower Systems in Australia developed BioWAVE and bioSTREAM technologies to mimic the movements of sea kelp and tuna tails (Goss, 2009; Zari, 2010). BioWAVE is installed on the ocean floor, with a pivot connected to a collection of buoyant blades that interact with the rise and fall of the water surface and the alternating underwater movement. The motion of the pivoting structure creates mechanical energy which is converted from fluid pressure in a power conversion module to electricity by rotating a generator. Efficient, clean electricity is transferred to shore through underwater cables (BioPower Systems, 2022). This example of biomimicry is eco-friendly, concealed and in harmony with nature (Aanuoluwapo & Ohis, 2017).

Although carbon dioxide production is an undesirable consequence of burning fossil fuels, CO_2 capture and sequestration methods prevent the release of CO_2 into the atmosphere (Coley, 2012). The mimicry of processes and functions of natural organisms that accumulate, sequester or reprocess CO_2 have influenced innovative technologies for industrial processes and the built and the human environment (Zari, 2010). Trees provide practical, easy-to-replicate biomimetic models for carbon sequestration and storage. One example of biomimicry based on trees is the Treepods Initiative designed by Influx Studio to create clean air in urban areas with artificial trees that capture CO_2 (Aanuoluwapo & Ohis, 2017). The Treepods, manufactured with recycled content (Archello, 2022), mimic the dragon tree because they contain a broad canopy to provide maximum shade and structural support for solar panels which power the air cleaning system (Rao, 2014).

Discussion

Although the environmental effects of climate change are becoming increasingly catastrophic, climate change is also an economic and social problem. While the environmental impacts are increasingly visible, the economic and social impacts are often more subtle and unevenly distributed. News reports about climate change–induced heat waves and flash flooding in developing nations are frequently overshadowed in developed countries by reports about blockbuster movie releases, celebrity lawsuits and political scandals.

Modern civilisation has at least partially alienated humankind from nature, enclosing us within buildings, neighbourhoods, cities and nations.

Nature is perceived as something external that can be visited and admired. However, solving our climate problems requires that we return to a perspective based on acknowledging and appreciating natural environmental systems (Beehner, 2020). System leaders are capable of understanding and respecting natural environmental systems, seeing the big picture and influencing across entire systems. However, existing leadership and decision making concerning climate change mitigation have been limited with respect to these attributes.

System leadership has received considerable attention in the education sector (Boylan, 2016; Fullan, 2004, 2005; Hopkins & Higham, 2007) and modest attention in health care (Hunter, 2017). System leaders in education recognised the need to sustain improvements in reading and mathematics, while simultaneously initiating fundamental reform in the overall educational system (Fullan, 2005). The proposed systemic changes required leaders who could lead within their own schools or systems, while interfacing and engaging with the broader educational system. These system leaders recognised that transforming the overall system required purposeful engagement, combined with local-level transformation (Hopkins & Higham, 2007). Although educational system leaders have been successful within the context of initiating and sustaining systemic transformation, the skills are relevant for achieving sustainability within curricula and facilities (Hopkins & Higham, 2007). While literature concerning system leadership in health care is limited, Hunter (2017) determined that enabling primary care practitioners to develop system leadership skills was crucial for facilitating meaningful change.

Although the application of system leadership in environmental settings has received limited attention (Beehner, 2020, 2022) and its applicability to climate change mitigation is theoretical, the effectiveness of system leadership in the education sector adds credibility to the potential of this model to enhance climate change mitigation efforts. Achieving climate change mitigation is similar to improving and transforming educational systems, because both activities require significant systemic change, engaging internal and external stakeholders and influencing broad behavioural change. The system leadership achievements in the education sector are relevant and transferrable to other areas and fields. Leaders in climate change mitigation can apply the skills and competencies of system leadership, which can be learnt and developed through their practical application.

Rickards et al. (2014) found that senior decision makers (SDMs) in government and business are actively fixated with their 'local' professional circumstances and immediate concerns, such as reputation among colleagues, relationships with competitors and current financial status. They exist collectively within a generally closed system and interpret the world from a relatively narrow perspective. The narrow focus of SDMs combined with the complexity and entrenched nature of existing systems hinders a more systemic or spontaneous approach.

Rickards et al. (2014) suggested three far-reaching climate change mitigation strategies, which are most effective when implemented together. The 'inside track' strategy requires establishing relationships with SDMs to identify anticipated constraints, apply subtle influence and refocus resources and effort. The 'outside track' approach functions from a strategic distance and requires drawing attention to the biases and decisions of SDMs to expand the conversation, encourage scrutiny and take advantage of opportunities. The 'middle out' approach may be the most promising, because this strategy operates at the meso level (network, organisations and institutions), seeking to 'combine the influence of an insider with the independence and credibility of an outsider' (Rickards et al., 2014, p. 766). The 'middle out' strategy attempts to change both formal and informal institutions by reducing the influence of a utilitarian ethic in developing identity and organisational norms. This approach focuses on SDM relationships with colleagues to instil individual involvement and collective action as the new, dominant norm (Rickards et al., 2014).

The 'outside track' and 'middle out' approaches proposed by Rickards et al. (2014) require leaders capable of influencing organisations and entities from the outside. Boundaryless leadership, which is characteristic of system leaders, is useful for influencing change from outside an organisation. These two approaches also require an understanding of systems thinking which is a characteristic of system leadership.

System leadership research and application are still in the developmental stage, especially with regard to wicked problems such as climate change. However, the urgency of climate change necessitates the use of all available tools, models and resources to achieve mitigation prior to reaching a crucial and irreversible tipping point. Many leaders possess some of the characteristics of system leadership and apply them absent any formal knowledge of or training on the subject. Increased awareness of system leadership may result in additional system leaders emerging within the area of climate change mitigation.

Conclusion

Mitigating climate change requires a paradigm shift in how we conduct business and in how we interact with and influence stakeholders. Business as usual and traditional business and leadership models have created the current climate dilemma. These models must be repurposed if we are to succeed in reversing climate change. Contemporary leadership faces the challenges of being agile and innovative, while continuing to operate in an era of transition from an established paradigm to a more ambiguous future (Harris & Jones, 2015). System leadership offers a promising alternative to existing short-term, short-sighted leadership models.

Chris Castro is a prominent example of a system leader within the field of climate change mitigation. Castro currently serves as CHIEF OF STAFF, Office of State and Community Energy Programs within the U.S. Department of Energy. Prior to accepting that role in the Biden administration, he served as director of sustainability and resilience for the City of Orlando, Florida. In that role, he developed a comprehensive collection of policies and programmes to transform Orlando into one of the leading U.S. cities in advancing sustainability, resiliency and climate change mitigation action. His influence extended beyond Central Florida through motivating leaders across the United States and globally to undertake governmental sustainability initiatives. Castro also co-founded the global sustainability non-profit IDEAS For Us, clean energy consulting firm Citizen Energy and the urban farming social enterprise Fleet Farming. Castro was featured in the 2018 National Geographic documentary *Paris to Pittsburgh*, which was inspired by President Trump's comment announcing his decision to exit the Paris Climate Agreement: 'I was elected to represent Pittsburgh, not Paris' (Owen, 2018). This climate change documentary has been viewed by millions globally. Castro's efforts demonstrate how one individual can influence systemic change across multiple stakeholders through system leadership without formal training on how to be a system leader.

System leadership is a viable leadership model for addressing complex, complicated, wicked problems. Leaders who can influence across boundaries and systems to mitigate the adverse effects of climate change are emerging from many regions, sectors and generations. In addition to Chris Castro, other examples include Greta Thunberg, who began climate change activism in Sweden at age 15, or 25-year-olds Vanessa Nakate in Uganda and Marinel Sumook Ubaldo in the Philippines. These climate change leaders build on the work of earlier climate change pioneers, such as Native American Tom Goldtooth, Elders Climate Action Co-chair Geri Freedman, and Sir David Attenborough of England, who continues to influence across boundaries and systems at the age of 96. Their level of success is dependent on how that model is perceived and the capacity of members of their teams, organisations and systems to embrace, embed and extend the proposed transformation (Harris & Jones, 2015). Their leadership will determine and shape the destiny, and possibly existence, of current and future generations.

Discussion Points

- Which of the system leadership skills, qualities and behaviours do you believe are the most common amongst contemporary leaders and why?
- What system leadership skills, qualities and behaviours are the most difficult to develop or acquire, and what suggestions could you offer for developing and acquiring them?

Suggested Reading

Beehner, C. G. (2020). *System leadership for sustainability.* Routledge.

Dreier, L., Nabarro, D., & Nelson, J. (2019). *Systems leadership for sustainable development: Strategies for achieving systemic change.* Kennedy School, Harvard University. https://www.hks.harvard.edu/sites/default/files/centers/mrcbg/files/Systems%20Leadership.pdf

Fiksel, J. (2006). Sustainability and resilience: Toward a systems approach. *Sustainability: Science, Practice, & Policy,* 2(2), 14–21. http://ejournal.nbii.org

Ross, D., Leonard, B., & Inayatullah, S. (2022). Leadership beyond the great pause: Climate change and other wicked problems. *Journal of Future Studies,* 26(4), 15–22. https://jfsdigital.org/2022-2/vol-26-no-4-june-2022/leadership-beyond-the-great-pause-climate-change-and-other-wicked-problems/

Senge, P., Hamilton, H., & Kania, J. (2015). The dawn of system leadership. *Stanford Social Innovation Review,* 13(1), 27–33. https://ssir.org/articles/entry/the_dawn_of_system_leadership

Siebert, M. (2018). *Systems thinking and how it can help build a sustainable world*. Post Carbon Institute. https://www.resilience.org/stories/2018-07-11/systems-thinking-and-how-it-can-help-build-a-sustainable-world/

Stroh, D. P. (2015). *Systems thinking for social change*. Chelsea Green.

References

Aanuoluwapo, A. A., & Ohis, A.C. (2017). Biomimetic strategies for climate change mitigation in the built environment, *Energy Procedia, 105*, 3868–3875. https://doi.org/10.1016/j.egypro.2017.03.792

Ambler, G. (2013). *Systems thinking as a leadership practice*.

Archello. (2022). *Boston TreePods*. https://archello.com/project/boston-treepods

Beehner, C. G. (2020). *System leadership for sustainability*. Routledge.

Beehner, C. G. (2022). System leadership for a circular economy. In C. Hinske (Ed.), *Factor X: Studies in sustainable natural resource management: The impossibilities of the circular economy* (pp. 156–166) Umweltbundesamt (German Environment Agency) and Routledge/Taylor & Francis.

Benyus, J. M. (1997). *Biomimicry: Innovation inspired by nature*. William Morrow.

Biomimicry Institute. (2019). *What is biomimicry?* https://biomimicry.org/what-is-biomimicry/

BioPower Systems. (2022). *About BPS*. https://bps.energy/

Boylan, M. (2016). Deepening system leadership: Teachers leading from below. *Educational Management Administration & Leadership, 44*(1), 57–72. https://doi.org/10.1177/1741143213501314

Coley, D. (2012). Energy efficiency: Alternative routes to mitigation. In C. A. Booth, F. N. Hammond, J. E. Lamond, & D. G. Proverbs (Eds.), *Solutions for climate change challenges in the built environment* (pp. 153–161). Blackwell.

Dreier, L., Nabarro, D., & Nelson, J. (2019). *Systems leadership for sustainable development: Strategies for achieving systemic change*. Kennedy School, Harvard University. https://www.hks.harvard.edu/sites/default/files/centers/mrcbg/files/Systems%20Leadership.pdf

Equal Measure & Harder+Company. (2017). *Cultivating systems leadership in cross-sector partnerships: Lessons from the Linked Learning Regional Hubs of Excellence*. https://www.equalmeasure.org/wp-content/uploads/2017/08/Systems-Leadership-Issue-Brief-081017-FINAL.pdf

European Academy for Executive Education. (n.d.). Interpersonal competencies of global leaders and how to develop them. *Global Leadership Magazine*. https://eurac.com/interpersonal-competencies-of-global-leaders/#:~:text=Interpersonal%20competence%20is%20the%20ability, capacity%20for%20interdependence%20and%20collaboration

Fullan, M. (2004). *Systems thinkers in action: Moving beyond the standards plateau.* DfES Innovation Unit/NCSL.

Fullan, M. (2005). *Leadership and sustainability: System thinkers in action.* Sage.

Ghate, D. (2015). *System leadership: Expanding understanding of leadership drivers in whole systems.* The Colebrooke Centre for Evidence and Implementation. http://www.cevi.org.uk

Goss, J. (2009). *Biomimicry: Looking to nature for design solutions.* Corcoran College of Art Design.

Hannon, V. (2014). *Can transforming education systems be led?* CSE Seminar Series (Paper No. 231). Centre for Strategic Education.

Harris, A., & Jones, M. S. (Eds.). (2015). *Leading futures: Global perspectives on educational leadership.* SAGE Publications India.

Hopkins, D., & Higham, R. (2007). System leadership: Mapping the landscape. *School Leadership and Management, 27*(2), 147–166. https://doi.org/10.1080/13632430701237289

Hunter, D. (2017). The system leadership challenge facing the primary healthcare workforce. *European Journal of Public Health, 27*(Suppl. 3). https://doi.org/10.1093/eurpub/ckx187.772

Kassel, K. (2014). *The thinking executive's guide to sustainability.* Business Expert Press.

Northouse, P. G. (2018). *Leadership: Theory and practice* (8th ed.). Sage.

Owen, R. (2018, December 6). Tuned In: A Trump quote inspires title of Nat Geo's 'Paris to Pittsburgh' documentary. *Pittsburgh Post-Gazette.* https://www.post-gazette.com/ae/tv-radio/2018/12/06/Tuned-In-A-Trump-quote-inspires-title-of-Nat-Geo-s-Paris-to-Pittsburgh-documentary/stories/201812050159

Peirce, M. (2011). Introduction. In M. Peirce (Ed.), *A journey of a thousand miles: The state of sustainability leadership 2011* (pp. 6–8). Cambridge Institute for Sustainability Leadership.

Rao, R. (2014). Biomimicry in architecture. *International Journal of Advanced Research in Civil, Structural, Environmental and Infrastructure Engineering and Developing, 1*(3), 101–107. https://biomimicryforhumanity.com/assets/files/biomimicry-architecture2.pdf

Rickards, L., Wiseman, J., & Kashima, Y. (2014). Barriers to effective climate change mitigation: The case of senior government and business decision makers. *Wiley Interdisciplinary Reviews: Climate Change, 5*(6), 753–773. https://doi.org/10.1002/wcc.305

Ross, D., Leonard, B., & Inayatullah, S. (2022). Leadership beyond the great pause: Climate change and other wicked problems. *Journal of Future Studies, 26*(4), 15–22. https://jfsdigital.org/2022-2/vol-26-no-4-june-2022/

leadership-beyond-the-great-pause-climate-change-and-other-wicked-problems/

Senge, P., Hamilton, H., & Kania, J. (2015). The dawn of system leadership. *Stanford Social Innovation Review, 13*(1), 27–33. https://ssir.org/articles/entry/the_dawn_of_system_leadership

Siebert, M. (2018). *Systems thinking and how it can help build a sustainable world.* Post Carbon Institute. https://www.resilience.org/stories/2018-07-11/systems-thinking-and-how-it-can-help-build-a-sustainable-world/

Sørensen, E., & Torfing, J. (2022). Co-creating ambitious climate change mitigation goals: The Copenhagen experience. *Regulation & Governance, 16*(2), 572–587. https://doi.org/10.1111/rego.12374

Srinivas, H. (2015). *Life cycle analysis.* Global Development Research Center. http://www.gdrc.org/sustdev/concepts/17-lca.html

Stroh, D. P. (2015). *Systems thinking for social change.* Chelsea Green.

Timmins, N. (2015). *The practice of system leadership: Being comfortable with chaos.* The King's Fund. https://www.kingsfund.org.uk/sites/default/files/field/field_publication_file/System-leadership-Kings-Fund-May-2015.pdf

Visser, W., & Courtice, P. (2011). *Sustainability leadership: Linking theory and practice.* Cambridge Institute for Sustainability Leadership.

Zari, M. P. (2010). Biomimetic design for climate change adaptation and mitigation. *Architectural Science Review, 53*(2), 172–183. https://doi.org/10.3763/asre.2008.0065

15

ADAPTATION LEADERSHIP

A KEY CAPABILITY FOR ORGANISATIONAL INNOVATION

Johanna Nalau

Chapter Summary

Climate change is one of the largest challenges facing organisations worldwide. While more is known about different ways to tackle greenhouse gas reductions across organisations, there is also a need to start focusing on how an organisation can adapt to the emerging impacts of climate change across its portfolios. Climate change brings significant threats to business viability (impacts on supply chains) and operations but also to the well-being of staff who might themselves become impacted by floods, fires and other extreme events. Climate change adaptation is about preparing now to face future threats that arise from climate change; it is the second pillar of any sensible climate policy or strategy. Yet, most organisations do not understand adaptation given the strong focus on reducing emissions, and hence leadership in adaptation remains an unexplored yet crucial area in climate risk management. This chapter focuses specifically on what climate change adaptation is, which specific qualities and capabilities can support robust climate change adaptation at different levels in organisations and

DOI: 10.4324/9781003343011-18

what steps are already being taken globally by different organisations to adapt. It will provide a key scholarly contribution in defining climate adaptation leadership and its different components and principles and provide a robust set of principles for organisations to consider in adapting to both short- and long-term climate change.

Introduction

Climate change is fast becoming a mainstream topic in the world of business, organisational management and leadership. Part of this change is due to the global pressure for governments and the private sector to act on climate change and reduce their greenhouse gas emissions (mitigation) and show robust sustainability credentials. Yet, increasing climate change impacts are already occurring across many areas and regions across the world, with significant impacts on supply chains and staff well-being and capabilities. These impacts include, for example, rising sea levels, increases in the number of heatwaves, increases in the intensity and frequency of storms and overall extreme weather events, while some regions are experiencing prolonged droughts and water scarcity (Intergovermental Panel on Climate Change [IPCC], 2022).

The Sixth Assessment Report of the IPCC makes it clear that many of these climate impacts are likely to intensify in the near future (IPCC, 2022). This means that we no longer can expect a business-as-usual scenario for our plans and decisions but a changed world with increases in uncertainty. This in turn requires new skills but also a new mindset in how we approach the future and how we adapt to the ongoing and upcoming changes and challenges (Dowds & McRae, 2021; Chapter 6) and how we lead.

While businesses are starting to take serious measures in mitigation – for example, transitioning towards low-carbon and more sustainable modes of operations – climate change adaptation still remains less well understood issue at the organisational level (Nalau, 2019). Reluctance to pay attention to adaptation is generally confounded by three key heuristics (aka rules of thumb) that are used to justify inaction or delayed focus on adaptation. First, adaptation is often seen as a novel issue for which there is no experience inside the organisation and for which no action should be taken until there is more knowledge (Preston et al., 2015). A second misinterpretation about adaptation also continues to persist: that adaptation is about accepting failure to solve the climate crises and thus reduces the ambition to mitigate (Nalau & Verrall, 2021). Third, adaptation is seen as a future issue and hence it does not require action in the present time (Preston et al., 2015).

Despite this, emerging discussions show the importance of climate adaptation investments for all organisations (Chidambaram & Khanna, 2022) and the many technologies and strategies that are already available (New et al., 2022; Noble et al., 2014). Adaptation, at its core, is about finding ways to adapt to these impacts now while also considering the future projections of change and making strategic decisions on how to deal with them. Early action and investments in adaptation can reduce future vulnerabilities significantly while delivering also a range of benefits that enable the building of climate-resilient communities and industries (Chidambaram & Khanna, 2022; IPCC, 2022). For example, many countries are investing in more climate-resilient crops that better withstand drought or excess rain (depending on location), increasing early warning system functionality and availability for heatwaves and extreme storms and revising coastal building and planning regulations in response to rising sea levels.

Even though the scientific knowledge about climate change adaptation has rapidly increased in recent years and now provides many new insights into what adaptation can, should or could look like (Nalau & Verrall, 2021), its implementation and incorporation into organisational management decisions is still only emerging. Many existing organisational decision-making methods such as cost–benefit analysis, scenario-based planning, probabilistic decision trees and others can accommodate also better adaptation-related decision making (Siders & Pierce, 2021). In this context, a better understanding of what climate change adaptation is (Dilling et al., 2019; Nalau et al., 2021; Preston et al., 2015; Singh et al., 2021), and subsequently the skills needed to develop, plan and implement adaptation (including adaptation leadership), can open up new opportunities and ways of doing things that build on successful change management and enable companies and organisations to stay relevant in a changing climate.

Theory and Basic Concepts

What Is Climate Change Adaptation?

Climate change adaptation is about preparing now to face future threats and risks that arise from climate change. The IPCC's (2014, p. 1758) definition of climate adaptation describes adaptation as a process:

> The process of adjustment to actual or expected climate and its effects. In human systems, adaptation seeks to moderate or avoid harm or exploit beneficial opportunities. In some natural systems, human intervention may facilitate adjustment to expected climate and its effects.

Adaptation is not an endpoint in itself: it cannot be viewed as a one-off decision or one-off strategy but rather as continuous management of change.

Others have defined adaptation as 'helping people, animals, and plants to survive despite rising climate volatility' (Chidambaram & Khanna, 2022, p. 2). Chidambaram and Khanna (2022) also pointed to the many benefits that proactive climate adaptation can bring to companies: investing early in technologies and strategies can address emission reductions and other sustainability goals at the same time. Adaptation can also be defined as 'actions that make an organisation more resilient in the face of ongoing and forecasted changes in the earth's systems' and a dynamic process (Forest & Toffel, 2017, p. 105). Indeed, this dual consideration of ongoing and forecasted risks and opportunities is the fine balance that climate adaptation initiatives seek to achieve (Carmin et al., 2013). Adaptation is, however, a fundamental shift in mindsets and will require fundamental changes in our values and behaviours (O'Brien, 2009).

Climate change adaptation has been researched since the 1970s and by now has amassed a wealth of knowledge (Nalau & Verrall, 2021). This knowledge is often instilled in *adaptation heuristics*, which are rules of thumb that help to grasp quickly what adaptation is and how it should be implemented (Nalau et al., 2021; Preston et al., 2015). For example, adaptation is often interpreted as a local-level issue that is mainly the responsibility of local actors such as local governments and/or communities (Nalau et al., 2015). Yet, most of the research shows that adaptation is not just local: it is a multi-level governance issue where all stakeholders and levels need to act together (Nalau et al., 2021). The regional scale is often more relevant for infrastructure decisions and plans rather than the local level. Balancing these different scales and knowing which decision is best made at what scale remains an important part of understanding adaptation decision making.

What makes climate adaptation to human-influenced climate change a novel challenge is the unforeseen speed of observed and projected climatic changes where business-as-usual approaches are no longer adequate (Preston et al., 2015; Schipper & Burton, 2009). This speed of change is also why there is an increasing attention on 'transformational adaptation' that seeks to fundamentally change the existing processes and ways of doing things (Kates et al., 2012; Nalau & Handmer, 2015). The fact that the operational and strategic context and environment are changing sits at the core of how we view the future and adaptation in particular (Nalau & Cobb, 2022). Incremental adaptation is often something that occurs slowly over time with minor changes made, whereas transformational adaptation introduces fundamental shifts in how we think, behave and act (Ara Begum et al., 2022). IPCC in particular discusses 'deliberate transformations', which are intentional changes made by actors in order to thrive in a changing climate (Ara Begum et al., 2022). For example, using new economic models such as doughnut economics or green new deals can open up new opportunities for more sustainable practices while also opening up new product and job markets.

Key concepts relating to adaptation are vulnerability and the different ways it can be understood and the concept of adaptive capacity (Vincent & Cundill, 2022). In particular, questions are often raised as to 'who is the most vulnerable and how much' (R. J. T. Klein, 2009); for example, who is most affected by climate change (Thomas et al., 2019), how that vulnerability is changing due to climate, the level of adaptive capacity needed for communities and countries to adapt (Siders, 2019) and the financial and technological resources needed (Vincent & Cundill, 2021). Another key question is whether the adaptation actions and strategies that are being implemented are actually effective (Singh et al., 2021), what effective adaptation looks like (Owen, 2020) and how we can determine 'successful adaptation (Dilling et al., 2019). For example, a successful adaptation strategy for a coastal community could include several adaptation options (e.g., sea wall, strengthening the coastal areas with coastal vegetation) that clearly reduce erosion and protect housing and other infrastructure with a clear monitoring and evaluation plan. In the business context, this can mean being able to reduce damages to supply chains from extreme weather events by changing transport routes or packaging components differently (Woetzel et al., 2020). This also requires identification of who is best placed to lead which adaptation effort (Becker & Kretch, 2019).

Adaptation to climate change, however, does not occur in a vacuum. While adaptation is often posed as a separate issue for research and policy, there are increasing calls to integrate adaptation as part of normal operations and strategic planning (Dupuis & Biesbroek, 2013). This is to make sure that both the short- and long-term perspectives are embedded in decision making at both the operational and strategic levels, while also understanding the interlinkages between adaptation and mitigation (IPCC, 2022). This linkage is particularly important so that our adaptation actions (e.g., installing air conditioners to help with heatwaves) do not increase emissions disproportionately. This broader integration, and its linkage to innovation in particular, is where organisations can make a difference (Mitchell, 2021).

Methods, Techniques and Applications

Examples of Climate Adaptation in Organisations and Sectors

The business case for climate adaptation is clear: the more resilient and adaptive a business or an organisation can be, the less impacted it will be by the changing climate. For example, the government of New South Wales offers specific advice complemented by case studies in how businesses can adapt to climate change (Department of Climate Change and Environment, 2022). This includes understanding business vulnerability and coping with extreme events but also considering the impacts that climate change can have on staff, their well-being and ability to work. Being prepared also includes understanding the changing nature of disasters and location and supply chain–specific risks. The United Nations Framework Convention on Climate Change (UNFCCC) has an *Adaptation Private Sector Initiative* that enables the private sector, such as companies and organisations, to consider climate adaptation as part of their operational and strategic decision making and sharing information on climate adaptation strategies and initiatives (UNFCCC, 2022a).

The finance sector is taking climate risk management more seriously than ever. Moodys Corporation, which gives credit ratings to governments, has bought a significant part of a firm that models and measures physical climate risks (Flavelle, 2019). This further signals the level of seriousness that the investment community has for climate change impacts and their implications for credit ratings, risk transparency and reporting. This is further driven by the Task Force on Climate-Related Financial Disclosures (TCFD), which aims to increase transparency of climate risk management reporting across organisations (TCFD, 2022). The TCFD framework covers governance (how climate risks are governed), strategy (how impacts will affect the business), risk management (how the organisations aims to manage these risks) and metrics and targets (how these risks are assessed and managed). In New Zealand, large publicly listed companies, banks, investment managers, insurers and non-bank deposit takers are now legally required to disclose their climate related risks (Ministry for the Environment, 2022).

The U.S. Navy is already considering climate adaptation in their operations and strategic planning (Forest & Toffel, 2017). The U.S. Navy delivers critical humanitarian services while managing billions of dollars in assets that will be heavily impacted by the changing climate, bringing new challenges to what they can do and have capacity for. Hence, the U.S. Navy has to

> understand now what sorts of missions it may be required to perform in 10, 20, or 30 years and what assets and infrastructure it will need to carry out those missions ... it needs to plan for the world that will exist at that time.
>
> (Forest & Toffel, 2017, p. 103)

They have to consider both the potential increases in demand for their humanitarian and military services due to increasing climate impacts and also their potentially reduced capacity to do so due to increasing climate impacts on key infrastructure and assets. For example, thinning of sea ice in the Arctic will pose new challenges but also opportunities for maritime and defence operations while increased flooding might impair some defence infrastructure that needs relocating (Forest & Toffel, 2017).

In the United States, the Department of Defense's Draft Climate Adaptation Plan outlines the Climate Adaptation Strategy Framework and its five priority areas while identifying climate change as a national security issue, threat multiplier and significant management challenge (Department of Defense, Office of the Undersecretary of Defense [Acquisition and Sustainment], 2021). Its four enablers are worth noting here: (a) continuous monitoring and data analytics, (b) aligning incentives to reward innovation, (c) climate literacy and (d) environmental justice. For example, under climate literacy, the enabling condition is of a climate-informed workforce that understands how climate change and adaptation considerations can be included in day-to-day operations but also in the longer-term strategic planning. Likewise, continuous monitoring of changing conditions (Enabler 1) and future scenarios provide access to data that can help in making decisions. The environmental justice component reflects the critical attention that needs to be paid so that climate adaptation actions do not disadvantage minority groups or low-income groups, a concern that is often raised in terms of maladaptation and unintended consequences (Atteridge & Remling, 2018; Magnan et al., 2016; Thomas et al., 2019).

In the private sector, adaptations are already ongoing in thinking how to secure supply chain resilience rather than efficiency. For example, hurricanes and other extreme weather events can severely disrupt production and supply chains. Adaptation options include investing in more resilient and disaster-proof production facilities, broadening the sourcing processes to multiple producers of parts and investing in insurance (Woetzel et al., 2020).

In Australia, Climate Planning's Informed.City tool enables organisations to develop a clear picture of their adaptation baseline and progress (Climate Planning, 2022). Informed.City has assessed climate change adaptation governance across over 360 local governments in Australia and several state departments and is also increasingly used in the private sector (banks, insurance). It combines both quantitative and qualitative indicators to assess how climate adaptation is being considered in asset management, land use management and emergency management and areas such as public risk disclosure, while also surveying the current staff capabilities and understanding of managing climate risks. Using the tool gives organisations real-time data-driven understanding of how much of their current strategies, policies and processes are in fact helping them to chart a path towards a climate-resilient and adaptive future (Nalau, 2019).

Having a whole-of-organisation view of adaptation will become increasingly important especially as adaptation requires multiple decisions across all levels of organisational management and operations. Likewise, many cities across the world are already being recognised for their climate adaptation leadership, including developing climate adaptation plans and conducting vulnerability and risk assessments and aiming to plan under uncertainty of future change and scenarios (Carmin et al., 2013). In fact, setting forward-looking indicators and vision are becoming increasingly important for climate adaptation at different scales (Nalau & Cobb, 2022; UNFCCC, 2022b).

Leadership Skills Needed in a Changing Climate

Twenty-first-century leadership will be determined by how fast leaders can respond to change, how they react overall and whether they are capable of detecting changes (both challenges and opportunities) both inside and outside their organisations (Chavez & Palsule, 2020). Many organisations are already developing key capacities in agile management, premortem scenarios and adaptive decision making (G. Klein, 2007, 2009), understanding inflection points and innovation (McGrath, 2019) and future-back thinking (Johnson & Suskewicz, 2021). All of these skill sets enable organisations to shift perspectives and open themselves up for innovation in diverse areas. Capacities in these areas will also well serve actions, strategies and decisions in climate change adaptation.

There are strong interlinkages between organisational leadership, innovation and climate change adaptation. While some of the core skills required for effective climate adaptation are specific to climate change, there are also other broader skills that enable organisations to respond in and plan for a changing context (Table 15.1). Key skills can be grouped into three broad categories: (a) accepting change, understanding risks and adaptation; (b) vision of the future; and (c) information literacy, flow and accessibility. Using and developing skills across all three areas will be key in going forward in an uncertain future.

To lead well on adaptation, the first step for any leader is to accept the realities of a changing climate. This includes a strong recognition across the whole organisation that climate change is occurring and that there is an urgent need to map climate impacts and risks to current and future operations and strategies. Existing guidance under the TCFD (2022) provides first steps on how to assess and report on climate-related risks, including identification of potential transition risks as the world shifts towards low carbon pathways. However, this alone is not enough: accepting change and identifying risks are the necessary first steps in the adaptation leadership journey.

Another key part of climate adaptation is *future visioning*: the way we construct, aspire to and plan to deal with the future impacts of climate change (Nalau & Cobb, 2022). Developing skills in this area will become crucial as people and organisations grapple in how to plan for something that is uncertain. For example, it is common knowledge from innovation literature that you need more perspectives to find richer and more diverse solutions. A recent UNFCCC report, for example, highlighted a four-tier approach to future visioning, where Level 1 is focused on survival and Level 4 is about thriving in a changing climate (UNFCCC, 2022b). Finding forward-looking indicators does remain a challenge, but there are several strategies available, such as the future-back thinking (Johnson & Suskewicz, 2021) that focuses on view of the future statements that are data-driven imaginations of what potential different future scenarios could look like. Similarly, Rita McGrath's work on understanding inflection points and innovation (McGrath, 2019) is another useful approach, especially on information flows and understanding the on-the-ground data that can give early indications of changing markets, market demand and opportunities.

In this context, I define adaptation leadership as 'the set of skills and mindset needed to consider both short- and long-term ramifications of climate change, make decisions on how to adapt, while taking charge of new opportunities in an inclusive manner'. This definition includes and emphasises openness to innovation, capacity to read emerging trends and making decisions on how to adapt to the changing strategic and operational environment. While leadership is most commonly equated to a position, a leader can be 'anyone who takes responsibility for finding the potential in people and processes, and who has the courage to develop that potential' (Brown, 2018, p. 4). In this manner, adaptation leadership is not position-based leadership but rather a combination of insight and courage that an individual or an organisation can exercise in adapting to climate change. This has a strong relationship with self-efficacy (belief in one's capability to adapt) and other concepts such as risk perception, negative affect, descriptive norms and outcome efficacy (van Valkengoed & Steg, 2019). Leaders could find ways to increase these in their organisations by discussing climate change as a real and relevant issue, emphasising the options available and the capability of the organisation to undertake adaptation.

Commitment of the organisational and political leadership plays a key role whether adaptation is taken seriously (Carmin et al., 2013). For example, when Boston's climate adaptation plan was discussed at an event, the presence of the city's mayor throughout the whole event was a public example of the organisational commitment that the strategy had at the highest level. Championing adaptation therefore becomes part of a role of the leader and sends an important message as to how valued the issue is.

Table 15.1 Areas and Connections Between Generic Leadership Skills and Those Specifically Required for Climate Change Adaptation

General Leadership	*Adaptation Specific*
Accepting change, understanding risks and adaptation	
• *Acceptance of change*: Accepting that the future will no longer be business as usual but characterised by change and uncertainty	• *Acceptance of change*: Accepting that the future will no longer be business as usual but characterised by change and uncertainty
• *Understanding vulnerability, risks and adaptive capacity* to change overall (which parts of the organisational system are most vulnerable to diverse shocks)	• *Understanding vulnerability, risks and adaptive capacity*; for example, differential vulnerability and adaptive capacity (which groups/sectors are most vulnerable and why; where gaps exist in adaptive capacity; staff well-being)
• *Business strategies*: how to compete in a changing context; general organisational strategies	• *Adaptation strategies*: specific understanding of the kinds of climate adaptation strategies that can be used to lessen impacts of climate change and/or take charge of emerging opportunities
Vision of the future	
• *Vision setting*: Setting a strong vision and aligning goals	• *Vision setting*: Setting a strong vision for adaptation and aligning goals
• *'Seeing the future'*: Understanding emerging trends of the marketplace, artificial intelligence, innovation, technologies	• *'Seeing the future'*: Understanding emerging trends of climate change and how these might change in the future
• *Bringing others along to the future*: Participatory future visioning and scenario planning in business	• *Bringing others along to the future*: participatory future-visioning and scenario planning in adaptation
Information literacy, flows, and accessibility	
• *Information flows*: Having a channel for information flows from the frontline (operational context → emerging threats and opportunities) across the organisation and to top-level leadership	• *Information flows*: Having a channel for information flows from those implementing adaptation to those designing and funding adaptation → emerging lessons to improve climate adaptation outcomes, processes and project/program design
• *Information literacy* (skills in data access, availability, interpretation and analysis)	• *Climate adaptation information literacy* (understanding climate adaptation and climate science; data access, availability, interpretation and analysis)

Vignola et al. (2017) likewise have assessed the different kinds of leadership styles that are needed across the adaptation cycle when we move from initial planning stage to implementation and to monitoring and evaluation. Leaders need to understand the kind of leadership that is necessary at different phases of adaptation (Vignola et al., 2017) and the range of barriers that might arise (New et al., 2022).

CASE STUDY ON FUTURE VISIONING FOR CLIMATE ADAPTATION

Many leaders are afraid to do future visioning, especially given the many uncertainties that exist about the future state of the world, the future trends in particular business sectors and trying to navigate through different sets of assumptions in finding a competitive edge in a rapidly changing marketplace. Yet, future visioning has multiple benefits, especially when dealing with issues such as climate adaptation. There are several key benefits in engaging staff, shareholders and external collaborators on visioning processes. Here, in this brief case study, I explain some of the challenges and opportunities as seen in the field of climate change adaptation in a recent study (Nalau & Cobb, 2022) and the lessons these offer for broader management and leadership. We reviewed 62 case studies in depth that reported on using scenario exercises with stakeholders to discuss climate adaptation.

1. *Stakeholder diversity and inclusion*: Our research shows that many projects had involved diverse stakeholder groups especially at regional and local scales but, overall, most studies did not explicitly report who was in the room. Innovation and management research has consistently shown that to have the best ideas, diverse perspectives should be valued (Syed, 2019). Including people with different roles across the organisation and even outside adds value to what the envisioned future can be like. In addition, paying attention to representation and inclusion is important: including women, people with disabilities and other minority groups can enrich the conversation and provide additional perspectives.
2. *Tools and methods*: There are a range of tools and methods that can be used for future visioning. In our research, we found that drawings and expert-solicitated quantitative scenarios on climate impacts were the most popular ones. But one should always consider what is fit for purpose: using virtual reality or videos can also be powerful in setting a scene and helping participants

to imagine alternative scenarios or futures. Some studies used multiple methods and tools (e.g., landscape mapping by walking in the environment, virtual reality, expert scenarios on future change). Also, unpacking together the core assumptions that people have – for example, about why future change might occur, where, when and how – is useful as this exposes underlying assumptions and can help to foster critical conversations about how to move forward if X, Y and Z are correct or not. On timelines, we found no common ground: people used for example, 20-, 100- or 70-year time horizons for the discussions. The futures literature is also divided on this: some suggest picking a very specific time, whereas others encourage more open-ended exploration of the future.

3. *Opportunities and challenges*: We found multiple benefits and opportunities resulting from running visioning scenarios for climate adaptation. Many participants reported increases in adaptation literacy (in understanding what climate adaptation is and means) that supported their intended actions afterwards to take adaptation-related decisions. Scenario exercises also provided opportunities for new social networks and broader collective thinking as to what the future of the whole community, whole region or whole country could look like. In other words, the participation changed the way people thought about individual vs. collective scale. We also found, however, that some exercises were confusing to participants given the long timescales involved and not having adequate background on future visioning thinking, which then made the participation challenging.

While there are many more lessons drawing from this research, the bottom line is that creating spaces for discussions on future scenarios and change remains a critical step in any leadership or management role. There is clearly no one-size-fits-all approach as the purpose and fit are based on what the organisation is seeking to create, who they decide to invite into these discussions and what the aim is. A key lesson is that whatever methods or tools are used, the leader must be clear as to what the scenario visioning process is for: is it just to increase connections across the organisations or expose underlying assumptions, or does the process actually feed into real decisions that are taken afterwards? Giving and having clarity on the actual outcomes of the process will help in managing expectations of the process and engagement.

Conclusion

How to adapt to climate change is becoming one of the most urgent and challenging questions for many leaders and organisations. While the reduction of greenhouse gas emissions and transitioning to more sustainable forms of operations are now understood, climate adaptation is still a less familiar concept. This chapter has unpacked what climate adaptation is, given examples of organisations already in applying adaptation thinking and defined leadership capabilities and skills that are relevant in a changing climate. This chapter has also shown the many similarities between common leadership and management thinking and those relevant to adapting to climate change, yet there are also important differences in the focus and lens that each apply. Responding to climate change is not about only mitigation or only adaptation: a balanced approach looks at both as key strategies to live and do business in a changing climate.

Discussion points

- What does climate change adaptation mean to our company and operations?
- What does a resilient company look like in your sector?
- What climate impacts are likely to reduce performance and increase vulnerability now and in the future?

Suggested reading

Informed City. (2019). South Australia Pilot Climate Change Adaptation Governance Assessment: Climate Change Adaptation Governance Assessment Report for the City of Marion, https://cdn.marion.sa.gov.au/sp/Climate-Change-Adaptation-Governance-Assessment-Report-for-Marion.pdf

References

Ara Begum, R., Lempert, R., Ali, E., Benjaminsen, T. A., Bernauer, T., Cramer, W., Cui, X., Mach, K., Nagy, G., Stenseth, N. C., Sukumar, R., & Wester, P. (2022). Point of departure and key concepts. In H.-O. Pörtner, D. C. Roberts, M. Tignor, E. S. Poloczanska, K. Mintenbeck, A. Alegría, M. Craig, S. Langsdorf, S. Löschke, V. Möller, A. Okem, B. Rama (Eds.), *Climate change 2022: Impacts, adaptation and vulnerability. Contribution of Working Group II to the Sixth Assessment Report of the Intergovernmental*

Panel on Climate Change (pp. 121–196). Cambridge University Press. doi:10.1017/9781009325844.003

Atteridge, A., & Remling, E. (2018). Is adaptation reducing vulnerability or redistributing it? *Wiley Interdisciplinary Reviews: Climate Change, 9*(1). doi:10.1002/wcc.500

Becker, A., & Kretsch, E. (2019). The leadership void for climate adaptation planning: Case study of the Port of Providence (Rhode Island, United States). *Frontiers in Earth Science, 7*(29). doi:10.3389/feart.2019.00029

Brown, B. (2018). *Dare to lead: Brave work, tough conversations, whole hearts.* Random House.

Carmin, J., Dodman, D., & Chu, E. (2013). Urban climate adaptation and leadership: From conceptual understanding to practical action (OECD Regional Development Working Papers, 2013/26). OECD Publishing. http://dx.doi.org/10.1787/5k3ttg88w8hh-en

Chavez, M., & Palsule, S. (2020). *Rehumanizing leadership: Putting purpose back into business.* LID Publishing.

Chidambaram, R., & Khanna, P. (2022, August 1). It's time to invest in climate adaptation. *Harvard Business Review.* https://hbr.org/2022/08/its-time-to-invest-in-climate-adaptation https://hbr.org/2022/08/its-time-to-invest-in-climate-adaptation

Climate Planning. (2022). Informed.City. https://climateplanning.com.au/informedcity/#:~:text=CityTM%20which%20is%20an, Agencies%20and%20the%20private%20sector

Department of Climate Change and Environment. (2022). *How businesses can adapt to climate change.* https://www.climatechange.environment.nsw.gov.au/how-business-can-adapt

Department of Defense, Office of the Undersecretary of Defense (Acquisition and Sustainment). (2021). *Department of Defense draft climate adaptation plan.* Report Submitted to National Climate Task Force and Federal Chief Sustainability Officer. https://www.sustainability.gov/pdfs/dod-2021-cap.pdf

Dilling, L., Prakash, A., Zommers, Z., Ahmad, F., Singh, N., de Wit, S., ... Bowman, K. (2019). Is adaptation success a flawed concept? *Nature Climate Change, 9*(8), 572–574. doi:10.1038/s41558-019-0539-0

Dowds, J., & McRae, G. (2021, July). *Workforce development needs of the transportation sector climate adaptation professionals.* White Paper, National Centre for Sustainable Transportation.

Dupuis, J., & Biesbroek, R. (2013). Comparing apples and oranges: The dependent variable problem in comparing and evaluating climate change adaptation policies. *Global Environmental Change, 23*(6), 1476–1487. http://dx.doi.org/10.1016/j.gloenvcha.2013.07.022

Flavelle, C. (2019, July 24). Moody's buys climate data firm, signalling new scrutiny of climate risks. *New York Times*. https://www.nytimes.com/2019/07/24/climate/moodys-ratings-climate-change-data.html

Forest, R., & Toffel, M. W. (2017). Managing climate change: Lessons from the U.S. Navy. *Harvard Business Review, 95*(4), 102–111.

Intergovernmental Panel on Climate Change. (2014). Annex II: Glossary. In K. J. Mach, S. Planton, & C. von Stechow (Eds.), *Climate change 2014. Contribution of Working Groups I, II and III to the Fifth Assessment Report of the Intergovernmental Panel on Climate Change* (pp. 1757–1776). https://www.ipcc.ch/site/assets/uploads/2018/02/WGIIAR5-AnnexII_FINAL.pdf

Intergovernmental Panel on Climate Change. (2022). Summary for policymakers. In H.-O. Pörtner, D. C. Roberts, M. Tignor, E. S. Poloczanska, K. Mintenbeck, A. Alegría, M. Craig, S. Langsdorf, S. Löschke, V. Möller, A. Okem, & B. Rama (Eds.), *Climate change 2022: Impacts, adaptation, and vulnerability. Contribution of Working Group II to the Sixth Assessment Report of the Intergovernmental Panel on Climate Change*. Cambridge University Press.

Johnson, M. W., & Suskewicz, J. (2020). *Lead from the future: How to turn visionary thinking into breakthrough growth*. Harvard Business Review Press.

Kates, R. W., Travis, W. R., & Wilbanks, T. J. (2012). Transformational adaptation when incremental adaptations to climate change are insufficient. *PNAS, 109 (19), 7156–7161.*

Klein, G. (2007). Performing a project premortem. *Harvard Business Review, 85*(9), 18–19.

Klein, G. (2009). *Streetlights and shadows: Searching for the keys to adaptive decision making*. MIT Press.

Klein, R. J. T. (2009). Identifying countries that are particularly vulnerable to the adverse effects of climate change: An academic or a political challenge? *Carbon & Climate Law Review, 3*(3), 284–291.

Magnan, A. K., Schipper, E. L. F., Burkett, M., Bharwani, S., Burton, I., Eriksen, S., ... Ziervogel, G. (2016). Addressing the risk of maladaptation to climate change. *WIREs Climate Change, 7*(5), 646–665. doi:10.1002/wcc.409

McGrath, R. (2019). Seeing around corners: How to spot inflection points in business before they happen. Houghton Mifflin Harcourt.

Ministry for the Environment. (2022). *Mandatory climate-related disclosures*. https://environment.govt.nz/what-government-is-doing/areas-of-work/climate-change/mandatory-climate-related-financial-disclosures/

Mitchell, T. (2021, January 25). Boosting climate adaptation with innovation. Climate-KIC. https://www.climate-kic.org/opinion/boosting-climate-adaptation-with-innovation/

Nalau, J. (2019). Climate adaptation and businesses: The case for private sector leadership in the Asia Pacific. In C. Byrne & L. West (Eds.), *State of the neighbourhood 2019* (pp. 48–56). Asia Institute, Griffith University. https://www.griffith.edu.au/__data/assets/pdf_file/0022/901912/W6-Nalau-Ch5-WEB.pdf

Nalau, J., & Cobb, G. (2022). The strengths and weaknesses of future visioning approaches for climate change adaptation: A review. *Global Environmental Change, 74*, 102527. https://doi.org/10.1016/j.gloenvcha.2022.102527

Nalau, J., & Handmer, J. (2015). When is transformation a viable policy alternative? *Environmental Science and Policy, 54*, 349–356. doi:10.1016/j.envsci.2015.07.022

Nalau, J., Preston, B. L., & Maloney, M. C. (2015). Is adaptation a local responsibility? *Environmental Science & Policy, 48*, 89–98. https://doi.org/10.1016/j.envsci.2014.12.011

Nalau, J., Torabi, E., Edwards, N., Howes, M., & Morgan, E. (2021). A critical exploration of adaptation heuristics. *Climate Risk Management, 32*, 100292. https://doi.org/10.1016/j.crm.2021.100292

Nalau, J., & Verrall, B. (2021). Mapping the evolution and current trends in climate change adaptation science. *Climate Risk Management, 32*, 100290. https://doi.org/10.1016/j.crm.2021.100290

New, M., Reckien, D., Viner, D., Adler, C., Cheong, S.-M., Conde, C., Constable, A., Coughlan de Perez, E., Lammel, A., Mechler, R., Orlove, B., & Solecki, W. (2022). Decision-making options for managing risk. In H.-O. Pörtner, D. C. Roberts, M. Tignor, E. S. Poloczanska, K. Mintenbeck, A. Alegría, M. Craig, S. Langsdorf, S. Löschke, V. Möller, A. Okem, B. Rama (Eds.), *Climate change 2022: Impacts, adaptation and vulnerability. Contribution of Working Group II to the Sixth Assessment Report of the Intergovernmental Panel on Climate Change* (pp. 2539–2654). Cambridge University Press. doi:10.1017/9781009325844.026

Noble, I. R., Huq, S., Anokhin, Y. A., Carmin, J., Goudou, D., Lansigan, F. P., ... Mastrandrea, P. R. (2014). Adaptation needs and options. In V. R. Barros, C. B. Field, D. J. Dokken, M. D. Mastrandrea, K. J. Mach, T. E. Bilir, M. Chatterjee, K. L. Ebi, Y. O. Estrada, R. C. Genova, B. Girma, E. S. Kissel, A. N. Levy, S. MacCracken, P. R. Mastrandrea, & L. L. White (Eds.), *Climate change 2014: Impacts, adaptation, and vulnerability. Part A: Global and sectoral aspects. Contribution of Working Group II to the Fifth Assessment Report of the Intergovernmental Panel on Climate Change* (pp. 833–868). Cambridge University Press.

O'Brien, K. (2009). Do values subjectively define the limits to climate change adaptation? In N. W. Adger, I. Lorenzoni, & K. O'Brien (Eds.), *Adapting to climate change: Thresholds, values, governance* (pp. 164–180). Cambridge University Press.

Owen, G. (2020). What makes climate change adaptation effective? A systematic review of the literature. *Global Environmental Change, 62*, 102071. doi:10.1016/j.gloenvcha.2020.102071

Preston, B. L., Mustelin, J., & Maloney, M. C. (2015). Climate adaptation heuristics and the science/policy divide. *Mitigation and Adaptation Strategies for Global Change, 20*(3), 467–497. doi:10.1007/s11027-013-9503-x

Schipper, E. L. F., & Burton, I. (2009). Understanding adaptation: origins, concepts, practice and policy. In E. L. F. Schipper & I. Burton (Eds.), *The Earthscan reader on adaptation to climate change* (pp. 1–8). Earthscan.

Siders, A. R. (2019). Adaptive capacity to climate change: A synthesis of concepts, methods, and findings in a fragmented field. *Wiley Interdisciplinary Reviews: Climate Change, 10*(3), e573. doi:10.1002/wcc.573

Siders, A. R., & Pierce, A. L. (2021). Deciding how to make climate change adaptation decisions. *Current Opinion in Environmental Sustainability, 52*, 1–8. https://doi.org/10.1016/j.cosust.2021.03.017

Singh, C., Iyer, S., New, M. G., Few, R., Kuchimanchi, B., Segnon, A. C., & Morchain, D. (2021). Interrogating 'effectiveness' in climate change adaptation: 11 Guiding principles for adaptation research and practice. *Climate and Development, 14*, 1–15. doi:10.1080/17565529.2021.1964937

Syed, M. (2019). *Rebel ideas: The power of diverse thinking.* Hachette.

Task Force on Climate-Related Financial Disclosures. (2022). Task Force on Climate-Related Financial Disclosures. https://www.fsb-tcfd.org

Thomas, K., Hardy, R. D., Lazrus, H., Mendez, M., Orlove, B., Rivera-Collazo, I., … Winthrop, R. (2019). Explaining differential vulnerability to climate change: A social science review. *Wiley Interdisciplinary Reviews: Climate Change, 10*(2), e565. doi:10.1002/wcc.565

United Nations Framework Convention on Climate Change. (2022a). *Adaptation Private Sector Initiative (PSI).* https://unfccc.int/topics/resilience/resources/adaptation-private-sector

United Nations Framework Convention on Climate Change. (2022b). *Compilation and synthesis of indicators, approaches, targets and metrics for reviewing overall progress in achieving the global goal on adaptation.* UNFCCC Secretariat Technical Paper. https://unfccc.int/sites/default/files/resource/ReportGGATP_final.pdf

van Valkengoed, A. M., & Steg, L. (2019). Meta-analyses of factors motivating climate change adaptation behaviour. *Nature Climate Change, 9*(2), 158–163. doi:10.1038/s41558-018-0371-y

Vignola, R., Leclerc, G., Morales, M., & Gonzalez, J. (2017). Leadership for moving the climate change adaptation agenda from planning to action. *Current Opinion in Environmental Sustainability, 26–27*, 84–89. https://doi.org/10.1016/j.cosust.2017.03.005

Vincent, K., & Cundill, G. (2022). The evolution of empirical adaptation research in the Global South from 2010 to 2020. *Climate and Development, 14*(1), 25–38. doi:10.1080/17565529.2021.1877104

Woetzel, J., Pinner, D., Samandari, H., Engel, H., Krishnan, M., Kampel, C., & Graabak, J. (2020, August 6). *Could climate become the weak link in your supply chain?* McKinsey Global Institute. https://www.mckinsey.com/capabilities/sustainability/our-insights/could-climate-become-the-weak-link-in-your-supply-chain

Part IV

ACTIONS

16

SUSTAINABLE GOAL SETTING FOR CLIMATE ACTION

WHAT LEADERS VALUE DEFINES HOW THEY TAKE ACTION

Donald Eubank

Chapter Summary

While the science of climate change has long been settled, the business case and existential urgency for companies to take action have been lacking until recently. Spurred by investors and recognition of threats to their operations, now visionary company leaders are setting sustainable business goals to thrive and survive in a rapidly changing environment. Their choices are part of a broader movement that has been guided by the United Nations (UN), international organisations and standards bodies such as the World Food Programme, the International Financial Reporting Standards Foundation and regional bodies such as the European Union (EU). Investors, too, in order to preserve their capital, are pushing boards and executives to be aware of the physical and business threats arising from a world heading toward a 2°C increase. To advance sustainable business transformations, leading companies in this movement are outlining organisation-wide strategies with specific actions and targets based on the long-term (2050) and mid-term time frames

DOI: 10.4324/9781003343011-20

(2030–2035), utilising frameworks such as Science-Based Targets for reducing carbon emissions and the Task Force for Climate-Related Disclosure. As a benefit, not only do these leaders' efforts make their organisations more resilient but research shows that such businesses are more competitive in their markets.

Introduction

The science on climate change is settled – if you don't believe the scientists, go have a chat with reinsurance companies, credit rating agencies and corporate risk committees. What's lacking in many quarters is progress in reducing societal contributions to the problem.

Setting sustainability goals is one of the most effective actions businesses can take to reduce their contribution to climate change. For goal setting for climate action to be meaningful, though, organisations and leaders have to understand three key points:

1. Setting targets is just the start – specific plans and actions must be put in place to advance toward and meet those goals.
2. Establishing goals for climate action doesn't happen in a silo within the company – to achieve such goals, the business must transform as a whole, which frequently requires setting internal organisational targets for how, and how quickly, that transformation proceeds.
3. Environmental actions are social actions, and social actions are environmental actions – when it comes to climate action, the goals of the Paris Agreement and the Sustainable Development Goals (SDGs) don't exist in parallel, they're intimately intertwined in the cause of a just transition.

*****

While the Congress of Parties (COP) negotiations on the Paris Agreement rulebook make progress on outlining a policy pathway for halting global warming, albeit in fits and starts, it's proving difficult for some national governments to provide the business world guidance. Counterintuitively, perhaps, business has stepped into this void with a helping hand from international standard-setting bodies. Jump starting this movement are 'enlightened' managers of capital, who are recognising the potential long-term – and short-term – risk to their capital.

Pension funds have led the way, due to their unique nature. Pension funds' fiduciary duty is to the communities they serve, not any single asset owner. As such, they have a responsibility to grow capital under their management over a long-term time frame encompassing the lives of pension contributors. As well, the size of many of these funds turns them into 'universal owners' – their portfolio is inevitably composed of businesses in every industry, some even in every company. Thus, they don't have the luxury of betting on winners and losers from the effects of climate change, as it's in their interest for all companies and industries perform well.

Businesses aren't far behind in adopting a sustainability mindset, due to a range of pressures on previously successful business practices. In our 2020 book *Leading Sustainably – The Path to Sustainable Business and How the SDGs Changed Everything* (Bridges & Eubank, 2020), my co-author Trista Bridges and I outlined eight factors that are forcing businesses to adopt more sustainable business models, three internal and five external (see Figure 16.1):

- **Organisational Factors**
    - New leaders assuming control
    - New opportunities
    - Core value challenges from within

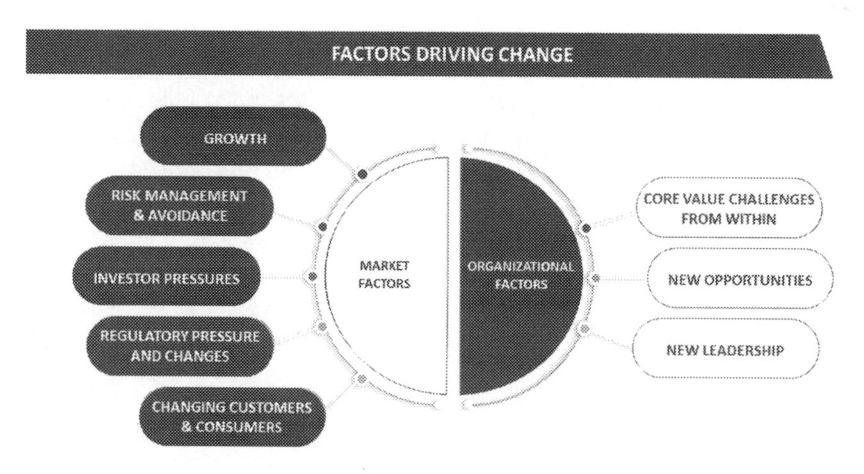

Figure 16.1 Factors Driving Change

- **Market Factors**
  - Slowing growth in existing business lines
  - Risk management and avoidance
  - Investor pressures
  - Regulatory pressures and changes
  - Changing customer and consumer behaviour and expectations

Businesses that will be best prepared for the impacts of climate change are the ones that have recognised these new sustainability-related pressures and are responding with changes to their core strategy. Any of the factors can be a motivating reason, but the initiation of actions to address one makes an organisation better prepared to deal with others.

Getting started isn't easy, though, and requires a base level understanding of fundamental sustainability concepts. For 'sustainability' itself, in Bridges and Eubank (2020, p. 26) we defined it in the following manner:

> In a business context, 'Sustainability' is a *continuous process* in which an organisation strives to reduce and ultimately eliminate its negative impacts on societal and environmental resources, and increase the benefits that it provides society in the course of its commercial activities, while maintaining or improving its profitability and market performance.

Two key concepts that represent the latest thinking on sustainable business practices elaborate this definition further: *double materiality* and *impact*. Collectively, business leaders, investors and standard-setting bodies such as the Science Based Targets initiative (SBTi) and the International Financial Reporting Standards Foundation (IFRS) develop their frameworks with these fundamental concepts in mind to improve disclosure around sustainability and decarbonisation efforts and, even more important, to drive target setting and planning to achieve such targets (Science Based Targets, n.d.a, n.d.b).

When business leaders apply these as the foundation of their thinking, they're able to outline strategies that create resilient, sustainable organisations, as we will see in the cases of health and nutrition leader DSM and insurer AXA.

Theory and Basic Concepts

Double Materiality

Materiality is an accounting term that covers any data that would affect an investor's decisions about a potential investment. The Sustainability Accounting Standards Board (SASB, n.d.) took the concept and applied it to environmental, social and governance (ESG) issues, thus developing a framework for determining the relevance – the materiality – of different sustainability dimensions to investment or business decisions. (SASB now exists within the newly launched International Sustainability Standards Board, itself under the IFRS.)

SASB's sustainable materiality framework creates a shared language among investors, CFOs, regulators and sustainability experts, making it possible to compare the importance of issues affecting business performance with other non-financial factors. The framework identifies important issues from environment, social and human capital, to business models, innovation and leadership – such as business ethics, competitive behavior or systemic risk management – that can impact risk profiles and business performance. These could include impacts on the cost of materials, products or services or on the cost of capital, assets and intangible assets.

In practice, there has been a fundamental failure in applying materiality in the sustainability space – specifically in terms of including all stakeholders. Many investors and business leaders have used ESG and materiality only to determine the risks *to* the operation of businesses from climate change–related risks. What they have left out is how their own business can create negative outcomes for external stakeholders – and possible positive ones (more on this next).

To resolve this, double materiality looks at both risks to operations as well as risks of the organisation causing problems to society. Many outcries against 'greenwashing' come from the failure to incorporate both types of materiality into planning and communications. With a robust public discussion occurring among investors, activists and businesses, the lens used to judge the sustainability performance of companies going forward necessarily will be guided by double materiality.

Impact

ESG materiality is a risk management tool. With ESG, one 'considers' certain aspects of companies alongside various financial factors. But ESG doesn't provide a holistic view. Approached in the right manner, *it's possible* for businesses to make decisions about how to create positive outcomes internally and externally by identifying ESG risks. Yet there are better ways to frame efforts to achieve positive results. The concept of impact shifts the focus from risk to intentions and opportunities.

Impact Frontiers (formerly the Impact Management Project), a consensus-driven group that created standards around the concept, defines *impact* as 'positive and negative changes in outcomes for people and the planet' (Impact Frontiers, n.d.). For business, impact is most often elaborated upon as an investing practice, for which The GIIN (Global Impact Investing Network) defines *impact investing* as 'investments made with the intention to generate positive, measurable social and environmental impact *alongside* a financial return' (GIIN, n.d.).

The idea is that there is the no compromise to be made – investors can achieve market-matching (or greater) financial returns while also driving positive social or environmental impact for the communities in which they operate.

'Intentionality' is core to impact investing. Those applying impact to guide their business activities are fundamentally *intending* to create positive outcomes. Investors are *intentionally* setting out to create positive social or environmental impact by funding businesses. Those businesses themselves are founded as 'purpose-driven' organisations that seek to generate positive impacts with products or services sold for financial returns, such as ECOncrete, the Israeli company that offers environmentally safe solutions for coastal and marine construction (ECOncrete, n.d.), or Re-Nuble, the U.S. business that creates fertiliser from food waste (Re-Nuble, n.d.).

Thus, the impact perspective is how businesses and investors can contribute to the SDGs. Applying an impact lens to your business guides you towards providing products and services that address the societal failures and issues that the SDGs make explicit in their goals and targets. (You could view the SDGs as 17 'intentions' that countries have to improve society and the environment.)

The opportunity here is easily quantified. According to Peter Bakker, president of the World Business Council for Sustainable Development, 'There are huge incentives available … at least USD 12 trillion of market value which could be opened up by 2030 if the SDGs are realised, creating 380 million jobs in the process' (Bakker, 2019). To focus just on two industries, the UN estimates that $4.3 trillion in market value could be unlocked in energy and materials, and for food and agriculture, $2.3 trillion (Bakker, 2019).

To conclude, with double materiality, executives can understand the risks to their company from climate change and societal shifts. With impact, leaders have a guide for building new business models and products that will create revenue as they contribute solutions to humankind's most wicked problems.

Sustainable Finance Seeks Action

The world of finance has seen a rapid transformation in recent years. From 2012 to 2020, the sustainable investments in the United States nearly quadrupled according to the U.S. SIF Foundation (2020). The Global Sustainable Investment Alliance reported that investment in sustainable assets rose to $35.3 trillion in the year 2020 (GSIA, 2020). While long led by Europe, the United States surpassed the EU in total sustainable assets under management, at $17.1 trillion in 2020.

Investors use sustainability-focused investing practices as they're recognising two types of risks to capital: physical risks that climate change poses to the operations of businesses and transition risks – or risks in the business environment. Transition risks include whether the company you're investing today will exist in 10 years or be replaced by a new one with a better market solution, such as a renewable energy business replacing a natural gas company. They also include regulatory risks, such as carbon pricing mechanisms (emissions trading systems or carbon taxes) or the possibility of future polices regarding human or natural capital.

There is profit to be made backing companies with higher ESG ratings. Many reports have looked at how ESG effects performance, such as Nissay Asset Management's analysis of companies in Japan's TOPIX exchange that broke them into buckets – high overall ESG rating, average and low – and compared their market performance from 2008 to 2019 (Nissay Asset Management, n.d.). The basket of companies with high-quality ESG ratings saw a 60% appreciation in stock price. The average ESG bucket underperformed the simple average, and the low ESG group saw depreciation of around 45%. Even more telling, when Nissay looked at companies that were performing highest on the social aspect alone, those businesses saw 100% appreciation.

From the risk perspective, Bank of America Merrill Lynch (2019) reported that poor ESG performance can result in disaster: '90 percent of bankruptcies in the S&P 500 between 2005 and 2015 were of companies with poor E&S [environmental and social] scores five years prior to the bankruptcies'.

The rapid rise of sustainable finance, powered by recognition of climate- and sustainability-related risks, has driven development of disclosure and target-setting frameworks by international standard bodies. CDP (originally Carbon Disclosure Project), SBTi and the Task Force on Climate-Related Disclosure are investor-initiated campaigns designed to improve access to ESG data, create awareness among executives on climate change issues and extract commitments to take action. These developments flow down through the investment field, gaining support from global accounting standards bodies such as IFRS in its creation of the International Sustainability Standards Board and being adopted by stock exchanges in listing requirements (IFRS, n.d.).

Five Steps to a Sustainable Business Model

So, what kind of organisation are sustainable investors looking for? In analysing the experiences of companies that we researched for *Leading Sustainably* (Bridges & Eubank, 2020), we identified five steps that most companies typically go through to become a sustainable organisation (see Figure 16.2). Businesses need:

1. A base level of understanding about sustainable business concepts to establish a foundation from which to start their transformation.
2. C-level engagement and to make initial choices about what they will do.
3. To start taking action and experience 'first wins'.
4. To share these successes to achieve buy-in and establish their priorities across the organisation.
5. Total alignment and process integration, with sustainability embedded in all decision making in the organisation.

At Steps 2 and 3 is where executives start formulating the sustainability goals that their organisations will pursue. These can be internal changes that are necessary to implement strategies or publicly declared targets with investor-backed organisations such as SBTi and CDP. Such disclosures of performance, targets and commitments generally start with greenhouse gas (GHG) emissions, energy and water use, waste management and employee injuries and turnover. More ambitious organisations include

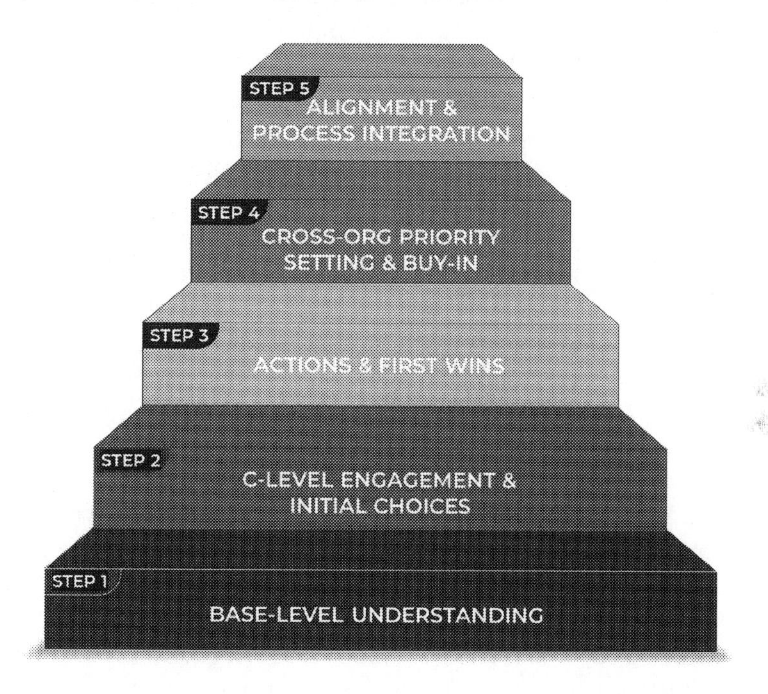

Figure 16.2 Five Steps to a Sustainable Business Model

commitments to progress across multiple SDG targets and transformational business changes to achieve such goals.

The reality is that most companies today are only at Steps 2 and 3 in their transformation. Some have reached Step 4 more recently, and there are very few at Step 5. But what would it look like if you made it to Step 5?

CASE STUDY

DSM and Sustainable Business Models for Addressing Climate Change

DSM, the world's largest food ingredient supplier and vitamin producer, is no stranger to change, having been established as the Royal Dutch Mining Company in 1902, before pivoting to trading chemicals in the middle of the 20th century and then, at the turn of the century, refocusing on nutrition solutions based on scientific innovations.

Yet perhaps its biggest organisational transition came when Feike Sijbesma, soon after becoming DSM CEO in 2007, participated in a discussion led by the World Food Programme (WFP) on the complexities around food assistance in Africa. While the West was supplying valuable food to communities to combat hunger, the food supplied didn't improve recipients' basic health. Sijbesma saw that other businesses were taking action to address these issues and that his company needed to follow suit. Thus, DSM's sustainability journey to climate action began with a social and adaptation issue but went on to become something much more all-encompassing (DSM, 2018).

That DSM was able to take this journey is testament, first, to the importance of C-level engagement in sustainability initiatives. It was the CEO, Sijbesma, who recognised the need to change and led the effort to do so. Secondly, as to the factors that prepared DSM to make such changes, the injection of new leadership under Sijbesma created an institutional desire to discover new opportunities for the company, to implement risk management and avoidance around climate change and to prepare for new regulatory pressures.

When a leader proposes to transition their organisation toward a sustainable business model, decisive action is essential. The leader must clearly communicate the benefits of sustainability and provide a clear roadmap for achieving it. Teams may be uncertain about how sustainability initiatives will impact their work or how it might create new opportunities. A true leader must have the courage to confront new challenges and prepare their organisation to make the necessary changes. While the decisions they have to make may be difficult, they are necessary to steer the organisation into uncharted territory. Clear strategic decisions, communicated properly, are key to success.

To start the process, Sijbesma communicated clearly to DSM's business group leaders that the company would focus on using its vast scientific knowledge about vitamins and nutrients to create solutions for malnutrition, while transforming the business itself into a leading model for sustainable operations. Once he had established buy-in from his executive teams and cross-organisation support with the help of 'sustainability champions' who stepped up when they understood the new mission their CEO was proposing, he rolled out a series of programs to align the business's core activities with the new sustainability-driven strategic direction.

The company established a requirement that all business lines must contribute to advancing toward DSM's sustainability goals, at around two-thirds achievement of annual targets. Those that failed would no longer be DSM companies and would be spun out. DSM also committed to assessing its performance against *all* 17 SDGs, not just those considered appropriate or favourable to its underlying business activities.

DSM systemised assessment through its Brighter Living Solutions Plus (BLS+) program (DSM, n.d.). BLS+ is a 'sustainable portfolio steering methodology' designed to identify products and services that deliver 'a sustainability benefit whilst doing no significant harm to people or planet' (DSM, 2023).

The focus of the sustainable portfolio is on nutrition and health, climate and energy and circularity solutions and resources, with inclusion in BLS+ based on assessment across 11 'impact drivers': health through nutrition, health through care, health protection, health recovery, sustainable livelihoods, animal welfare, low carbon future, reduced resource use, circular economy, biodiversity and ecosystems and water stewardship.

DSM applies a product life cycle approach to candidate solutions, evaluating environmental effect across the value chain from raw material extraction, production, manufacturing and transport to their ultimate use, end-of-life and recycling. As well, candidates' positive environmental and social impacts are compared to main competing solutions, with comparative ecological- and people-based life cycle assessments and expert insights. DSM reported that 64% of 2021 sales came from products designated as BLS+ (DSM, 2022).

Looking at human resources and organisational incentives, managers and teams were given ambitious sustainability-focused key performance indicators (KPIs) to drive their actions towards solutions that would make a difference, rather than just support the financial successes. Not everyone was onboard with changes like these and the new mission; some of those who felt that the new direction was not appropriate for a business chose to leave on their own accord. Yet, that allowed the company to be certain that those who stayed were true believers in the shift who would make it happen.

With these changes, it became crucial for everyone to integrate knowledge about sustainability into their functional roles. Rather than have standalone sustainability officers in siloed departments, knowledge and ability were spread throughout the organisation.

And finally, DSM partnered with relevant organisations – such as WFP – or acquired new businesses where it lacked whatever it required to accomplish its goals. Today, DSM has one of the best-defined sustainability strategies and annual assessments of its performance in achieving sustainability and SDG-related goals.

There has been no sacrifice in financial performance. If you judge DSM against three exchange-traded funds that break out different aspects of the company's core business – XLB, the largest exchange-traded funds of basic materials companies in the S&P 500; MOO, the most popular fund for agriculture materials; and VAW, a diversified chemicals fund – DSM's stock has outperformed them by three to five times from 2011 to 2021, achieving 364% appreciation versus VAW's 121% and MOO's 74%. So in DSM, you see a company that has taken significant steps to become sustainable, and yet not only did it not suffer financially for pursuing this new strategy but it was able to financially outperform its cohort.

Sustainable Business Solutions

The solution DSM developed to resolve the 'hidden hunger' problem Sijbesma encountered at the WFP meeting was a nutritional aid for people in Africa who have access to staple foods but don't receiving enough nutrients. DSM produced mineral and vitamin-rich porridge as part of the social enterprise Africa Improved Foods, a public–private partnership between the company, the Rwandan government and international development funds. The first market-ready supplements were made in Rwanda, from local agricultural sources where possible, creating jobs and economic opportunities. The products were targeted not at the most desperate communities but at those that were moving from poverty to more 'middle-class' lifestyles yet still didn't have access to a healthy diet. DSM has followed up the Africa Improved Foods program with products that fortify rice across Africa and Asia to combat micronutrient deficiencies.

DSM has a number of activities that it undertakes to provide industry leadership specifically in climate change, through advocacy, GHG emissions reductions and adaptation to the changing natural environment.

In 2018, Sijbesma chaired the High-Level Leadership Forum on Carbon Pricing and Competitiveness, which released a report at the UN's 2019

Climate Action Summit, providing guidance to governments on how to address policy issues around climate change (Carbon Pricing Leadership Coalition, 2019).

Sijbesma's successors, DSM Co-CEOs Geraldine Matchett and Dimitri de Vreeze, continue this work. Matchett speaks frequently about what DSM does to advance the global goals and Paris Agreement targets and is a board of director of Focusing Capital on the Long Term, an initiative to shift from short-termism to the deployment of capital for more sustainable outcomes (FCLTGlobal, n.d.). Before COP27, de Vreeze announced he had joined 100 CEOs, as a member of the Alliance of CEO Climate Leaders, in signing an open letter to world leaders on the urgency taking bold action on climate change (de Vreeze, 2022; World Economic Forum, 2022).

de Vreeze also shared an update on SBTi validation of DSM's emissions reduction plans being aligned with the Paris Agreement's 1.5°C target. As of August 2022, DSM had committed to a 59% GHG emissions reduction target by 2030 over its baseline of 2016, accelerating the previous 50% commitment, and a 100% renewable electricity ambition by 2030.

DSM uses an internal carbon price of €50/ton CO_2 equivalent in valuations of investment projects and internal business group profit–loss statements to advance decarbonisation efforts. Internal carbon prices act as a 'shadow' target price on potential investments or as a cost added for embodied carbon in transactions between business units. This encourages companies to incentivise resource allocation toward low carbon activities such as energy efficiency improvements and emissions reductions over high carbon activities. For example, DSM has the halved the carbon footprint in production of its Akulon line of polyamide 6 thermoplastic material products.

DSM is also designing new products with an eye towards reducing GHG emissions in their very use. The company has developed the cattle feed additive Bovaer, which reduces methane emissions from cows' digestion of grasses and grains by 30%, and collaborated with agtech leader Syngenta to develop innovative microbial-based agricultural solutions such as bio-pesticides and bio-stimulants to replace more energy-intensive and harmful chemical-based treatments.

DSM is an inspiring success story of what happens when a business sets target for its own operations and for it impact on society. Among the factors that led to this success, a couple were key to creating meaningful targets and driving their achievement:

- Business units, divisions and managers were given KPIs that are based on advancing towards the organisation's shared sustainability goals.
- DSM determines its targets, strategy and actions based on a systematic annual assessment of the 11 'impact drivers' in its company-wide Brighter Living Solutions Plus portfolio methodology.
- The company takes a product life cycle approach that looks across the whole value chain.

Methods, Techniques and Applications

Applying Impact for Climate Action and Circular Solutions

While more businesses are starting to follow the lead of companies such as DSM, these groundbreakers are simultaneously expanding the scope of what it means to be sustainable.

DSM achieved two crucial changes in its transformation, in re-targeting its organisation and internal resources towards becoming a sustainable organisation as a company and in systemising solution development based on achieving positive impact.

This second achievement represents a new way of deciding how budgets are allocated for new business development by *basing them on sustainability*. To return to impact, this is an application of that concept to internal business planning. As they say in politics, 'Show me your budget, and I'll tell you what you value'.

There are a growing number of businesses – across industries as diverse as fashion, automotive, insurance and energy – that are becoming impact investors in fields core to their operations.

The BMW Foundation Herbert Quandt, via its Eberhard von Kuenheim Fund, has been conducting research to examine 'bold alternatives within the existing financial and economic system' (BMW Foundation, n.d.) and supports impact-driven start-ups pursuing sustainable business models via its RESPOND Accelerator program. The family office of the Persson family, founders of fashion giant H&M, invested $100 million in the social impact funds of the Norrsken Foundation (Familyofficehub.io, 2021). Norrsken operates social innovation hubs in Europe and Africa supporting start-ups focused on social tech entrepreneurship.

Closer to its core business, the H&M corporation invests in circular economy solutions such as Worn Again Technologies, a polymer recycling start-up, and HKRITA (the Hong Kong Research Institute of Textiles and Apparel), which has developed a hydrothermal method for recycling cotton and polyester blends that is able to maintain the structural quality of the materials.

Besides L'Oréal having an industry-leading organisational approach to sustainability much like DSM's, the world's leading cosmetics brand is actively targeting investments in areas that are vital to its operations and customer base. L'Oreal has created three funds totalling €150 million focused on impact investing to make certain that natural environments are able to regenerate so that the company can source for its own products. One is for solutions targeting the restoration of marine and terrestrial ecosystems, another for advancing circular economy solutions and the third is a charitable endowment fund to support vulnerable women.

Each of these impact investing efforts can be tracked against specific SDG targets, whereby these organisations can show how they're contributing to achievement of the global goals. The United Nations Global Compact (UNGC), which acts as the UN's interface with the business world, supports these activities, with a focus on helping corporate CFOs to incorporate thinking about the SDGs into their planning.

In 2020, UNGC released *Introducing the CFO Principles on Integrated SDG Investments and Finance*, and in March of 2022 it launched the CFO coalition for the SDGs with 89 businesses as signatories 'to drive more private sector investment towards sustainable development'. UNGC (2020) stated:

> Our goal is to inspire a new meaning for the role of CFOs as the architects of long-term sustainable value creation. ... We also aspire to create a market for corporate SDG investments and finance ... to channel trillions of dollars of financial investments towards effective private-sector solutions for the SDGs.

A Shift to 'Intended' Core Outcomes

The approach of one of the three top international insurers, AXA Group, to impact investing is instructive to how such CFOs and executives can view their decision making.

AXA allocates €508 billion of its total €815 billion 'insurance float' – the funds that the companies receive from customers when they pay insurance premiums – based on ESG criteria with AXA Investor Managers (AXA IM). In 2019, AXA Investor Managers launched three impact investment funds (for micro-insurance, financial education, climate and biodiversity protection) backed by €350 to €400 million of AXA capital (AXA, n.d.).

The investment funds' strategies focus on companies addressing sustainability issues, aligning their corporate social responsibility (CSR) activities with core operations and advancing SDG achievement. They were created both to transform AXA's investment knowledge and strategies, as well as to move the broader investment community to seek societal returns alongside financial ones.

Within these funds, AXA IM invests in public equities through an impact lens. First, standard ESG filters narrow down the pool of targets, and then managers assess five dimensions of the company: operations, CSR activities, negative externalities, products and services and R&D. The first two dimensions exist within the ESG spectrum, looking at the basics of what a business does and how that may create risks or indicate the maturity of its sustainability initiatives. Examining negative externalities moves into the realm of double materiality, where AXA IM is looking beyond ESG risks to the company, to potential negative impacts it might have on society.

When it comes to assessing products and services and R&D, AXA IM applies an impact lens by determining a company's *intended* core external effects. Here the process is prioritising the 'intentionality' of the company by asking questions such as 'Do the particular products and services the company sells create a positive impact?', 'Are R&D decisions and budgets supporting the creation of products that advance sustainability goals?' and 'What are the negative externalities that the company creates in its business activities?'

These questions are important because they drill down on this question of 'what the company values' in its budgeting and how much attention it's paying to the positive or negative effects of these decisions on their stakeholders. This represents a significant shift from an ESG perspective to an impact perspective.

A process like this should quickly identify a company such as DSM as a desirable target investee. Just as relevant for executives, taking this view on their operations and planning, they can assess the direction to steer their business and the opportunities they have to create positive solutions and avoid future sustainability issues.

Conclusion

From Target Setting to Taking Action

To set ambitious targets and take meaningful action towards becoming sustainable businesses, most of the companies discussed here followed a similar playbook. Their leaders looked internally at where their company was today and externally at how the business, investment and regulatory environment was changing and determined the new priorities to which they had to respond. These leaders then started by making clear strategic choices. By doing so, they were able to align their internal and external stakeholders with the outcomes they look to achieve.

They pursued a multi-stakeholder approach to understand what was material across all parties so they could prioritise important issues and opportunities to maintain long-term viability.

And, critically, these leaders took a systematic approach to building sustainability capabilities. Some did so by adopting an impact approach to developing business lines and allocating funding, others by adopting disclosure and target-setting frameworks or performance metrics judged against the SDGs or, most effectively, incentivising knowledge-building and action by establishing sustainability-aligned KPIs, as DSM did.

What's Next?

While there has been exciting progress made by multi-nationals, small and medium-sized enterprises need more help in making the transition. For listed companies, this will be especially urgent as pressure from investors isn't going to let up. To the contrary, it's becoming more organised with the evolution of ESG reporting, digital sustainability data management solutions and the harmonisation of international non-financial standards.

Today the world is behind schedule – and budget – for achieving the Paris Agreement goals and the SDGs. There are positive signs, though, that realistic decarbonisation pathways do exist to reduce GHG emissions, especially in Europe, and including in the United States and Japan (Reuters, 2021). These countries made reductions in emissions from both consumption and production of products while growing their gross domestic product, an example that can show other nations how to take climate action. At the same time, policies are being developed, such as the EU's Carbon Border Adjustment Mechanism, to prevent carbon leakage by charging a levy on carbon emissions produced in the manufacture of a product (European Commission – Press Corner, 2022). These are supported by EU industry, as they protect companies in the economic block that have made investments to reduce the carbon profile of their own products.

For businesses, making progress on protecting the environment will take industry-wide action. SBTi supports this with its sectorial decarbonisation approach that provides sectoral guidance for setting targets in high-GHG emission, hard-to-abate industries.

A groundbreaking effort at Harvard Business School, the Impact-Weighted Accounting Initiative, is making possible an industry-level view on impact metrics (Harvard, n.d.). Impact-weighted accounting looks to increase non–equity holder value at the same time as equity holder value, by creating 'financial accounts that reflect a company's financial, social, and environmental performance' (Harvard, n.d.). The initiative's pilots currently focus on environmental impact, employment impact and product impact across eight industries, including aviation, oil and gas and consumer packaged goods, and an independent organisation, the International Foundation for Valuing Impacts, has been launched 'to drive the global integration of impacts in financial analysis to promote effective resource allocation and achieve long-term financial stability' (Harvard Business School, 2022).

Business should be aware that this view will assess the positive and negative effects of their organisations on society *with financial values*, making it simple to compare their performance against competitors. On the flip side, they can apply impact-weighted accounting to make business decisions that make them more resilient and competitive.

Another next-generation model is being developed at Doshisha University's Value Research Center (VRC) in Kyoto under the leadership of Professor Philip Sugai. VRC has analysed the more than 700 impact measurements included in 20 different sustainability reporting and measurement frameworks, such as SASB, the SDGs and GRI. These were distilled into 81 shared goals across 27 themes for seven stakeholder groups that include the organisation itself and the planet (see Figure 16.3). VRC (n.d.)

DEFINING MACRO INDICATOR CATEGORIES

Value Actors	Macro Indicators	Micro Indicators	Frameworks
Employee *114*	Employee: Diversity & Equity	13	8
	Employee: Fair Wages	10	5
	Employee: Health, Welfare and Safety	33	10
	Employee: Development	29	8
	Employee: Engagement and Satisfaction	16	6
	Employee: Human Rights	13	6
Environment *89*	Environment: Waste and Pollution	28	8
	Environment: Water	20	6
	Environment: Energy	9	5
	Environment: Products	19	8
	Environment: Biodiversity	10	7
	Environment: Buildings and Land	3	3
Society *46*	Society: Appropriate Taxes	5	2
	Society: Local Community Development	20	7
	Society: Local Employment and Engagement	15	6
	Society: Charity and Volunteerism	6	3
Firm *50*	Firm: Transparent Financial Reporting	13	5
	Firm: Governance and Firm Structure	37	5
	Firm: Management Capability	0	0
Customer *29*	Customer: Truth in Communications	3	1
	Customer: Privacy	9	5
	Customer: Satisfaction, Health and Safety	17	7
Partner *29*	Partner: Reporting	7	4
	Partner: Structure	6	3
	Partner: Environment & Society	8	5
	Partner: Fair Labor	8	4
Shareholder	Shareholder: EVA	0	0

Figure 16.3 Defining Macro Indicator Categories

posits that no organisation can assess a goal separate from the whole and are working on model that allows businesses to see how they create (or destroy) value against the whole host of themes.

These new frameworks from the Impact-Weighted Accounting Initiative and VRC will help drill down further on how companies are performing against goals for climate action. Furthermore, they will make it evident that setting a target isn't enough.

Evidence that efforts are being made to achieve stated goals is needed to make true progress. Some industries have been accused of setting targets just to follow custom but then ignore them as being 'unachievable'. For any target to be meaningful, it has to be accompanied by leadership outlining a plan to achieve it and initiating actual real-world activities that put that plan into action. Only when leadership, targets, plans and actions come together can real change in a corporation can be achieved.

Discussion Points

- How can leaders start the process of transforming their companies from 'business-as-usual' models to sustainable business models?
- What is the difference between the ESG perspective and that of an impact organisation or investor?
- What were the new business practices that DSM CEO Feike Sijbesma implemented when he directed his executive teams to adopt a more sustainable business model?
- What has to change within a business for it to adopt a sustainable business model? What has to stop, and what needs to be done differently? What would you prioritise? How would you choose to align with particular SDGs?
- What is the danger to companies if the Impact-Weighted Accounting Initiative approach becomes widespread and publicly reported? How can businesses respond?

Suggested Reading

Edmans, A. (2023) *The end of ESG*. Wiley Periodicals LLC on behalf of Financial Management Association International.

Hubbard, D. W. (2010). *How to measure anything: Finding the value of 'intangibles' in business*. Wiley.

Pistor, K. (2019). *The code of capital*. Princeton University Press.

Serafeim G., Zochowski, T. R., & Downing, J. (2019). *Impact-weighted financial accounts: The missing piece for an impact economy*. Harvard Business School.

Sugai, P., Koizumi, R., Linnan, N., Phattanaprayoonvong, S., & Phetharn, J. (2022). *A value model for responsible business*. Doshisha University.

References

AXA. (n.d.). *Towards a 'low carbon' investment strategy*. https://www.axa.com/en/commitments/low-carbon-investment

Bank of America Merrill Lynch. (2019, September 23). *ESG Matters – U.S., 10 reasons you should care about ESG*.

Bakker, P. (2019, May 10). *A global coming of age: How the Sustainable Development Goals can help transform the world we live in*. World Business Council for Sustainable Development. https://www.wbcsd.org/Overview/

News-Insights/Insights-from-the-CEO/How-the-Sustainable-Development-Goals-can-help-transform-the-world-we-live-in

BMW Foundation Herbert Quandt. (n.d.). *Investing with impact*. https://bmw-foundation.org/en/our-work/investing-with-impact

Bridges, T., & Eubank, D. (2020). *Leading sustainably: Sustainable business and how the SDGs have changed everything* (1st ed.). Routledge.

Carbon Pricing Leadership Coalition. (2019). *Report on the High-Level Commission on Carbon Pricing and Competitiveness*. https://openknowledge.worldbank.org/bitstream/handle/10986/32419/141917.pdf

de Vreeze, D. (2022, November 17). *It was announced during #COP27 that, if emissions continue unchecked, it's 50% likely global temperatures will cross* [Post]. LinkedIn. https://www.linkedin.com/posts/dimitri-de-vreeze-b52a8a1_cop27-sustainability-climateemergency-activity-6998932429411393536-UrTu?utm_source=share&utm_medium=member_desktop

Doshisha University Value Research Center. (n.d.). *Home*. https://www.valueresearchcenter.com/

DSM. (n.d.). *Brighter Living Solutions Plus*. https://www.dsm.com/corporate/sustainability/brighter-living-solutions.html

DSM. (2018, October 26). *Purpose-led business: A new model to fight malnutrition* [Video]. YouTube. https://youtu.be/qCcVNQA_40Y

DSM. (2022). *DSM integrated annual report 2021, combating hidden hunger through rice fortification*. https://annualreport.dsm.com/ar2021/case-studies/combating-hidden-hunger-through-rice-fortification.html

DSM. (2023). *DSM integrated annual report 2022: Sustainable portfolio steering*. https://www.dsm.com/corporate/sustainability/brighter-living-solutions.html

ECOncrete. (n.d.). *We bring concrete to life*. https://econcretetech.com/

European Commission – Press Corner. (2022, 13 December). *European Green Deal: Agreement reached on the Carbon Border Adjustment Mechanism (CBAM)*. https://ec.europa.eu/commission/presscorner/detail/en/ip_22_7719

Familyofficehub.io. (2021, October 8). *Persson single family office invests in €100M social impact fund*. https://familyofficehub.io/blog/persson-single-family-office-invests-in-e100m-social-impact-fund/

FCLTGlobal. (n.d.). *Board of directors: Geraldine Matchett*. https://www.fcltglobal.org/team-member/geraldine-matchett/

The Global Impact Investing Network. (n.d.). *Global Impact Investing Network*. https://thegiin.org/

Global Sustainable Investment Alliance. (2020). *Global sustainable investment review 2020*. http://www.gsi-alliance.org/wp-content/uploads/2021/08/GSIR-20201.pdf

Harvard Business School. (n.d.). *Impact-weighted accounts*. https://www.hbs.edu/impact-weighted-accounts/Pages/default.aspx

Harvard Business School. (2022, July 12). *International foundation for valuing impacts holds inaugural board meeting*. https://www.hbs.edu/news/releases/Pages/IFVI-IAWI.aspx

IFRS. (n.d.). *About the International Sustainability Standards Board*. https://www.ifrs.org/groups/international-sustainability-standards-board/

Impact Frontiers. (n.d.). *Impact for investment decision-making*. https://impactfrontiers.org/

Nissay Asset Management. (n.d.). *Case study 1: Japanese ESG leader's excess return vs. TOPIX*. https://www.nam.co.jp/pri/html/effectiveness.html

Re-Nuble. (n.d.). *Re-Nuble: Converting food waste into organic hydroponic nutrients*. https://www.re-nuble.com/

Reuters. (2021, December 10). *Japan's greenhouse gas emissions drop to record low in year to March 2021*. https://www.reuters.com/markets/commodities/japans-greenhouse-gas-emissions-drop-record-low-year-march-2021-2021-12-10/

Science Based Targets. (n.d.a). *Ambitious corporate climate action*. https://sciencebasedtargets.org/

Science Based Targets. (n.d.b). *Sector guidance*. https://sciencebasedtargets.org/sectors

Sustainability Accounting Standards Board. (n.d.). *SASB*. https://www.sasb.org/

United Nations Global Compact. (2020). *Introducing CFO principles on integrated SDG investments and finance*. https://globalcompact.no/app/uploads/2020/10/CFO_Principles_on_Integrated_SDG_Investments_and_Finance_20200921.pdf

United Nations Global Compact. (2022, March 29). *UN Global Compact launches CFO coalition for the SDGs to drive more private sector investment towards sustainable development*. https://www.unglobalcompact.org/news/4887-03-29-2022

U.S. SIF: The Sustainable Investment Forum. (2020). *Report on U.S. sustainable and impact investing trends 2020*. https://www.ussif.org/files/US%20SIF%20Trends%20Report%202020%20Executive%20Summary.pdf

World Economic Forum. (2022, November 16). *The Alliance of CEO Climate Leaders' open letter to COP27*. https://www.weforum.org/agenda/2022/11/cop27-alliance-of-ceo-climate-leaders

17

CORPORATE CARBON TARGETS

THE ROLE OF GOAL SETTING IN DRIVING ORGANISATIONAL CHANGE FOR CLIMATE ACTION

Frederik Dahlmann

Chapter Summary

This chapter examines the role and effectiveness of corporate carbon targets. Corporate carbon targets are part of a growing range of sustainability announcements that are aimed at conveying plans about how companies intend to mitigate their greenhouse gas emissions (GHGs) over time. This chapter discusses the key theoretical arguments used for understanding how and why companies might set such goals. It develops a framework for critically evaluating key characteristics of corporate carbon targets before providing an overview of key insights from a range of studies that have examined the effectiveness of these managerial approaches to climate change. This chapter helps readers understand that setting targets may well be the first and easiest part of organisational responses to climate change. Given the emergence of a diversity of related concepts and approaches such as science-based and net zero targets as well as wider sustainability concerns, critically understanding their role

DOI: 10.4324/9781003343011-21

and relevance is more important than ever for business management and leadership in the 21st century.

Introduction

Climate change presents the most complex and urgent challenge of our time, affecting people, the planet and business (and other) organisations (Howard-Grenville et al., 2014; Rockström et al., 2017). Organisational responses to this grand challenge have, for a long time at least, largely been characterised by inertia, if not outright hostility designed to undermine global policy efforts to tackle its causes and impacts (Slawinski et al., 2017; Wright & Nyberg, 2016). In recent years, however, some companies (and other non-state actors) have started to engage with the technological, organisational, behavioural, managerial and financial issues and implications that climate change poses for their strategies, business models and leadership approaches. Driven by increasing media, customer, employee and investor pressures, companies have begun to respond to growing demands for more and detailed information about their risk perceptions of and strategic positions on climate change (Backman et al., 2017; Hahn et al., 2015). Beyond the initial act of measuring and disclosing their direct and indirect carbon footprints, a growing number of companies have started to address climate change and their carbon performance as issues that need to be managed effectively and to avoid a wide range of concerns and critiques, or even in recognition of significant commercial opportunities (Busch et al., 2020; Kolk & Pinkse, 2005). As part of this process, declaring a 'climate emergency' and announcing a wide range of corporate carbon targets has become widespread (Dahlmann et al., 2019).

This chapter examines the role and effectiveness of these corporate carbon targets by discussing key theoretical arguments used for understanding how and why organisations might set such goals. Moreover, it provides an overview of key insights from different studies that have examined the effectiveness of these managerial approaches to climate change. This chapter helps readers appreciate that while setting targets may well be the first step in organisations' responses to climate change, understanding their respective differences and effectively implementing them raises new challenges for managers and leaders.

Conceptual Background

Measuring Carbon Footprints

Under pressure from society to engage with and mitigate their impacts on climate change, one of the most pressing challenges for organisations relates to the widespread absence of reliable and comparable data about their carbon footprints. While national-level reporting of GHGs has been in existence for decades, understanding the respective contributions from individual organisations has been a continuing problem for policymakers and others. Apart from specific industry requirements (especially in the power sector), initially only the (then-called) Carbon Disclosure Project aimed at providing insight and data on large public companies' stance on climate change. The CDP sends out annual surveys within which such organisations are invited to provide information on their strategic responses to climate change and, if possible, to detail their levels of carbon performance for the previous year (Depoers et al., 2016). Recently, various jurisdictions have made the reporting of GHGs a requirement for larger companies, and similar efforts are being debated in the context of specific stock exchange listings and disclosures (e.g., Department for Business, Energy & Industrial Strategy, 2022).

The emphasis on measuring and reporting organisational carbon footprints reflects the widespread adage among business practitioners that 'what gets measured gets managed'. In other words, there is a firm belief that in the absence of clear and accurate data on the scale of the emissions at an organisational level, managers are unable to develop effective strategies for addressing them. Consistent with organisational information processing theory, there is a need for gathering, processing and disseminating information internally to devise appropriate organisational responses (Dahlmann & Roehrich, 2019). These approaches also align with the widely held managerial tenet of ensuring that they follow the process of 'plan, do, check, act' when it comes to managing organisational change (Deming, 1986).

Understanding the scale of an organisation's 'problem' – that is, the size of its carbon footprint – however, is only the first critical step when it comes to climate change mitigation. Knowing how an organisation contributes to global GHGs provides a baseline from which to consider how to proceed. Consequently, and under pressure from a range of different stakeholders, many companies have started to declare their ambitions for seeking to reduce their emissions over time. In recent years, companies have announced a plethora of statements that are aimed at conveying plans about how they intend to mitigate their corporate carbon footprints, known as corporate climate change targets. Many of these are framed around addressing the climate emergency as an urgent call for organisational change. Quite what these targets entail, why they were formulated and, more important, whether they are effective remains subject to speculation and evaluation, which is the topic of this chapter.

Corporate Carbon Target Characteristics

The concept of target setting generally is well established, in terms of both individual goals (Nowack, 2017) and shaping team or organisational contexts more broadly, especially when expressed as 'stretch goals' (Hamel & Prahalad, 1993) or 'Big Hairy Audacious Goals' (Collins, 1999, p. 70) designed to drive increased performance outcomes or success chances. However, the effectiveness of such goal setting approaches has been questioned and remains subject to vigorous debates, not least in terms of the extent to which such goals can be accurately measured and evaluated but also given concerns about the psychological impacts of such aspirations. Scholars and others argue that rather than driving commitment and optimism, in certain circumstances the extreme difficulty and/or novelty of stretch goals may have significant (and negative) side effects. These side effects may include a reduced likelihood of targets being acted on as well as increased chances of causing organisational disruption because people may believe that, despite these high-level aspirations, they have neither the necessary resources and requisite know-how nor motivation to overcome personal and organisational inertia (Sitkin et al., 2011).

Academic research on the process and effectiveness of goal setting generally and in the context of environmental management specifically therefore points to important issues and considerations that are necessary when assessing corporate carbon targets. Most important, there are significant concerns that setting targets may provide several benefits to organisations, not all of which necessarily align with the scientific imperatives of addressing climate change. In particular, borne out of research evidence on target setting in other social and environmental domains, scholars argue that some organisations set targets to communicate a superficial concern for such wider ethical issues without any real intention of actively wanting to address them. By announcing plans to make improvements on climate change, companies seek to enhance their image and reputation among stakeholders to ensure general legitimacy from a societal perspective for their existence and operations (Delmas & Montes-Sancho, 2010). At the same time, making such announcements is seen as a cost-effective and instant means of attracting positive attention that does not require significant further effort and investments. Many such announcements therefore reflect a decoupling of message from action that has become synonymous with the concept of *greenwashing* (Aragón-Correa et al., 2016).

Such symbolic forms of engagement with climate change stand in contrast to more substantive intentions on taking this global and urgent grand challenge seriously and which are underpinned by a real commitment to reducing GHGs over time. However, at least initially, from an outside perspective it is difficult to determine the true motivations and intentions behind the announcement of corporate carbon targets.

To provide guidance, my colleagues and I developed a framework that examines more specific and observable characteristics of corporate carbon targets. The purpose of this framework is to distinguish the extent to which targets might reveal something about the true intentions and thus their likelihood of being effective in reducing organisational GHGs. Specifically, the framework distinguishes between the *type*, *scope*, *ambition* of and *time frame* covered by corporate carbon targets to determine whether they are likely to have been devised as a means of gaining superficial legitimacy only or whether they reflect a more genuine motivation for mitigating climate change at the organisational level (Figure 17.1).

Type

Corporate carbon targets typically tend to be specified in one of two different formats, either as intensity-based targets or as absolute targets. This difference is critical for understanding how organisations intend to make progress (and the extent to which these targets allow meaningful contributions to climate change mitigation). Specifically, intensity-based targets specify commitments to reducing GHG emissions relative to a specific measure of production or output. Common examples include emissions

Figure 17.1 Corporate Carbon Target Characteristics

reductions per kilowatt hour of electricity produced, per unit of product manufactured (e.g., per car), per passenger revenue kilometre (for airlines), per square meter built (for housing developers) or per number of employees. The benefit of specifying intensity-based targets is that they essentially anticipate efficiency improvements across production without constraining business growth. While this is advantageous from an economic perspective (highlighting the self-interest from reducing waste in production and operation processes), achieving such goals at the same time as increasing output does not reduce an organisation's level of GHG emissions overall; that is, in absolute terms.

As a result, while intensity-based targets make welcome contributions to avoiding emissions, on their own they do not lead to a decoupling of business operations from emissions growth. For that, organisations must specify absolute targets that provide a hard limit no matter what level of output, production or organisational growth is achieved. Consequently, when companies purely rely on intensity-based targets, there is a strong risk that these are viewed as primarily symbolic announcements which, while serving their organisation's self-interest, are insufficient for achieving broader scientific and policy goals regarding climate change mitigation. At the very least, intensity-based targets must appear in combination with absolute targets to provide a meaningful limit to and decline in overall emissions at the organisational level.

This also matters in the context of certain hard-to-abate industry sectors such as steel, concrete, aviation and shipping. There was recognition once that these industries were either part of a globalised sector that was difficult to regulate without resulting in competitive disadvantages and/or were facing significant challenges to identify technological solutions in the short term to reduce emissions in absolute terms. Here, therefore, an argument could temporarily be made that an intensity-based approach is favourable to having no targets at all. Increasingly, however, these sectors are under pressure to work hard to implement emissions reductions in absolute terms.

Scope

A second important specification of corporate carbon targets relates to the underlying scopes of emissions covered. Internationally, organisations are encouraged to categorise and measure the emissions they generate and are responsible for with reference to the globally recognised GHG Protocol, which distinguishes between scopes 1, 2 and 3. The standard 'covers the accounting and reporting of seven greenhouse gases covered by the Kyoto Protocol – carbon dioxide (CO_2), methane (CH_4), nitrous oxide (N_2O), hydrofluorocarbons (HFCs), perfluorocarbons (PCFs), sulphur hexafluoride (SF_6) and nitrogen trifluoride (NF_3)' and also includes 'emissions from purchased or acquired electricity, steam, heat, and cooling' (GHG Protocol, 2011).

- Scope 1 GHG emissions are those created through direct combustion of fossil fuels and other industrial processes.
- Scope 2 GHG emissions are all those that are indirectly created by the provision of electricity, heat, cooling and steam which are then consumed by the organisation on site.
- Scope 3 GHG emissions entail a much more complex range of emissions resulting from all of those processes, both upstream and downstream as well as during the product life cycle, that are necessary for an organisation's operations. They include 15 categories of activities that broadly capture both the indirect GHG emissions related to purchased or acquired goods and services and the indirect GHG emissions related to sold goods and services (GHG Protocol, 2011). In many

sectors, scope 3 emissions are on average 11.4 times greater than the volume of scope 1 and 2 emissions (CDP, 2022b). Given that they are generated by customers, suppliers and others, the level of control over such emissions is significantly lower.

While there are significant differences between sectors, generally, the broader the scopes targeted, the more likely that an organisation is aware of and intent on reducing its emissions overall. A specific focus on a single scope of emissions (e.g., scope 2 only) or even a self-defined target scope (for example, for a specific project, facility or product only) suggests that a company is highly selective, 'cherry-picking' its target scope potentially because it provides the greatest level of control or chances of success. Despite still being relevant, a narrow scope targeted is suggestive of a more symbolic form of engagement compared to a set of broader scopes targeted, which indicates that an organisation fully appreciates and addresses its wide-ranging levels of impact and responsibility.

Ambition

One of the key reasons for developing organisational targets is their quantitative nature, which lends them a certain sense of objectivity with regard to evaluating performance and progress. Unlike broad, qualitative visions or intentions, corporate climate change targets typically specify a measurable rate of improvement expressed in percentage terms. Quite what this level of ambition is or should be again provides insights into the extent to which companies are serious about their commitments to reducing GHG emissions. Arguably, given the scale and urgency of climate change, the higher the percentage, the greater the level of ambition and thus a more substantive commitment towards mitigation (Newell, 2020). Such large-scale targets are also more reflective of the need for significant innovation and re-organisation that are necessary to decouple economic growth from GHG emissions at a global level. By contrast, minor reduction targets may follow the general spirit of doing something on climate but are more likely a sign of symbolic efforts.

Yet context matters, and setting such targets needs to acknowledge the organisational origins and achievements, fluctuating growth patterns and future strategic ambitions of the company in light of in industry and (inter) national contexts (Pinkse & Kolk, 2009). Some companies may be very reluctant to take on a front-runner role given levels of competition in their sectors. Others may be more mindful of the message such targets send to end consumers who may wish to align themselves with organisations that share their environmental concerns. More often, companies will also evaluate the extent to which there are technological and operational alternatives available when committing to such targets. The question therefore is do targets incentivise and motivate employees to search for and develop innovation, or will overly ambitious targets backfire by demotivating those that hang on to the status quo (Ioannou et al., 2016)? The level of ambition – that is, the percentage of emissions reductions targeted – therefore also needs to be examined closely together with the three other target characteristics to ensure that it is clear where and how they apply.

Time Frame

Finally, the last characteristic of corporate climate targets relates to the time frame or the period over which they are intended to be implemented. This is an area where organisational planning processes encounter significant tensions, since most internal processes tend to be driven by monthly (or even less), quarterly and annual timelines (for example, annual financial reporting, personal performance evaluation, budgeting, project time frames, etc.). While some processes, particularly on business strategy and innovation, exceed those timelines (from multiple years up to a decade in the context of large capital investments, particularly in the extractive resource sectors), the nature of climate change and the need for significant GHG emissions reductions pose a certain conundrum: Should companies approach this with a long-term view, aiming for major reductions to be achieved in decades ahead, or should they treat this as an annual challenge, hoping that incremental improvements add up over time?

In line particularly with the target level of ambition, are longer time frames more effective in stimulating broad-ranging organisational change through innovation and collaboration, and thus reflective of a substantive commitment to making improvements regarding carbon footprints? Or do they effectively lead to continued inertia by passing responsibility for their achievement to future leaders and managers while relying on business as usual in the short term?

By contrast, are short-term targets meaningful enough to incentivise significant levels of innovation and organisational change? Or do they again reflect 'cherry-picking', whereby organisations set themselves targets that they believe can be reasonably easily achieved with existing knowledge and technology? Particularly when targets are combined with (financial) incentives for executives and others (Dahlmann et al., 2017), there is risk that short-term targets will primarily be designed around symbolic efforts to harvest the 'low-hanging fruit' of the easier organisational changes needed to meet them.

In this context, there are two further considerations. The first pertains to the question of establishing a suitable baseline. Aligned with the initial efforts of determining an organisation's carbon footprint, companies variously reference their targets to both different years in the future, as well as to different base years in the present or past. This makes comparison across companies extremely challenging. So far, there seems to be no consensus on how to set this in the private sector except for the importance of explicitly stating the base year used for carbon target setting in any case.

The second consideration includes responsibility for historical emissions to ensure that greater climate justice for pollution occurred in the past (that is, before the base year used for future targets). A front-runner in this regard is the software company Microsoft, which has not only pledged to reduce future scope 1 to 3 emissions through various efforts, investments and initiatives by 2030 but which has also committed by 2050 to remove its historical emissions since the company's founding in 1975 (Microsoft, 2020). Such aspirations are, of course, easier to achieve for organisations whose own direct carbon footprints are comparatively lighter and that have the necessary financial and other resources to commit action in this area. As the global climate policy negotiations begin to acknowledge the need for compensation of 'loss and damage' caused by climate change (United Nations Framework Convention on Climate Change, 2022) and as companies are being (successfully) sued for a lack of progress with cutting their GHG emissions in line with climate science (BBC, 2021), companies' targets may increasingly also have to address and reflect such historical responsibilities and injustices.

Measurement and Practice

Having outlined our conceptual framework for evaluating the characteristics of corporate carbon targets, one key question facing policymakers, managers, investors and society at large is do they actually work? What evidence is there to suggest that setting corporate targets in all of their diverse manifestations leads to significant reductions in organisational GHGs over time and as required by international scientific and policy consensus?

Our own research studied these questions using a large sample of organisations from around the world and a variety of different industry sectors for the period 2009 to 2014 (Dahlmann et al., 2019). We leveraged data obtained through the CDP, a leading non-profit that is backed by investors seeking to increase transparency in and understanding of the effects of climate change on business and, more important, the extent to which companies are starting to respond and mitigate their impacts (CDP, 2022a). Our analysis found that corporate climate change target types, ambitiousness and time frame were all associated with significant reductions in GHG emissions, at least over the period under our observation. By contrast, there was no evidence to suggest that the breadth of emissions scope targeted had any effect on emissions reductions.

Broadly, the research findings therefore aligned with our conceptual framework in that only substantive climate change goals, as expressed through targets defined in absolute terms, with larger percentage levels of ambitions and over longer time frames, were ultimately linked to carbon performance improvements. Conversely, targets defined in relative terms, with smaller percentage levels of ambition and shorter time frames, were not seen to be effective in terms of driving reductions in GHG emissions levels (at least in the short term). The latter group of targets therefore seemed to express a more symbolic form of engagement with the challenge of climate change, effectively paying lip service to its urgency without initiating a strategically meaningful organisational change process through clear and substantive targets. Given the voluntary nature of these target-setting efforts, it is thus important to be aware of the ethical and strategic implications of such organisational announcements and to question both their motivations and effectiveness more generally. It is important to stress, however, that during our period of observation, most companies made little, if any, progress in terms of reducing their emissions. The interpretation of our findings was therefore shaped by the wider context of firms barely reducing their GHG emissions at all.

Since then, other research has continued to investigate to what extent corporate carbon targets are effective tools in helping organisations reduce their

GHG emissions. For example, Malen (2022) focused his research on Japanese companies over the period 2011 and 2017 and, specifically, the question of what organisations do when they start missing their corporate carbon targets. Results suggested that when failing to realise GHG targets, companies simply 'reoperationalise' their aspirations by making immediate changes to the measurement type, change type, and/or level of ambition. Companies were, in effect, 'moving the goalposts' (Malen, 2022, p. 378). This research therefore illustrates another concern with corporate carbon targets, namely, the fact that such voluntarily set ambitions may be subject to adjustment to reflect specific organisational changes in circumstances, rather than align with the needs of the wider planetary climate system to which their emissions contribute.

From a climate change perspective, it is thus important that targets not only be stated in substantive terms but also adhered to over time, regardless of changing circumstances, and particularly when organisations have failed to achieve them in the short term. Interestingly, in this context, there is, so far, no empirical evidence of the opposite, the so-called ratchet effect whereby an organisation that exceeds a target in one period might subsequently feel compelled to revise its target further upward (Leone & Rock, 2002). This stands in contrast to the ambitions of the Paris Agreement whereby countries commit to increase their climate policy commitments every 5 years as part of the 'ratchet mechanism' to ensure that they close the gap between the effects of their policies and the requirements of keeping global temperature increase to no more than 1.5°C.

At this point, however, there are substantial doubts that this form of target-setting process is working as intended (Grant, 2022). In fact, debates among scientists highlight the challenges of adopting the language of 'targets' in this context more generally. While some argue that the political target of 1.5°C is no longer achievable and should be abandoned because it leads to purely symbolic commitments without any real action (McGuire, 2022), others stress that this is neither a target nor a goal at all but rather a natural limit that must not be breached to avoid catastrophe (Rockström, 2022).

Science-Based Targets and Net Zero – Towards Reliable and Effective Assessment

In response to many of these early issues and concerns, organisations have increasingly been advised and driven towards a stronger, more consistent and comparable approach of defining their corporate carbon targets. Two specific terms and initiatives are gaining widespread popularity: science-based targets and net zero.

Science-Based Targets

To better evaluate whether corporate carbon targets are actually meaningful and effective, a coalition of non-governmental organisations including CDP, the United Nations Global Compact, World Resources Institute and the World Wide Fund for Nature developed a methodology to help organisations set targets that are in line with the Paris Agreement on Climate Change (United Nations Framework Convention on Climate Change, 2015). Advocating a five-step process, the Science-Based Targets initiative (SBTi) seeks to help organisations set corporate climate targets that are 'in line with what the latest climate science deems necessary to meet the goals of the Paris Agreement – limiting global warming to well-below 2°C above pre-industrial levels and pursuing efforts to limit warming to 1.5°C' (Science Based Targets [SBT], 2022). The framework provides sector-based guidance and offers organisations an opportunity to review these science-based targets so they can be publicly listed on its website. The SBTi distinguishes between near-term, long-term and net zero targets whereby *near-term* refers to 2030 and *long-term* to 2050.

Since its inception in 2015 and as of December 2022, 4,237 companies were listed, of which 2,080 companies had approved science-based targets. Currently, an emerging stream of academic research is again trying to evaluate the effectiveness of this target-setting framework, suggesting refinements and changes to the way in which organisational, sectoral and national targets and emissions are allocated through the SBTi to ensure greater comparability and, importantly, effectiveness (Bjørn et al., 2021; Rekker et al., 2022). Aligned with the framework proposed in this chapter, concerns persist that even with the framework of the SBT it remains difficult to distinguish between substantive and symbolic target setting and the extent to which companies will actually be able to achieve their corporate climate targets (Bjørn et al., 2022; Giesekam et al., 2021).

Similarly, research by the non-profit ClimateAction100+ (2022) suggests that despite progress in terms of more and more companies making climate commitments such as setting long-term carbon targets, these are not matched by credible plans for short- and medium-term decarbonisation, largely exclude scope 3 emissions or are characterised by a lack of capital expenditure commitments to achieve these carbon targets. In that sense, there is growing recognition that for carbon targets to be substantive and meaningful they must cover the full breadth of emissions scopes and embrace a combination of a long-term targets and more short-term interim aspirations to enable evaluation of progress along the way.

Net Zero Targets

Adding further confusion to the debate and evaluation, organisations are also beginning to define their own corporate carbon targets with reference to net zero. While this ambition essentially recognises the wider role of ecological systems in contributing to and absorbing GHG emissions through natural cycles, the increasingly widespread adoption of net zero targets by organisations and industries is leading to increased ambiguity rather than clarity. Again, part of the issue is that much depends on how net zero targets are effectively defined, since 'choosing different gases, different timing for net-zero emissions and different methods of aggregating emissions can have very different outcomes' (Rogelji et al., 2021, p. 366). These authors provided a checklist of considerations that should help companies understand the extent to which their corporate carbon targets are rigorous and clear. Such conceptual clarity is even more important when trying to avoid further obfuscation through the use of alternative terms (e.g., carbon neutrality), as well as aiming for statistical achievement of the concept through complementary processes, practices and investments, including carbon capture, storage and use; carbon removal (e.g., direct air capture); and carbon offsetting through nature-based solutions (Fankhauser et al., 2021).

Fundamentally, there is agreement that the term net zero as defined by geophysical sciences needs to remain meaningful primarily at the planetary level. Further, while national territories contribute towards this goal through their national policies as part of the Paris Agreement, other entities including regions, cities and organisations and their products play very differentiated roles. As such, the French Environment and Energy Management Agency argued that nonstate actors such as cities and companies should not adopt the language of net zero and instead focus their efforts on reducing both their direct and indirect emissions (including scope 3) as much and as quickly as possible (ADEME, 2021).

Similarly, while carbon offsetting investments and projects are welcome and strongly encouraged as efforts to contribute to clean energy development or the restoration of nature, some argue that they should not be counted towards overall emissions reductions at the company level (Carbone4, 2021). This matters because the development and voluntary use of carbon offsetting schemes and projects remain highly controversial and fraught with ethical and operational challenges, such as questions over their scientific legitimacy and the avoidance of additionality in this unregulated market (Dhanda & Hartman, 2011; Hyams & Fawcett, 2013). As voluntary offsets have allowed companies to claim that they have achieved carbon neutrality for marketing purposes, critics argue that they serve as a distraction from the difficult choices involved in reducing direct operational emissions without helping climate change. Some companies are beginning to wind down their offsetting schemes accordingly (Bloomberg, 2022).

Recognising these continuing issues and challenges, the United Nations High-Level Expert Group on the Net Zero Emissions Commitments of Non-State Entities (UNHLEG, 2022) therefore developed several recommendations which also align with some of the key ideas outlined in this chapter:

- Net zero pledges must contain stepping-stone targets for every 5 years and set out concrete ways to reach net zero in line with the Intergovernmental Panel on Climate Change or other scientific assessment regarding the limit of 1.5°C global temperature increase.
- Pledges must cover emissions across scopes 1, 2 and 3, including end-use emissions.
- Companies cannot focus on reducing the intensity of their emissions but rather must reduce their absolute emissions.
- Emissions reductions must start now, rather than be left for implementation later this century.
- While carbon credits through offsetting schemes are allowable, they must not be counted towards interim emissions reductions required by companies' net zero pathways.

CASE STUDY

Global brewer Carlsberg commits to achieving zero GHG emissions from its breweries by 2030, from a 2015 base year, which is equivalent to reducing total scope 1 and 2 GHG emissions by 92%. This is supported by a 2022 target to reduce the GHG emissions from breweries by 50%, which is equivalent to reducing total scope 1 and 2 emissions by 46%. This includes a focus on 100% low climate impact cooling.

Carlsberg also commits to reducing its beer-in-hand value chain GHG emissions (scopes 1, 2 and 3) 30% by 2030, from a 2015 base year, with a 2022 target to reduce GHG emissions by 15%. All renewable electricity for scope 2 must come from new assets (or via power purchase agreements). By 2040, the brewer aims to have achieve net zero emissions across its entire value chain by decarbonising thermal energy storage, producing on-site renewable electricity, ensuring that agricultural raw materials are cultivated using regenerative agricultural practices, using circular packaging systems, using electrified transport vehicles for short distances and renewable fuels for long-distance transport and using renewable energy–powered, efficient cooling systems. The company is also working on launching glass bottles with up to 90% lower carbon impact as well as trialling bio-based and fully recyclable bottles to reduce the embedded emissions(Carlsberg, 2023; Edie, 2022).

For other case studies, please see SBT (2023).

Conclusion

Addressing climate change is the most urgent and complex challenge of our time (Howard-Grenville et al., 2014; Rockström et al., 2017). Companies are under pressure to demonstrate meaningful and effective engagement with this issue by developing strategies, processes, products and services designed to reduce GHGs and keep global temperature rise to below 1.5°C. As organisations begin setting goals and targets aligned with such scientific assessments, it becomes ever more important to review them critically and to examine the extent to which they represent substantive, rather than symbolic, acts of intent.

At the same time, it is important to recognise that climate change is but one out of many critical sustainability issues and concerns of importance to humanity and our economies. From an ecological perspective, climate change is captured within the wider planetary boundaries framework designed to highlight the perilous state of the global natural environment. This 'global dashboard for sustainability' also counts significant impacts such as loss of biodiversity, widespread land use change, freshwater availability, man-made pollutants including plastics and excessive biochemical flows of phosphorous and nitrogen as the key indicators flashing red and threatening the safe operating space for humanity (Rockström et al., 2009). Companies should therefore consider the extent to which target setting needs to be applied much more widely to acknowledge such wider concerns.

One potential avenue for such recognition is through the 17 United Nations Sustainable Development Goals (SDGs). Designed as successor to the Millennium Development Goals and agreed by all nations in 2015, they provide a broader sustainable development framework that integrates the abovementioned environmental concerns with significant social issues and challenges including poverty, inequality and a variety of human rights within a wide-ranging set of policy targets. Given the private sector's involvement in shaping this framework, there are great hopes and ambitions riding on companies integrating these SDGs into their business strategies through effective targets, innovation activities and, importantly, partnerships with various stakeholders to develop economies that are ecologically safe and socially just. While SDG13 specifically encourages climate action from all sectors, the remaining 16 SDGs provide a comprehensive agenda for target setting designed to ensure that businesses recognise their broader roles and responsibilities within this complex nexus of sustainability issues (Folke et al., 2016; Mio et al., 2020). Companies must therefore integrate sustainability efforts strategically across all parts and functions of their organisations, where target setting forms part of a wider sustainable management approach designed to ensure accountability and deliver demonstrable progress. This also is included within the UNHLEG (2022) recommendations.

This chapter provided a framework with which to distinguish the key characteristics of corporate carbon targets and to assess their likelihood of being effective. Early evidence suggests that while there is some progress, the voluntary nature of corporate carbon target setting still provides a lot of flexibility that leads to weak enforcement and implementation. While other target initiatives potentially provide a more robust and rigorous framework, they inadvertently also risk further obfuscation of companies' true impact and progress. For some, therefore, the time has come for a mandatory policy framework to ensure that all companies are setting comparable corporate carbon targets and actually meet their ambitions. In the meantime, however, it is investors and other stakeholders that must hold companies to account for the effectiveness of their organisational targets.

Discussion Points

- Has your organisation set itself targets in relation to climate change mitigation (and/or broader sustainability ambitions)?
- How were these targets decided upon? That is, who was involved in the process? What was the underlying motivation for defining them? On what basis were these targets defined?
- Using the framework proposed in this chapter, would you characterise your climate change targets as substantial or as symbolic?
- What impact have these targets had on your organisation so far (in terms of both GHG emissions reductions and wider organisational actions and decisions)?

Suggested Reading

Science-Based Targets. (2023). *SBT case studies*. https://sciencebasedtargets.org/companies-taking-action/case-studies

United Nations' High-Level Expert Group. (2022). *Integrity matters: Net zero commitments by businesses, financial institutions, cities and regions*. https://www.un.org/sites/un2.un.org/files/high-level_expert_group_n7b.pdf

References

ADEME. (2021, April 1). *Tous les acteurs doivent agir collectivement pour la neutralité carbone, mais aucun acteur ne devrait se revendiquer neutre en carbone*. https://presse.ademe.fr/2021/04/avis-de-lademe-tous-les-acteurs-doivent-agir-collectivement-pour-la-neutralite-carbone-mais-aucun-acteur-ne-devrait-se-revendiquer-neutre-en-carbone.html

Aragón-Correa, J. A., Marcus, A., & Hurtado-Torres, N. (2016). The natural environmental strategies of international firms: Old controversies and new evidence on performance and disclosure. *Academy of Management Perspectives, 30*(1), 24–39.

Backman, C. A., Verbeke, A., & Schulz, R. A. (2017). The drivers of corporate climate change strategies and public policy: A new resource-based view perspective. *Business & Society, 56*(4), 545–575.

BBC. (2021). *Shell: Netherlands court orders oil giant to cut emissions.* https://www.bbc.co.uk/news/world-europe-57257982

Bjørn, A., Lloyd, S., & Matthews, D. (2021). From the Paris Agreement to corporate climate commitments: evaluation of seven methods for setting 'science-based' emission targets. *Environmental Research Letters, 16*(5), 054019.

Bjørn, A., Tilsted, J. P., Addas, A., & Lloyd, S. M. (2022). Can science-based targets make the private sector Paris-aligned? A review of the emerging evidence. *Current Climate Change Reports, 8*, 53–69. https://doi.org/10.1007/s40641-022-00182-w

Bloomberg. (2022, November 21). *Junk carbon offsets are what make these big companies 'carbon neutral'.* https://www.bloomberg.com/graphics/2022-carbon-offsets-renewable-energy

Busch, T., Johnson, M., & Pioch, T. (2022). Corporate carbon performance data: Quo vadis? *Journal of Industrial Ecology, 26*(1), 350–363.

Carbone4. (2021, July 12). Decoding ADEME's opinion on carbon neutrality. https://www.carbone4.com/en/decoding-ademe-carbon-neutrality

Carlsberg. (2023). *Zero carbon footprint.* https://www.carlsberggroup.com/sustainability/our-esg-programme/zero-carbon-footprint/

CDP. (2022a). *Climate change.* https://www.cdp.net/en/climate

CDP. (2022b, February). *Engaging the chain: Driving speed and scale.* https://www.cdp.net/ja/reports/downloads/6106

ClimateAction100+. (2022, October 13). *Climate action 100+ net zero company benchmark shows continued progress on net zero commitments is not matched by development and implementation of credible decarbonisation strategies.* https://www.climateaction100.org/news/climate-action-100-net-zero-company-benchmark-shows-continued-progress-on-net-zero-commitments-is-not-matched-by-development-and-implementation-of-credible-decarbonisation-strategies/

Collins, J. (1999). Turning goals into results: The power of catalytic mechanisms. *Harvard Business Review, 77*, 70–84.

Dahlmann, F., Branicki, L., & Brammer, S. (2017). 'Carrots for corporate sustainability': Impacts of incentive inclusiveness and variety on environmental performance. *Business Strategy and the Environment, 26*(8), 1110–1131.

Dahlmann, F., Branicki, L., & Brammer, S. (2019). Managing carbon aspirations: The influence of corporate climate change targets on environmental performance. *Journal of Business Ethics, 158*(1), 1–24.

Dahlmann, F., & Roehrich, J. K. (2019). Sustainable supply chain management and partner engagement to manage climate change information. *Business Strategy and the Environment, 28*, 1632–1647.

Delmas, M. A., & Montes-Sancho, M. J. (2010). Voluntary agreements to improve environmental quality: Symbolic and substantive cooperation. *Strategic Management Journal, 31*(6), 575–601.

Deming, W. E. (1986). *Out of the crisis*. Massachusetts Institute of Technology, Center for Advanced Engineering Study.

Department for Business, Energy & Industrial Strategy. (2022). *Mandatory climate-related financial disclosures by publicly quoted companies, large private companies and LLPs. Non-binding guidance.* https://assets.publishing.service.gov.uk/government/uploads/system/uploads/attachment_data/file/1056085/mandatory-climate-related-financial-disclosures-publicly-quoted-private-cos-llps.pdf

Depoers, F., Jeanjean, T., & Jérôme, T. (2016). Voluntary disclosure of greenhouse gas emissions: Contrasting the carbon disclosure project and corporate reports. *Journal of Business Ethics, 134*(3), 445–461.

Dhanda, K. K., & Hartman, L. P. (2011). The ethics of carbon neutrality: A critical examination of voluntary carbon offset providers. *Journal of Business Ethics, 100*(1), 119–149.

Edie. (2022, June 29). 'Something this radical is not easy': Inside Carlsberg's quest for a fully fibre-based beer bottle. https://www.edie.net/something-this-radical-is-not-easy-inside-carlsbergs-quest-for-a-fully-fibre-based-beer-bottle/

Fankhauser, S., Smith, S. M., Allen, M., Axelsson, K., Hale, T., Hepburn, C., Kendall, J. M., Khosla, R., Lezaun, J., Mitchell-Larson, E., & Obersteiner, M. (2022). The meaning of net zero and how to get it right. *Nature Climate Change, 12*(1), 15–21. https://doi.org/10.1038/s41558-021-01245-w

Folke, C., Biggs, R., Norström, A. V., Reyers, B., & Rockström, J. (2016). Social–ecological resilience and biosphere-based sustainability science. *Ecology and Society, 21*(3), 41. http://dx.doi.org/10.5751/ES-08748-210341

GHG Protocol. (2011, September). *Corporate value chain (scope 3) accounting and reporting standard.* World Business Council for Sustainable Development (WBCSD) and World Resources Institute (WRI). https://ghgprotocol.org/standards/scope-3-standard

Giesekam, J., Norman, J., Garvey, A., & Betts-Davies, S. (2021). Science-based targets: On target? *Sustainability, 13*(4), 1657.

Grant, N. (2022). The Paris Agreement's ratcheting mechanism needs strengthening 4-fold to keep 1.5° C alive. *Joule, 6*(4), 703–708.

Hahn, R., Reimsbach, D., & Schiemann, F. (2015). Organizations, climate change, and transparency: Reviewing the literature on carbon disclosure. *Organization & Environment, 28*(1), 80–102.

Hamel, G., & Prahalad, C. K. (1993). Strategy as stretch and leverage. *Harvard Business Review, 71*(2), 75–84.

Howard-Grenville, J., Buckle, S. J., Hoskins, B. J., & George, G. (2014). Climate change and management. *Academy of Management Journal, 57*(3), 615–623.

Hyams, K., & Fawcett, T. (2013). The ethics of carbon offsetting. *WIREs Climate Change, 4*, 91–98. doi:10.1002/wcc.207

Ioannou, I., Li, S. X., & Serafeim, G. (2016). The effect of target difficulty on target completion: The case of reducing carbon emissions. *The Accounting Review, 91*, 1467–1492.

Kolk, A., & Pinkse, J. (2005). Business responses to climate change: Identifying emergent strategies. *California Management Review, 47*(3), 6–20.

Leone, A. J., & Rock, S. (2002). Empirical tests of budget ratcheting and its effect on managers' discretionary accrual choices. *Journal of Accounting & Economics, 33*(1), 43–67.

Malen, J. (2022). Moving the goalposts: Aspiration reoperationalization in response to failure to achieve environmental performance targets. *Academy of Management Discoveries, 8*(3), 357–383.

McGuire, B. (2022, November 12). The 1.5C climate target is dead – To prevent total catastrophe, Cop27 must admit it. *The Guardian*. https://www.theguardian.com/commentisfree/2022/nov/12/climate-target-cop27-breakdown-fossil-fuel

Microsoft. (2020, January 16). *Microsoft will be carbon negative by 2030*. https://blogs.microsoft.com/blog/2020/01/16/microsoft-will-be-carbon-negative-by-2030/

Mio, C., Panfilo, S., & Blundo, B. (2020). Sustainable development goals and the strategic role of business: A systematic literature review. *Business Strategy and the Environment, 29*(8), 3220–3245.

Newell, P. (2020). The business of rapid transition. *Wiley Interdisciplinary Reviews: Climate Change, 11*(6), e670.

Nowack, K. (2017). Facilitating successful behavior change: Beyond goal setting to goal flourishing. *Consulting Psychology Journal: Practice and Research, 69*(3), 153.

Pinkse, J., & Kolk, A. (2009). *International business and global climate change*. Routledge.

Rekker, S., Ives, M. C., Wade, B., Webb, L., & Greig, C. (2022). Measuring corporate Paris compliance using a strict science-based approach. *Nature Communications, 13*(1), 1–11. https://doi.org/10.1038/s41467-022-31143-4

Rockström, J. [@jrockstrom]. (2022, October 25). *I just get tired...Tired of hearing that 1.5°C is a "target" or "goal". IT IS NOT. It is a limit. The only real goal is 0°C. And not bad 1.5°C, when we LIKELY tip GIS, WAIS, Tropical Coral Reefs and Abrupt Boreal Permafrost, and get more floods, droughts, heat, disease, storms* [Tweet]. Twitter. https://twitter.com/jrockstrom/status/1584811163329523712

Rockström, J., Gaffney, O., Rogelj, J., Meinshausen, M., Nakicenovic, N., & Schellnhuber, H. J. (2017). A roadmap for rapid decarbonization. *Science, 355*(6331), 1269–1271.

Rockström, J., Steffen, W., Noone, K., Persson, Å., Chapin, F. S. I., Lambin, E., Lenton, T., Scheffer, M., Folke, C., Schellnhuber, H. J., Nykvist, B., de Wit, C., Hughes, T., van der Leeuw, S., Rodhe, H., Sörlin, S., Snyder, P., Costanza, R., Svedin, U., ... Foley, J. (2009). Planetary boundaries: Exploring the safe operating space for humanity. *Ecology and Society, 14*(2). https://doi.org/10.5751/ES-03180-140232

Rogelj, J., Geden, O., Cowie, A., & Reisinger, A. (2021). Net-zero emissions targets are vague: Three ways to fix. *Nature, 591*, 365–368. https://doi.org/10.1038/d41586-021-00662-3

Science Based Targets. (2022). *How it works.* https://sciencebasedtargets.org/how-it-works

Science Based Targets. (2023). *SBT case studies.* https://sciencebasedtargets.org/companies-taking-action/case-studies

Sitkin, S. B., See, K. E., Miller, C. C., Lawless, M. W., & Carton, A. M. (2011). The paradox of stretch goals: Organizations in pursuit of the seemingly impossible. *Academy of Management Review, 36*(3), 544–566.

Slawinski, N., Pinkse, J., Busch, T., & Banerjee, S. B. (2017). The role of short-termism and uncertainty avoidance in organizational inaction on climate change: A multi-level framework. *Business & Society, 56*(2), 253–282.

United Nations Framework Convention on Climate Change. (2015). *The Paris Agreement.* https://unfccc.int/process-and-meetings/the-paris-agreement/the-paris-agreement

United Nations Framework Convention on Climate Change. (2022). *Introduction to loss and damage.* https://unfccc.int/topics/adaptation-and-resilience/the-big-picture/introduction-to-loss-and-damage

United Nations' High-Level Expert Group on the Net Zero Emissions Commitments of Non-State Entities. (2022). *Integrity matters: Net zero commitments by businesses, financial institutions, cities and regions.* https://www.un.org/sites/un2.un.org/files/high-level_expert_group_n7b.pdf

Wright, C., & Nyberg, D. (2017). An inconvenient truth: How organizations translate climate change into business as usual. *Academy of Management Journal, 60*(5), 1633–1661.

18

COACHING IN THE ANTHROPOCENE

Joel A. DiGirolamo

Chapter Summary

Coaching leaders has been important for decades, but with the potential existential threat of dramatic climate change, its importance has increased even more. This threat of climate change has forced organisations and governments to work together in ways that could not be envisioned even a few short years ago. Coaching leaders to enhance their team's performance, to share leadership responsibilities and to span the combined work into a single focus can be a powerful tool. To be effective in this realm, it is essential that coaches enhance their knowledge and skills to include team dynamics, cross-cultural effectiveness, strategic goal alignment and effectively sharing leadership responsibilities across multiple teams and organisations.

DOI: 10.4324/9781003343011-22

Introduction

Coaching inside organisations has mostly been focused on individual development as well as team and organisation performance (e.g., Jones et al., 2016; Pavur, 2013). While this has served us well during the Industrial and Information ages, it is time to bring a broader perspective to coaching leaders (Western, 2010). Our species can no longer afford to research, develop and produce goods and services in isolation. The new perspective must take into account the plethora of systems, or ecosystems, and evolve to more collaborative (Gallagher, 2018) and shared leadership (MacKie, 2019) models. Gallagher summed it up well in a report on the June 2012 United Nations Rio +20 Conference on Sustainable Development of leaders, stating that we must have leaders in:

> committed partnerships with like-minded others engaged in joint problem solving. The existential global climate crisis motivated members to consider innovative approaches to leadership, in which personal, titular power would not be the sole source of change. These exercises of environmental leadership that occurred post-Rio were not sustained by personal charisma, motivated by desires to transform organisational relationships, or rooted in visions of heroic actions, but rather grounded in a sense that humility and collaboration are critical to the survival of the planet.
>
> (Gallagher, 2018, p. 129).

Theory and Basic Concepts

Leadership

Leadership in various forms of conceptualisation has been seen amongst our primal ancestors (Furuichi, 2019; Van Vugt et al. 2008) and evolved with our species' development through phases of city-state development with agriculture and writing (Teng, 2013). The industrial revolution and the rise of capitalism further evolved the construct of leadership to be primarily focused on organisations (Day, 2001; Van Vugt et al. 2008). However, Western (2010) encouraged us to look deeper into the construct of leadership, to eco-leadership, which, 'implies leadership in relation to the ecosystems in which we live and work' (p. 36). Perhaps more important,

Wielkiewicz and Stelzner (2005) pointed out that 'specific leaders are less important than they appear because the ecological context is more important than what leaders decide to do' (p. 326). In other words, while leaders in organisations have collectively changed the planet, our ecological environment will ultimately win any conflict with *Homo sapiens.*

The concept of 'tragedy of the commons,' where natural resources are used for the benefit of a few but to the detriment of the many, was developed by Lloyd (1833) and popularised by Hardin (1968) over a century later. A tragedy of the commons happens when there is a lack of direction, leadership and governance. Large participative and strong governance approaches have been suggested to meet these difficult challenges (Ferraro et al., 2015; Orr & Hill, 1978). The tragedies that Lloyd and Hardin envisioned were local or regional, but we are now concerned with a tragedy at the global – and existential – level.

Fundamentally, leadership is about aligning individuals and teams in working towards a vision, in a strategic direction (Kotter, 2008). In the context of a tragedy of the commons, while this alignment may benefit an organisation, failure to consider the broader implications of decisions and actions can be to the detriment of the many. Consequently, it is imperative that leaders explore and consider these broader implications and work collaboratively with other teams, leaders and organisations – in addition to applying responsible and ethical leadership.

Leaders exhibit leadership behaviours. An individual does not need to have the title 'leader' to be a leader. In an early treatise on leadership, Gibb (1954) made the distinction between leadership 'functions' and leader roles. He went on to coin the term 'distributed leadership' and stated that he felt that leadership is actually a group quality rather than an individual quality, as it is typically thought of today. Taggar et al. (1999) observed 94 autonomous (initially leaderless) teams to evaluate leader emergence and team performance, among other elements. In their conclusion, they wrote, 'Our results suggest that human resource practitioners should seek to maximise the number of people in a team who exhibit leadership behaviour, such as performance management, goal setting, and synthesis of ideas' (Taggar et al., 1999, p. 922). Jackson et al. (2018) provided an outline of six perspectives through which leadership can be observed: the person, the position, performance, process, place and purpose. Coaches, when working with leaders of all types, may find any of these elements useful in their work.

To solve big problems we need a compelling vision and motivated and aligned teams. Take, for example, the vision U.S. President John F. Kennedy provided in a speech on May 25, 1961, with the goal of landing a man on the moon before the end of that decade (National Aeronautics and Space Administration: NASA History Office, 2013). Creating the vision itself involved multiple teams and, of course, the enormous effort to achieve that goal required leadership and alignment of individuals across teams of NASA personnel, contractors and government.

It is incumbent upon leaders to develop compelling visions. Clearly this should involve consultation with experts in pertinent areas (Locke, 2003). Achieving that vision requires the use of leadership skills by all participants. Locke (2003) illustrated a useful 'integrated' leadership model wherein leadership is shared amongst team members along with a designated leader. In addition to creating a compelling vision, at times the leader must be leaned upon to make important and sometimes controversial decisions. DiGirolamo and Tkach (2019) described a spectrum across which managers and leaders may move from directive to participative. At one end, leaders need to set a vision and direction – and align individuals and sub-group tasks towards that vision. At the other end of the spectrum, the participative activities can bring in new ideas and ways to work together.

On a more granular basis, Day et al. (2004) provided a valuable model that illustrates the contribution of individual knowledge, skills and abilities to teamwork and ultimately to team leadership capacity. In an experimental study with MBA students, Carson et al. (2007) saw positive effects of shared leadership contributing to team performance.

At the most fundamental level, to solve the big, compelling problems such as climate change and work productively within and across teams and organisations, enhanced collaboration is necessary (Glaser, 2005). This takes effort and practice, as Glaser suggested:

> But despite its current appeal, collaboration and collegiality do not happen spontaneously. As we will see, it requires habits and a discipline that obligates a public leader to be much more facilitative and far less directive than our learned practice may have been.
>
> (Glaser, 2005, p. 5)

As indicated above, moving beyond conventional leadership requires new thinking and willingness to adopt new leadership models, such as shared leadership. Pearce et al. (2014) provided an eloquent description: 'Shared leadership moves beyond the moribund myth of leadership being a solely top-down hierarchical affair into the idea that leadership can be systemically fluid and simultaneously multi-versional based on a dynamic give-and-take relationship' (p. 277). In short, leadership skills can be used by everyone when appropriate.

In the climate change context, large, significant initiatives will be necessary, and shared leadership can provide the enhanced drive and momentum necessary to build and align large teams to make progress on climate change. The importance of vision and goals was discussed above, and coalitions of teams and organisations will need to develop a joint vision and strategy. Nonaka and Takeuchi (2021) provided a compelling approach to making strategy more human-centric and future focused with a set of best practices, including living with nature. Tasks will need to align to the coalition vision and to each organisation's vision, mission and strategy. Individuals within each team and organisation will need to show leadership related to their specific task and team while at the same time contributing on the overall vision. MacKie (2019) provided a comprehensive mediator and moderator model illustrating the potential effects of a variety of team elements, such as team strengths, empowering leadership, leader humility and shared leadership on team performance. In a more recent study, Cho et al. (2021) verified the importance of leader humility and shared leadership in team performance.

Morgeson et al. (2010) provided a comprehensive list of team leadership functions that are compiled into a transition phase and an action phase. Functions in the transition phase relate to recruiting and selecting team members, training, setting goals, training and much more. Functions in the action phase are related to continuous improvement, securing resources, social climate and more. No matter how small or large the teams, no matter how widely dispersed the members are or disparate their expertise or task, the leadership can be shared – and all of the functions covered.

Importance of Systems and Context

When considering the idea of involving many teams, organisations and governments in a project, context and mental models are important in two ways. First, it is important for the vision and project charter to clearly articulate models of the envisioned future. This can go a long way towards achieving the goals and vision. Secondly, it is important to understand what context and models each team, organisation and government might be working within and with. An entity's own context or models may limit their understanding, participation and ability to move forward in the project.

Mental models and a common understanding of them among individuals and teams can elevate group performance (Mathieu et al., 2000; Senge, 2006). Glaser (2005) referred to this as 'coherence,' which he considered to be a significant factor in successful collaboration. When multiple teams, organisations and governments are involved, such as with large climate change perspectives and projects, shared mental models can be critical to success. This is important to ensure high productivity and prevent incorrect assumptions and misalignment in tasks. Similarly, taking context into account is an important element in successful leadership (B. Berman & Bradt, 2021) just as it is in coaching (International Coaching Federation [ICF], 2019b; Stelter, 2014).

A Compelling Vision

Developing a compelling vision to work towards mitigation of climate change is difficult. We as *Homo sapiens* generally will change because we wish to move away from something painful or towards something of great value to us (Kuhlen, 1963; Schlossberg, 1984). While our current climate change is certainly rapid in paleoclimate terms (Working Group I of the Intergovernmental Panel on Climate Change, 2021), it is imperceptibly slow in *Homo sapiens* terms.

Those of us living outside the equatorial region of our planet may have anecdotal evidence of climate change, such as a slightly longer summer season, but we still have significant seasonal shifts and don't think too much about this. Therefore, innately, our daily behaviours are not consciously driven by a focus on climate change. To more effectively orient our behaviours in sustainable directions, we must spend time acquiring knowledge on the topic and in reflection on how our daily behaviours can be modified. In other words, for us *Homo sapiens* there is no palpable stimulus–response connection whereby actions such as driving a fossil fuel–powered automobile leads immediately and directly to an undesirable outcome such as difficulty breathing or intense heat. Further, humans have an evolutionary bias to discount future events (temporal myopia), such as potentially climate-induced disasters

(Palomo-Vélez & Van Vugt, 2021). As a result, it is difficult to motivate individuals to adopt ecologically sustainable behaviours, which begs the need for leadership beyond what has been conventionally accepted.

In an attempt to understand the factors most likely to change or adapt behaviour to reduce or avoid the impacts of climate change, van Valkengoed and Steg (2019) undertook a meta-analysis of studies relating to 13 possible factors. The results indicated that self-efficacy (extent to which people believe they are able to engage in adaptive behaviours), outcome efficacy (extent to which people believe that their adaptive behaviours will be effective), negative affect (how possible negative emotional outcomes from climate change may influence adaptive behaviours) and descriptive norms (perception of the extent to which others are adopting adaptive behaviours) are the strongest predictors of adaptive behaviour. By working together across organisations and groups, the adaptive behaviours can become the norm and build perceived self- and outcome efficacy.

We need two things: a vivid and compelling illustration of the existential threat that climate change is and a grand vision of how we can mitigate this threat with realistic aligned and potent efforts of individuals, teams, organisations and governments. The vision should motivate individuals to put forth energy and intention towards it and to harness individual agency; that is, compelling individuals to align towards that vision. Until we have a compelling grand vision that illuminates a path forward, we all must provide some level of leadership within our sphere of influence while at the same time expanding that sphere. We will all need to work more collaboratively across organisations and governments to build a sustainable future.

While we frequently hear catastrophic news reports of conflict, across the globe we can find evidence of growing collaboration, such as the United Nations, the creation and expansion of the European Union, the Group of Seven countries, the United Nations Climate Change Conference, the Association of Southeast Asian Nations, the Geneva conventions and a variety of nuclear arms treaties.

Client-Directed and Coach-Guided

Some individuals regard Socrates as the founder of coaching as we know it today, given his penchant for asking a myriad of questions (Wildflower, 2013). But there is more. The word *coaching* is now being used in a broad set of circumstances – from sports coaching to sales coaching to executive coaching to team coaching to life coaching – and more.

Coaching is about change, about helping clients to move forward and progress along their own growth path. The ICF (n.d.) defined coaching as 'partnering with clients in a thought-provoking and creative process that inspires them to maximise their personal and professional potential'.

Consider for a moment the pivotal insights from humanistic psychology (Kosslyn & Rosenberg, 2004) and client-centred therapy (Rogers, 1951) where the client leads the way. This can result in therapy and coaching as minimally directive modalities. However, in some types of coaching, the coach will be providing performance knowledge and motivation (e.g., sports coaching), broader perspectives (e.g., leadership coaching), resources (e.g., health and wellness coaching), process knowledge (e.g., agile and sales coaching) and so on. But a common element to all types of coaching is the individual's development of and work towards goals.

So, we can ponder the idea that coaching may be viewed through a lens of providing knowledge and guidance and also through a lens of allowing the client to lead the way. Figure 18.1 illustrates a conceptual spectrum from a guiding agile coaching approach to a non-directive coaching approach where the client leads the way.

Over the years the ICF has developed a model of coaching – core competencies – which come close to this idea of a client-centred coaching model (ICF, 2019b). While it can be argued that guiding a client through a coaching process is inherently an influence on the client, the only overt role of guidance to the client in the ICF core competency model is the sub-competency 'shares observations, insights and feelings, without attachment, that have the potential to create new learning for the client'.

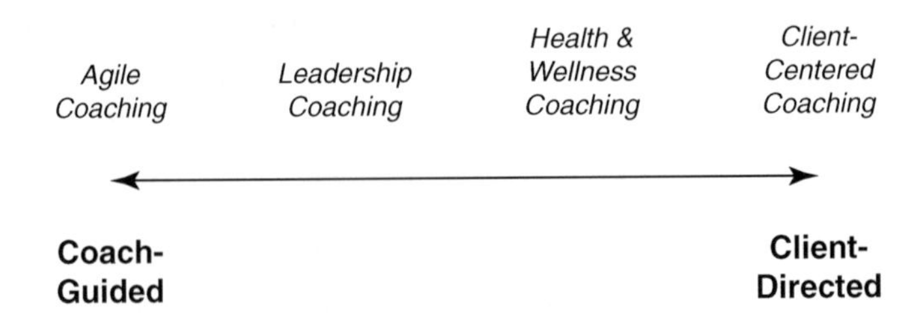

Figure 18.1 A Conceptual Perspective of Various Types of Coaching Along a Spectrum From Coach Guided to Client Directed

Targeted coaching practices, such as executive, business, health and wellness coaching, have indicated the need for some input from coaches, with content education (Sohl et al., 2021) and business knowledge (W. H. Berman, 2019) being just a few. We can anticipate (and hope) for more desired knowledge in the area of sustainability or eco-leadership (Western, 2010). As we move farther to the left on the spectrum in Figure 18.1, the coaching modalities have more guidance from the coach. At an even greater extreme, for adult athletes there is an expectation for coaches to 'share knowledge' in addition to helping the athletes define and work towards their goals (Callary et al., 2017; Ferrari et al., 2016).

When, why, how and to what extent a coach provides knowledge or shares wisdom is dependent on the type of coaching, the coach–client agreement, the coach–client power dynamics and a myriad of other factors. What is important is the intention of helping the client 'without attachment' within the context of our greater society, and specifically toward climate change since that is our topic of focus here. It is important to consider the ICF code of ethics viewpoint, 'I am aware of my and my client's impact on society. I adhere to the philosophy of doing good versus avoiding bad.' (ICF 2019a, p. 7).

Looking at ethical issues more broadly in the context of coaching for climate change, it can be seen that this is a matter of applied ethics as well as justice (Klinsky & Dowlatabadi, 2009). In coaching leaders, the coach can certainly interject questions about the ethics of proposed actions and the equity involved for all affected parties or stakeholders. This can bring greater awareness to the client of broad implications for specific actions.

Whybrow et al. (2023) took the issue even further and suggested an entirely new paradigm for coaching, one which makes a transition from client- or organisation-centric to an exploration of 'what life is requiring'. In this paradigm, service is valued more highly than personal success. It is such a shift that is required developing norms such as those suggested by van Valkengoed and Steg (2019) above.

Measuring Progress

Following the axiom that what gets measured gets attention, it may be good to ask leaders how they want to measure progress towards their goals, including those related to climate change. One of the ICF core competencies

(2019b) is 'facilitates client growth.' This competency includes several sub-competencies with elements of accountability and measurement.

Additional considerations are to ask leaders how they might be more effective in their climate change efforts by engaging with more individuals, teams and groups both inside and outside their organisation. When coaching teams, consideration should be given to when interventions might take place (Hackman & Wageman, 2005), how to measure team progress and when to check in with team sentiment.

Practice: Methods, Techniques & Application

Coaching the Leaders

Now it's time to consider all of these elements together to understand how to effectively coach leaders with climate change as an important consideration. The ICF has developed a set of team coaching competencies that may also provide guidance here (ICF, 2020). By reviewing some of those elements, coaches may gain inspiration for one-on-one coaching with team leaders in a sustainability context.

To be an effective team coach, it is essential that the coaches enhance their knowledge and skills to include team dynamics, cross-cultural effectiveness, ability to move in and out of the team dialog and much more (ICF, 2020). Teams generally effect greater change given their size, thus providing an opening for the entrance of climate change ramifications of team action or inaction. One of a team coach's goals should be to build internal leadership capacity within the team so that the team coach is no longer needed for effective team development.

Given the desire for teams to learn to work effectively without a team coach, team leaders should be acquiring skills similar to the team coaches. It is important for team leaders to learn how to develop strategic goals and align work activity towards those goals. To effectively achieve broad and significant goals, especially across multiple teams and organisations, team leaders must be sensitive to multiple cultures – organisational as well as geographic.

It is important to balance working with a team as a single entity while also promoting team member empowerment and shared leadership. A study by DiGirolamo and Tkach (2019) found that empowerment was an important element for managers and leaders to have a positive impact on team members' career development or job performance. Promoting and communicating to the team that it is working as a single entity with a single identity can maintain team member motivation towards the goal and enhance team member collaboration. In support of both sides, it is important to provide a safe space for open and honest team interaction.

On the one hand, it is important to promote empowerment and shared leadership; on the other, there are times when the leader must take charge and provide direction, help to remove obstacles, provide structure, build the team and facilitate appropriate core values (Locke, 2003). These two roles are not mutually exclusive but build on each other. In addition, the team leader should be challenging the team's assumptions, behaviours and meaning-making processes to enhance their collective awareness or insight. This may be especially important in light of the factors offered by van Valkengoed and Steg (2019): self-efficacy, outcome efficacy, negative affect and descriptive norms. Skillfully applying these factors to interactions with team members may significantly enhance effectiveness of integrating climate change issues into the team tasks and goals.

Moving from the team level down to the personal level, it is important for each team member to feel valued by the team leader and that they feel the leader is present for them. Each team member, as well as the entire team, should feel free to express their feelings, perceptions, concerns, beliefs, hopes and suggestions. Elements of climate change can often be brought into these conversations at appropriate times. Good communications paths should be established no matter what the size of the team is, especially when multiple organisations or governments are involved given the potential mismatch in culture and different first languages.

Conflicts should be resolved quickly through dialog to everyone's satisfaction. While this might mean that everybody doesn't get what they'd most like, hopefully everybody will at least be able to live with issues and decisions that arise. A good leader will be aware of how team members relate to each other and how they impact the team energy, engagement and focus with climate change in mind. Hackman and Wageman (2005) identified that the beginning, mid-point and end of team projects are likely good times for reflection and a review of sentiment and progress.

Pulling It All Together

As indicated at the outset, coaching is primarily client directed but, depending on the type of coaching, a coach may inquire about context, the bigger picture and broader implications, especially when it relates to climate change. Team dynamics, shared leadership and collaboration across multiple teams and organisations may help to achieve greater goals.

It is important to remember that, ultimately, coaching is about focusing on client goals and direction, and the coach will need to work within that framework to the best of their ability. When coaching teams, explore the team dynamics to understand how you might engage with the positive dynamics and direct them towards the goals and bring in the effects to climate change when appropriate. It is also imperative to discern team dynamics that may be obstacles in progress towards the goals, including those affecting our climate. Empowering both teams and individuals may also enhance performance and professional development.

Inquire about broader perspectives and context when appropriate and without attachment to ensure that they are being considered, including elements of climate change, of course. Along with this, it is important to inquire about leadership actions and behaviours to bring awareness to the significance of these elements. And finally, reflect on when, why, how and to what extent you might provide vital knowledge or wisdom to your client.

Discussion Points

- Discuss a scenario where a coach has an opportunity to bring greater awareness to a leader client of the broader circumstances such as climate change.
- Describe how a coach might build shared mental models with leaders and their team members.
- Suggest how coaches could bring awareness of the idea of shared leadership to clients.
- Discuss how coaches might explore with leader clients the idea of collaborating and leading towards greater, more significant goals, such as climate change, with additional groups.
- Discuss how coaches might work with a team as a single entity and also work with individuals on the team to enhance their capabilities and leadership skills.

Suggested Reading

Berman, B., & Bradt, G. (2021). *Influence and impact: Discover and excel at what your organization needs from you the most*. John Wiley & Sons.

Glaser, J. (2005). *Leading through collaboration: Guiding groups to productive solutions*. Sage.

Mazutis, D., & Eckardt, A. (2017). Sleepwalking into catastrophe: Cognitive biases and corporate climate change inertia. *California Management Review, 59*(3), 74–108. https://doi.org/10.1177/0008125617707974

Senge, P. M. (2006). *The fifth discipline: The art & practice of the learning organization*. Crown Business.

References

Berman, B., & Bradt, G. (2021). *Influence and impact: Discover and excel at what your organization needs from you the most*. John Wiley & Sons.

Berman, W. H. (2019). Coaching C-suite executives and business founders. *Consulting Psychology Journal: Practice and Research, 71*(2), 72–85. https://doi.org/10.1037/cpb0000128

Callary, B., Rathwell, S., & Young, B. W. (2017). Alignment of masters swim coaches' approaches with the andragogy in practice model. *International Sport Coaching Journal, 4*(2), 177–190.

Carson, J. B., Tesluk, P. E., & Marrone, J. A. (2007). Shared leadership in teams: An investigation of antecedent conditions and performance. *Academy of Management Journal, 50*(5), 1217–1234.

Cho, V., Roll, L. C., Wu, C. H., & Tang, V. (2021). Changing digital age in the wake of COVID-19: How does humility impact on virtual leaderless teams? *Journal of Global Information Management, 30*(4), 1–23.

Day, D. V. (2001). Leadership development: A review in context. *The Leadership Quarterly, 11*(4), 581–613.

Day, D. V., Gronn, P., & Salas, E. (2004). Leadership capacity in teams. *The Leadership Quarterly, 15*(6), 857–880.

DiGirolamo, J. A., & Tkach, J. T. (2019). An exploration of managers and leaders using coaching skills. *Consulting Psychology Journal: Practice and Research, 71*(3), 195–218. http://dx.doi.org/10.1037/cpb0000138

Ferrari, G., Bloom, G. A., Gilbert, W. D., & Caron, J. G. (2016). Experiences of competitive masters swimmers: Desired coaching characteristics and perceived benefits. *International Journal of Sport and Exercise Psychology, 15*(4), 409–422.

Ferraro, F., Etzion, D., & Gehman, J. (2015). Tackling grand challenges pragmatically: Robust action revisited. *Organization Studies, 36*(3), 363–390.

Furuichi, T. (2019). *Bonobo and chimpanzee: The lessons of social coexistence.* Springer.

Gallagher, D. R. (2018). Heroes no more: Businesses practice collaborative leadership to confront climate change innovation in environmental leadership. In B. W. Redekop, D. R. Gallagher, & R. Satterwhite (Eds.), *Innovation in environmental leadership: Critical perspectives* (pp. 128–144). Routledge.

Gibb, C. A. (1954). Leadership. In G. Lindzey (Ed.), *Handbook of social psychology* (Vol. 2). Addison-Wesley.

Glaser, J. (2005). *Leading through collaboration: Guiding groups to productive solutions.* Sage.

Hackman, J. R., & Wageman, R. (2005). A theory of team coaching. *Academy of Management Review, 30*(2), 269–287.

Hardin, G. (1968). The tragedy of the commons. *Science, 162*(3859), 1243–1248.

International Coaching Federation. (n.d.). *ICF definition of coaching.* https://coachingfederation.org/about

International Coaching Federation. (2019a). *ICF code of ethics.* https://coachfederation.org/code-of-ethics

International Coaching Federation. (2019b). *Updated ICF core competency model.* https://coachingfederation.org/core-competencies

International Coaching Federation. (2020). *ICF team coaching competencies: Moving beyond one-to-one coaching.* https://coachingfederation.org/app/uploads/2020/11/Team-Coaching-Competencies-2.pdf

Jackson, B., Nicoll, M., & Roy, M. J. (2018). The distinctive challenges and opportunities for creating leadership within social enterprises. *Social Enterprise Journal, 14*(1), 71–91.

Jones, R. J., Woods, S. A., & Guillaume, Y. R. F. (2016). The effectiveness of workplace coaching: A meta-analysis of learning and performance outcomes from coaching. *Journal of Occupational and Organizational Psychology, 89*(2), 249–277. https://doi.org/10.1111/joop.12119

Klinsky, S., & Dowlatabadi, H. (2009). Conceptualizations of justice in climate policy. *Climate Policy, 9*(1), 88–108. https://doi.org/10.3763/cpol.2007.0468

Kosslyn, S. M., & Rosenberg, R. S. (2004). *Psychology: The brain, the person, the world* (2nd ed.). Pearson Education.

Kotter, J. P. (2008). *A force for change: How leadership differs from management.* Free Press.

Kuhlen, R. G. (1963). Motivational changes during the adult years. In R. G. Kuhlen (Ed.), *Psychological backgrounds for adult education* (pp. 77–113). Center for the Study of Liberal Education for Adults.

Lloyd, W. F. (1833). *Two lectures on the checks to population.* S. Collingwood.

Locke, E. A. (2003). Leadership: Starting at the top. In C. L. Pearce & J. A. Conger (Eds.), *Shared leadership: Reframing the hows and whys of leadership* (pp. 271–283). Sage.

MacKie, D. (2019). Models of shared leadership and team coaching. In D. Clutterbuck, J. Gannon, S. Hayes, I. Iordanou, K. Lowe, & D. MacKie (Eds.), *The practitioner's handbook of team coaching* (pp. 53–62). Routledge.

Mathieu, J. E., Heffner, T. S., Goodwin, G. F., Salas, E., & Cannon-Bowers, J. A. (2000). The influence of shared mental models on team process and performance. *Journal of Applied Psychology, 85*(2), 273–283.

Morgeson, F. P., DeRue, D. S., & Karam, E. P. (2010). Leadership in teams: A functional approach to understanding leadership structures and processes. *Journal of Management, 36*(1), 5–39. https://doi.org/10.1177/0149206309347376

National Aeronautics and Space Administration: NASA History Office. (2013). *The decision to go to the moon: President John F. Kennedy's May 25, 1961 speech before a joint session of Congress.* https://history.nasa.gov/moondec.html

Nonaka, I., & Takeuchi, H. (2021). Humanizing strategy. *Long Range Planning, 54*(4), 102070. https://doi.org/10.1016/j.lrp.2021.102070

Orr, D. W., & Hill, S. (1978). Leviathan, the open society, and the crisis of ecology. *Western Political Quarterly, 31*(4), 457–469.

Palomo-Vélez, G., & Van Vugt, M. (2021). The evolutionary psychology of climate change behaviors: Insights and applications. *Current Opinion in Psychology, 42*, 54–59. https://doi.org/10.1016/j.copsyc.2021.03.006

Pavur, E. J. J. (2013). Why do organizations want their leaders to be coached? *Consulting Psychology Journal: Practice and Research, 65*(4), 289–293.

Pearce, C. L., Wassenaar, C. L., & Manz, C. C. (2014). Is shared leadership the key to responsible leadership? *Academy of Management Perspectives, 28*(3), 275–288.

Rogers, C. R. (1951). *Client-centered therapy: Its current practice, implications, and theory.* Houghton Mifflin.

Schlossberg, N. K. (1984). *Counseling adults in transition: Linking practice with theory.* Springer.

Senge, P. M. (2006). *The fifth discipline: The art & practice of the learning organization.* Crown Business.

Sohl, S. J., Lee, D., Davidson, H., Morriss, B., Weinand, R., Costa, K., Ip, E. H., Lovato, J., Rothman, R. L., & Wolever, R. Q. (2021). Development of an observational tool to assess health coaching fidelity. *Patient Education and Counseling, 104*(3), 642–648.

Stelter, R. (2014). Third generation coaching: Reconstructing dialogues through collaborative practice and a focus on values. *International Coaching Psychology Review, 9*(1), 51–66.

Taggar, S., Hackew, R., & Saha, S. (1999). Leadership emergence in autonomous work teams: Antecedents and outcomes. *Personnel Psychology, 52*(4), 899–926.

Teng, J. (2013). *Musket, map and money: How military technology shaped geopolitics and economics*. Versita.

van Valkengoed, A. M., & Steg, L. (2019). Meta-analyses of factors motivating climate change adaptation behaviour. *Nature Climate Change, 9*(2), 158–163. https://doi.org/10.1038/s41558-018-0371-y

Van Vugt, M., Hogan, R., & Kaiser, R. B. (2008). Leadership, followership, and evolution: Some lessons from the past. *American Psychologist, 63*(3), 182–196.

Western, S. (2010). Eco-leadership: Towards the development of a new paradigm. In B. W. Redekop (Ed.), *Leadership for environmental sustainability* (Vol. 3, pp. 36–54). Routledge.

Whybrow, A., Turner, E., McLean, J., & Hawkins, P. (Eds.). (2023). *Ecological and climate-conscious coaching: A companion guide to evolving coaching practice*. Routledge. https://www.routledge.com/Ecological-and-Climate-Conscious-Coaching-A-Companion-Guide-to-Evolving/Whybrow-Turner-McLean-Hawkins/p/book/9780367722005

Wielkiewicz, R. M., & Stelzner, S. P. (2005). An ecological perspective on leadership theory, research, and practice. *Review of General Psychology, 9*(4), 326–341.

Wildflower, L. (2013). *The hidden history of coaching*. Open University Press.

Working Group I of the Intergovernmental Panel on Climate Change. (2021). *Technical summary*. https://www.ipcc.ch/report/ar6/wg1/downloads/report/IPCC_AR6_WGI_TS.pdf

19

DEVELOPING CLIMATE CHANGE LEADERSHIP IN ORGANISATIONS

Doug MacKie

Chapter Summary

Developing climate change leadership (CCL) in organisations has become of critical importance in closing the gap between the impact and intent of current corporate sustainability. However, whilst the qualities of effective climate change leadership remain relatively under-researched, it is challenging to know which capabilities and competencies to prioritise in terms of development. This chapter focuses on the current research in this area and outlines the foundational and complementary skills necessary for individuals, teams and organisations in their quest to develop the necessary leadership structures and capabilities for a thriving and responsible corporation in the context of a healthy and regenerative planetary environment. In addition, developing CCLs will be discussed at both the individual and programmatic levels, and the balance between inner development (mindsets, values and worldviews) and external development (purpose, structure and governance) will be discussed in pursuit of

DOI: 10.4324/9781003343011-23

a business sector that actively promotes and aligns with the Sustainable Development Goals (SDGs).

Introduction: The Context of Climate Change Leadership Development

The integration of sustainability development into leadership is not new, with the Brundtland Report in 1987 challenging leaders to envision a world that does not compromise the needs of future generations (Hajan & Kashani, 2021). The characteristics of climate change leadership (CCL) have not been systematically researched, but successful exemplars have been described and articulated in a qualitative methodology (Quinn & Dalton, 2009). However, reviewing the evolution of leadership development over the past decade since the decline of the Friedman doctrine that emphasised the purpose of corporations as vehicles for shareholder wealth creation, certain themes become apparent (Chapter 7). Firstly, the context in which leadership occurs has become paramount (McManus et al., 2018). No longer the preserve of a dyadic interaction between leader and follower independent of context, leadership has been extended and grounded in a finite naturalistic environment and intolerant of discounting of negative externalities and planetary pollution (Chapter 11). Ecological embeddedness brings with it the second critical development in leadership theory, that of stakeholder inclusion. Stakeholder inclusion inevitably democratizes the leadership process and makes ethical decision making more likely by ensuring multiple voices are heard in the strategizing and operations of contemporary corporations (Biglan, 2020; McManus et al., 2018). Thirdly and most critical, the illusion that economic growth and material consumption is the foundation of human prosperity has been broken, with significant data over the last 2 decades confirming that after a relatively small amount of affluence, any additional income has no impact on well-being and the materialistic values that are so often the concomitants of economic growth in fact undermine well-being and sustainable prosperity (Jackson, 2021; Kasser, 2016). It is self-transcendent values, a critical part of the inner dimensions that mediate sustainability actions, that are most highly correlated with individual well-being and environmental sustainability (Isham & Jackson, 2022). These critical contextual factors of naturalistic context, stakeholder inclusion and self-transcendent values provide the scaffolding on which post-conventional leadership development is built.

Theory and Concepts

In addition to the contextual factors outlined above, there are several key conceptual factors that are necessary to assimilate in expediting the development of effective climate change leaders.

Inner Versus Outer Dimensions

Firstly, the concept of inner versus outer development has gained significant traction in the field of sustainability leadership development (Ives et al., 2020; Wamsler et al., 2021). As a counterpoint to the extensive research on Sustainable Development Goals (SDGs), the concept of inner development goals has been suggested as a reason for the relative lack of progress against the 17 SDGs (Jordan, 2021). Awareness and understanding of what skills, abilities, virtues and character strengths are necessary for effective climate change leadership has lagged the identification of necessary environmental changes, resulting in a capability gap between external goals and targets and the leadership necessary to achieve them (Bridges & Eubank, 2020).

Adult Development and Maturity

The second key concept in developing effective climate change leaders is that of vertical development. Vertical development attempts to move the leadership development paradigm beyond the incremental acquisition of greater awareness, skills and capabilities and instead defines and develops different stages of adult development of increasing perspective and maturity (Berger & Fitzgerald, 2002; Kegan, 1998). This approach is similar to levelised leadership where the necessary leadership capabilities are defined by the complexity of the role in which the individual is expected to function (Lord & Hall, 2005; Mumford et al., 2007). However, adult development's focus is foremost on the individual's developmental stage and less prescriptive about which role may fit the individual's capability set. Implicit in the focus on adult development is the recognition that the development of effective climate change leaders may be a lifelong process where leaders build expertise in managing complex and wicked problems over the duration of their careers (Rooke & Tolbert, 2005). This is a fundamental challenge to a profession that is frequently organized and structured around the provision of short-term leadership courses that have minimal impact on the character development, wisdom and maturity of the participant (Hoffman, 2021).

Shared Leadership

The third significant construct in the development of effective climate change leaders is the awareness that, for some time, the leadership development field has been moving away from its historical leader centricity and embracing more collective, distributed and democratic models (Kellerman, 2021; MacKie, 2019). This has led to a renewed focus on team leadership and effectiveness (Clutterbuck et al., 2019). This appreciation of the relative abundance of leadership capability is critical for the successful development of climate change leaders as it emphasises that both leaders and followers have a critical role to play in the pursuit of sustainability corporations with the capacity to reduce consumption, support transitions and model self-transcendent and sustainable values. There is significant empirical support for the more distributed leadership approach in high-performing teams, with shared leadership explaining an additional 6% of team performance (Nicolaides et al., 2014).

Measurement

Given the number of possible models and approaches that are nested under the rubric of CCL, it is not practical here to define reliable and valid individual psychometrics for each approach. Instead, it is more effective to describe the existing methodologies by which data can be gathered and a preliminary assessment of relative capability under the relevant domain achieved.

1. *Psychometric inventories* – see Table 19.1 for a review of some of the available psychometrics for elements of CCL.

Table 19.1 Assessing Climate Change Leadership

Leadership Domain	*Psychometric*	*Key Constructs*	*Key Reference/Source*
Virtues	Values in Action	6 domains of virtues/24 character strengths including wisdom, humanity and transcendence	Peterson et al. (2009) https://www.viacharacter.org/
Values	Human Values Test	10 domains of human values divided into self-enhancing and self-transcendent	Schwartz (2012) https://www.idrlabs.com/human-values/test.php
Personality	HEXACO	Honesty, humility, emotionality extraversion, agreeableness, conscientiousness, openness to experience	Lee and Ashton (2018) www.hexaco.org
Sustainability mindset	Sustainability Mindset Indicator	Ecological worldview, systems perspective, emotional intelligence, spiritual intelligence	Rimanoczy and Klingenberg (2021) https://smindicator.com
Responsible leadership	Competency Assessment for Responsible Leadership	Stakeholder relations Ethics and values Self-awareness Systems thinking Change and innovation	Muff et al. (2020) https://carl2030.org/
Environmentally specific transformational leadership	EFTL 12-item scale	Transformational leadership with an environmental focus	Robertson (2018)
Adult development	Subject–Object Interview	Kegan's five stages of adult development, including self-authoring and self-transforming minds	Berger (2010) Kegan (1998)

2. *Individual psychological assessment* – a comprehensive assessment process that is oriented around a structured or semi-structured interview methodology (Stamoulis, 2010). This methodology inevitably relies more on the judgements of the interviewer, but the benefits are that it can be easily modified to include many of the core constructs outlined in this chapter. The downside is that, unlike with psychometrics, it does not provide the developing climate change leader with a single metric to chart their development.
3. *Multi-rater assessment* – designed to address many of the self-serving biases inherent in self-assessment by averaging the impact of assessed competencies across a number of external raters. They also provide an index of self-awareness by comparing self-assessment with that of the average of all others, known as *self–other alignment* (Sosik & Jung, 2011).

Practice: Methods, Techniques and Applications

Following the theme of this book, the development of climate change leaders can be usefully divided into foundation factors like character and values and the transition of contemporary leadership models like transformational leadership into concepts that have a more environmental focus; for example, environmentally specific transformational leadership and progressions, where new and innovative models of leadership have been developed precisely because the complexity and sophistication of wicked problems like climate change have exposed the limitations of contemporary leadership development.

Foundations

The foundations of sustainable and effective leadership have been conceptualized in a number of ways. Much of the inner dimension including mindsets, values and virtues sits at the foundational level (MacKie, 2021; Chapter 6). Also included here are an awareness of the cognitive biases that are so effective in reducing the intensity of the perception of climate change (Chapter 3) and an appreciation of the evolutionary origins of these cognitive biases that can mediate the temporal myopia and excessive positivity that undermine a commitment to transformational change (Chapter 5).

The core components of a sustainability mindset have been expertly covered in Chapter 6, but the development of prosocial and ecological orientated values is also essential for the developing climate change leader. Values tend to describe areas of personal importance but lack the inherent moral goodness of virtues. This is an issue because values predict behaviour, and materialistic values are not only destructive for an individual's mental health (Kasser, 2016) but also correlate with reduced environmental concerns and unsustainable lifestyles (Isham & Jackson, 2022). The cultivation of prosocial and sustainable values is consequently essential for both individual and planetary health (Atkins et al., 2019; Ewest, 2021).

The cultivation of character strengths or virtues has also received significant attention in the leadership development literature (Crossan et al., 2013; Niemiec, 2013). However, character strengths, like all elements of character, are subject to the laws of proportionality where the titration of each virtue sits within the golden mean. Excessive utilisation of any virtue leads to non-monotonic effects and counterproductive excess (MacKie, 2016b). Teaching techniques such as role-plays and experiential learning do seem to affect character development and increase moral awareness (Crossan et al., 2013). However, the converse is also true, with MBA students reporting an increase in self-oriented values after attending a 2-year program (Krishnan, 2008). The negative impact of attending further education in business and economics on the student's values and character is one of the many reasons for the significant contemporary attempts underway to fundamentally reform management and leadership education; for example, Principles of Responsible Management Education. The link between virtuous behaviour and sustainability has been comprehensively summarised by Corral-Verdugo et al. (2015) and includes humility, self-regulation and equity.

Finally, the concept of self-regulation is a core component of the foundations of CCL, especially when mediated through the process of mindfulness meditation. Self-regulation is a critical element of the inner dimension, and mindfulness has been recently linked to enhanced compassion for others, including the environment (Wamsler & Brink, 2018). Mindfulness may also be the antidote to cognitive bias and reflexive consumption through its promotion of non-reactivity and acting with awareness (K. W. Brown & Kasser, 2005).

Transitions

The fundamental orientation of leadership models that sit in the transition domain is their repurposing for the age of sustainability. Transformational leadership is one of the most researched and applied models of contemporary leadership (Sosik & Jung, 2011). However, it has been subject to a number of criticisms, including an excessive focus on individual agency and being environmentally agnostic when it comes to the context in which transformational leadership is applied (Tourish, 2013). Consequently, transformational leadership has recently been repurposed with an additional focus on environmental concerns and ethical behaviour that aims to cultivate environmental and prosocial values within the developing leader (Chapter 9).

Ethical decision making is a core construct in CCL and one that becomes increasingly prevalent and complex as leaders move through the stages of adult development (B. C. Brown, 2013; Day et al., 2008). Ethical decision making can be enhanced by both traditional training methods through the use of case studies and experiential methods where role-playing in ethically challenging business scenarios can simulate the application of virtues and character strengths in real world scenarios (Crossan et al., 2013). One of the challenges of virtue-based leadership development is that many of the contemporary assessment models have been developed in the absence of environmental and sustainability challenges. The VIA Survey, for example, is composed of six virtues, none of which align specifically with environmentalism or sustainability. There is a compelling case for extending these inventories to include stewardship and sustainability (MacKie, 2021).

Responsible leadership (RL) is another conceptual model that is being actively repurposed for the climate crisis (Chapter 10). RL emphasises both the interconnectivity of all living systems and the importance of stakeholder inclusion to ensure no group is disadvantaged by a company's activities. RL has been consolidated into the Globally Responsible Leadership Initiative (2023), which defined RL as "the global exercise of ethical, values-based leadership in the pursuit of economic and societal progress and sustainable development'. The emphasis on values and ethical decision making was then extended to include respectful stakeholder relationships (Muff, 2013; Muff et al., 2020). RL also combines the inner dimensions outlined above, with its focus on increased awareness and reflective capacity. RL has recently been operationalised into stakeholder relations, ethics and values, self-awareness, systems thinking and change and innovation (Muff et al., 2020). Each of these domains is then broken down into the necessary knowledge, skills and attitudes for their application. Elsewhere, other advocates of the approach have emphasised the ongoing transformation of character and the need for compassion, humility and restraint in responsible leaders (Kempster & Carroll, 2016). Case studies of the developmental trajectory of responsible leaders often point to particular crucible experiences that have been formative in the development of critical components (Blakeley & Higgs, 2014). Place-based leadership and managed retreats are the latest iteration and extension of the RL domain (Kempster & Jackson, 2021).

Progressions

The focus of those models that sit within the progressions domain of CCL is primarily the innovation and development of models capable of positively influencing complex and wicked problems that are beyond the scope of contemporary leadership models. These include models of vertical development, maturity, systems thinking and adaptation to a dynamic and uncertain ecological context.

There is a general consensus in the adult development literature that the majority of leaders do not in their own ontogeny reach the necessary levels of maturity to comprehend and manage complex and systemic problems like climate change, with some estimates suggesting that only 1% do (Rooke, 2018; Rooke & Torbert, 2005). How to accelerate the development of transformation with the necessary maturity to manage complex challenges is a matter of significant debate, but individualised leadership coaching rather than generic training or programmatic work appears to be the most effective pathway to catalyse these types of complex development (Lewin et al., 2019). A number of stages of adult development have been suggested, from the instrumental with its focus on individual desires and needs to the self-transforming with its focus on ethical development and societal progress. Moving between these stages is a process known as subject–object shift where what the individual leader was subject to becomes object or apparent, similar to the process of making underlying assumptions explicit (Kegan & Lahey, 2009). Individualised coaching, with its capacity to titrate development to the specific stage of the leader, is the ideal mechanism for making the underlying assumptions of the coachee more explicit in the context of directive and normative development (Di-Girolamo, 2022; Pannell, 2021).

Cannon et al. (2015) have suggested a competency-based progression towards a more self-transforming leadership approach including humility, commitment to the mission, perspective including the balcony view and seeing systems, curiosity and expertise beyond their role, authentic and reflexive, inspiring to followers and capacity for collaborative innovation. Boiral et al. (2018) found that the higher the stage of adult development in a leader, the more like they were to engage in organisational citizenship behaviours for the environment and that these were mediated by greater altruism and collaboration typical of the post-conventional stages of development.

Systems leadership is another concept that sits in the progressions domain (Chapter 14). Systems leadership takes its inspiration from the ecological perspective by emphasising both the interconnectedness of living things and a broader perspective that includes cross-boundary collaboration and intergenerational empathy (Senge et al., 2015). To what extent these qualities are products of adult development rather than processes to be acquired through targeted leadership development is a question for future research. The broader perspective comes with the ethical awareness that sustainable prosperity now must not compromise the well-being of other stakeholders or future generations (Middlebrooks et al., 2009).

The majority of research on developing CCL looks at the behaviours, values and competencies necessary to mitigate the destructive effects of climate change, including sea level rise and coastal erosion. Adaptation leadership is defined by its application but still contains familiar components of CCL, including complex and ethical decision making (Siders & Pierce, 2021) and visioning the future (Nalau & Cobb, 2022). Given the complexity of adaptation to climate change, it is no surprise that different types of leadership have been applied to different stages of adaptation (Vignola et al., 2017) and by function from policy to connectivity and sustainability (Meijerink & Stiller, 2013). These internal adaptations to context mirror the external stages that organisations progress through from weak to strong sustainability (Chapter 12).

The Loci of CCL Development

So far we have primarily been focused on the development of the climate change leader, but this emphasis is challenged by both the general trend for more distributed forms of leadership (MacKie, 2019) and by the recognition that both the teams in which leaders operate and the cultural context of their corporation are significant determinants of leadership effectiveness (MacKie, 2016a).

Climate Change Leadership in Teams

Many of the existing conceptual models of high-performing teams (Hawkins, 2021; Wageman et al., 2008) can also be repurposed for the age of sustainability. High-performing teams are assessed by their structure, process and models of leadership. Wageman et al. (2008) developed a model of the structure of high-performing teams that consisted of three essential and three enabling factors. Of the three essential factors, compelling purpose is by far the most relevant for the development of climate change capability. Once a sustainable purpose is articulated, the remaining two essential factors, a real inter-dependent team and the right people, can be orchestrated around this. When the three essential factors are in place, the three enabling factors can be developed. The enabling structure component includes both task design, which, again, can be developed around meaningful components of the sustainable purpose, and team norms including transparency, commitment and participation. Norms can be both injunctive (will adaptive climate behaviour be valued and approved by others?) and descriptive (are others behaving like climate change leaders?), and both correlate significantly with climate adaptation behaviour (van Valkengoed & Steg, 2019). The second enabling factor is having a supportive organisational context, which includes alignment with purposeful and self-transcendent values and the provision of the necessary education to develop the team's climate leadership. Once these five factors are in place, the final element of team coaching can be introduced. There is no doubt that a climate-aware coach who is prepared to be directive and prescriptive in terms of the alignment of internal and external sustainable goals will assist the team's evolution and enhance its effectiveness (DiGirolamo, 2022).

Team process is the description of the behaviours that high-performing teams engage in to be effective (Hawkins, 2021). Team process also includes the importance of purpose or the 'why' the team has been commissioned. Analogous to structural models, a sustainable purpose here will help catalyse the team's engagement and impact on broader environmental and social metrics. Once the team clarifies its purpose and aligns strengths to individual roles, the co-creation or how they work together will also offer the opportunity for the cultivation of sustainable values and norms. Informal roles such as a sustainability champion can also ensure that the team's development is aligned with its sustainable purpose. Teams also need to connect with their stakeholders, and this provides the opportunity to include communities, the environment and other key stakeholders in alignment with the principles of responsible leadership (Hawkins & Turner, 2019).

Team leadership is invariably distributed, shared and collaborative in nature to fully utilise the strengths, talents and capabilities of its members (MacKie, 2019). There is significant empirical support for this approach, with studies reporting that shared leadership is a meaningful predictor of team effectiveness and that collective approaches explain addition variance over other leadership approaches (Barnett & Weidenfeller, 2016). Distributed models of leadership are the antidote to individual exceptionalism and ensure that egalitarianism prevails over more autocratic styles. The consequent plurality of voices safeguards against the promotion of self-enhancing agendas, and the distribution of responsibility ensures that those whose informal role includes sustainability will always have a platform and influence on the leadership team (MacKie, 2019).

Cultivating a Culture of CCL

Organisational culture has been described as the 'tacit social order' where the patterns of beliefs and shared expectations are found (Groysberg et al., 2018, p. 48). Schein and Schein (2018) suggested that the role of culture was to solve the problems of 'external adaptation and internal integration' (p. 45). Organisational cultures need to adapt urgently to the changing environmental circumstances in which they function. In a similar way to high-performing teams which have their own culture, organisations need to promote behaviour aligned with the norms, rules and practices of sustainability. Leadership has a significant role in the development of organisation culture, but its role is mediated by the presence of the need for change and the capability and maturity of the relevant leaders (Hsieh et al., 2018). If these external and internal enabling conditions are present, it then requires a precipitating factor and a triggering event to effect change. Climate change is clearly one such event that can be both an external enabler of cultural change and a proximate condition. In terms of the types of organisational culture most conducive to sustainability concerns, Groysberg et al. (2018) outlined eight types of culture ranging along two axes of interdependence and flexibility. Purpose- and caring-orientated cultures most closely aligned with the values of sustainability are high on both these criteria.

Sustainable Goal Setting

The ultimate purpose of CCL is to acquire and enhance the capabilities necessary to make meaningful progress on the external criteria of sustainable prosperity such as the SDGs (Dahlmann et al., 2019). Linking leadership development to the SDGs is a useful metric to ensure that activities are meaningfully connected with relevant and valid external criteria. Sustainable goal setting involves a process of enlightenment, encouragement and enablement (Nowack, 2017). Enlightenment involves raising awareness of character strengths and virtues, whilst encouragement involves building self-efficacy and other necessary skills required to maintain motivation in the face of overwhelming complexity. Enablement involves supporting adherence to goals and maintaining gains made. Not all of the SDGs are equally attended to by corporations, but the following have particular resonance for corporate leaders:

- SDG 3: employee well-being, anxiety and depression; especially 3.4 (promotion of mental health)
- SDG 4: education and lifelong learning, including business schools and climate change education; especially 4.7 (promotion of sustainable development)
- SDG 6: sustainable management of water; especially 6.6 (protect and restore water-related ecosystems)

- SDG 7: affordable and clean energy, including electrification; especially 7.2 (increasing renewable energy in the global mix)
- SDG 8: decent work and economic growth; especially 8.4 (resource efficiency and decoupling growth from environmental degradation)
- SDG 9: industry innovation and infrastructure; especially 9.5 (research and development)
- SDG 10: reduce inequalities; especially 10.2 (empower social, economic and political inclusion)
- SDG 11: Sustainable cities and communities; especially 11.4 (safeguard the world's cultural and natural heritage)
- SDG 12: responsible consumption and production; especially 12.6 (integrate sustainability into the reporting cycle)
- SDG 13: Climate action, waste treatment, clean air and biodiversity; especially 13.3 (enhance mitigation and adaptation capacity)
- SDG 15: life on land; especially 15.5 (preserve natural habitats and prevent extinction)
- SDG 16: peace, justice and strong institutions; especially 16.7 (enhance participatory and representative decision making at all levels)

Corporate activity is not done in isolation but is predicated on the natural resource base of SDGs 13, 14 and 15. The totality of the SDGs also reminds us that each alone in isolation is insufficient for sustainable prosperity. Six transformations are necessary to achieve the SDGs (Sachs et al., 2019), only one of which is related to energy decarbonization, the most common focus of many contemporary corporate sustainability programs. The gap frame methodology (Muff et al., 2017) has been specifically developed to assist organisations in developing the SDGs into specific indicators of organisational and societal progress. These, when combined with the inner development goals, offer a powerful synergy for organisational change.

Conclusion

Climate change leadership development is complex, multi-faceted and challenging to conventional models of development, which have tended to focus on the development of singular domains or capabilities. One way to reduce this complexity is to attempt to deduce patterns in the data and consider the overall system rather than fragmented components of leadership capability.

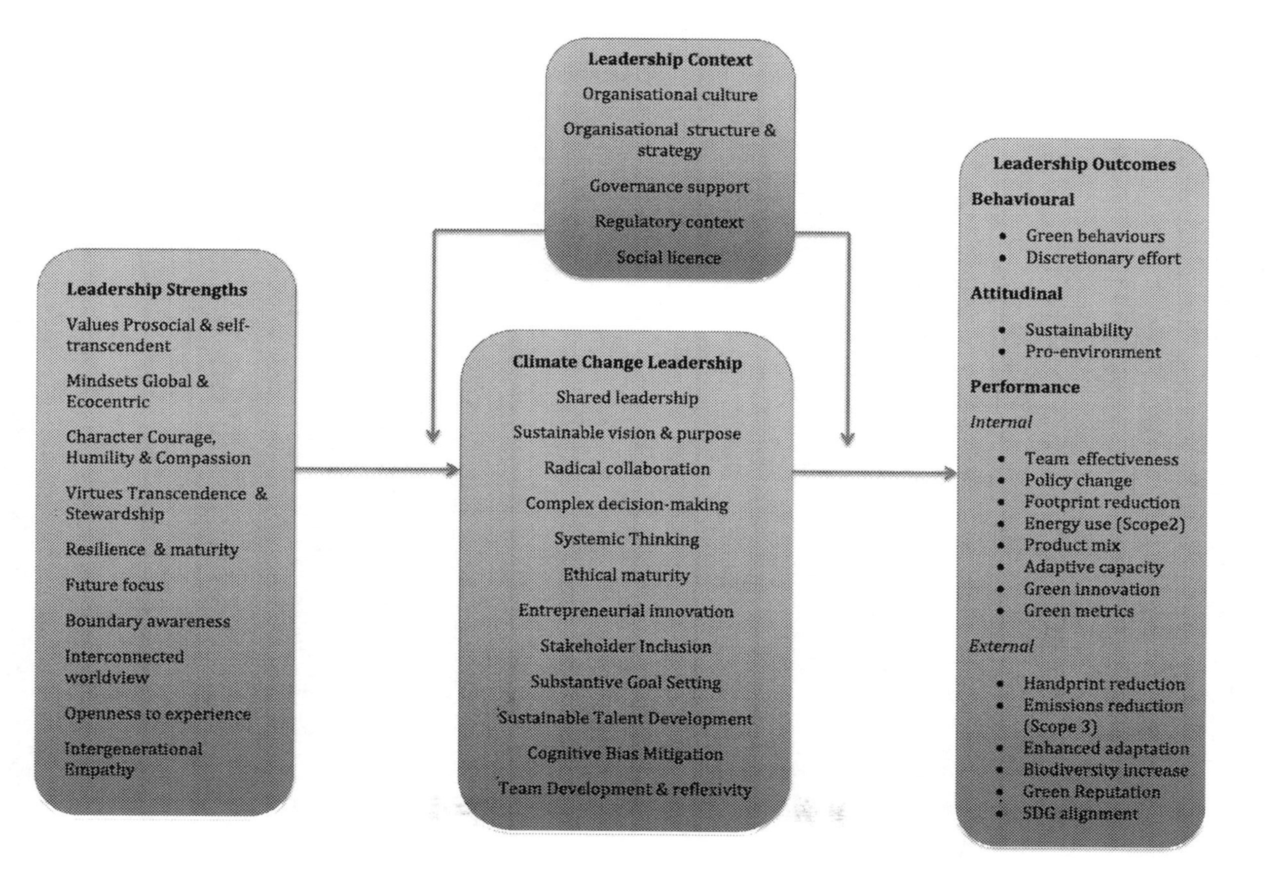

Figure 19.1 Potential Mediators and Moderator of Climate Change Leadership in Organisations

Figure 19.1 outlines a model of CCL development that attempts to incorporate the foundational aspects, including character and values development, as well as transitional and progressive components, including systems thinking and complex decision making. This occurs in a social and organisational context that can moderate the effectiveness of any development process. The critical consequences of this development are positive environmental outcomes at the attitudinal and behavioural levels as well as performance criteria that can be internal, including policy development, and external, including impact on biodiversity. Future research will determine the criticality of each component, but the research base on which many models are transitioning to a greater focus on sustainability is compelling enough to warrant the urgent and immediate focus on developing CCL to support the ongoing evolution towards more sustainable and regenerative organisations.

Discussion Points

- Outline some of the key theoretical developments that have influenced the evolution of CCL.
- What are some of the challenges of assessing CCL, and how might they be overcome?
- What are some of the foundational, transitional and progressive models of CCL that can inform its development?
- How does sustainable goal setting support the development of CCL?

Suggested Reading

Beehner, C. G. (2020). *System leadership for sustainability*. Routledge.

Muff, K. (2018). *Five superpowers for co-creators: How change makers and business can achieve the Sustainable Development Goals*. Routledge.

Redekop, B. W., Gallagher, D. R., & Satterwhite, R. (Eds.). (2018). *Innovation in environmental leadership: Critical perspectives*. Routledge.

References

Atkins, P. W., Wilson, D. S., & Hayes, S. C. (2019). *Prosocial: Using evolutionary science to build productive, equitable, and collaborative groups*. New Harbinger.

Barnett, R. C., & Weidenfeller, N. K. (2016). Shared leadership and team performance. *Advances in Developing Human Resources, 18*(3), 334–351.

Berger, J. G. (2010). Using the subject–object interview to promote and assess self-authorship. In M. B. B. Magolda, P. S. Meszaros, & E. G. Creamer (Eds.), *Development and assessment of self-authorship: Exploring the concept across cultures* (pp. 245–264). Taylor & Francis.

Berger, J. G., & Fitzgerald, C. (2002). Leadership and complexity of mind. In J. G. Berger & C. Fitzgerald (Eds.), *Executive coaching: Practices and perspectives* (pp. 27–57). Davies-Black Publications.

Biglan, A. (2020). *Rebooting capitalism: How we can forge a society that works for everyone.* Values to Action.

Blakeley, K., & Higgs, M. (2014). Responsible leadership development – Crucible experiences and power relationships in a global professional services firm. *Human Resource Development International, 17*(5), 560–576.

Boiral, O., Raineri, N., & Talbot, D. (2018). Managers' citizenship behaviors for the environment: A developmental perspective. *Journal of Business Ethics, 149*, 395–409.

Bridges, T., & Eubank, D. (2020). *Leading sustainably: The path to sustainable business and how the SDGs changed everything.* Routledge.

Brown, B. C. (2013). *The future of leadership for conscious capitalism. A white paper.* MetaIntegral Associates.

Brown, K. W., & Kasser, T. (2005). Are psychological and ecological well-being compatible? The role of values, mindfulness, and lifestyle. *Social Indicators Research, 74*, 349–368.

Cannon, S., Morrow-Fox, M., & Metcalf, M. (2015). The strategist competency model: The future of leadership development. In M. Sowcik, A. C. Andenoro, M. McNutt, & S. E. Murphy (Eds.), *Leadership 2050: Critical challenges, key contexts, and emerging trends* (pp. 176–189). Emerald.

Clutterbuck, C., Gannon, J., Hayes, S., Iordanou, I., Lowe, K., & MacKie, D. (Eds.). (2019). *The practitioner's handbook of team coaching.* Routledge.

Corral-Verdugo, V., Tapia-Fonllem, C., & Ortiz-Valdez, A. (2015). On the relationship between character strengths and sustainable behavior. *Environment and Behavior, 47*(8), 877–901.

Crossan, M., Mazutis, D., Seijts, G., & Gandz, J. (2013). Developing leadership character in business programs. *Academy of Management Learning & Education, 12*(2), 285–305.

Dahlmann, F., Branicki, L., & Brammer, S. (2019). Managing carbon aspirations: The influence of corporate climate change targets on environmental performance. *Journal of Business Ethics, 158*(1), 1–24.

Day, D. V., Harrison, M. M., & Halpin, S. M. (2008). *An integrative approach to leader development: Connecting adult development, identity, and expertise.* Routledge.

DiGirolamo, J. A. (2022). Coaching for sustainability. In S. Greif, H. Möller, W. Scholl, J. Passmore, & F. Müller (Eds.), *International handbook of evidence-based coaching: Theory, research and practice* (pp. 163–172). Springer International.

Ewest, T. (2021). The prosocial leadership development process and its applications to business and education. In A. A. Ritz & I. Rimanoczy (Eds.), *Sustainability mindset and transformative leadership: A multidisciplinary perspective* (pp. 93–115). Springer Nature.

Globally Responsible Leadership Initiative. (2023). *Guiding principles.* https://grli.org/about/global-responsibility/#guiding-principles

Groysberg, B., Lee, J., Price, J., & Cheng, J. (2018). The leader's guide to corporate culture. *Harvard Business Review, 96*(1), 44–52.

Hajian, M., & Kashani, S. J. (2021). Evolution of the concept of sustainability. From Brundtland Report to Sustainable Development Goals. In C. M. Hussain (Ed.), *Sustainable resource management* (pp. 1–24). Elsevier.

Hawkins, P. (2021). *Leadership team coaching: Developing collective transformational leadership* (4th ed.). Kogan Page.

Hawkins, P., & Turner, E. (2019). *Systemic coaching: Delivering value beyond the individual.* Routledge.

Hoffman, A. J. (2021). Business education as if people and the planet really matter. *Strategic Organization, 19*(3), 513–525.

Hsieh, N. H., Lange, B., Rodin, D., & Wolf-Bauwens, M. L. (2018). Getting clear on corporate culture: conceptualisation, measurement and operationalisation. *Journal of the British Academy, 6*(1), 155–184.

Isham, A., & Jackson, T. (2022). Finding flow: Exploring the potential for sustainable fulfilment. *The Lancet Planetary Health, 6*(1), e66–e74.

Ives, C. D., Freeth, R., & Fischer, J. (2020). Inside-out sustainability: The neglect of inner worlds. *Ambio, 49*, 208–217.

Jackson, T. (2021). *Post growth: Life after capitalism.* John Wiley & Sons.

Jordan, T. (2021). *Inner development goals – Background, method and the IDG framework.* Growth That Matters AB. https://static1.squarespace.com/static/600d80b3387b98582a60354a/t/61aa2f96dfd3fb39c4fc4283/1638543258249/211201_IDG_Report_Full.pdf

Kasser, T. (2016). Materialistic values and goals. *Annual Review of Psychology, 67*, 489–514.

Kegan, R. (1998). *In over our heads: The mental demands of modern life.* Harvard University Press.

Kegan, R., & Lahey, L. L. (2009). *Immunity to change: How to overcome it and unlock potential in yourself and your organization.* Harvard Business Review Press.

Kellerman, B. (2021). Introduction on systems approaches to leadership. *Journal of Leadership Studies, 15*(2), 36–38.

Kempster, S., & Carroll, B. (Eds.). (2016). *Responsible leadership: Realism and romanticism.* Routledge.

Kempster, S., & Jackson, B. (2021). Leadership for what, why, for whom and where? A responsibility perspective. *Journal of Change Management, 21*(1), 45–65.

Krishnan, V. R. (2008). Impact of MBA education on students' values: Two longitudinal studies. *Journal of Business Ethics, 83*, 233–246.

Lee, K., & Ashton, M. C. (2018). Psychometric properties of the HEXACO-100. *Assessment, 25*(5), 543–556.

Lewin, L. O., McManamon, A., Stein, M. T., & Chen, D. T. (2019). Minding the form that transforms: Using Kegan's model of adult development to understand personal and professional identity formation in medicine. *Academic Medicine, 94*(9), 1299–1304.

Lord, R. G., & Hall, R. J. (2005). Identity, deep structure and the development of leadership skill. *The Leadership Quarterly, 16*(4), 591–615.

MacKie, D. (2016a). Positive leadership development. In L. G. Oades, M. F. Steger, D. E. Fave, & J. Passmore (Eds.), *The Wiley Blackwell handbook of the psychology of positivity and strengths-based approaches at work* (pp. 297–316). Wiley.

MacKie, D. (2016b). *Strength-based leadership coaching in organizations: An evidence-based guide to positive leadership development.* Kogan Page.

MacKie, D. (2019). Shared leadership and team coaching. In C. Clutterbuck, J. Gannon, S. Hayes, I. Iordanou, K. Lowe, & D. MacKie (Eds), *The practitioner's handbook of team coaching* (pp. 53–62). Routledge.

MacKie, D. (2021). Strength-based coaching and sustainability leadership. In W. A. Smith, I. Boniwell, & S. Green (Eds.), *Positive psychology coaching in the workplace* (pp. 375–396). Springer.

McManus, R. M., Ward, S. J., & Perry, A. K. (Eds.). (2018). *Ethical leadership: a primer.* Edward Elgar.

Meijerink, S., & Stiller, S. (2013). What kind of leadership do we need for climate adaptation? A framework for analyzing leadership objectives, functions, and tasks in climate change adaptation. *Environment and Planning C: Government and Policy, 31*(2), 240–256.

Middlebrooks, A., Miltenberger, L., Tweedy, J., Newman, G., & Follman, J. (2009). Developing a sustainability ethic in leaders. *Journal of Leadership Studies, 3*(2), 31–43.

Muff, K. (2013). Developing globally responsible leaders in business schools: A vision and transformational practice for the journey ahead. *The Journal of Management Development, 32*(5), 487–507.

Muff, K., Kapalka, A., & Dyllick, T. (2017). The gap frame – Translating the SDGs into relevant national grand challenges for strategic business opportunities. *The International Journal of Management Education, 15*(2), 363–383.

Muff, K., Liechti, A., & Dyllick, T. (2020). How to apply responsible leadership theory in practice: A competency tool to collaborate on the Sustainable Development Goals. *Corporate Social Responsibility and Environmental Management, 27*(5), 2254–2274.

Mumford, T. V., Campion, M. A., & Morgeson, F. P. (2007). The leadership skills strataplex: Leadership skill requirements across organizational levels. *The Leadership Quarterly, 18*(2), 154–166.

Nalau, J., & Cobb, G. (2022). The strengths and weaknesses of future visioning approaches for climate change adaptation: A review. *Global Environmental Change, 74*, 102527.

Nicolaides, V. C., LaPort, K. A., Chen, T. R., Tomassetti, A. J., Weis, E. J., Zaccaro, S. J., & Cortina, J. M. (2014). The shared leadership of teams: A meta-analysis of proximal, distal, and moderating relationships. *The Leadership Quarterly, 25*(5), 923–942.

Niemiec, R. M. (2013). *Mindfulness and character strengths*. Hogrefe.

Nowack, K. (2017). Facilitating successful behavior change: Beyond goal setting to goal flourishing. *Consulting Psychology Journal: Practice and Research, 69*(3), 153.

Pannell, B. (2021). Adult development and positive psychology coaching. In W. A. Smith, I. Boniwell, & S. Green (Eds.), *Positive psychology coaching in the workplace* (pp. 357–373). Springer.

Peterson, C., Stephens, J. P., Park, N., Lee, F., & Seligman, M. E. (2009). *Strengths of character and work*. Oxford University Press.

Quinn, L., & Dalton, M. (2009). Leading for sustainability: Implementing the tasks of leadership. *Corporate Governance: The International Journal of Business in Society, 9*(1), 21–38.

Rimanoczy, I., & Klingenberg, B. (2021). The Sustainability Mindset Indicator: A personal development tool. *Journal of Management for Global Sustainability, 9*(1).

Robertson, J. L. (2018). The nature, measurement and nomological network of environmentally specific transformational leadership. *Journal of Business Ethics, 151*(4), 961–975.

Rooke, D. (2018). Transformational leadership capabilities for medical leaders. *BMJ Leader, 2*(1).

Rooke, D., & Torbert, W. R. (2005). Seven transformations of leadership. *Harvard Business Review, 83*(4), 66–76.

Sachs, J. D., Schmidt-Traub, G., Mazzucato, M., Messner, D., Nakicenovic, N., & Rockström, J. (2019). Six transformations to achieve the sustainable development goals. *Nature Sustainability, 2*(9), 805–814.

Schein, E. H., & Schein, P. A. (2018). *Humble leadership: The power of relationships, openness, and trust*. Berrett-Koehler.

Schwartz, S. H. (2012). An overview of the Schwartz theory of basic values. *Online Readings in Psychology and Culture, 2*(1), 2307–0919.

Senge, P., Hamilton, H., & Kania, J. (2015). The dawn of system leadership. *Stanford Social Innovation Review, 13*(1), 27–33.

Siders, A. R., & Pierce, A. L. (2021). Deciding how to make climate change adaptation decisions. *Current Opinion in Environmental Sustainability, 52*, 1–8.

Sosik, J. J., & Jung, D. (2011). *Full range leadership development: Pathways for people, profit and planet*. Psychology Press.

Stamoulis, D. (2010). *Senior executive assessment: A key to responsible corporate governance*. John Wiley & Sons.

Tourish, D. (2013). *The dark side of transformational leadership: A critical perspective*. Routledge.

van Valkengoed, A. M., & Steg, L. (2019). Meta-analyses of factors motivating climate change adaptation behaviour. *Nature Climate Change, 9*(2), 158–163.

Vignola, R., Leclerc, G., Morales, M., & Gonzalez, J. (2017). Leadership for moving the climate change adaptation agenda from planning to action. *Current Opinion in Environmental Sustainability, 26*, 84–89.

Wageman, R., Nunes, D. A., Burruss, J. A., & Hackman, J. R. (2008). *Senior leadership teams: What it takes to make them great*. Harvard Business Review Press.

Wamsler, C., & Brink, E. (2018). Mindsets for sustainability: Exploring the link between mindfulness and sustainable climate adaptation. *Ecological Economics, 151*, 55–61.

Wamsler, C., Osberg, G., Osika, W., Herndersson, H., & Mundaca, L. (2021). Linking internal and external transformation for sustainability and climate action: Towards a new research and policy agenda. *Global Environmental Change, 71*, 102373.

20

CASE STUDY

THE ROLE OF LEADERSHIP AND ENABLING CHANGE – SPECIFIC TO THE CLUSTER AND ENERGY TRANSITION

Kevin Reeves and Rik Irons-Mclean

Industry Need

Climate change represents significant economic risk, with the 2006 *Stern Review* (Nordhaus, 2006) highlighting a 5% annual loss of gross domestic product from the impacts of severe weather and climate-related challenges. The last 5 years have seen many of the *Stern Review* predictions come to fruition, with severe drought, flooding and hurricanes reaching record levels. These challenges create a detrimental impact on economic performance. Biodiversity and other aligned sustainability development goals require governments and business leaders globally to take concerted action. Clean energy is a fundamental pathway to a sustainable economy, and decarbonising industry, which collectively equates to two thirds of the net zero journey, is a key priority. Realising the UK's net zero policy ambitions requires systemic change to overcome significant challenges, where new approaches to leadership are fundamental.

DOI: 10.4324/9781003343011-24

Challenges

Faced with this vast challenge, the UK Government established a programmatic approach to decarbonise heavy industries to reduce the risk of introducing new technologies. This core enabler of the UK's net zero strategy (HM Government, 2021) led to the formation of industrial clusters located in the UK's main industrial regions. Initially formed to decarbonise coal-fired power stations, the model evolved to incorporate exploration of various strategic technologies: hydrogen, carbon capture, utilisation and storage (CCUS) and renewables (Department for Business, Energy & Industrial Strategy, 2021). Zero Carbon Humber, the largest of the industrial clusters, requires leaders to consider future impacts of climate change, such as the potential for £27.5 billion in carbon taxes by 2040 and the need to protect 55,000 jobs in heavy industries within the region.

Three key enablers to this model have emerged:

- **Turning ideation into action:** The UK Government recognises that individual organisations acting alone will not achieve UK strategic policy, nor unlock required investment for regional growth. Government investment is prioritised to catalyse clean energy technology creation and adoption only where collaborative leadership is witnessed, with collaborative industry bids into cluster funding opportunities encouraged.
- **Data sharing:** To accelerate the development of new markets including hydrogen and CCUS, leaders are required to make decisions with little historical evidence. Access to data collated through scientific means can provide leaders a foundation for decision making and support ongoing governance in collaborative ecosystems.
- **Internal profit vs. broader impact:** Modern leaders need to consider more than just financial success, particularly where public investment is provided. Social and environmental value are fundamental measures of success to support corporate environmental, social and governance goals. In collaborative ventures like the clusters, this also requires consideration of partners. The World Economic Forum and Accenture describe multi-stakeholder collaboration as essential to align on cluster-level goals, enabling the development and implementation of roadmaps to net zero (Accenture, 2021).

Personas and Leadership

Overcoming the challenges and unlocking the three key enablers require a different approach to leadership, one that combines the driver of commercial success with the need to consider environmental and social value. Taking account of partner needs can create tension when managing internal and external stakeholders, such as government and shareholders who have differing expectations.

The modern leader must manage these tensions through articulation of shared benefits, whilst protecting the commercial interests of multiple stakeholders, particularly relevant in industrial clusters which combine the demand, supply and governance actors within a collaborative environment. Competitive advantage must be married with public good outcomes and aligned to sustainability goals for the cluster to succeed. Taking Zero Carbon Humber (ZCH) as an example, there are 15 organisations across the value chain that compete in terms of access to government funding and market share. At the same time, the ZCH partners need to collaborate to reduce investment risk and deliver new hydrogen and CCUS technology into the existing energy market. Companies like Equinor and SSE are partnering in the Humber to accelerate offshore wind for use in green hydrogen production. Likewise, Centrica and Equinor have agreed to form a co-operative to develop a low carbon hydrogen plant in Easington as another part of the ZCH value chain. Combined with off-takers such as British Steel and SSE's Keadby power stations, the ZCH ecosystem represents an outstanding example of industry leaders collaborating across the value chain to unlock business value.

Another facet for consideration is the need to democratise leadership; such is the scale of the challenges we face that it is imperative for businesses to empower employees to take a lead. Highly collaborative and networked organisations challenge traditional hierarchical business structures (Moldoveanu & Narayandas, 2019), where cross-organisational 'enterprises' are demonstrating value in UK infrastructure. This highly collaborative approach, as outlined in the Infrastructure Client Groups Project 13 initiative, is being implemented across major programmes to reduce cost and risk and align parties in terms of outcomes (Project13, 2016).

Opportunity

Early adopters tend to be those organisations willing to embrace innovation and demonstrate industry leadership. The industrial clusters can be considered collaborative ventures enacting through early adopter networks, where we see some key themes emerge:

- **Systemic thinking:** Hydrogen and CCUS are new technologies that must integrate with the wider energy system and need careful consideration. Concerns around energy system flexibility and market reforms remain, and the introduction of new technologies risks burdening an already complex picture.
- **Digital as an enabler:** This complexity can be managed using modern digital approaches, such as the use of digital twins to model and simulate scenarios before build and during operations and artificial intelligence to help simplify complex systems and present relevant and useful insight that puts the human back in the loop. As an example, early digital twin demonstrators for ZCH (Figure 20.1) have focused on economic modelling, to help the various partners understand the impact on the value chain as hydrogen demand changes. Importantly, supply chain analysis using digital twin methodologies is helping identify key suppliers, supply constraints over time, gaps in supply chain capability and resilience. Given the ambitious UK targets, analysis of the energy at a national scale has become an imperative, with potential for the ZCH foundation to evolve into a national solution hosted by the Advanced Manufacturing Research Centre, an academic partner in ZCH.
- **Stakeholder engagement and collaboration:** Leaders in ZCH need to engage with a broad range of stakeholders, such as policymakers, local authorities, key interest groups and the general public. This is a vital part of the planning and consent process, with the added complexity of new, largely mis-understood technologies. Leaders must articulate the expectation that these technologies support the wider net zero agenda but also protect local environments and deliver social value within the region.
- **Next-gen workforce, local regeneration:** A key driver for social value is the creation of new, higher value jobs within the local region (Gardiner, 2021), a focus in the Humber region as part of wider regeneration plans under the government's levelling up agenda. This next-generation workforce needs to be armed with the digital skills needed to work within a more integrated energy market, underpinned by a digital foundation and leveraging leading-edge artificial intelligence capability to manage complexity (Microsoft, 2020).

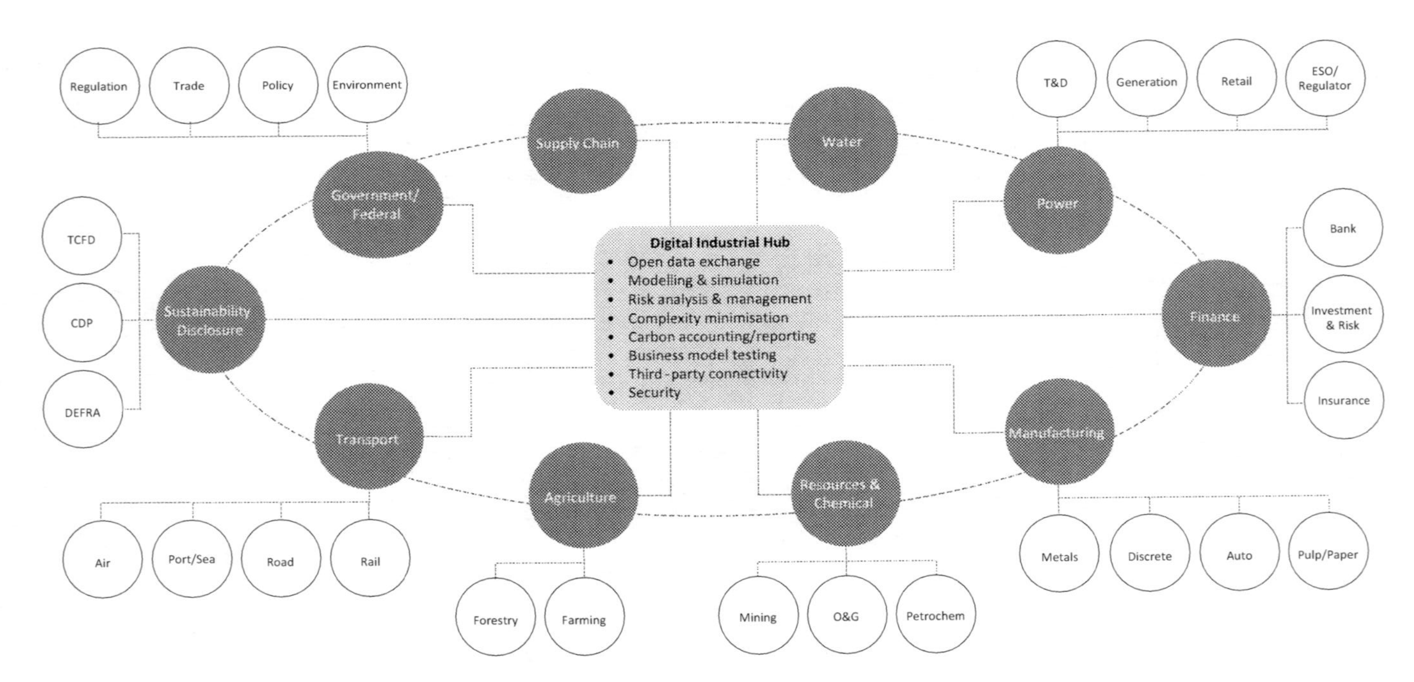

Figure 20.1 Example Digital Enablers in an Industrial Cluster at Zero Carbon Humber

- **Resilience – local supply chain model and workforce:** The next-generation workforce requirement extends into the supply chain, which must evolve and mature as the market develops. As clients drive internal intelligence, there is a risk of leaving their supply chains behind; therefore, concerted efforts are needed to drive strategic alignment across diverse ecosystems.
- **Net new business models:** The evolution of ecosystems fosters an environment for success, with alliancing in UK infrastructure becoming a dominant model across transport, water and defence. Whilst the energy market still relies heavily on traditional engineering, procurement and construction contracts, there is recognition that alliancing presents opportunity in pace of delivery and reduction of risk. The clusters model develops this further by encouraging collaborative models at the industry level, with the potential to develop a new standard for accelerated market development, leveraging technology.

Recommendation

Delivering a new approach to realise the energy transition requires system change, where the role of leadership must adapt and evolve. Traditional hierarchical leadership models cannot deliver the scale and pace required. Our recommendation, supported by Microsoft and Accenture (2020), therefore is that digital and data technologies be leveraged to democratise leadership, arming people with the information required at all levels to make effective decisions based on scientific fact. We consider leadership in the round, seamlessly integrating policy, regulatory, academic and industrial decisions in concert, recognising the impact across a diverse value chain where collaboration is imperative to success.

Our suggested model (Figure 20.2) draws upon existing best practice, such as the Project 13 enterprise model (Project13, 2016), which has successfully demonstrated collaborative approaches for major infrastructure projects. The Project 13 'enterprise' moves away from transactional relationships with investors, advisors and supply chains to a collaborative, long-term, strategic partnership where all partners are aligned in terms of outcomes and incentive.

We propose demonstration through test beds to deliver tangible outcomes and catalyse the market by showing real-world benefits. This approach allows

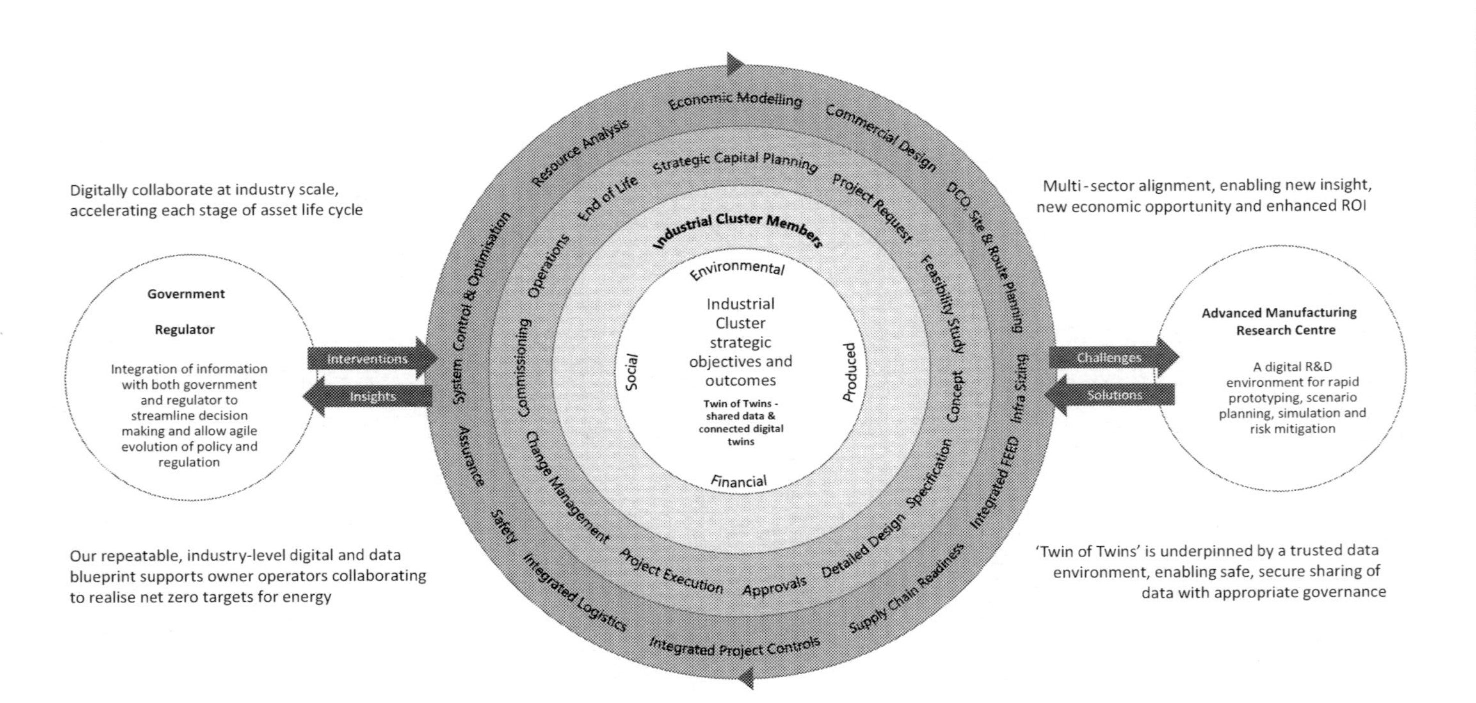

Figure 20.2 Digital and Data Blueprint for Industrial Clusters

organisations to de-risk investments and explore priority use cases in a safe, secure environment before considering deployment at scale.

Most important, our recommendation fosters collaboration across government, industry and academia to work collectively on the planet's more pressing challenges.

Conclusion

UK net zero targets in the energy sector are ambitious, requiring a different approach to the delivery of new energy infrastructure and the introduction of hydrogen, CCUS and scaling of renewables.

In excess of £300 million has been invested by the UK Government to date, through the Net Zero Hydrogen Fund and Cluster Sequencing bids, catalysing both hydrogen and CCUS developments, expected to create in excess of 25,000 jobs per year between 2023 and 2050 across the east coast.

Zero Carbon Humber and the other industrial clusters present an opportunity to collaborate at the industry level to move at pace and reduce the risks from climate change. This new delivery paradigm requires a shift in leadership principles, empowering people within organisations to re-think traditional methods and approaches underpinned by digital technology.

References

Accenture. (2021, March 1). *Achieving net-zero future with industrial clusters.* https://www.accenture.com/content/dam/accenture/final/a-com-migration/r3-3/pdf/pdf-147/accenture-wef-industrial-clusters.pdf#zoom=40

Department for Business, Energy & Industrial Strategy. (2021, April 7). *Industrial decarbonisation strategy.* Gov.uk. https://www.gov.uk/government/publications/industrial-decarbonisation-strategy/industrial-decarbonisation-strategy-accessible-webpage

Gardiner, W. (2021, July 7). *The Zero Carbon Humber project is decarbonizing UK's highest industrial CO_2 emissions area.* World Economic Forum. https://www.weforum.org/agenda/2021/07/net-zero-carbon-humber-uk-industry/

HM Government. (2021, October). *Net zero strategy: Build back greener.* Gov.uk. https://assets.publishing.service.gov.uk/government/uploads/system/uploads/attachment_data/file/1033990/net-zero-strategy-beis.pdf

Microsoft. (2020). *Unlocking the UK's potential with digital skills.* https://info.microsoft.com/rs/157-GQE-382/images/Unlocking-the-UKs-potential-with-digital-skills_131120__v3.pdf

Microsoft & Accenture. (2020). *Driving sustainability in industrial clusters.* https://www.accenture.com/content/dam/accenture/final/a-com-migration/r3-3/pdf/pdf-168/accenture-industrial-clusters-and-sustainability-white-paper-v7.pdf#zoom=40

Moldoveanu, M., & Narayandas, D. (2019, March–April). The future of leadership development. *Harvard Business Review.* https://hbr.org/2019/03/the-future-of-leadership-development

Nordhaus, W. D. (2006, December). *The 'Stern Review' on the economics of climate change.* NBER. https://www.nber.org/papers/w12741

Project13. (2016). *About Project 13.* https://www.project13.info/about-project13/

INDEX

Note: **Bold** page numbers refer to tables; *italic* page numbers refer to figures and page numbers followed by "n" denote endnotes.

Printed in the United States
by Baker & Taylor Publisher Services